Kaplan Publishing are constantly finding n
difference to your studies and our exciting
offer something different to students look

C000173475

This book comes with free MyKaplan onlin
study anytime, anywhere. **This free online**
separately and is included in the price of the book.

Having purchased this book, you have access to the following online study materials:

CONTENT	ACCA (including FBT, FMA, FFA)		FIA (excluding FBT, FMA, FFA)	
	Text	Kit	Text	Kit
Electronic version of the book	✓	✓	✓	✓
Knowledge checks with instant answers	✓		✓	
Material updates	✓	✓	✓	✓
Latest official ACCA exam questions*		✓		
Timed questions with an online tutor debrief using video icon***		✓		
Consolidation Test including questions and answers	✓		✓	

* Excludes BT, MA, FA, FBT, FMA, FFA; for all other papers includes a selection of questions, as released by ACCA

*** Excludes BT, MA, FA, LW, FBT, FMA and FFA

How to access your online resources

Kaplan Financial students will already have a MyKaplan account and these extra resources will be available to you online. You do not need to register again, as this process was completed when you enrolled. If you are having problems accessing online materials, please ask your course administrator.

If you are not studying with Kaplan and did not purchase your book via a Kaplan website, to unlock your extra online resources please go to www.mykaplan.co.uk/addabook (even if you have set up an account and registered books previously). You will then need to enter the ISBN number (on the title page and back cover) and the unique pass key number contained in the scratch panel below to gain access. You will also be required to enter additional information during this process to set up or confirm your account details.

If you purchased through the Kaplan Publishing website you will automatically receive an e-mail invitation to MyKaplan. Please register your details using this email to gain access to your content. If you do not receive the e-mail or book content, please contact Kaplan Publishing.

Your Code and Information

This code can only be used once for the registration of one book online. This registration and your online content will expire when the final sittings for the examinations covered by this book have taken place. Please allow one hour from the time you submit your book details for us to process your request.

Please scratch the film to access your unique code.

4WYk-PNwg-Bxzm-2vLu

Please be aware that this code is case-sensitive and you will need to include the dashes within the passcode, but not when entering the ISBN.

KAPLAN

PUBLISHING

ACCA

Applied Skills

Performance Management (PM)

EXAM KIT

British Library Cataloguing-in-Publication Data

A catalogue record for this book is available from the British Library.

Published by:

Kaplan Publishing UK
Unit 2 The Business Centre
Molly Millar's Lane
Wokingham
Berkshire
RG41 2QZ

ISBN: 978-1-83996-147-2

© Kaplan Financial Limited, 2022

Printed and bound in Great Britain.

Acknowledgements

These materials are reviewed by the ACCA examining team. The objective of the review is to ensure that the material properly covers the syllabus and study guide outcomes, used by the examining team in setting the exams, in the appropriate breadth and depth. The review does not ensure that every eventuality, combination or application of examinable topics is addressed by the ACCA Approved Content. Nor does the review comprise a detailed technical check of the content as the Approved Content Provider has its own quality assurance processes in place in this respect.

The past ACCA examination questions are the copyright of the Association of Chartered Certified Accountants. The original answers to the questions from June 1994 onwards were produced by the examiners themselves and have been adapted by Kaplan Publishing.

We are grateful to the Chartered Institute of Management Accountants and the Institute of Chartered Accountants in England and Wales for permission to reproduce past examination questions. The answers have been prepared by Kaplan Publishing.

CONTENTS

Section

Key features in this edition

In addition to providing a wide ranging bank of practice questions, we have also included in this edition:

- An analysis of all of the recent examinations.

- Exam-specific information and advice on exam technique.

- Our recommended approach to make your revision for this particular subject as effective as possible.

- This includes step by step guidance on how best to use our Kaplan material (Study text, pocket notes and exam kit) at this stage in your studies.

- Enhanced tutorial answers packed with specific key answer tips, technical tutorial notes and exam technique tips from our experienced tutors.

- Complementary online resources including full tutor debriefs to point you in the right direction when you get stuck

You will find a wealth of other resources to help you with your studies on the following sites:

www.MyKaplan.co.uk

www.accaglobal.com

Quality and accuracy are of the utmost importance to us so if you spot an error in any of our products, please send an email to mykaplanreporting@kaplan.com with full details.

Our Quality Co-ordinator will work with our technical team to verify the error and take action to ensure it is corrected in future editions.

INDEX TO QUESTIONS AND ANSWERS

INTRODUCTION

Following the introduction of the revised exam format, all previous ACCA constructed response (long) exam questions within this kit have been adapted.

The specimen exam is included at the end of the kit.

KEY TO THE INDEX

EXAM ENHANCEMENTS

We have added the following enhancements to the answers in this exam kit:

Key answer tips

All answers include key answer tips to help your understanding of each question.

Tutorial note

Many answers include more tutorial notes to explain some of the technical points in more detail.

Top tutor tips

For selected questions, we 'walk through the answer' giving guidance on how to approach the questions with helpful 'tips from a top tutor', together with technical tutor notes.

These answers are indicated with the 'footsteps' icon in the index.

Within the questions in the exam kit you will see the following icons, shown in the question requirements:

⌨ = word processing

▦ = spreadsheet

The icons highlighting the constructed response workspace tool alongside some of the questions are for guidance only – it is important to recognise that each question is different and that the answer space provided by ACCA in the exam is determined by both the technical content of the question as well as the quality assurance processes ACCA undertakes to ensure the student is provided with the most appropriate type of workspace.

ONLINE ENHANCEMENTS

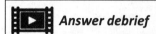 *Answer debrief*

For selected questions, we recommend that they are to be completed in full exam conditions (i.e. properly timed in a closed book environment).

In addition to the examining team's technical answer, enhanced with key answer tips and tutorial notes in this exam kit, online you can find an answer debrief by a top tutor that:

- works through the question in full

- explains key elements of the answer

- ensures that the easy marks are obtained as quickly as possible.

These questions are indicated with the 'video' icon in the index.

Answer debriefs will be available on MyKaplan at:

www.mykaplan.co.uk

SECTION A – OBJECTIVE TEST QUESTIONS

Page number

Question *Answer*

SECTION B – OBJECTIVE TEST CASE STUDY QUESTIONS

SECTION C – CONSTRUCTED RESPONSE QUESTIONS

ANALYSIS OF PAST EXAMS

The table below summarises the key topics that have been tested within sections B & C in the examinations. A much wider range of topics will now be examined following the introduction of objective test questions.

	M18/J18	S18/D18	M19/J19	S19/D19	M20/J20	S20/D20	M21/J21	S21/D21
Specialist cost and management accounting techniques								
ABC								
Target costing								
Lifecycle costing		✓				✓		
Throughput accounting								
Decision making techniques						✓		
Key factor analysis	✓	✓					✓	✓
Linear programming								✓
Pricing								
Relevant costing								
Uncertainty and risk				✓				
Budgeting								
Budgeting	✓			✓				
Forecasting								
Learning curves								
Standard costing and variance analysis		✓						
Standard costing		✓ ✓						
Variances			✓				✓	
Mix		✓	✓		✓			
Planning and operational							✓	
Performance measurement and control				✓	✓			
Performance measurement	✓		✓	✓	✓		✓	✓
ROI/RI		✓						
Transfer pricing	✓							
Not for profit organisations				✓		✓		

KAPLAN PUBLISHING

EXAM TECHNIQUE

GENERAL COMMENTS

- Read the examination questions carefully

- **Divide the time** you spend on questions in proportion to the marks on offer:

  - one suggestion for this examination is to allocate 1.8 minutes to each mark available, so a 20 mark question should be completed in approximately 36 minutes.

  - within that, try to allow time at the end of each question to review your answer and address any obvious issues.

  Whatever happens, always keep your eye on the clock and **do not over run on any part of any question!**

- If you **get completely stuck** with a question:

  - flag the question and

  - **return to it later.**

- Stick to the question and **tailor your answer** to what you are asked.

  - Pay particular attention to the verbs in the question.

  - Try to apply your comments to the scenario where possible.

- If you do not understand what a question is asking, **state your assumptions**.

  Even if you do not answer in precisely the way the examiner hoped, you should be given some credit, if your assumptions are reasonable.

- You should do everything you can to make things easy for the marker.

  The marker will find it easier to identify the points you have made if your **answers are legible and well labelled**.

OBJECTIVE TEST QUESTIONS

- Decide whether you want to attempt these at the start of the exam or at the end.

- No credit for workings will be given in these questions, the answers will either be correct (2 marks) or incorrect (0 marks).

- Read the question carefully, as any alternative answer choices will be given based on common mistakes that could be made in attempting the question.

- If a question looks particularly difficult or time consuming, then miss it out first time through (make sure you flag it) and come back to it later.

CONSTRUCTED RESPONSE (LONG) QUESTIONS

- **Written elements**:

  Your answer should have:

  - a clear structure

  - short paragraphs containing short, succinct sentences.

  - heading and sub-headings (where possible).

  Be concise.

  Cover a range of points but make sure you can provide evidence and justification from the scenario.

  Where possible, try to relate comments to the specific context given rather than your answer looking like it was simply copied out of the textbook.

- **Computations**:

  It is essential to include all your workings in your answers.

COMPUTER-BASED EXAMS – ADDITIONAL TIPS

- Do not attempt a CBE until you have **completed all study material** relating to it.

- On the ACCA website there is a CBE demonstration. It is **ESSENTIAL** that you attempt this before your real CBE. You will become familiar with how to move around the CBE screens and the way that questions are formatted, increasing your confidence and speed in the actual exam.

- Be sure you understand how to use the **software** before you start the exam. If in doubt, ask the assessment centre staff to explain it to you.

- Questions are **displayed on the screen** and answers are entered using keyboard and mouse.

- In addition to the traditional multiple choice question type, CBEs will also contain other types of questions, such as number entry questions, multiple correct answers (select two or more), matching labels to targets, stem questions with multiple parts and written questions requiring text entry.

- You need to be sure you **know how to answer questions** of these types before you sit the exam, through practice.

EXAM SPECIFIC INFORMATION

THE EXAM

FORMAT OF THE EXAM

The exam will be in **THREE sections**, and will be a mix of narrative and computational answers.

All questions are compulsory.

		Number of marks
Section A:	Fifteen objective test questions of 2 marks each	30
Section B:	Three objective test case studies	
	– five questions per case study of 2 marks each	30
Section C:	Two constructed response (long) questions	
	Question 1	20
	Question 2	20
		———
		100
		———

Total time allowed: 3 hours. Prior to the exam, candidates are given an extra 10 minutes to read the exam instructions.

Note that:

- the Performance Management exam will have both a discursive and computational element. The objective test questions and the objective test case study questions will therefore include a mix of calculation-based and explanation-based questions.

- there is likely to be a discussion element included in the constructed response questions in Section C.

- Section C questions only come from syllabus areas C, D and E (with potentially a bit of syllabus area A), but not from syllabus area B. In this Exam Kit, section C questions from syllabus areas B and the 20 mark questions from syllabus area A are just there for practice of the topics, but could not come up in the actual exam.

PASS MARK

The pass mark for all ACCA Qualification examinations is 50%.

SECTION A QUESTIONS

The computer-based exam will include different question styles, as described in the previous section on exam technique.

A mixture of these question types is included within this exam kit.

APPROACH TO THIS EXAM

Performance Management is divided into three different sections, requiring the application of different skills to be successful.

Section A

Stick to the timing principle of 1.8 minutes per mark. This means that the 15 OT questions in Section A (30 marks) should take 54 minutes.

Work steadily. Rushing leads to careless mistakes and the OT questions are designed to include answers which result from careless mistakes.

If you don't know the answer, eliminate those options you know are incorrect and see if the answer becomes more obvious.

Remember that there is no negative marking for an incorrect answer. After you have eliminated the options that you know to be wrong, if you are still unsure, guess.

Section B

There is likely to be a significant amount of information to read through for each case. You should begin by reading the OT questions that relate to the case, so that when you read through the information for the first time, you know what it is that you are required to do.

Each OT question is worth two marks. Therefore, you have 18 minutes (1.8 minutes per mark) to answer the five OT questions relating to each case. It is likely that all of the cases will take the same length of time to answer, although some of the OT questions within a case may be quicker than other OT questions within that same case.

Once you have read through the information, you should first answer any of the OT questions that do not require workings and can be quickly answered. You should then attempt the OT questions that require workings utilising the remaining time for that case.

All of the tips for Section A are equally applicable to each Section B question.

Section C

The constructed response questions in Section C will require a written response rather than being OT questions. Therefore, different techniques need to be used to score well.

Unless you know exactly how to answer the question, spend some time planning your answer. Stick to the question and tailor your answer to what you are asked. Pay particular attention to the verbs in the question e.g. 'Calculate', 'State', 'Explain'.

As stated earlier, if you **get completely stuck** with a question, leave space in your answer and return to it later.

If you do not understand what a question is asking, state your assumptions. Even if you do not answer in precisely the way the examining team hoped, you should be given some credit, provided that your assumptions are reasonable.

You should do everything you can to make things easy for the marker. The marker will find it easier to identify the points you have made if your answers are legible.

Computations: It is essential to include all your workings in your answers. Many computational questions require the use of a standard format. Be sure you know these formats thoroughly before the examination and use the layouts that you see in the answers given in this book and in model answers.

Remember you can use the spreadsheet function to help you with the layout and calculation of your answers. Markers are able to see the formula you are using.

Adopt a logical approach and cross reference workings to the main computation to keep your answers tidy.

All sections

Don't skip any parts of the syllabus. The PM exam has 32 different questions so the examination can cover a very broad selection of the syllabus each sitting.

Spend time learning the rules and definitions.

Practice plenty of questions to improve your ability to apply the techniques and perform the calculations.

Spend the last five minutes reading through your answers and making any additions or corrections.

 Always keep your eye on the clock and do not over run on any part of any question!

DETAILED SYLLABUS, STUDY GUIDE AND CBE SPECIMEN EXAM

The detailed syllabus and study guide written by the ACCA, along with the specimen exam, can be found at:

https://www.accaglobal.com/my/en/student/exam-support-resources/fundamentals-exams-study-resources/f5.html

KAPLAN'S RECOMMENDED REVISION APPROACH

QUESTION PRACTICE IS THE KEY TO SUCCESS

Success in professional examinations relies upon you acquiring a firm grasp of the required knowledge at the tuition phase. In order to be able to do the questions, knowledge is essential.

However, the difference between success and failure often hinges on your exam technique on the day and making the most of the revision phase of your studies.

The **Kaplan study text** is the starting point, designed to provide the underpinning knowledge to tackle all questions. However, in the revision phase, poring over text books is not the answer.

Kaplan Online fixed tests help you consolidate your knowledge and understanding and are a useful tool to check whether you can remember key topic areas.

Kaplan pocket notes are designed to help you quickly revise a topic area, however you then need to practice questions. There is a need to progress to full exam standard questions as soon as possible, and to tie your exam technique and technical knowledge together.

The importance of question practice cannot be over-emphasised.

The recommended approach below is designed by expert tutors in the field, in conjunction with their knowledge of the examiner and their recent real exams.

The approach taken for the fundamental exams is to revise by topic area. However, with the professional stage exams, a multi topic approach is required to answer the scenario based questions.

You need to practice as many questions as possible in the time you have left.

OUR AIM

Our aim is to get you to the stage where you can attempt exam standard questions confidently, to time, in a closed book environment, with no supplementary help (i.e. to simulate the real examination experience).

Practising your exam technique on real past examination questions, in timed conditions, is also vitally important for you to assess your progress and identify areas of weakness that may need more attention in the final run up to the examination.

In order to achieve this we recognise that initially you may feel the need to practice some questions with open book help and exceed the required time.

The approach below shows you which questions you should use to build up to coping with exam standard question practice, and references to the sources of information available should you need to revisit a topic area in more detail.

Remember that in the real examination, all you have to do is:

- attempt all questions required by the exam

- only spend the allotted time on each question, and

- get them at least 50% right!

Try and practice this approach on every question you attempt from now to the real exam.

EXAMINER COMMENTS

We have included the examiners comments to the specific new syllabus examination questions in this kit for you to see the main pitfalls that students fall into with regard to technical content.

However, too many times in the general section of the report, the examiner comments that students had failed due to:

- "not answering the question"

- "a poor understanding of why something is done, not just how it is done"

- "simply writing out numbers from the question. Candidates must understand what the numbers tell them about business performance"

- "a lack of common business sense" and

- "ignoring clues in the question".

Good exam technique is vital.

ACCA SUPPORT

For additional support with your studies please also refer to the ACCA Global website.

THE KAPLAN PERFORMANCE MANAGEMENT (PM) EXAMINATION REVISION PLAN

Stage 1: Assess areas of strengths and weaknesses

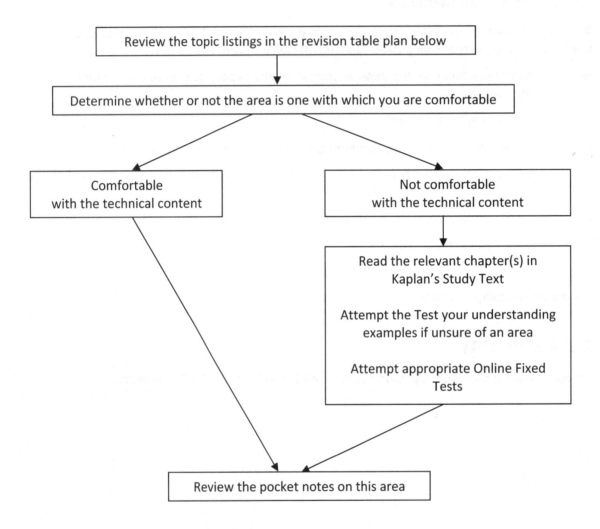

Stage 2: Practice questions

Follow the order of revision of topics as recommended in the revision table plan below and attempt the questions in the order suggested.

Try to avoid referring to text books and notes and the model answer until you have completed your attempt.

Try to answer the question in the allotted time.

Review your attempt with the model answer and assess how much of the answer you achieved in the allocated exam time.

Fill in the self-assessment box below and decide on your best course of action.

Note that:

 The "footsteps questions" give guidance on exam techniques and how you should have approached the question.

Stage 3: Final pre-exam revision

We recommend that you **attempt at least one three hour mock examination** containing a set of previously unseen exam standard questions.

It is important that you get a feel for the breadth of coverage of a real exam without advanced knowledge of the topic areas covered – just as you will expect to see on the real exam day.

Ideally this mock should be sat in timed, closed book, real exam conditions and could be:

- a mock examination offered by your tuition provider, and/or

- the specimen exam at the back of this exam kit, and/or

- the last real examination (available shortly afterwards on MyKaplan with "enhanced walk through answers" and a full "tutor debrief").

Topic	Study Text Chapter	Pocket note Chapter	Questions to attempt	Tutor guidance	Date attempted	Self assessment
Information, technologies and systems for organisational performance						
– Information systems and data analytics	2,3	2,3	Questions 15 to 28 in Section A. Question 241 in Section B. Question 272 in Section C.	Questions on systems and information will serve as excellent preparation for any exam question on this area, which has become all-important in this exam.		
– Sources of information			Questions 6 to 15 in Section A			
– Managing information			Questions 1 to 5 in Section A			
Specialist cost and management accounting techniques						
– ABC	4	4	Questions 29 to 41 inclusive in Section A. Question 245 in Section B.	Activity-based Costing (ABC) is a key costing technique. In many questions, you will be asked to calculate the cost per unit using both full absorption costing, and an ABC approach. Be ready to explain the reasons for the development of ABC, its pros and cons and its implications.		

Topic	Study Text Chapter	Pocket note Chapter	Questions to attempt	Tutor guidance	Date attempted	Self assessment
— Target costing	4	4	Questions 42 to 47 inclusive in Section A. Question 246 Helot Co in Section B.	Calculations for target costing are key, but they're not everything: Exam questions may ask for a discussion of the implications of target costing or of the use of target costing in the service industry.		
— Life-cycle costing	4	4	Questions 48 to 54 inclusive in Section A. Question 242 in Section B. Question 277 in Section C.	This is a relatively straightforward technique but it is still important to practice at the very least one long question to ensure you have the required knowledge.		
— Environmental management accounting	4	4	Questions 62 to 70 in Section A. Question 249 in Section B	It is important that you can explain what is meant by EMA and that you understand how it should be used.		

Topic	Study Text Chapter	Pocket note Chapter	Questions to attempt	Tutor guidance	Date attempted	Self assessment
– Throughput accounting	4	4	Questions 55 to 61 inclusive in Section A. Question 250 in Section B. Question 277 in Section C.	Good Section B question ('Sweet treats bakery') covering the different calculations that could be examined on throughput accounting. This is a more difficult costing technique and it is therefore important to complete these questions before the exam.		
Decision making techniques						
– Cost volume profit analysis	3	3	Questions 82 to 96 inclusive in Section A. Question 252 in Section B. Question 281 in Section C.	A good question ('Mango Leather') covering multi-products breakeven charts. Even if you are not going to be requested to draw a graph in the exam, constructing one in revision will help consolidate your understanding. A complete question with well-split requirements that also refer to an article on the ACCA website – an absolute must.		
– Linear programming	4	4	Questions 97 to 108 inclusive in Section A. Question 255 in Section B. Question 285 in Section C.	Excellent questions on linear programming. In addition to the six step approach, the examiner is likely to examine some peripheral areas such as shadow prices, slack or linear programming assumptions.		

Topic	Study Text Chapter	Pocket note Chapter	Questions to attempt	Tutor guidance	Date attempted	Self assessment
– Pricing	5	5	Questions 109 to 119 inclusive in Section A. Question 256 in Section B. Question 300 in Section C.	The Section C question, 'TR Co', is a very recent question testing pricing and learning curves. It also mixes calculations with written parts. An excellent question to practice as part of your revision programme.		
– Relevant costing	6	6	Questions 71 to 81 inclusive in Section A. Question 251 in Section B. Question 293 in Section C.	This is a tricky area but a methodical approach to answering questions should help. If you are not sure about a particular number, take a guess and move on. The aim is not to get the question 100% correct but to get through the question in time and to score a pass in the question.		
– Dealing with risk and uncertainty	7	7	Questions 126 to 140 inclusive in Section A. Question 258 in Section B. Question 296 in Section C.	The calculations are important and the decision trees techniques must be well rehearsed. Look for other questions to practice in this area as you must also be prepared to discuss the various methods of managing risk. Some of the terms, e.g. minimax regret, make this area appear difficult but the underlying concepts are relatively straightforward.		

Budgeting and control

Topic	Study Text Chapter	Pocket note Chapter	Questions to attempt	Tutor guidance	Date attempted	Self assessment
– Budgeting systems and types of budget	8	8	Questions 141 to 156 inclusive in Section A. Question 262 in Section B. Question 303 in Section C.	Do not overlook this area. Knowledge of the written areas of budgeting can help you to score relatively easy marks in the exam, like most well-prepared candidates do when narrative questions are set. 'Static Co' is very important when it comes to testing the topic of rolling budgets.		
– Quantitative techniques	9	9	Questions 157 to 171 inclusive in Section A. Question 263 in Section B. Question 316 in Section C.	Excellent questions on learning curves and representative of what you should expect in the exam. Be prepared to discuss the reservations with the learning curve. Forecasting techniques – such as linear regression, correlation and time series are making an appearance again.		
– Mix and yield variances	10	10	Questions 179 to 190 inclusive in Section A. Question 264 in Section B. Question 314 in Section C.	These require a calculation of mix and yield variances and are good preparation for the exam. Question 319, for example, is a very good one to practice and also a very recent exam question (Sept 2018). Sales mix and quantity variances should not be omitted either.		

Topic	Study Text Chapter	Pocket note Chapter	Questions to attempt	Tutor guidance	Date attempted	Self assessment
– Planning and operational variances	10	10	Questions 197 to 203 inclusive in Section A. Question 261 in Section B. Question 309 in Section C.	This is representative of the type of question that may come up on this area. 'Medical Temp Co' is a must-practice question on revision.		
Performance measurement and control						
– ROI/RI	12	12	Questions 220, and 222 to 226 inclusive in Section A. Question 321 in Section C.	It is important that you can calculate the ROI and RI but you must also be able to discuss the pros and cons of each of these methods. Some of these questions are challenging but necessary, testing your knowledge of how ROI and RI are affected by different transactions which may take place.		
– Transfer pricing	12	12	Questions 219, 221, and 227 to 229 inclusive in Section A. Question 325 in Section C.	For all questions on transfer pricing, you will require an in-depth understanding of the information contained in the scenario.		

Topic	Study Text Chapter	Pocket note Chapter	Questions to attempt	Tutor guidance	Date attempted	Self assessment
Performance analysis in not-for-profit organisations and the public sector	13	13	Questions 230 to 235 inclusive in Section A. Question 336 in Section C.	Questions on not-for-profit organisations will serve as excellent preparation for any exam question on this area. You should focus on understanding and applying the 'Value For Money' (or 3Es) framework.		

Note that not all of the questions are referred to in the programme above. We have recommended a large number of exam standard questions and successful completion of these should reassure you that you have a good grounding of all of the key topics and are well prepared for the exam.

The remaining questions are available in the kit for extra practice for those who require more questions and focus on some areas.

FORMULAE

Performance Management (PM)
Formulae sheet

Regression analysis

$$y = a + bx$$

$$a = \frac{\sum y}{n} - \frac{b \sum x}{n}$$

$$b = \frac{n \sum xy - \sum x \sum y}{n \sum x^2 - (\sum x)^2}$$

$$r = \frac{n \sum xy - \sum x \sum y}{\sqrt{(n \sum x^2 - (\sum x)^2)(n \sum y^2 - (\sum y)^2)}}$$

Learning curve

$$Y = ax^b$$

Where Y = cumulative average time per unit to produce x units

a = the time taken for the first unit of output

x = the cumulative number of units produced

b = the index of learning (log LR/log2)

LR = the learning rate as a decimal

Demand curve

$$P = a - bQ$$

$$b = \frac{\text{change in price}}{\text{change in quantity}}$$

a = price when Q = 0

MR = a − 2bQ

Section 1

OBJECTIVE TEST QUESTIONS – SECTION A

INFORMATION, TECHNOLOGIES AND SYSTEMS FOR ORGANISATIONAL PERFORMANCE

MANAGING INFORMATION

1   Which TWO of the following are typical advantages of investing in a new information system?

- Enhanced compatibility with other systems

- Enhanced information processing capacity

- Enhanced information processing efficiency

- Enhanced staff training needs

2   An airline wants to provide access to a select group of travel agents to real time information held by the airline regarding flights which may have the potential for passenger seat upgrades.

Which of the following is likely to be used to achieve this?

A   Intranet

B   Extranet

C   Internet

D   Email

3   A government department generates information which should not be disclosed to anyone who works outside of the department. There are many other government departments working within the same building.

Which of the following would NOT be an effective control procedure for the generation and distribution of the information within the government department?

A   If working from home, departmental employees must use a memory stick to transfer data, as laptop computers are not allowed to leave the department.

B   All departmental employees must enter non-disclosed and regularly updated passwords to access their computers.

C   All authorised employees must swipe an officially issued, personal identity card at the entrance to the department before they can gain access.

D   All hard copies of confidential information must be shredded at the end of each day or locked overnight in a safe if needed again.

4   A small doctors' surgery is considering providing a wireless network for use by nurses to access patient data in real time.

Which of the following is a DISADVANTAGE of using a wireless network in this way?

A   Access to the network cannot be limited

B   The network cannot match the coverage of a wired network

C   The network will be less stable than a wired network

D   It will be necessary to buy lots of new user devices

5   **Which of the following methods would be LEAST effective in ensuring the security of confidential information?**

A   Monitoring emails

B   Encryption of files

C   Dial back facility

D   Universal passwords

SOURCES OF INFORMATION

6   **Identify by placing a tick in the correct boxes in the table below, whether the information gathered is from an internal or external source.**

	Internal	External
Interviewing potential customers		
Reading business magazines		
Listing employee records from the company's payroll system		
Looking through sales records for the last year		

7 Identify by placing a tick in the correct boxes in the table below, whether the information gathered is from an internal or external source.

	Internal	External
Number of people clicking on the 'Coming soon' link on the company's website		
How likely one of our customers is to recommend our business to a friend or colleague		
Share prices of different competitors over time		
Average household income in Mumbai in 20X0		

8 Which of the following statement(s) regarding the use of external information is/are true?

(1) External information is usually more reliable than internal information.

(2) External information can be general and vague, and may not really help an organisation with decision making.

A (1) only

B (2) only

C Neither (1) nor (2)

D Both (1) and (2)

9 Which of the following would show information on the frequency of machine breakdowns causing lost productions?

A The non-current asset register

B The machine maintenance schedule

C Production output reports

D The purchase ledger account for the supplier that provides replacement machine parts

10 **D plc is wishing to improve staff morale so the HR department intend to use an online questionnaire that all staff are expected to complete to gather information. Completing the questionnaire will take approximately 30 minutes and staff have been told that they must do this during their lunch break.**

The following costs of producing this information have been identified:

I	Paying for an external consultancy to design the questionnaire
II	Paying wages for people to email staff with instructions on how to complete the survey
III	Loss of staff morale due to loss of lunch break time
IV	Delays caused in other parts of the business due to staff filling in the survey when they should be working

Which of these costs would be considered as "indirect" costs of producing the information?

A   III only

B   IV only

C   III and IV only

D   I, III and IV

11 **Which of the following is the most reliable source of information on a country's inflation rate?**

A   Spending on groceries by a family from one point of time to the next

B   Journalist reports concerning the difficulties local families are having making ends meet

C   Average house prices measured across the country from one point of time to the next

D   The government figures for retail price index (RPI)

12 The qualities of good information contained in reports are more easily remembered using the mnemonic ACCURATE.

Which one of the following is NOT normally associated with a quality of good information?

A   Adaptable to the needs of the user

B   Acceptable to the user

C   Accurate

D   Understandable by the user

13 An accountant wants to determine the increase in average usage of paper per employee from printing out of emails. She is concerned that paper usage in her business has risen by 10% in the last year to $40,400.

She has estimated that it will take 4 weeks of her time to prepare the report. As well as other incremental costs she has estimated that the total cost of preparing the report will be $28,000.

This report is an example of bad information. Which one of the principles of good information does it breach?

A   Relevant

B   Complete

C   Cost beneficial

D   Understandable

14 Local managers within organisations often use operational reports.

Which of the following features of reports would be most true of an operational report?

A   Summarised information

B   Mainly external information on local competition

C   Accurate information on current position

D   Infrequent

INFORMATION SYSTEMS AND DATA ANALYTICS

15 **Strategic reports have many features, which of the following is the most likely feature of a strategic report?**

A   Prepared regularly

B   Total accuracy of past and forecast data

C   Highly summarised showing overall trends

D   Demonstrates only the company's current position

16 **Which of the following statements regarding planning and control as described in the three tiers of Robert Anthony's decision-making hierarchy is/are true?**

(1)   Strategic planning is concerned with making decisions about the efficient and effective use of existing resources.

(2)   Operational control is about ensuring that specific tasks are carried out efficiently and effectively.

A   (1) only

B   (2) only

C   Neither (1) nor (2)

D   Both (1) and (2)

17 **Long-term sales forecasts are an example of accounting information used at which level of control in an organisation?**

A   Strategic planning

B   Management control

C   Tactical control

D   Operational control

18 Information systems described below may or may not be suited to all levels of management.

Identify by placing a tick in the relevant boxes in the table below, the suitability of the systems for all levels of management.

	Suited to all levels of management	Not suited to all levels of management
A Management Information System producing management accounts showing margins for individual customers		
An Expert System holding specialist tax information		
An Executive Information System giving access to internal and external information in summarised form, with the option to drill down to a greater level of activity		

19 A manufacturer and retailer of kitchens introduces an enterprise resource planning system.

Which of the following is NOT likely to be a potential benefit of introducing this system?

A   Schedules of labour are prepared for manufacturing

B   Inventory records are updated automatically

C   Sales are recorded into the financial ledgers

D   Critical strategic information can be summarised

20 **Which of the following is an example of an Expert Systems (ES)?**

A   A Customer Relationship Management (CRM) software to identify trends and marketing opportunities

B   A database management system

C   A computer networking installation

D   A tax system that solves problems dealing with business tax planning.

21 You have been presented with a summary report of sales in the last month, with a breakdown of totals per product, and with variances from the corresponding monthly sales plan.

Which of the following systems would generate such a report?

A   A transaction processing system

B   A management information system

C   An executive Information system

D   None of the above

22 **Which of the following could be described as an expert system?**

A   An ATM dispensing cash provided there is enough money in the account

B   A stock management system, which highlights stock-outs

C   A marketing database holding records of past advertising campaigns and the sales generated by those campaigns

D   A tax calculator which predicts the level of tax payable in different scenarios

23 **Which of the following is NOT normally considered to be a feature of big data?**

A   Volume

B   Velocity

C   Variety

D   Vicinity

24 **Which TWO of the following statements regarding big data are true?**

*   It is more reliable than other sources of data

*   It can change very quickly

*   It can take multiple forms

*   It involves dealing with large financial numbers

25 **Which of the following statements regarding big data is true?**

A   It is only useful for big organisations

B   It is all contained on the internet

C   It is all generated external to the organisation

D   It can lead to a competitive advantage

26   It is often said that big data enhances business decisions.

      Which of the following statements regarding big data and decision making is/are true?

      (i)   Decisions which include big data analytics can lead to a competitive edge over rivals.

      (ii)   Big data analytics cannot account for competitors' expected actions.

      A   Statement (i) only

      B   Statement (ii) only

      C   Both statements

      D   Neither statement

27   **Which TWO of the following statements are thought to be benefits when using big data to enhance business decisions?**

      •   There is no need to have a deep understanding of the industry in order to interpret the data

      •   Customer relationship management can be improved resulting in better repeat business and customer loyalty

      •   Business performance can be better tracked and analysed against a wider set of criteria

      •   All available big data will create value for an organisation when analysed

28   **Which of the following is NOT considered a risk when using big data to enhance business decision making?**

      A   The veracity of the data is difficult to assess

      B   Traditional sources of data are ignored

      C   The data may be distorted by data outliers

      D   The benefits may be outweighed by the financial costs

SPECIALIST COST AND MANAGEMENT ACCOUNTING TECHNIQUES

ACTIVITY-BASED COSTING

29   **Which TWO of the following are NOT usually a characteristic of a modern manufacturing environment?**

      •   Shorter production cycles

      •   A greater emphasis on quality

      •   A greater use of advanced technology

      •   Reduced levels of employee participation

      •   Increased rigidity in processes

30 A company produces a range of products and uses an absorption costing system. Which two of the following are UNLIKELY to be a consequence of the company switching to an activity based costing (ABC) system?

- Indirect overheads will be shared between products on fairer bases

- Product pricing decisions will be improved

- The prime production cost of each product will fall

- Cost control on indirect overheads will be harder to achieve

- Total production cost of each product will change

31 A company which makes two products, Alpha and Zeta, uses activity-based costing to absorb its overheads. It has recently identified a new overhead cost pool for inspection costs and has decided that the cost driver is the number of inspections.

The following information has been provided:

		Alpha	Zeta
Total inspection costs	$250,000		
Production volume (units)		2,500	8,000
Machine hours per unit		1	1.5
Units per batch		500	1,000
Inspections per batch		4	1

What is the inspection cost per unit of product Alpha? Select from the list below.

List options are as follows:

- $23.81

- $17.24

- $71.43

- $80.00

32 Which of the following statements are true regarding activity-based costing (ABC) and cost drivers?

(1) A cost driver is any factor that causes a change in the cost of an activity.

(2) For long-term variable overhead costs, the cost driver will be the volume of activity.

(3) Traditional absorption costing tends to under-allocate overhead costs to low-volume products.

A (1) and (3) only

B (2) and (3) only

C (1) and (2) only

D (1), (2) and (3)

33 A company makes products A and B. It is experimenting with activity-based costing. Production set-up costs are $12,000; total production will be 20,000 units of each of products A and B. Each run is 1,000 units of A or 5,000 units of B.

Using activity-based costing, what is the set-up cost per unit of A? (Give your answer to the nearest cent.)

$ [   ]

34 Which of the following statement(s) is/are true regarding activity-based costing?

(1) A cost pool is an activity which consumes resources and for which overhead costs are identified and allocated.

(2) An activity-based costing overhead absorption rate (OAR) is calculated in the same way as an absorption costing OAR, and will result in the same OAR being calculated for each cost pool.

A (1) only

B (2) only

C Neither (1) nor (2)

D Both (1) and (2)

35 A company uses activity-based costing to calculate the unit cost of its products. The figures for Period 3 are as follows: production set-up costs are $84,000. Total production is 40,000 units of each of products A and B, and each run is 2,000 units of A or 5,000 units of B.

What is the set-up cost per unit of B (to 2 decimal places)?

$ [   ]

36 The ABC Company manufactures two products, product Alpha and Product Beta. Both are produced in a very labour-intensive environment and use similar processes. Alpha and Beta differ by volume. Beta is a high-volume product, while Alpha is a low-volume product. Details of product inputs, outputs and the costs of activities are as follows:

	Direct labour hours/unit	Annual output (units)	Number of purchase orders	Number of set-ups
Alpha	5	1,200	75	40
Beta	5	12,000	85	60
			160	100

Fixed overhead costs amount to a total of $420,000 and have been analysed as follows:

	$
Volume-related	100,000
Purchasing related	145,000
Set-up related	175,000

Using a traditional method of overhead absorption based on labour hours, what is the overhead cost per unit for each unit of product Alpha (to two decimal places)?

$ [   ]

37   The ABC Company manufactures two products, product Alpha and Product Beta. Both are produced in a very labour-intensive environment and use similar processes. Alpha and Beta differ by volume. Beta is a high-volume product, while Alpha is a low-volume product. Details of product inputs, outputs and the costs of activities are as follows:

	Direct labour hours/unit	Annual output (units)	Number of purchase orders	Number of set-ups
Alpha	5	1,200	75	40
Beta	5	12,000	85	60
			160	100

Fixed overhead costs amount to a total of $420,000 and have been analysed as follows:

	$
Volume-related	100,000
Purchasing related	145,000
Set-up related	175,000

Using a traditional method of overhead absorption based on labour hours, what is the overhead cost per unit for each unit of product Beta (to two decimal places)?

A $6.36

B $22.75

C $31.82

D $122.55

38   The ABC Company manufactures two products, Product Alpha and Product Beta. Both are produced in a very labour-intensive environment and use similar processes. Alpha and Beta differ by volume. Beta is a high-volume product, while Alpha is a low-volume product. Details of product inputs, outputs and the costs of activities are as follows:

	Direct labour hours/unit	Annual output (units)	Number of purchase orders	Number of set-ups
Alpha	5	1,200	75	40
Beta	5	12,000	85	60
			160	100

Fixed overhead costs amount to a total of $420,000 and have been analysed as follows:

	$
Volume-related	100,000
Purchasing related	145,000
Set-up related	175,000

Using Activity-based costing as the method of overhead absorption, what is the overhead cost per unit for each unit of product Alpha (to two decimal places)?

A $6.36

B $22.75

C $122.55

D   Cannot be determined without more information

39 A company makes two products using the same type of materials and skilled workers. The following information is available:

	Product A	Product B
Budgeted volume (units)	1,000	2,000
Material per unit ($)	10	20
Labour per unit ($)	5	20

Fixed costs relating to material handling amount to $100,000. The cost driver for these costs is the volume of material purchased.

General fixed costs, absorbed on the basis of labour hours, amount to $180,000.

Using activity-based costing, what is the total fixed overhead amount to be absorbed into each unit of product B (to the nearest whole $)?

A $113

B $120

C $40

D $105

40 A company is changing its costing system from traditional absorption costing based on labour hours to activity-based costing. It has overheads of $156,000 which are related to taking material deliveries.

The delivery information about each product is below.

Product:	X	Y	Z
Total units required	1,000	2,000	3,000
Delivery size	200	400	1,000

Total labour costs are $360,000 for 45,000 hours. Each unit of each product takes the same number of direct hours.

Assuming that the company uses the number of deliveries as its cost driver, what will be the effect on the costs per unit following the change from absorption costing to activity-based costing?' Place a tick in the boxes in the table below where appropriate.

	Increase	Decrease
Product X		
Product Y		
Product Z		

41 DRP Ltd has recently introduced an activity-based costing (ABC) system. It manufactures three products, details of which are set out below:

Product:	D	R	P
Budgeted annual production (units)	100,000	100,000	50,000
Batch size (units)	100	50	25
Machine set-ups per batch	3	4	6
Purchase orders per batch	2	1	1
Processing time per unit (minutes)	2	3	3

Three cost pools have been identified. Their budgeted costs for the year ending 30 June 20X3 are as follows:

Machine set-up costs	$150,000
Purchasing of materials	$70,000
Processing	$80,000

What is the budgeted machine set-up cost per unit of product R?

A $6.52

B $0.52

C $18.75

D $1.82

TARGET COSTING

42 **In target costing, which of the following would be an appropriate strategy to reduce a cost gap for a product that existed in a competitive industry with demanding shareholders?**

A Increase the selling price

B Reduce the expectation gap by reducing the selling price

C Reducing the desired margin on the product

D Mechanising production in order to reduce average production cost

43 **Which of the following strategies would be an immediately acceptable method to reduce an identified cost gap?**

A Reduce the desired margin without discussion with business owners

B Reduce the predicted selling price

C Source similar quality materials from another supplier at reduced cost

D Increase the predicted selling price

44   The predicted selling price for a product has been set at $56 per unit. The desired mark-up on cost is 25% and the material cost for the product is estimated to be $16 before allowing for additional materials to allow for shrinkage of 20% (for every 10 kg of material going in only 8 kg comes out).

If labour is the only other cost and 2 hours are needed what is the most the business can pay per hour if a cost gap is to be avoided?

The maximum rate per hour is (2 d.p) $ [   ]

45   **Which of the following techniques is NOT relevant to target costing?**

A   Value analysis

B   Variance analysis

C   Functional analysis

D   Activity analysis

46   The selling price of product Zigma is set to be $250 for each unit and sales for the coming year are expected to be 500 units. The company requires a return of 15% in the coming year on its investment of $250,000 in product Zigma.

What is the target cost for each unit of Zigma for the coming year? Select from the list as appropriate.

List options are as follows:
- $145
- $155
- $165
- $175

47   VC Co is a company of opticians. It provides a range of services to the public, such as eye tests and contact lens consultations, and has a separate dispensary selling glasses and contact lenses. Patients book appointments with an optician in advance.

A standard appointment is 30 minutes long, during which an optician will assess the patient's specific requirements and provide them with the eye care services they need. After the appointment, patients are offered the chance to buy contact lenses or glasses from the dispensary.

Which of the following describes a characteristic of the services provided by an optician at VC Co during a standard appointment?

A   Tangible

B   Homogeneous

C   Non-perishable

D   Simultaneous

LIFE-CYCLE COSTING

48 A company has produced the following information for a product it is about to launch. The product is expected to have a life of three years.

Year	1	2	3
Expected sales units	2,000	5,000	7,000
Variable production cost per unit	$2.30	$1.80	$1.20
Fixed production costs	$3,000	$3,500	$4,000
Variable selling cost per unit	$0.50	$0.40	$0.40
Fixed selling costs	$1,500	$1,600	$1,600
Administrative costs	$700	$700	$700

What is the life-cycle cost per unit?

A $2.81

B $2.32

C $3.22

D $3.07

49 A manufacturing company which produces a range of products has developed a budget for the life-cycle of a new product, P. The information in the following table relates exclusively to product P:

	Lifetime total	Per unit
Design costs	$800,000	
Direct manufacturing costs		$20
Depreciation costs	$500,000	
Decommissioning costs	$20,000	
Machine hours		4
Production and sales units	300,000	

The company's total fixed production overheads are budgeted to be $72 million each year and total machine hours are budgeted to be 96 million hours. The company absorbs overheads on a machine hour basis.

What is the budgeted life-cycle cost per unit for product P?

A $24.40

B $25.73

C $27.40

D $22.73

50 SNT is a Japanese electronics giant specialising in the production of game consoles. SNT is planning to introduce the latest 'next-generation' console and range of games in the summer of 20X0. Development of the new console is due to commence on January 1st, 20X0 and SNT is currently working out at what price the new console should be sold then.

The new console is expected to incur the following costs in the four years it will be developed and commercialised:

	20X0	20X1	20X2	20X3
Consoles manufactured and sold	10,000	12,000	11,100	3,000
R&D costs	$950,000	$0	$0	$0
Marketing costs	$230,000	$120,000	$20,000	$5,000
Production cost per console	$450	$430	$290	$290
Warranty costs per console	$30	$30	$40	$45
End of life costs	$0	$0	$0	$125,000

Market research has indicated that customers will be prepared to pay an average price of $420 per console, but SNT's Chief Executive believes this will not be sufficient to make production worthwhile.

Which of the following statements, made by the Chief Executive, are true regarding the costs of the console?

(1) The cost per console, calculated using life-cycle costing principles, is higher than the price customers are prepared to pay.

(2) More attention to R&D costs in 20X0 could reduce warranty costs in later years.

A (1) only

B (2) only

C Neither (1) nor (2)

D Both (1) and (2)

51 While a drag and drop style question is impossible to fully replicate within a paper based medium, some questions of this style have been included for completeness.

Which FOUR of the following are said to be benefits of life-cycle costing?

- It provides the true financial cost of a product
- The length of the life-cycle can be shortened
- Expensive errors can be avoided in that potentially failing products can be avoided
- Lower costs can be achieved earlier by designing out costs
- Better selling prices can be set
- Decline stages of the life-cycle can be avoided

Drag the items selected into the box below:

52   Which of the following statements are true regarding the justification of the use of life cycle costing?

(1)   Product life cycles are becoming increasingly short. This means that the initial costs are an increasingly important component in the product's overall costs.

(2)   Product costs are increasingly weighted to the start of a product's life cycle, and to properly understand the profitability of a product these costs must be matched to the ultimate revenues.

(3)   The high costs of (for example) research, design and marketing in the early stages in a product's life cycle necessitate a high initial selling price.

(4)   Traditional capital budgeting techniques do not attempt to minimise the costs or maximise the revenues over the product life cycle.

A   (1), (2) and (4) only

B   (2) and (3) only

C   (1) and (3) only

D   (1), (2), (3) and (4)

53   Which of the following statement(s) is/are true regarding life-cycle costing?

(1)   Life cycle costing takes into account all costs incurred in a product life cycle with exception of sunk costs incurred on research and development.

(2)   Life cycle costing ensures a profit is generated over the life of the product.

(3)   Life cycle costing is most useful for products with an even weighting of costs over their life.

A   (1) and (3) only

B   (2) only

C   (2) and (3) only

D   (1), (2) and (3)

54   Company B is about to start developing a new product for launch in its existing market. They have forecast sales of 20,000 units and the marketing department suggest a selling price of $43/unit. The company seeks to make a mark-up of 40% product cost. It is estimated that the lifetime costs of the product will be as follows:

(1)   Design and development costs $43,000.

(2)   Manufacturing costs $15/unit.

(3)   Plant decommissioning costs $30,000.

What is the life cycle cost per unit of the new product?

A $18.65

B $22

C $22.87

D $24

THROUGHPUT ACCOUNTING

55   When demand exceeds supply, which one of the following situations would increase the throughput accounting ratio?

A   An increase in the speed of the fastest machine in the production process

B   An unexpected increase in the factory rent

C   A 5% wage increase linked to an 8% improvement in productivity

D   A 10% sales discount to stimulate demand by 20%

56   A manufacturing company decides which of three mutually exclusive products to make in its factory on the basis of maximising the company's throughput accounting ratio.

Current data for the three products is shown in the following table:

	Product X	Product Y	Product Z
Selling price per unit	$60	$40	$20
Direct material cost per unit	$40	$10	$16
Machine hours per unit	10	20	2.5

Total factory costs (excluding direct materials) are $150,000. The company cannot make enough of any of the products to satisfy external demand entirely as machine hours are restricted.

What would be the effect of the following actions on the company's throughput accounting ratio (TPAR)?' Place a tick in the appropriate boxes in the table below.

	Would improve the company's existing TPAR	Would NOT improve the company's existing TPAR
Increase the selling price of product Z by 10%		
Increase the selling price of product Y by 10%		
Reduce the material cost of product Z by 5%		
Reduce the material cost of product Y by 5%		

57 Skye Limited operates in an environment where products go through two processes and details of their capacity are below:

Process P

There are 8 machines operating at 90% capacity. Each machine produces 6 units per hour.

Process Q

There are 6 machines operating at 85% capacity. Each machine produces 9 units per hour.

Skye Limited produces the 'Cloud' which is not a popular product. The marketing manager has therefore decided to apply a price discount of 15% on the selling price of $20 per unit. The material cost per unit is $5 and the direct labour cost per unit is twice that of the material costs for the 'Cloud'. It currently takes 0.2 hours and 0.3 hours to make a unit of the 'Cloud' on the machines in process P and process Q respectively.

What is the Cloud's throughput per hour of the bottleneck resource (to two decimal places)?

$ [   ]

58 A manufacturing company uses machine C, which is operational for five hours a day to manufacture four products: W, X, Y and Z. Factory costs are $150,000 per day. The company uses throughput accounting and its objective is to maximise profits.

Information relating to these products is as follows:

Product	Production rate per machine hour (units)	Selling price per unit ($)	Material cost per unit ($)	Conversion cost per unit ($)
W	200	350	120	40
X	500	190	95	25
Y	400	270	160	20
Z	350	215	75	35

If the company is not able to increase the availability of machine C's operational hours, what is the production ranking of product Y?

A   First

B   Second

C   Third

D   Fourth

59 A manufacturing company uses three processes to make its two products, X and Y. The time available on the three processes is reduced because of the need for preventative maintenance and rest breaks.

The table below details the process times per product and daily time available:

Process	Hours available per day	Hours required to make one unit of product X	Hours required to make one unit of product Y
1	22	1.00	0.75
2	22	0.75	1.00
3	18	1.00	0.50

Daily demand for product X and product Y is 10 units and 16 units respectively.

Which of the following will improve throughput?

A   Increasing the efficiency of the maintenance routine for Process 2

B   Increasing the demand for both products

C   Reducing the time taken for rest breaks on Process 3

D   Reducing the time product X requires for Process 1

60   **Which ONE of the below statements is NOT true of throughput accounting?**

A   Throughput accounting considers that the only variable costs in the short run are materials and components.

B   Throughput accounting considers that time at a bottleneck resource has value, not elsewhere.

C   Throughput accounting views stock building as a non-value-adding activity, and therefore discourages it.

D   Throughput accounting was designed as a decision-making tool for situations where there is a bottleneck in the production process.

61   **Which of the following is a definition of the throughput accounting ratio?**

A   Throughput contribution/hours on bottleneck

B   Costs per factory hour/return per factory hour

C   Return per factory hour/costs per factory hour

D   Total costs/total throughput

ENVIRONMENTAL ACCOUNTING

62   **Which TWO of the following activities are environmental INTERNAL failure costs?**

   A   Quality control inspections to monitor pollution levels in water leaving a production process.

   B   Water purification treatment to clean waste water before it leaves the factory

   C   Fitting of carbon filters to machine processes to reduce carbon emissions

   D   Power usage measuring system to monitor energy consumption within the factory

   E   Payment of fines for breaching environmental regulations in the industry

   F   Insulation of heating pipes in the factory to reduce heat loss

   G   Public relations costs to remedy reputational damage caused by accidental river pollution

   H   Capturing and recycling of waste exhaust gases to generate energy

63   The monthly budget for process X shows the following input/output analysis:

   INPUTS

Description	Comment	Weight (kg)	$
Materials		1,000	(50,000)
System costs	Labour, utilities and other overheads	–	(30,000)
Total		1,000	(80,000)

   OUTPUTS

Description	Comment	Weight (kg)	$
Good output	Expected good output is 70% of input and can be sold for $120 per kg	700	84,000
Waste	Expected waste is 10% of input and must be scrapped at a cost of $10 per kg	100	(1,000)
Scrap	Expected scrap is 20% of input and can be sold for $15 per kg	200	3,000
Total		1,000	86,000

   Monthly profit is thus expected to be $6,000.

   The company is looking at introducing new quality systems that will increase system costs by $5,000 per month but will reduce waste from 10% to 4% of input. Scrap is expected to stay at 20% of input.

   What would be the impact on monthly profit of implementing the proposal?

   A $4,400 reduction in profit

   B $200 increase in profit

   C $2,200 increase in profit

   D $2,800 increase in profit

64 Different management accounting techniques can be used to account for environmental costs.

One of these techniques involves analysing costs under three distinct categories: material, system, and delivery and disposal.

What is this technique known as?

A   Activity-based costing

B   Life-cycle costing

C   Input-output analysis

D   Flow cost accounting

65 **Which TWO of the following statements about the advantages of using Activity-based costing for Environmental Management Accounting are correct?**

- Higher environmental costs can be reflected in higher prices
- Cost savings achieved through environmental policies can be measured
- It is simple to determine the environmental costs and cost drivers
- It considers all environmental effects of the company's actions

66 The monthly budget for process X shows the following input/output analysis:

INPUTS

Description	Comment	Weight (kg)	$
Materials		1,000	(50,000)
System costs	Labour, utilities and other overheads	–	(30,000)
Total		1,000	(80,000)

OUTPUTS

Description	Comment	Weight (kg)	$
Good output	Expected good output is 70% of input and can be sold for $120 per kg	700	84,000
Waste	Expected waste is 10% of input and must be scrapped at a cost of $10 per kg	100	(1,000)
Scrap	Expected scrap is 20% of input and can be sold for $15 per kg	200	3,000
Total		1,000	86,000

The company is looking at adopting environmental flow cost accounting, in which all material and system costs will be apportioned on the basis of weight.

Calculate the total net cost of waste and scrap using flow cost accounting. Give you answer to the nearest $.

$ [   ]

67 **Which TWO of the following statements about flow cost accounting are correct?**

- Manufacturing costs are categorised into material costs, system costs and delivery and disposal costs

- Flow cost accounting records material inflows and balances this with outflows both in terms of physical quantities and, at the end of the process, in monetary terms too, so that businesses are forced to focus on environmental costs

- In flow cost accounting, output costs are allocated between positive and negative product costs

- The aim of flow cost accounting is to increase the quantity of materials which, as well as having a positive effect on the environment, should have a positive effect on a company's total costs in the long run

68 **Which of the following statements is/are true regarding the issues faced by businesses in the management of their environmental costs?**

(1) The costs involved are difficult to define.

(2) Environmental costs can be categorised as quality related costs.

(3) Cost control can be an issue, in particular if costs have been identified incorrectly in the first place.

A   (1) only

B   (2) and (3) only

C   None of them

D   All of them

69 Flow cost accounting is a technique which can be used to account for environmental costs. Inputs and outputs are measured through each individual process of production.

Which of the following is NOT a category used within flow cost accounting?

A   Material flows

B   System flows

C   Delivery and disposal flows

D   Waste flows

70 Accountants usually find it difficult to deal with environmental costs.

Which of the following is NOT a reason for this?

A   Costs are often hidden

B   Costs are mostly minor

C   Costs are often very long term

D   Accounting systems rarely split off these costs automatically

DECISION-MAKING TECHNIQUES

RELEVANT COST ANALYSIS

71 UU Company has been asked to quote for a special contract. The following information about the material needed has been given:

Material X:

Original cost	Scrap value	Replacement cost
$5.00 per kg	$0.50 per kg	$5.50 per kg

The contract requires 10 kgs of Material X. There are 250 kgs of this material in inventory which was purchased in error over two years ago. If Material X is modified, at a cost of $2 per kg, it could then be used as a substitute for material Y which is in regular use and currently costs $6 per kg.

What is the relevant cost of the materials for the special contract?

A $5

B $40

C $50

D $55

72 VV Company has been asked to quote for a special contract. The contract requires 100 hours of labour. However, the labourers, who are each paid $15 per hour, are working at full capacity.

There is a shortage of labour in the market. The labour required to undertake this special contract would have to be taken from another contract, Z, which currently utilises 500 hours of labour and generates $5,000 worth of contribution.

If the labour was taken from contract Z, then the whole of contract Z would have to be delayed, and such delay would invoke a penalty fee of $1,000.

What is the relevant cost of the labour for the special contract?

A $1,000

B $1,500

C $2,500

D $7,500

73 An organisation is considering the costs to be incurred in respect of a special order opportunity. The order would require 1,250 kgs of material D, that is readily available and regularly used by the organisation on its normal products.

There are 265 kgs of material D in inventory which cost $795 last week. The current market price is $3.24 per kg. Material D is normally used to make product X. Each unit of X requires 3 kgs of material D, and if material D is costed at $3 per kg, each unit of X yields a contribution of $15.

What is the relevant cost of material D to be included in the costing of the special order?

A $3,990

B $4,050

C $10,000

D $10,300

74 In order to utilise some spare capacity, K is preparing a quotation for a special order which requires 2,000 kgs of material J.

K has 800 kgs of material J in inventory (original cost $7.00 per kg). Material J is used in the company's main product L. Each unit of L uses 5 kgs of material J and, based on an input value of $7.00 per kg of J, each unit of L yields a contribution of $10.00.

The resale value of material J is $5.50 per kg. The present replacement price of material J is $8.00 per kg. Material J is readily available in the market.

What is the relevant cost of the 2,000 kgs of material J to be included in the quotation?

A $11,000

B $14,000

C $16,000

D $18,000

75 A company is calculating the relevant cost of the material to be used on a particular contract. The contract requires 4,200 kgs of material H and this can be bought for $6.30 per kg. The company bought 10,000 kgs of material H some time ago when it paid $4.50 per kg. Currently 3,700 kgs of this remains in inventory. The inventory of material H could be sold for $3.20 per kg.

The company has no other use for material H other than on this contract, but it could be modified it at a cost of $3.70 per kg and use it as a substitute for material J. Material J is regularly used by the company and can be bought for $7.50 per kg.

What is the relevant cost of the material for the contract?

A $17,210

B $19,800

C $26,460

D $30,900

76 Ace Limited is considering a new project that will require the use of a currently idle machine. The machine has a current book value of $12,000 and a potential disposal value of $10,500 (before $200 disposal costs) and hence has been under depreciated by $1,500 over its life to date. If the machine is to be fit for purpose on the new project it will have to be relocated at a cost of $500 and refitted at a further cost of $800.

What is the relevant cost of using the machine on the new project?

A $9,000

B $10,300

C $11,600

D $13,300

77 Blunt is considering a new project but is unsure how much overhead to include in the calculations to help him decide whether or not to proceed. Existing fixed overheads are absorbed at the rate of $8 per hour worked. Blunt is certain that the project will involve an incremental 500 labour hours.

The project will involve extra machine running costs and these variable overheads cost him $4 per hour. The number of extra machine hours is expected to be 450 hours. The difference between this figure and the 500 labour hours above is expected idle time.

The project will require a little more temporary space that can be rented at a fixed cost of $1,200 for the period of hire. This overhead is not included in the fixed overhead absorption rate above.

What is the overhead to be charged to the project?

A $3,000

B $3,200

C $7,000

D $7,200

78 Cleverclogs is short of labour for a new one-off project needing 600 hours of labour and has choices as to where to source this. They could hire new people temporarily from an agency at a cost of $9 per hour. Alternatively, they could recruit new temporary staff at a fixed cost of advertising of $1,200 but then only pay $6 per hour for the time. They could also redirect some staff from existing work who are currently paid $7 per hour and who make sandals that generate a contribution of $3 per hour after all variable costs. Sandals are a good selling product and Cleverclogs will lose the production and the related sales whilst staff is working on the new one-off project.

What is the relevant cash flow?

A $1,800

B $3,600

C $4,200

D $4,800

79 Drippy is producing a list of relevant cash flows regarding a decision they have to make. They are considering launching a new type of USB memory stick that guarantees better protection to the host computer.

Drippy manages many existing products and has a standing arrangement with a technology magazine for advertising space entitling them to advertise each month. The contract has just been signed and covers the next twelve months. Payment is made in the month following an advert appearing. Drippy is going to use the magazine to advertise their exciting new USB stick.

As regards to relevant costing principles, what would be the best description for the cost of the advertising space?

A   Sunk cost

B   Historic cost

C   Relevant cost

D   Committed cost

80 **Which of the following terms would NOT normally be used to describe a relevant cost for a decision?**

A   Incremental

B   Future

C   Material

D   Cash flow

81 X plc intends to use relevant costs as the basis of the selling price for a special order: the printing of a brochure. The brochure requires a particular type of paper that is not regularly used by X plc although a limited amount is in X plc's inventory which was left over from a previous job. The cost when X plc bought this paper last year was $15 per ream and there are 100 reams in inventory. The brochure requires 250 reams. The current market price of the paper is $26 per ream, and the resale value of the paper in inventory is $10 per ream.

What is the relevant cost of the paper to be used in printing the brochure?

A $2,500

B $4,900

C $5,400

D $6,500

COST VOLUME PROFIT ANALYSIS

82   A company makes and sells product X and product Y. Twice as many units of product Y are made and sold as that of product X. Each unit of product X makes a contribution of $10 and each unit of product Y makes a contribution of $4. Fixed costs are $90,000.

What is the total number of units which must be made and sold to make a profit of $45,000?

A   7,500

B   22,500

C   15,000

D   16,875

83   Betis Limited is considering changing the way it is structured by asking its employed staff to become freelance. Employees are currently paid a fixed salary of $240,000 per annum, but would instead be paid $200 per working day. On a typical working day, staff can produce 40 units. Other fixed costs are $400,000 per annum.

The selling price of a unit is $60 and material costs are $20 per unit.

What will be the effect of the change on the breakeven point of the business and the level of operating risk?

A   The breakeven point reduces by 6,000 units and the operating gearing goes down

B   The breakeven point reduces by 4,571 units and the operating gearing goes down

C   The breakeven point reduces by 4,571 units and the operating gearing goes up

D   The breakeven point reduces by 6,000 units and the operating gearing goes up

84   P Co makes two products – P1 and P2 – budgeted details of which are as follows:

	P1	P2
	$	$
Selling price	10.00	8.00
Cost per unit:		
Direct materials	3.50	4.00
Direct labour	1.50	1.00
Variable overhead	0.60	0.40
Fixed overhead	1.20	1.00
Profit per unit	**3.20**	**1.60**

Budgeted production and sales for the year ended 30 November 20X5 are:

Product P1   10,000 units

Product P2   12,500 units

The fixed overhead costs included in P1 relate to apportionment of general overhead costs only. However P2 also includes specific fixed overheads totalling $2,500.

If only product P1 were to be made, how many units (to the nearest unit) would need to be sold in order to achieve a profit of $60,000 each year?

85 An organisation manufactures and sells a single product, the G. It has produced the following budget for the coming year:

	$000	$000
Sales revenue (20,000 units)		5,000
Manufacturing costs		
Fixed	1,600	
Variable	1,400	
Selling costs		
Fixed	1,200	
Variable	400	
Cost of sales		(4,600)
Profit		400

If inventory levels are negligible, what is the breakeven point in units?

A   13,634

B   13,750

C   17,500

D   28,000

86 A company manufactures and sells a single product with a variable cost per unit of $36. It has a contribution to sales ratio (C/S ratio) of 25%. The company has weekly fixed costs of $18,000.

Which of the following is the weekly breakeven point in units? Pick from list

List options are as follows:

- 1,500
- 1,600
- 1,800
- 2,000

87   A company makes a single product with the following data:

	$	$
Selling price		25
Material	5	
Labour	7	
Variable overhead	3	
Fixed overhead	4	
		(19)
Profit per unit		6

Budgeted output is 30,000 units.

In relation to this data, which of the following statements is correct?

A   The margin of safety is 40%

B   The contribution to sales ratio is 24%

C   The volume of sales needed to make a profit of $270,000 is 45,000 units

D   If budgeted sales increase to 40,000 units, budgeted profit will increase by $100,000

88   The management accountant of Caroline plc has calculated the firm's breakeven point from the following data:

Selling price per unit	$20
Variable costs per unit	$8
Fixed overheads for next year	$79,104

It is now expected that the product's selling price and variable cost will increase by 8% and 5.2% respectively.

By how much will Caroline's breakeven point for next year change by as a result of these changes?

A   Rise by 9.0%

B   Rise by 2.8%

C   Fall by 2.8%

D   Fall by 9%

89 Edwards sells two products with selling prices and contributions as follows:

	Product F	**Product G**
Selling price per unit	$40	$20
Contribution per unit	$10	$4
Budgeted sales units	150,000	100,000

Edwards' fixed costs are $1,400,000 per year.

What is Edwards' current breakeven revenue (to the nearest $)?

A $100,000

B $200,000

C $5,600,000

D $5,894,737

90 Edwards sells two products with selling prices and contributions as follows:

	Product F	**Product G**
Selling price	$40	$20
Contribution	$10	$4
Budgeted sales units	150,000	100,000

Edwards' fixed costs are $1,400,000 per year.

Edwards now anticipates that more customers will buy the cheaper product G and that budgeted sales will be 150,000 units for each product.

What would be the impact on the break-even revenue if the sales volume of G increases?

A   Increase by the extra revenue from G of 50,000 × $20 per unit, or $1,000,000

B   Decrease by the extra revenue from G of 50,000 × $20 per unit, or $1,000,000

C   Increase by a different amount

D   Decrease by a different amount

91

Units

What does the shaded area on the breakeven chart above represent?

A   Loss

B   Fixed cost

C   Variable cost

D   Profit

92   A company has produced the following Profit/Volume (P/V) chart for its sole product:

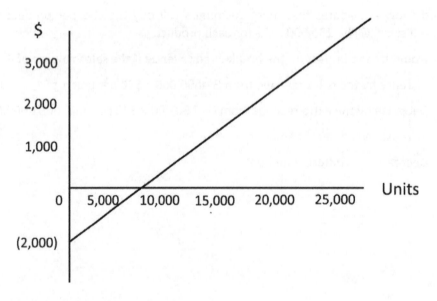

What are the total fixed costs for the product?

A $0

B $2,000

C $8,000

D $10,000

93   The following breakeven chart has been drawn for a company's single product:

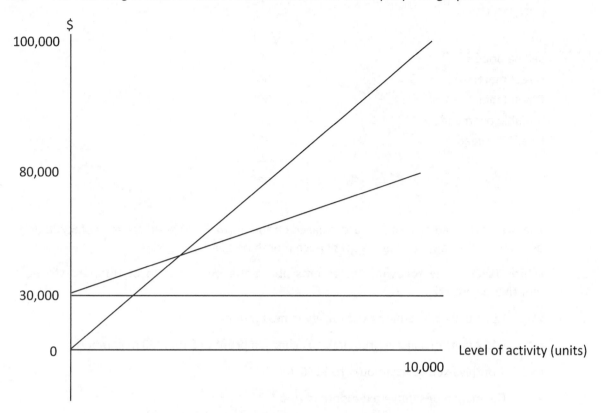

Which of the following statements about the product are correct?

(1)   The product's selling price is $10 per unit.

(2)   The product's variable cost is $8 per unit.

(3)   The product incurs fixed costs of $30,000 per period.

(4)   The product earns a profit of $70,000 at a level of activity of 10,000 units.

A   (2) and (3)

B   (1) and (3)

C   (1) and (4) only

D   (1), (2) and (4)

94   Hubbard Ltd manufactures and sells a single product that has the following cost and selling price structure:

	$/unit
Selling price	199
Direct material	54
Direct labour	50
Variable overhead	20
Fixed overhead	22
	—
	53
	—

The fixed overhead absorption rate is based on the normal budgeted capacity of 6,200 units per month. The same amount is spent each month on fixed overheads.

Which TWO of the following statements about the performance of Hubbard Ltd next month are correct?

- 1,921 units are required to breakeven next month

- 3,152 units of sales are required to achieve a profit of $100,000 next month

- Monthly fixed costs amount to $136,400

- The margin of safety next month is 75%

95   The following profit-volume chart for three products, has been prepared:

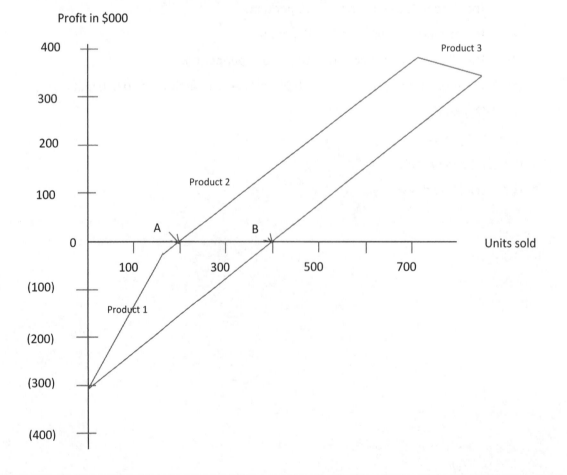

Which TWO of the following statements about the above chart are correct?

- Point A is the breakeven point if the company's products are sold in order of their C/S ratio

- Point B is the breakeven point if the company's products are sold in the budgeted sales mix

- Changing the product mix in favour of Product 3 would improve the overall c/s ratio

- If all three products are produced, then the company can expect sales revenues of $350,000

96 The contribution to sales (C/S) ratio for a business is 0.4 and its fixed costs are $1,600,000. Budget revenue has been set at 6 times the amount of the fixed costs.

What is the margin of safety % measured in revenue (to 1 decimal place)?

%

LIMITING FACTORS

97 A company has the following production planned for the next four weeks. The figures reflect the full capacity level of operations. Planned output is equal to the maximum demand per product.

	Product A	Product B	Product C	Product D
	$/unit	$/unit	$/unit	$/unit
Selling price	160	214	100	140
Raw material cost	24	56	22	40
Direct labour cost	66	88	33	22
Variable overhead cost	24	18	24	18
Fixed overhead cost	16	10	8	12
Profit	30	42	13	48
Planned output	300	125	240	400
Direct labour hours per unit	6	8	3	2

The direct labour force is threatening to go on strike for two weeks out of the coming four. This means that only 2,160 hours will be available for production, rather than the usual 4,320 hours.

If the strike goes ahead, which product or products should be produced if profits are to be maximised? Place a tick in the boxes in the table below as appropriate.

	Should be produced	Should not be produced
Product A		
Product B		
Product C		
Product D		

98 An organisation has the following contribution function:

Contribution = 5X + 10Y

where

X = the number of units of product X produced, and

Y = the number of units of product Y produced.

A graph has identified that the optimal production plan exists at the point where the following two constraints cross:

Skilled labour: 6X + 4Y ≤ 62,000

Unskilled labour: 2X + 5Y ≤ 50,000

There is a maximum demand of 12,000 units of each product.

What is the number of units of Product Y produced in order to maximise contribution (to the nearest whole unit)?

```
┌─────────────────────────────┐
│                             │
│                             │
└─────────────────────────────┘
```

99 A jewellery company makes rings (R) and necklaces (N).

The resources available to the company have been analysed and two constraints have been identified:

Labour time 3R + 2N ≤ 2,400 hours   Machine time   0.5R + 0.4N ≤ 410 hours

The management accountant has used linear programming to determine that R = 500 and N = 400.

Which of the following is/are slack resources?

(1)   Labour time available

(2)   Machine time available

A   (1) only

B   (2) only

C   Both (1) and (2)

D   Neither (1) nor (2)

100 Q plc makes two products – Quone and Qutwo – from the same raw material. The selling price and cost details of these products are as shown below:

	Quone	Qutwo
	$	$
Selling price	20.00	18.00
Direct material ($2.00 per kg)	6.00	5.00
Direct labour	4.00	3.00
Variable overhead	2.00	1.50
	12.00	9.50
Contribution per unit	8.00	8.50

The maximum demand for these products is 500 units per week for Quone, and an unlimited number of units per week for Qutwo.

What is the shadow price of these materials, if material were limited to 2,000 kgs per week? Pick from list

List options are:

- $nil
- $2.00 per kg
- $2.66 per kg
- $3.40 per kg

101 **The shadow price of skilled labour for CBV is currently $8 per hour. What does this mean?**

A   The cost of obtaining additional skilled labour resources is $8 per hour

B   There is a hidden cost of $8 for each hour of skilled labour actively worked

C   Contribution will be increased by $8 per hour for each extra hour of skilled labour that can be obtained

D   Total costs will be reduced by $8 for each additional hour of skilled labour that can be obtained

102 The following details relate to three services provided by RST Company:

	Service R	Service S	Service T
	$	$	$
Fee charged to customers	100	150	160
Unit service costs:			
Direct materials	15	30	25
Direct labour	20	35	30
Variable overhead	15	20	22
Fixed overhead	25	50	50

All three services use the same type of direct labour which is paid $25 per hour.

The fixed overheads are general fixed overheads that have been absorbed on the basis of machine hours.

What are the most and least profitable uses of direct labour, a scarce resource?

	Most profitable	Least profitable
A	S	R
B	S	T
C	T	R
D	T	S

103 A linear programming model has been formulated for two products, X and Y. The objective function is depicted by the formula C = 5X + 6Y, where C = contribution, X = the number of product X to be produced and Y = the number of product Y to be produced.

Each unit of X uses 2 kg of material Z and each unit of Y uses 3 kg of material Z. The standard cost of material Z is $2 per kg.

The shadow price for material Z has been worked out and found to be $2.80 per kg.

If an extra 20 kg of material Z becomes available at $2 per kg, what will the maximum increase in contribution be?

A   Increase of $96

B   Increase of $56

C   Increase of $16

D   No change

104 An organisation is experiencing a shortage of resources and has graphed a potential linear programming solution which shows its first product, televisions, on the horizontal axis and its other product, tablet computers, on the vertical axis.

The iso-contribution line to solve the linear programme is very flat and downward sloping.

Which of the following statements is likely to be true for the company?

A   The contribution per unit for tablet computers must be higher than that for televisions

B   The contribution per unit for televisions must be higher than that for tablet computers

C   The contribution per unit for each type of product is very similar

D   The contribution per unit for one of the products must be negative

105 A linear programming model has been formulated for two products, A and B, manufactured by J Co.

Which TWO of the following statements about linear programming are true?

•   J Co can use linear programming if it starts to manufacture another product, C.

•   J Co would not need to use linear programming if there was not a demand constraint.

•   J Co should ignore fixed costs when making decisions about how to utilise production capacity in the short run, using linear programming.

•   Linear programming models can be used when there is an experience curve, once the steady state has been reached.

106 An organisation has the following contribution function:

Contribution = 12A + 8B, where

A = the number of units of product A produced, and

B = the number of units of product B produced.

A graph has identified that the optimal production plan exists at the point where the following two constraints cross:

Material X: A + 2B ≤ 8,000

Material Y: 2A + B ≤ 13,000

There is a maximum demand of 10,000 units of each product.

How many units of Product A are produced in order to maximise contribution?

A   0

B   1,000

C   6,000

D   10,000

107 An organisation has graphed the following linear programming model:

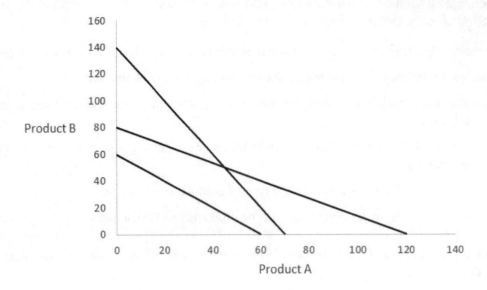

All constraints have less than or equal to constraints.

What is the maximum number of units of Product B which can be produced?

108 An organisation has created the following linear programming solution to represent the position it faces currently in the presence of short term scarce resources:

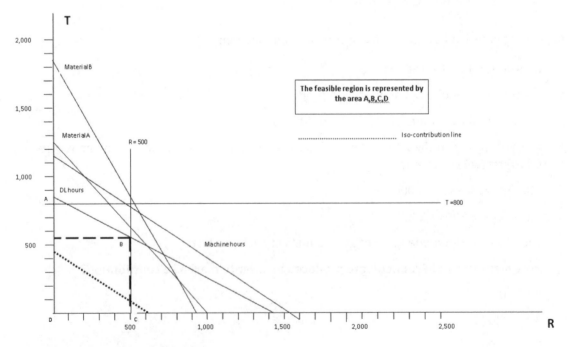

Note: DL = Direct labour hours

The point marked B has been determined to be the point which provides the optimal production plan.

Which of the following resources will have a shadow price greater than 0? (select all that apply)

- Direct labour hours

- Material A

- Material B

- Machine hours

PRICING DECISIONS

109 **Which of the following statements is true of pricing?**

A   Discrimination is always illegal so everyone should pay the same amount

B   Early adopters get a discount for being first in the market

C   Pricing against a similar competitor is important in the Internet age

D   Price to make the most sales in that way you will always get the most profit

110 **Which of the following statements regarding market penetration as a pricing strategy is/are correct?**

(1)   It is useful if significant economies of scale can be achieved.

(2)   It is useful if demand for a product is highly elastic.

A   (1) only

B   (2) only

C   Neither (1) nor (2)

D   Both (1) and (2)

111 **Which of the following conditions would need to be true for a price skimming strategy to be effective?**

A   An existing product where the owners have decided to increase prices to move the product up market

B   Where the product has a long life-cycle

C   Where the product has a short life-cycle

D   Where only modest development costs had been incurred

112 **Which TWO of the following circumstances (in relation to the launch of a new product) favour a penetration pricing strategy?**

- Demand is relatively inelastic

- There are significant economies of scale

- The firm wishes to discourage new entrants to the market

- The product life cycle is particularly short

113 **Which of the following conditions must be true for a price discrimination strategy to be effective?**

A   Buying power of customers must be similar in both market segments

B   Goods must not be able to move freely between market segments

C   Goods must be able to move freely between market segments

D   The demand curves in each market must be the same

114 The demand for product S is 50,000 units at the current price of $1,000. Market research has determined that there is a linear relationship between price and demand that can be calculated using the following function:

$P = 1,500 - 0.01Q$

The variable cost per unit of producing product S is $200, and fixed costs are $20 million.

What is the maximum total profit for product S?

A $13,000,000

B $22,250,000

C $42,250,000

D $55,250,000

115 A product has a prime cost of $12, variable overheads of $3 per unit and fixed overheads of $6 per unit.

Which pricing policy gives the highest price?

A   Prime cost + 80%

B   Marginal cost + 60%

C   Total absorption cost + 20%

D   Net margin of 14% on selling price

116 The demand for a product is 5,000 units when the price is $400 and 6,000 units when price is $380. The variable cost of the product is $200.

What is the optimum price to be charged in order to maximise profit?

A $150

B $200

C $350

D $700

117 While a drag and drop style question is impossible to fully replicate within a paper based medium, some questions of this style have been included for completeness.

A brand new game is about to be launched. The game is unique and can only be played on the Star2000 gaming console, another one of the businesses products. Students are entitled to a small discount.

Which THREE of the following pricing strategies could be used to price the game?

Drag the correct options into the box below:

- Penetration pricing
- Price skimming
- Complimentary product pricing
- Product line pricing
- Price discrimination
- Variable production cost + %

118 The following price and demand combinations have been given:

P1 = $400, Q1 = 5,000 units

P2 = $380, Q2 = 5,500 units

The variable cost is a constant at $80 per unit and fixed costs are $600,000 per annum.

What is the demand function?

A $P = 200 - 0.04Q$

B $P = 600 - 0.04Q$

C $P = 600 + 0.04Q$

D $P = 200 - 20Q$

119 The following price and demand combinations have been given:

P1 = $400, Q1 = 5,000 units

P2 = $380, Q2 = 5,500 units

The variable cost is a constant at $80 per unit and fixed costs are $600,000 per annum.

The optimal price is (to the nearest $):

$ [   ]

MAKE-OR-BUY AND OTHER SHORT TERM DECISIONS

120 Which FOUR of the following are to be correctly included in the considerations in a make or buy decision?

(i)   The amount of re-allocated rent costs caused by using the production space differently.

(ii)   The variable costs of purchase from the new supplier.

(iii)   The level of discount available from the new supplier.

(iv)   The redundancy payments to the supervisor of the product in question.

(v)   The saved labour costs of the production staff re-directed to other work.

(vi)   The materials no longer bought to manufacture the product.

121 Appler is considering the relevant cash flows involved in a short-term decision. An important client has asked for the minimum price for the processing of a compound. The compound involves the following:

Material A: Appler needs 500 kg of material for the compound but has 200 kg in stock at present. The stock items were bought 3 months ago for $5/kg but have suffered 10% shrinkage since that date. Material A is not regularly used in the business and would have to be disposed of at a cost to Appler of $400 in total. The current purchase price of material A is $6.25/kg.

Material B: Appler needs 800 kg of material B and has this in stock as it is regularly needed. The stock was bought 2 months ago for $4/kg although it can be bought now at $3.75/kg due to its seasonal nature.

Processing energy costs would be $200 and the supervisor says they would allocate $150 of their weekly salary to the job in the company's job costing system.

Based upon the scenario information, what is the total cost of material A and B to be built in to the minimum price calculation (to the nearest $)?

$ [   ]

122 Appler is considering the relevant cash flows involved in a short-term decision. An important client has asked for the minimum price for the processing of a compound. The compound involves the following:

Material A: Appler needs 500 kg of material for the compound but has 200 kg in stock at present. The stock items were bought 3 months ago for $5/kg but have suffered 10% shrinkage since that date. Material A is not regularly used in the business and would have to be disposed of at a cost to Appler of $400 in total. The current purchase price of material A is $6.25/kg.

Material B: Appler needs 800 kg of material B and has this in stock as it is regularly needed. The stock was bought 2 months ago for $4/kg although it can be bought now at $3.75/kg due to its seasonal nature.

Processing energy costs would be $200 and the supervisor says they would allocate $150 of their weekly salary to the job in the company's job costing system.

Based upon the scenario information, what is the total cost for processing and supervision to be included in the minimum price calculation (to the nearest $)?

$ [   ]

123 While a drag and drop style question is impossible to fully replicate within a paper based medium, some questions of this style have been included for completeness.

Ace Limited is considering whether or not to cease production of leather-bound diaries.

Which TWO of the following items are valid factors to consider in this decision?

- The diaries made a loss in the year just passed
- The diaries made a positive contribution in the year just passed
- The market outlook in the long term looks very poor
- The budget for next year shows a loss
- The business also sells pens and many diary buyers will often also buy a pen
- The business was founded to produce and sell diaries

Drag and drop the correct factors in the box below:

[   ]

124 Jorioz Co makes joint products X and Y. $120,000 joint processing costs are incurred.

At the split-off point, 10,000 units of X and 9,000 units of Y are produced, with selling prices of $1.20 for X and $1.50 for Y.

The units of X could be processed further to make 8,000 units of product Z. The extra costs incurred in this process would be fixed costs of $1,600 and variable costs of $0.50 per unit of input.

The selling price of Z would be $2.25.

What profit or loss will arise if product X is further processed? Pick from

List options are

- $600 loss

- $400 gain

- $3,900 gain

- $1,600 loss

125 P is considering whether to continue making a component or to buy it from an outside supplier. It uses 12,000 of the components each year.

The internal manufacturing cost comprises:

	$/unit
Direct materials	3.00
Direct labour	4.00
Variable overhead	1.00
Specific fixed cost	2.50
Other fixed costs	2.00
	———
	12.50
	———

If the direct labour were not used to manufacture the component, it would be used to increase the production of another item for which there is unlimited demand. This other item has a contribution of $10.00 per unit but requires $8.00 of labour per unit.

What is the maximum price per component, at which buying is preferable to internal manufacture?

A $8.00

B $10.50

C $12.50

D $15.50

DEALING WITH RISK AND UNCERTAINTY IN DECISION-MAKING

126 Shuffles Co uses fork-lift trucks in its warehouses. The management accountant is deciding which grade of trucks to buy based on the company's risk appetite. There are three grades of truck, the A series, B series and the C series. The decision for the truck is dependent on Shuffles Co's growth in its online market which could be at 15%, 30% or 40% for the next period.

The management accountant has correctly produced a pay-off table showing the daily contribution earned for each of the outcomes.

Pay-off table		Type of truck		
		A series	B series	C series
Growth rate	15%	$2,400	$1,800	$3,600
	30%	$1,400	$1,900	$4,500
	40%	$4,900	$2,800	$3,900

If Shuffles Co is risk averse, which grade of truck will it purchase?' Enter the letter only.

	series

127 Shuffles Co uses fork-lift trucks in its warehouses. The management accountant is deciding which grade of trucks to buy based on the company's risk appetite. There are three grades of truck, the A series, B series and the C series. The decision for the truck is dependent on Shuffles Co's growth in its online market which could be at 15%, 30% or 40% for the next period.

The management accountant has correctly produced a pay-off table showing the daily contribution earned for each of the outcomes.

Pay-off table		Type of truck		
		A series	B series	C series
Growth rate	15%	$2,400	$1,800	$3,600
	30%	$1,400	$1,900	$4,500
	40%	$4,900	$2,800	$3,900

If Shuffles Co is risk seeking, which grade of truck will it purchase?' Enter the letter only.

	series

128 Shuffles Co uses fork-lift trucks in its warehouses. The management accountant is deciding which grade of trucks to buy based on the company's risk appetite. There are three grades of truck, the A series, B series and the C series. The decision for the truck is dependent on Shuffles Co's growth in its online market which could be at 15%, 30% or 40% for the next period.

The management accountant has correctly produced a pay-off table showing the daily contribution earned for each of the outcomes.

Pay-off table		Type of truck		
		A series	B series	C series
Growth rate	15%	$2,400	$1,800	$3,600
	30%	$1,400	$1,900	$4,500
	40%	$4,900	$2,800	$3,900

If Shuffles Co adopt the minimax regret approach to decision-making, which grade of truck will it purchase? Enter the letter only.

	series

129 Shuffles Co uses fork-lift trucks in its warehouses. The management accountant is deciding which grade of trucks to buy based on the company's risk appetite. There are three grades of truck, the A series, B series and the C series. The decision for the truck is dependent on Shuffles Co's growth in its online market which could be at 15%, 30% or 40% for the next period.

The management accountant has correctly produced a pay-off table showing the daily contribution earned for each of the outcomes.

Pay-off table		Type of truck		
		A series	B series	C series
Growth rate	15%	$2,400	$1,800	$3,600
	30%	$1,400	$1,900	$4,500
	40%	$4,900	$2,800	$3,900

Based upon the scenario information, if the probabilities of the given growth rates are 15%: 0.4, 30%: 0.25 and 40%: 0.35, and Shuffles Co is risk neutral, which grade of truck will it purchase? Enter the letter only.

	series

130 **Which TWO of the following statements about sensitivity analysis are correct?**

    (1)   Sensitivity analysis can be used to gain insight into which assumptions or variables in a situation are critical

    (2)   Sensitivity analysis provides information on the basis of which decisions can be made but it does not point to the correct decision directly

    (3)   As well as identifying how far a variable needs to change, sensitivity analysis looks at the probability of such a change

    (4)   Sensitivity analysis not only assumes that variables can change independently, it also allows to change more than one variable at a time

    A   (1) and (2) only

    B   (2) and (3) only

    C   (1) and (4) only

    D   (2) and (4) only

131 **Indicate, by clicking in the relevant boxes, whether the following statements about simulation are true or not true:**

	True	Not true
Simulation models the behaviour of a system.		
Simulation models can be used to study alternative solutions to a problem.		
The equations describing the operating characteristics of the system are known.		
A simulation model cannot prescribe what should be done about a problem.		

132 A company has used expected values to evaluate a one-off project. The expected value calculation assumed two possible profit outcomes which were assigned probabilities of 0.4 and 0.6.

Which TWO of the following statements about this approach are correct?

    •   The expected value profit is the profit which has the highest probability of being achieved

    •   The expected value gives no indication of the dispersion of the possible outcomes

    •   Expected values are relatively insensitive to assumptions about probability

    •   The expected value may not correspond to any of the actual possible outcomes

133 Tree Co is considering employing a sales manager. Market research has shown that a good sales manager can increase profit by 30%, an average one by 20% and a poor one by 10%. Experience has shown that the company has attracted a good sales manager 35% of the time, an average one 45% of the time and a poor one 20% of the time. The company's normal profits are $180,000 per annum and the sales manager's salary would be $40,000 per annum.

Based on the expected value criterion, which of the following represents the correct advice which Tree Co should be given?

A   Do not employ a sales manager as profits would be expected to fall by $1,300

B   Employ a sales manager as profits will increase by $38,700

C   Employ a sales manager as profits are expected to increase by $100

D   Do not employ a sales manager as profits are expected to fall by $39,900

134 **Which of the following is the correct definition of IMPERFECT information?**

A   Information which costs more to collect than its value to the business

B   Information which is available only after preliminary decisions on a business venture have been taken

C   Information which does not take into account all factors affecting a business

D   Information which may contain inaccurate predictions

135 A company is considering the development and marketing of a new product. Development costs will be $2m. There is a 75% probability that the development effort will be successful, and a 25% probability that it will be unsuccessful. If development **is** successful and the product **is** marketed, it is estimated that:

	Profit	Probability
Product very successful	$6.0m	0.4
Product moderately successful	$1.8m	0.4
Product unsuccessful	($5.0m)	0.2

What is the expected value of profit for the new product?

A   ($0.41m)

B $2.12m

C $1.59m

D $0.41m

136 A company can make either of two new products, X and Y, but not both. The profitability of each product depends on the state of the market, as follows:

Market state	Profit from product		Probability of market state
	X $	Y $	
Good	20,000	17,000	0.2
Fair	15,000	16,000	0.5
Poor	6,000	7,000	0.3

What is the expected value of perfect information as to the state of the market?

$ [   ]

137 A business is considering investing in a project which is very dependent on whether a government grant is received.

Details on the project are as follows:

	Grant received	Grant not received	Overall expected value
Probability	30%	70%	
Expected profits/(loss)	$200,000	($80,000)	$4,000

It is now concerned that the expected loss when the grant is not received has been underestimated.

What would the expected loss when the grant is not received have to increase to in order to no longer make the project worthwhile?

A $84,000

B $85,714

C $114,286

D $200,000

138 An organisation is considering launching a new product, X. If the product is successful in its first month there will be an opportunity to either make a further investment or to outsource all future development to another company. The decision for the company is illustrated by the following decision tree:

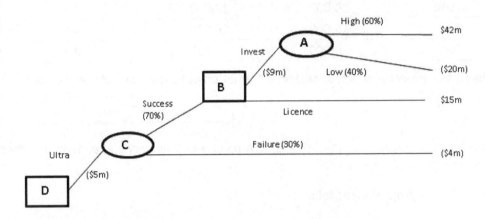

The profit outcomes do not include the cost of any investments made.

What is the expected value from investing in product X?

A $0

B $4.3m

C $6.2m

D $6.5m

139 An organisation is considering launching a new product, X. If the product is successful in its first month there will be an opportunity to either make a further investment or to outsource all future development to another company. The decision for the company is illustrated by the following decision tree:

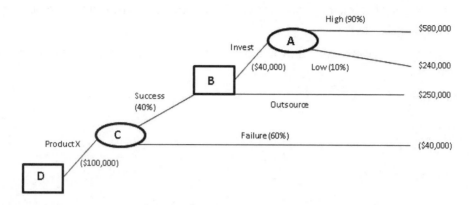

The profit outcomes do not include the cost of any investments made.

What is the expected value at point B on the decision tree (to the nearest $000)?

$ [   ]

140 **Which of the following is considered to be a form of secondary research?**

A Desk research

B Motivational research

C Measurement research

D Field research

BUDGETING AND CONTROL

BUDGETARY SYSTEMS AND TYPES OF BUDGET

141   Which of the following statements are true regarding activity-based budgeting (ABB)?

    (1)   The costs determined using activity-based costing (ABC) are used as a basis for preparing budgets.

    (2)   The aim of ABB is to control the number of units output rather than the costs themselves.

    A   (1) only

    B   (2) only

    C   Neither (1) nor (2)

    D   Both (1) and (2)

142   Which of the following statement(s) is/are true regarding budgetary systems in the performance hierarchy?

    (1)   Developing new products in response the changes in technology is a budgeting activity that would fall within operational planning and control.

    (2)   Budgetary systems at strategic planning levels look at the business as a whole and define resource requirements.

    A   (1) only

    B   (2) only

    C   Neither (1) nor (2)

    D   Both (1) and (2)

143   What is the purpose of a flexible budget?

    A   To allow budgets to be produced for virtually any level of production

    B   To reduce the total time in preparing the annual budget

    C   To allow management some latitude in meeting goals

    D   To eliminate cyclical fluctuations in production reports by ignoring variable costs

144   Which of the following statement(s) is/are true regarding feed-forward control budgetary systems?

    (1)   Feed-forward control systems have an advantage over other types of control in that it establishes how effective planning was.

    (2)   Feed-forward control can start as soon as actual results become available.

    A   (1) only

    B   (2) only

    C   Neither (1) nor (2)

    D   Both (1) and (2)

145 While a drag and drop style question is impossible to fully replicate within a paper based medium, some questions of this style have been included for completeness.

Incremental budgeting can sometimes be an appropriate methodology for setting budgets.

Which THREE of the following statements are true?

Incremental budgets could be appropriate when:

- The business is growing rapidly

- Applied to total sales in an international seasonal business

- Applied to stationery costs

- Applied to production costs

- The business is stable

- For administration costs when the experience of the managers is limited

Drag the correct answers in to the box:

146 **Which of the following best describes an incremental budgeting system?**

A a system that budgets only for the extra costs associated with a particular plan

B a system that budgets for the variable manufacturing costs only

C a system that prepares budgets only after the manager responsible has justified the continuation of the relevant activity

D a system that prepares budgets by adjusting the previous year's values by expected changes in volumes of activity and price/inflation effects

147 **Which of the following is an advantage of non-participative budgeting as compared to participative budgeting?**

A It increases motivation

B It is less time consuming

C It increases acceptance

D The budgets produced are more attainable

148 **Which of the following is a common feature of a beyond budgeting approach?**

    A   A greater use of rolling budgets

    B   A greater use of top-down budgets

    C   A greater emphasis on financial targets

    D   A greater focus on standardisation

149 EFG uses an activity-based budgeting system. It manufactures three products, budgeted details of which are set out below:

	Product E	Product F	Product G
Budgeted annual production (units)	75,000	120,000	60,000
Batch size (units)	200	60	30
Machine set-ups per batch	5	3	9
Purchase orders per batch	4	2	2
Processing time per unit (minutes)	3	4	4

Three cost pools have been identified. Their budgeted costs for the year ending 30 September 20X3 are as follows:

Machine set-up costs	$180,000
Purchasing of materials	$95,000
Processing	$110,000

Which of the following is the budgeted machine set-up cost per unit of product F? Pick from list

List options are:

- $0.1739

- $0.35

- $6.96

- Cannot be determined without any more information

150 **Which of the following best describes a master budget?**

    A   Budgeted Statement of profit or loss and budgeted cash flow only

    B   Budgeted Statement of profit or loss and budgeted Statement of financial position only

    C   Budgeted Statement of profit or loss and budgeted capital expenditure

    D   Budgeted Statement of profit or loss, budgeted Statement of financial position and budgeted cash flow

151 **Which TWO of the following are expected benefits from a beyond budgeting approach?**

- Coordination between activities becomes easier

- It is cheap and easy to introduce

- Innovation and continuous improvement become more likely

- The organisation becomes more customer focused

152 X Co uses rolling budgeting, updating its budgets on a quarterly basis. After carrying out the last quarter's update to the cash budget, it projected a forecast cash deficit of $400,000 at the end of the year. Consequently, the planned purchase of new capital equipment has been postponed.

Which of the following types of control is the sales manager's actions an example of?

A   Feedforward control

B   Negative feedback control

C   Positive feedback control

D   Double loop feedback control

153 **Which of the following statement(s) is/are true regarding different types of budget?**

(1)   A flexible budget can be used to control operational efficiency.

(2)   Incremental budgeting can be defined as a system of budgetary planning and control that measures the additional costs that are incurred when there are unplanned extra units of activity.

(3)   Rolling budgets review and, if necessary, revise the budget for the next quarter to ensure that budgets remain relevant for the remainder of the accounting period.

A   (1) and (3)

B   (2) and (3)

C   (3) only

D   (1) only

154 A definition of zero-based budgeting is set out below, with two blank sections.

"Zero-based budgeting: a method of budgeting which requires each cost element _____, as though the activities to which the budget relates _____."

Which combination of two phrases correctly completes the definition?

	Blank 1	Blank 2
A	to be specifically justified	could be out-sourced to an external supplier
B	to be set at zero	could be out-sourced to an external supplier
C	to be specifically justified	were being undertaken for the first time
D	to be set at zero	were being undertaken for the first time

155 **Which TWO of the following statements regarding zero-based budgeting are correct?**

- It is best applied to support expenses rather than to direct costs
- It can link strategic goals to specific functional areas
- It carries forward inefficiencies from previous budget periods
- It is consistent with a top-down budgeting approach

156 Which of the following statement(s) regarding the drawbacks of activity-based budgeting (ABB) is/are true?

(1) It is not always useful or applicable, as in the short term many overhead costs are not controllable and do not vary directly with changes in the volume of activity for the cost driver.

(2) ABB will not be able to provide useful information for a total quality management programme (TQM).

A (1) only

B (2) only

C Neither (1) nor (2)

D Both (1) and (2)

QUANTITATIVE TECHNIQUES

157 The following table shows the number of clients who attended a particular accountancy practice over the last four weeks and the total costs incurred during each of the weeks:

Week	Number of clients	Total cost ($)
1	400	36,880
2	440	39,840
3	420	36,800
4	460	40,000

Applying the high low method to the above information, which of the following could be used to forecast total cost ($) from the number of clients expected to attend (where x = the expected number of clients)?

A 7,280 + 74x

B 16,080 + 52x

C 3,200 + 80x

D 40,000/x

158 PT has discovered that, when it employs a new test engineer, there is a learning curve with a 75% rate of learning that exists for the first 12 customer assignments. A new test engineer completed her first customer assignment in 6 hours.

Note: The index for a 75% learning curve is −0.415.

Calculate the time that she should take for her 7th assignment to the nearest 0.01 hours.

A 1.52 hours

B 1.62 hours

C 2.68 hours

D 18.73 hours

159   The first unit of product A takes 50 hours to produce. The learning rate is 85%, meaning b is –0.234.

What is the total time taken to produce 17 units (to the nearest 0.01 hours)?

A   19.88 hours

B   25.77 hours

C   418.14 hours

D   438.02 hours

160   The time taken to produce the first batch of 50 units was 500 hours. The total time for the first 16 batches of 50 units was 5,731 hours.

What is the learning rate (to the nearest %)?

	%

161   The budgeted electricity cost for a business is $30,000 based upon production of 1,000 units. However, if 1,400 units were to be produced, the budgeted cost would rise to $31,600.

Using the high/low approach what would be the budgeted electricity cost if 2,100 units were to be produced (to the nearest $)?

$ | |
  | -- |

162   The time taken to produce the first unit produced was 100 hours. The time for the second unit was 90 hours.

What is the learning rate (to the nearest %)?

	%

163   The time taken to produce the first batch of 50 units was 400 hours but the labour budget is subject to a learning effect where the learning rate is 90%. The rate of pay for labour is $12 per hour.

The business had received and satisfied an order for 600 units but it has now received a second order for another 800 units.

The value of b is = –0.152

What will be the labour cost for the second order? (to the nearest $))

$ | |
  | -- |

164 The times taken to produce each of the first four batches of a new product were as follows:

Batch number	Time taken
1	100 minutes
2	70 minutes
3	59 minutes
4	55 minutes

What was the rate of learning closest to? (1 d.p)

	%

165 Kim Co has recently developed a new product. The nature of Kim Co's work is repetitive, and it is usual for there to be an 80% learning effect when a new product is developed. The time taken for the first unit was 22 minutes.

Note: For this question, use a value for b of -0.3219

How long would it take to make the fourth unit? Select from the list below.

List options are as follows:

17.6 minutes

14.08 minutes

15.45 minutes

9.98 minutes

166 Z plc has found that it can estimate future sales using time series analysis and regression techniques. The following trend equation has been derived:

$$y = 25,000 + 6,500x$$

where 'y' is the total sales units per quarter and 'x' is the time period reference number.

Z has also derived the following set of seasonal variation index values for each quarter using a multiplicative (proportional) model:

Quarter 1	70%
Quarter 2	90%
Quarter 3	150%
Quarter 4	90%

Assuming that the first quarter of year 1 is time period reference number 1, what would be the forecast sales units for the third quarter of year 7?

A   174,500 units

B   200,500 units

C   261,750 units

D   300,750 units

167 Hi-Tech plc is a mobile phone repair shop. The director is interested in the relationship between the amount that is spent on advertising and the sales revenue that is achieved. They have established that the regression equation y = 150 + 7x can be used, where y is the total sales revenue and x is the advertising spend (in $000s).

Which ONE of the following statements is a correct interpretation of the relationship?

A If $7,000 is spent on advertising, then sales revenue would be $150,000

B If no money is spent on advertising, then sales revenue would be $7,000

C If $150,000 is spent on advertising, then $7,000 sales revenue per month will be generated

D If no money is spent on advertising, then sales revenue would be $150,000

168 Production overhead costs at company MZ Ltd are assumed to vary in line with the number of labour hours worked. The following data has been collected:

Year	Total production overheads $	Number of labour hours	Cost index
20X4	205,000	4,200	189
20X5	226,180	4,700	205

If the line of best fit, based on current (20X5) prices is calculated as y = 127,000 + 18.6x, calculate the total expected overhead costs in 20X6 if expected production activity is 4,600 labour hours and the expected cost index is 225.

A $193,666

B $212,560

C $233,298

D $253,048

169 The overhead costs of RP have been found to be accurately represented by the formula:

$$y = \$10,000 + \$0.25x$$

where y is the monthly cost and x represents the activity level measured as the number of orders.

Monthly activity levels of orders may be estimated using a combined regression analysis and time series model:

$$a = 100,000 + 30b$$

where a represents the de-seasonalised monthly activity level and b represents the month number.

In month 240, the seasonal index value is 108.

The overhead cost for RP for month 240 is $_____ (round to the nearest $1,000)

170 Monthly sales of product R follow a linear trend of y = 9.72 + 5.816x, where y is the number of units sold and x is the number of the month. Monthly deviations from the trend follow an additive model.

The forecast number of units of product R to be sold in month 23, which has a seasonal factor of +6.5 is, to the nearest whole unit:

    A   134

    B   137

    C   143

    D   150

171 A company has calculated that the coefficient of determination between output and production costs over a number of months is 89%.

Which TWO of the following comments are correct?

	Correct?
89% of the variation in production costs from one month to the next can be explained by corresponding variation in output.	
Costs increase as output increases.	
The linear relationship between output and costs is very strong.	
An increase of 100% in output is associated with an increase of 89% in costs.	
An increase of 89% in output is associated with an increase of 100% in costs.	

STANDARD COSTING

172 **Which of the following best describes a 'basic standard' within the context of budgeting?**

    A   A standard which is kept unchanged over a period of time

    B   A standard which is based on current price levels

    C   A standard set at an ideal level, which makes no allowance for normal losses, waste and machine downtime

    D   A standard which assumes an efficient level of operation, but which includes allowances for factors such as normal loss, waste and machine downtime

173 **Which TWO of the following statements about budgets and standards are true?**

    •   Budgets can be used in situations where output cannot be measured, but standards cannot be used in such situations

    •   Budgets can include allowances for inefficiencies in operations, but standards use performance targets which are attainable under the most favourable conditions

    •   Budgets are used for planning purposes, standards are used only for control purposes

    •   Standards which remain unaltered for long periods of time are referred to as basic standards

174 **Which one of the following best defines standard costing in a system of budgeting?**

A   all activities are examined without reference to history each year

B   output level and costs are predetermined, actual results then compared with these predetermined costs and variances analysed

C   actual costs are compared with predetermined costs for the level of activity

D   costs are assigned to a manager in order that controllable and non-controllable costs are accounted for

175 The following are management accounting techniques:

(i)   Actual versus flexed budget calculations.

(ii)   Variance analysis.

(iii) Trend of costs analysis.

Which of the above techniques could be used by a company to control costs?

A   (i) and (ii) only

B   (i) and (iii) only

C   (ii) and (iii) only

D   (i), (ii) and (iii)

176 **When considering setting standards for costing, which of the following would NOT be appropriate?**

A   The normal level of activity should always be used for absorbing overheads

B   Average prices for materials should be used, encompassing any discounts that are regularly available

C   The labour rate used will be the rate at which the labour is paid

D   Average material usage should be established based on generally-accepted working practices

177 **Which of the following statements is/are true regarding standard costing and total quality management (TQM)?**

(1)   They focus on assigning responsibility solely to senior managers.

(2)   They work well in rapidly changing environments.

A   (1) only

B   (2) only

C   Neither (1) nor (2)

D   Both (1) and (2)

178 While a drag and drop style question is impossible to fully replicate within a paper based medium, some questions of this style have been included for completeness.

A business is expanding rapidly and buying its material in a variety of countries in a variety of currencies. It has an exclusive supply delivery contract whereby the same logistics expert makes all deliveries in to its warehouses on a cost plus basis. It pays all delivery charges on a per unit basis.

Which THREE of the following are valid explanations of an adverse material price variance measured to include delivery costs as part of the cost per kg delivered?

Drag the correct items into the box below:

- Exchange rate movements

- Extra discounts agreed

- Increased world-wide demand for the material

- Extra supply of the material becoming available from new suppliers

- World oil price rises

- Increases in the dividends paid by the delivery business

MIX AND YIELD VARIANCES

179 While a drag and drop style question is impossible to fully replicate within a paper based medium, some questions of this style have been included for completeness.

The following are potential causes of a material usage variance; drag the THREE reasons that could properly explain an adverse usage variance and at the same time indicate poor performance of the production manager into the box below.

The business has separate managers for production, material purchase and machine maintenance.

- Selection of a new supplier offering similar quality for lower prices

- Inadequate training of newly recruited staff in the production department

- Movements in the exchange rates causing more expensive materials

- Machine breakdown due to delays in the annual maintenance schedule

- Reduced quality materials bought

- Change in the production process causing extra losses of materials

180 Which of the following statements is/are true regarding the material mix variance?

(1) A favourable total mix variance would suggest that a higher proportion of a cheaper material is being used instead of a more expensive one.

(2) A favourable total mix variance will usually result in a favourable material yield variance.

A (1) only

B Both (1) and (2)

C (2) only

D Neither (1) nor (2)

181 Which of the following concerning a labour planning variance is true?

A A labour planning variance will always be adverse if actual labour rates increase

B A labour planning variance will be caused by a manager changing the labour mix during the year

C A labour planning variance will be caused by an unexpected government policy to increase labour rates

D A labour planning variance will always lead to a variable overhead planning variance

182 Which of the following statements is/are true regarding the materials yield variance?

(1) An adverse total yield variance would suggest that less output has been achieved for a given input, i.e. that the total input in volume is more than expected for the output achieved.

(2) A favourable total mix variance will usually result in an adverse material yield variance.

A (1) only

B Both (1) and (2)

C (2) only

D Neither (1) nor (2)

183 A business advisor had planned to use 3 hours of labour on 700 client services in June. Labour is paid $40 per hour.

In June there were actually 900 services provided. Total labour hours were 3,240 and the actual labour rate was $42 per hour.

The advisor has since discovered that, due to a change in legislation that meant extra client responsibilities, the budget should have provided for 3 ½ hours of labour per service.

What is the adverse planning labour efficiency variance for June (to the nearest $000)?

$ [   ]

184 Product GX consists of a mix of three materials, J, K and L. The standard material cost of a unit of GX is as follows:

		$
Material J	5 kg at $4 per kg	20
Material K	2 kg at $12 per kg	24
Material L	3 kg at $8 per kg	24

During March, 3,000 units of GX were produced, and actual usage was:

Material J	13,200 kg
Material K	6,500 kg
Material L	9,300 kg

What was the materials yield variance for March?

A $6,800 favourable

B $6,800 adverse

C $1,000 favourable

D $1,000 adverse

185 An organisation has recorded a favourable labour rate planning variance for the year of $40,000.

On investigation it has discovered that, whilst actual labour rates were $60 per hour, a revised standard rate for labour should have been $70 per hour for the actual hours worked of 20,000.

What was the original planned labour rate per hour for the year (to the nearest $)?

$ [   ]

186 JC Ltd mixes three materials to produce a chemical SGR. The following extract from a standard cost card shows the materials to be used in producing 100 kg of chemical SGR:

	kg		$
Material A	50	$10 per kg	500
Material B	40	$5 per kg	200
Material C	20	$9 per kg	180
	110		880

During October, 23,180 kg of SGR were produced using the following materials:

	kg
Material A	13,200
Material B	7,600
Material C	5,600
	26,400

What is the total material mix variance?

A $1,984 adverse

B $7,216 adverse

C $9,200 adverse

D $16,416 adverse

187 Mr. Green makes salads. The standard plate of salad has 30 g of lettuce (L), 50 g of peppers (P) and 80 g of beetroot (B). The standard prices of the three ingredients are $0.2/kg, 0.4/kg and 0.8/kg respectively. The actual prices were $0.22/kg, $0.38/kg and $0.82/kg.

Mr. Green has been experimenting and so in July he changed the mix of vegetables on the plate thus: 1,500 plates contained 62,000 grams of lettuce, 81,000 grams of peppers and 102,000 grams of beetroot.

What is the value of the total favourable material mix variance (to the nearest cent)?

$ [   ]

188 Mr. Green makes salads. The standard plate of salad has 30 g of lettuce (L), 50 g of peppers (P) and 80 g of beetroot (B). The standard prices of the three ingredients are $0.2/kg, 0.4/kg and 0.8/kg respectively.

Mr. Green has been experimenting and so in July he changed the mix of vegetables on the plate thus: 1,500 plates contained 62,000 grams of lettuce, 81,000 grams of peppers and 102,000 grams of beetroot.

What is the total material yield variance?

A $2.8125 favourable

B $2.8125 adverse

C $2,812.5 favourable

D $2,812.5 adverse

189 A company has a process in which the standard mix for producing 9 litres of output is as follows:

	$
4.0 litres of D at $9 per litre	36.00
3.5 litres of E at $5 per litre	17.50
2.5 litres of F at $2 per litre	5.00
Total	58.50

A standard loss of 10% of inputs is expected to occur. The actual inputs for the latest period were:

	$
4,300 litres of D at $9.00 per litre	38,700
3,600 litres of E at $5.50 per litre	19,800
2,100 litres of F at $2.20 per litre	4,620
Total	63,120

Actual output for this period was 9,100 litres.

What is the total material mix variance?

A $2,400 adverse

B $2,400 favourable

C $3,970 adverse

D $3,970 favourable

190 Operation B, in a factory, has a standard time of 15 minutes. The standard rate of pay for operatives is $10 per hour. The budget for a period was based on carrying out the operation 350 times. It was subsequently realised that the standard time for Operation B included in the budget did not incorporate expected time savings from the use of new machinery from the start of the period. The standard time should have been reduced to 12 minutes.

Operation B was actually carried out 370 times in the period in a total of 80 hours. The operatives were paid $850.

The operational labour efficiency variance was:

A $60 adverse

B $75 favourable

C $100 adverse

D $125 adverse

SALES MIX AND QUANTITY VARIANCES

191 Bloom Limited was the subject of the following press story:

"Bloom is proud to announce that it has managed to maintain its market share despite an overall increase in the market size by 10%." However, the sales director when challenged, by this journalist recently admitted having been forced to reduce prices by $1.50 per bunch on average on a budget volume of 12,000 bunches. All is not as rosy as it seems in Bloom's garden!" If the standard variable cost of a bloom bunch of flowers is $20 and the standard contribution gained is $5.

What is the adverse sales price variance (to the nearest $)?

$ [   ]

192 Bloom Limited was the subject of the following press story:

"Bloom is proud to announce that it has managed to maintain its market share despite an overall increase in the market size by 10%." However, the sales director when challenged, by this journalist recently admitted having been forced to reduce prices by $1.50 per bunch on average on a budget volume of 12,000 bunches. All is not as rosy as it seems in Bloom's garden!" If the standard variable cost of a bloom bunch of flowers is $20 and the standard contribution gained is $5.

What is the favourable sales volume variance (to the nearest $)?

$ [   ]

193 Yellow sells two types of squash balls: the type A and the type B. The standard contribution from these balls is $4 and $5 respectively and the standard profit per ball is $1.50 and $2.40 respectively. The budget was to sell 5 type A balls for every 3 type B balls.

Actual sales were 240,000 balls which is 20,000 balls higher than budgeted. The actual sales included 200,000 of the type A balls. Yellow values its stock of balls at standard marginal cost.

What is the value of the adverse sales mix variance (to the nearest $)?

$ _____

194 Yellow sells two types of squash ball, the type A and the type B. The standard contribution from these balls is $4 and $5 respectively and the standard profit per ball is $1.50 and $2.40 respectively. The budget was to sell 5 type A balls for every 3 type B balls.

Actual sales were 240,000 balls which is 20,000 balls higher than budgeted. The actual sales included 200,000 of the type A balls. Yellow values its stock of balls at standard marginal cost.

What is the value of the favourable sales quantity variance (to the nearest $)?

$ _____

195 Jones' monthly absorption costing variance analysis report includes a sales mix variance, which indicates the effect on profit of actual sales mix differing from the budgeted sales mix. The following data are available.

	Product X		Product Y	
	$	$	$	$
Selling price		12		11
Less Variable cost	6		2	
Fixed cost	2		3	
	—	(8)	—	(5)
Standard net profit per unit		4		6
July sales (units)				
Budget		3,000		6,000
Actual		2,000		8,000

Which one of the following best gives the favourable sales mix variance in July? Pick from list

List options include:

- $8,000
- $5,333
- $4,000
- $2,667

196 You have been provided with the following information relating to three products:

	Product X	Product Y	Product Z
Demand (units)	1,000	2,000	3,000
Selling price	$15	$20	$30
Profit per unit	$2	$5	$2

Actual sales for the year showed the following results.

	Product X	Product Y	Product Z
Units sold	1,100	2,050	2,800
Sales value	$17,050	$38,950	$86,800
Profit	$3,080	$10,455	$6,160

What is the sales quantity variance?

A $150 adverse

B $50 favourable

C $1,208 adverse

D $1,695 favourable

PLANNING AND OPERATIONAL VARIANCES

197 **Which of the following statements are true regarding material price planning variances?**

(1)   The publication of material price planning variances should always lead to automatic updates of standard costs.

(2)   The causes of material price planning variances do not need to be investigated by managers at any level in the organisation.

A   (1) only

B   (2) only

C   Neither (1) nor (2)

D   Both (1) and (2)

198 Leaf Limited has had a mixed year. Its market share has improved 2% to 20% but the overall market had contracted by 5% in the same period. The budgeted sales were 504,000 units and standard contribution was $12 per unit.

What is the level of actual sales?

A   Two percentage points up on budget at 510,080 units

B   Three percent down overall on budget at 488,880 units

C   Three percent up on budget at 519,120 units

D   Up by 5.55% to 532,000 units

199 Leaf Limited has had a mixed year. Its market share has improved 2% to 20% but the overall market had contracted by 5% in the same period. The budgeted sales were 504,000 units and standard contribution was $12 per unit.

The sales market size variance is:

A $1,680,000 favourable

B $1,680,000 adverse

C $302,400 adverse

D $302,400 favourable

200 A company manufactures a specific clinical machine used in hospitals. The company holds a 2% share of the market and the total market demand has been constant at 250,000 machines for the last few years. The budgeted selling price for each machine is $10,000 and standard contribution is equivalent to 10% of the budgeted selling price.

An initial performance review of the company's actual results showed a sales volume of 5,600 machines had been achieved. The total market demand for the machines, though, had risen to 300,000 units.

What is the market share variance for the clinical machines?

A $200,000 favourable

B $400,000 adverse

C $600,000 favourable

D $1,000,000 adverse

201 PlasBas Co uses recycled plastic to manufacture shopping baskets for local retailers. The standard price of the recycled plastic is $0.50 per kg and standard usage of recycled plastic is 0.2 kg for each basket. The budgeted production was 80,000 baskets.

Due to recent government incentives to encourage recycling, the standard price of recycled plastic was expected to reduce to $0.40 per kg. The actual price paid by the company was $0.42 per kg and 100,000 baskets were manufactured using 20,000 kg of recycled plastic.

What is the materials operational price variance?

A $2,000 favourable

B $1,600 favourable

C $400 adverse

D $320 adverse

202 A profit centre manager claims that the poor performance of her division is entirely due to factors outside her control. She has submitted the following table along with notes from a market expert, which she believes explains the cause of the poor performance:

Category	Budget this year	Actual this year	Actual last year	Market expert notes
Sales volume (units)	500	300	400	The entire market has decreased by 25% compared to last year. The product will be obsolete in four years
Sales revenue	$50,000	$28,500	$40,000	Rivalry in the market saw selling prices fall by 10%
Total material cost	$10,000	$6,500	$8,000	As demand for the raw materials is decreasing, suppliers lowered their prices by 5%

After adjusting for the external factors outside the manager's control, in which category/ categories is/are there evidence of poor performance?

A   Material cost only

B   Sales volume and sales price

C   Sales price and material cost

D   Sales price only

203 **Which of the following statement(s) is/are true regarding planning and operational variances?**

(1)   Planning and operational variances are calculated when it is necessary to assess a manager on results that are within his/her control.

(2)   Revised standards are required because variances may arise partly due to an unrealistic budget, and not solely due to operational factors.

A   (1) only

B   (2) only

C   Neither (1) nor (2)

D   Both (1) and (2)

PERFORMANCE ANALYSIS

204 The finance director of Paint Mixers Ltd has produced the table below showing the variance results for the first three months of the year:

	January	February	March
Material price variance	$3,000 adverse	$2,000 adverse	$1,000 adverse
Material mix variance	$2,000 adverse	$750 adverse	$100 favourable
Material yield variance	$4,000 adverse	$2,000 adverse	$50 favourable

Which of the following interpretations of the variances analysis exercise above is NOT correct?

A   The purchasing manager should be able to threaten to switch suppliers to get better deals and address the adverse material price variance

B   The materials mix variance is entirely under the control of the production manager

C   The favourable yield variance in March could be the result of operational efficiency

D   The responsibility for the initial poor performance must be borne by both the purchasing manager and the production manager

205 **Which of the following statement(s) regarding the use of standard costs in rapidly changing environments is/are true?**

(1)   Variance analysis results will take into account important criteria such as customer satisfaction or quality of production.

(2)   Achieving standards is suitable in most modern manufacturing environments.

A   (1) only

B   (2) only

C   Neither (1) nor (2)

D   Both (1) and (2)

PERFORMANCE MEASUREMENT AND CONTROL

PERFORMANCE ANALYSIS IN PRIVATE SECTOR ORGANISATIONS

206 The following are types of key performance indicators (KPIs):

(i)   Return on capital employed

(ii)   Gross profit percentage

(iii)   Acid test ratio

(iv)   Gearing ratio

Which of the above KPIs would be used to assess the liquidity of a company?

A   (i) and (ii)

B   (iii) only

C   (iv) only

D   (iii) and (iv)

207 Why would a company want to encourage the use of non-financial performance indicators?

    A   To encourage short-termism

    B   To look at the fuller picture of the business

    C   To enable results to be easily manipulated to the benefit of the manager

    D   To prevent goal congruence

208 Quotations have been sent to clients either late or containing errors. The department concerned has responded that it is understaffed, and a high proportion of current staff has recently joined the firm. The performance of this department is to be carefully monitored.

Which **ONE** of the following non-financial performance indicators would **NOT** be an appropriate measure to monitor and improve the department's performance?

    A   Percentage of quotations found to contain errors when checked

    B   Percentage of quotations not issued within company policy of three working days

    C   Percentage of department's quota of staff actually employed

    D   Percentage of budgeted number of quotations actually issued

209 Which **TWO** of the following key performance indicators would be appropriate to assess the customer perspective within a traditional balanced scorecard?

- Customer profitability analysis
- Customer retention rates
- Customer satisfaction ratings
- Customer ordering processing times

210 HH plc monitors the percentage of total sales that derives from products developed in the last year.

How would this be classified in the balanced scorecard? Pick from list

List options are as follows:

- Financial perspective
- Customer perspective
- Internal business process perspective
- Innovation and learning perspective

211 Which of the following is the best measure of quality to be included within a building block model in a rapidly growing clothing business?

A Number of returns in the month

B Number of faulty goods returned as a percentage of number of orders received in the month

C Average customer satisfaction rating where customers were asked a range of questions including quality, delivery and customer service

D Number of faulty goods returned as a percentage of deliveries made in the month

212 While a drag and drop style question is impossible to fully replicate within a paper based medium, some questions of this style have been included for completeness.

Drag the six dimensions of performance contained within the building block model into the box below:

- Customers
- Competitive Performance
- Learning
- Innovation
- Financial Performance
- Resource utilisation
- Flexibility
- Equity
- Controllability
- Quality of Service

213 The following extracts relate to Company X and Company Y for 20X1:

	Company X	Company Y
	$000	$000
Revenue	20,000	26,000
Cost of sales	(15,400)	(21,050)
Gross profit	4,600	4,950
Expenses	(2,460)	(2,770)
Operating profit	2,140	2,180

What is the operating profit margin for both companies for 20X1?

	Company X	Company Y
A	10.7%	8.38%
B	8.38%	10.7%
C	23%	19%
D	12%	10%

214 Companies A and B are both involved in retailing. Relevant information for the year ended 30 September 20X1 was as follows:

	A	B
	$000	$000
Sales revenue	50,000	200,000
Profit	10,000	10,000
Capital employed	50,000	50,000

Which of the following statements is true?

A The profit margin of both companies is the same

B Company B is generating more profit from every $1 of asset employed than Company A

C Company B is using its assets more efficiently

D Company B is controlling its costs better than Company A

215 The trading account of Calypso for the year ended 30 June 20X0 is set out below:

	$	$
Sales		430,000
Opening inventories	50,000	
Purchases	312,500	
Closing inventories	(38,000)	
Cost of sales		(324,500)
Gross profit		105,500

The following amounts have been extracted from the company's statement of financial position at 30 June 20X0.

	$
Trade receivables	60,000
Prepayments	4,000
Cash in hand	6,000
Bank overdraft	8,000
Trade payables	40,000
Accruals	3,000
Declared dividends	5,000

Which one of the following correctly gives the inventories holding period (using average inventories) and the current ratio for Calypso Ltd for the period?

	Inventory days	Current ratio
A	33 days	1.25:1
B	49 days	1.25:1
C	49 days	1.93:1
D	33 days	1.93:1

216 In an investment centre, a divisional manager has autonomy over negotiating all selling prices, has local functions set up for payables, inventory and cash management, and uses a full debt factoring service.

Which of the following should the divisional manager be held accountable for? Place a tick in the boxes in the table below as appropriate.

	Accountable	Not accountable
The generation of revenues		
Transfer prices		
Management of working capital		
Apportioned head office costs		

217 **Which TWO of the following matters would the manager of an investment centre have the power to make decisions over?**

- Granting credit to customers

- Settling inter-departmental disputes

- The apportionment of head office costs

- Inventory carrying decisions

218 Binny Co has annual sales of $960,000 and a current ratio of 3.2:1. All of its sales are for cash and are priced at a mark-up on cost of 50%. The average cash balance is $40,000 and the inventory holding period is 90 days.

Assuming 360 days in a year, what is Binny Co's quick ratio (acid test ratio)?

A   0.64

B   0.53

C   0.80

D   1.56

DIVISIONAL PERFORMANCE AND TRANSFER PRICING

219 Oxco has two divisions, A and B. Division A makes a component for air conditioning units which it can only sell to Division B. It has no other outlet for sales.

Current information relating to Division A is as follows:

Marginal cost per unit	$100
Transfer price of the component	$165
Total production and sales of the component each year	2,200 units
Specific fixed costs of Division A per year	$10,000

Cold Co has offered to sell the component to Division B for $140 per unit. If Division B accepts this offer, Division A will be shut down.

If Division B accepts Cold Co's offer, what will be the impact on profits per year for the group as a whole?

A   Increase of $65,000

B   Decrease of $78,000

C   Decrease of $88,000

D   Increase of $55,000

220 Dust Co has two divisions, A and B. Each division is currently considering the following separate projects:

	Division A	Division B
Capital required for the project	$32.6 million	$22.2 million
Sales generated by the project	$14.4 million	$8.8 million
Operating profit margin	30%	24%
Cost of capital	10%	10%
Current return on investment of division	15%	9%

If residual income is used as the basis for the investment decision, what decision is each division likely to make? Place a tick in the boxes in the table below as appropriate.

	Would choose to invest in the project	Would choose not to invest in the project
Division A		
Division B		

221 JB Ltd is a divisionalised organisation comprising a number of divisions, including divisions A and B. Division A makes a single product, which it sells on the external market at a price of $12 per unit. The variable cost of the product is $8 per unit and the fixed cost is $3 per unit. Market demand for the product considerably exceeds Division A's maximum production capacity of 10,000 units per month.

Division B would like to obtain 500 units of the product from Division A. If Division A does transfer some of its production internally rather than sell externally, then the saving in packaging costs would be $1.50 per unit.

What transfer price per unit should Division A quote in order to maximise group profit?

$ [   ]

222 Pro is a division of Mo and is an investment centre. The head office controls finance, HR and IT expenditure but all other decisions are devolved to the local centres.

The statement of financial position for Pro shows net value of all assets and liabilities to be $4,500m. It carries no debt itself although the group has debt liabilities.

The management accounts include the following:

	$m
Revenue	3,500
Cost of sales	1,800
Local administration	250
IT costs	50
Distribution	80
Central administration	30
Interest charges	90
Net profit	1,200

Ignore taxation.

If the cost of capital is 12%, what is the division's residual income (to the nearest $m)?

$ [   ]

223 Summary financial statements are given below for a division of a divisionalised company:

Statement of financial position		**Statement of profit or loss**	
	$000		$000
Non-current assets	2,400	Revenue	7,300
Current assets	1,000	Operating costs	(6,800)
Total assets	3,400	Operating profit	500
		Interest paid	(320)
Divisional equity	1,500	Profit before tax	180
Long-term borrowings	900		
Current liabilities	1,000		
Total equity and liabilities	3,400		

The cost of capital for the division is estimated at 11% each year. The annual rate of interest on the long-term loans is 9%. All decisions concerning the division's capital structure are taken by central management.

What is the divisional return on capital employed (ROCE) for the year ended 31 December (to 1 decimal place)?

%

224 Summary financial statements are given below for a division of a divisionalised company:

Statement of financial position		**Statement of profit or loss**	
	$000		$000
Non-current assets	2,400	Revenue	7,300
Current assets	1,000	Operating costs	(6,800)
Total assets	3,400	Operating profit	500
		Interest paid	(320)
Divisional equity	1,500	Profit before tax	180
Long-term borrowings	900		
Current liabilities	1,000		
Total equity and liabilities	3,400		

The cost of capital for the division is estimated at 11% each year. The annual rate of interest on the long-term loans is 9%. All decisions concerning the division's capital structure are taken by central management.

What is the divisional residual income (RI) for the year ended 31 December?

A   −$84,000

B $180,000

C $236,000

D $284,000

225 Pro is a division of Mo and is an investment centre. The head office controls finance, HR and IT expenditure but all other decisions are devolved to the local centres.

The statement of financial position for Pro shows net value of all assets and liabilities to be $4,500m at the start of the year and $4,890m at the end. It carries no debt itself although the group has debt liabilities.

The management accounts include the following:

	$m
Revenue	3,500
Cost of sales	1,800
Local administration	250
IT costs	50
Distribution	80
Central administration	30
Interest charges	90
Net profit	1,200

Ignore taxation.

What is the divisional ROI (1 d.p)? (The closing Capital Employed should be used to calculate the ROI).

%

226 At the end of 20X1, an investment centre has net assets of $1m and annual operating profits of $190,000. However, the bookkeeper forgot to account for the following:

A machine with a carrying value of $40,000 was sold at the start of the year for $50,000, and replaced with a machine costing $250,000. Both the purchase and sale are cash transactions. No depreciation is charged in the year of purchase or disposal. The investment centre calculates return on investment (ROI) based on closing net assets.

Assuming no other changes to profit or net assets, what is the return on investment (ROI) for the year (to 1 decimal place)?

%

227 Division B of a company makes units which are then transferred to other divisions. The division has no spare capacity, and sells units externally as well as internally.

Which of the following statement(s) regarding the minimum transfer price that will encourage the divisional manager of B to transfer units to other divisions is/are true?

(1) Any price above variable cost will generate a positive contribution, and will therefore be accepted.

(2) The division will need to give up a unit sold externally in order to make a transfer; this is only worthwhile if the income of a transfer is greater than the net income of an external sale.

A (1) only

B (2) only

C Neither (1) nor (2)

D Both (1) and (2)

228 Perrin Co has two divisions, A and B.

Division A has limited skilled labour and is operating at full capacity making product Y. It has been asked to supply a different product, X, to division B. Division B currently sources this product externally for $700 per unit.

The same grade of materials and labour is used in both products. The cost cards for each product are shown below:

Product	Y	X
	($)/unit	($)/unit
Selling price	600	–
Direct materials ($50 per kg)	200	150
Direct labour ($20 per hour)	80	120
Apportioned fixed overheads ($15 per hour)	60	90

Using an opportunity cost approach to transfer pricing, what is the minimum transfer price?

A $270

B $750

C $590

D $840

229 TM plc makes components which it sells internally to its subsidiary RM Ltd, as well as to its own external market.

The external market price is $24.00 per unit, which yields a contribution of 40% of sales. For external sales, variable costs include $1.50 per unit for distribution costs, which are not incurred on internal sales.

TM plc has sufficient capacity to meet all of the internal and external sales. The objective is to maximise group profit.

At what unit price should the component be transferred to RM Ltd (to 2 decimal places)?

$ [   ]

PERFORMANCE ANALYSIS IN NOT-FOR-PROFIT ORGANISATIONS AND THE PUBLIC SECTOR

230 **Which of the following statements regarding measurement of performance in not-for-profit organisations is/are true?**

(1)   Output does not usually have a market value, and it is therefore more difficult to measure effectiveness.

(2)   Control over the performance can only be satisfactorily achieved by assessments of 'value for money'.

A   (1) only

B   (2) only

C   Neither (1) nor (2)

D   Both (1) and (2)

231 Def Co provides accounting services to government. On average, each staff member works six chargeable hours per day, with the rest of their working day being spent on non-chargeable administrative work. One of the company's main objectives is to produce a high level of quality and customer satisfaction.

Def Co has set its targets for the next year as follows:

(1) Cutting departmental expenditure by 5%.

(2) Increasing the number of chargeable hours handled by advisers to 6.2 per day.

(3) Obtaining a score of 4.7 or above on customer satisfaction surveys.

Which of the above targets assesses economy, efficiency and effectiveness at Def Co? Place a tick in the boxes in the table below as appropriate.

	Economy	Efficiency	Effectiveness
Target (1)			
Target (2)			
Target (3)			

232 A government is looking at assessing hospitals by reference to a range of both financial and non-financial factors, one of which is survival rates for heart by-pass operations and another is 'cost per successfully treated patient'.

Which of the three E's in the 'Value For Money' framework is NOT measured here?

A Economy

B Effectiveness

C Efficiency

D Externality

233 **Which of the following statements, regarding the existence of multiple objectives in not-for-profit organisations, is/are correct?**

(1) They ensure goal congruence between stakeholders.

(2) Compromise between objectives can be problematic.

A (1) only

B (2) only

C Both (1) and (2)

D Neither (1) nor (2)

234 A government is trying to assess schools by using a range of financial and non-financial factors. One of the chosen methods is the percentage of students passing five exams or more.

Which of the three Es in the value for money framework is being measured here?

A   Economy

B   Efficiency

C   Effectiveness

D   Expertise

235 **Which of the following statement(s) about measuring effectiveness in not-for-profit organisations is/are true?**

(1)   Effectiveness targets cannot usually be expressed financially, and therefore non-financial targets must be used.

(2)   The effective level of achievement could be measured by comparing actual performance against target.

A   (1) only

B   (2) only

C   Neither (1) nor (2)

D   Both (1) and (2)

EXTERNAL CONSIDERATIONS AND THE IMPACT ON PERFORMANCE

236 The senior manager is suspicious of a local manager's accounts and thinks that the profit performance may have been overstated.

Which of the following would be a plausible explanation of an overstatement of profit?

A   Delaying payments to payables

B   Shortening the useful economic life of a non-current asset

C   Overstatement of a prepayment

D   Overstatement of an accrual

237 **Which of the following statements regarding standard setting is correct?**

A   Imposed standards are more likely to be achieved

B   Managers across the organisation should be targeted using the same standards

C   Standards should be set at an ideal level with no built in stretch

D   Participation in standard setting is more motivating than where standards are imposed

238 When setting performance measures, external factors should be taken into account.

Which THREE of the following statements regarding external factors is/are true?

A   Stakeholders will have different objectives and companies may deal with this by having a range of performance measures to assess the achievement of these objectives

B   A downturn in the industry or in the economy as a whole could have a negative impact on performance

C   It is only important for companies to take account of internal stakeholders when setting performance targets

D   Company performance could be affected if a competitor reduces its prices or launches a successful advertising campaign

E   Changes to government policy are irrelevant to measuring internal company performance, as they are an external factor

239 When setting performance measurement targets it should be considered that there is the possibility that managers will take a short-term view of the company and may even be tempted to manipulate results in order to achieve their targets.

Which of the following would assist in overcoming the problems of short-termism and manipulation of results?

A   Rewards should be linked to a wider variety of performance measures including some non-financial measures

B   Managers should only be rewarded for the results achieved in their own departments

C   Any capital investment decision should be judged using the payback method of investment appraisal

D   Setting targets involving the overall performance of the company will be more motivating for managers

240 Stakeholders will have different objectives and companies may deal with this by having a range of performance measures to assess the achievement of these objectives.

Which of the following statements is true in relation to stakeholders?

A   The aim of all performance measures should be to increase short term profit

B   The only interest of the government is that companies pay their taxes

C   Shareholders will be looking for increasing dividends and increased share price

D   Only internal stakeholders need to be considered by companies

Section 2

OBJECTIVE TEST CASE STUDY QUESTIONS – SECTION B

INFORMATION, TECHNOLOGIES AND SYSTEMS FOR ORGANISATIONAL PERFORMANCE

MANAGING INFORMATION

241 SILVERSAFE

Silversafe Co operates a number of care homes for the elderly in the county of Shineshire, and has expansion plans for more homes.

Silversafe Co has recently completed the installation of 'Beacon' ceiling lamps in all its residents' lodgings across all its current locations. Each lamp operates four motion sensors that illuminate dark rooms if the person moves around in the dark. The sensors can also detect falls and send out alerts to get help quickly. Beacon lamps are also meant to prevent falls in the first place with activity monitoring and helpful reminders to the resident in the room. The motion sensors feed information to an internal processor that understands different positions like sitting up or laying down. It can also detect furniture, so it knows if a person is laying on a bed versus on the floor.

If a fall occurs, a microphone within Beacon will ask if the person has fallen. A simple "no" response will stop the system from taking further action. Otherwise, Wi-Fi signals are sent from the room and are routed wirelessly through the company's network to the senior nurse on call at that time. The senior nurse can be operating from any of Silversafe's homes. The two-way microphone will allow the nurse to chat with the resident who has fallen and decide on the next steps. In the unlikely event of the nurse not responding, Beacon can also send abstract images to family, second-line caregivers or emergency services in order to get help.

The management of Silversafe has linked the computers of all its care homes together for data sharing and shared emergency care, such as telephone support as described above. That network unfortunately was recently hacked into by individuals posing as healthcare visitors, who were trying to obtain residents credit card details and personal information.

1   Which of the following is often used to protect information systems from unauthorised access by an external hacker?

   A   Anti-virus software

   B   A firewall

   C   A daily back up of data

   D   Passwords

2 Silversafe has networked its computers together to form a business-wide network across its Shineshire homes.

Which of the following is Silversafe operating?

A   An internet

B   An intranet

C   An ethernet

D   An extranet

3 **Which of the following statements made by Silversafe's CEO about the company's IT systems is/are true?**

(i)   All Silversafe employees should be able to change patients' medical records and personal details if they notice an error or omission.

(ii) Transmitted residents' data should be encrypted to prevent hackers gaining access to it.

A   (i) only

B   (ii) only

C   (i) and (ii)

D   Neither (i) nor (ii)

4 **Which of the following are benefits of wireless technology for Silversafe?**

(1)   It facilitates remote working and intervention.

(2)   It increases productivity, because employees across different homes can work together whenever they need to.

(3)   It gives a better understanding of the causes of overhead costs.

(4)   It will record reduced IT costs per site as Silversafe builds new homes.

A   (1), (2) and (3)

B   (2) and (3) only

C   (1) and (4) only

D   (1), (2) and (4)

5 **Which of the following controls would be appropriate in Silversafe homes to ensure the security of highly confidential information about its residents?**

(1)   A procedures manual.

(2)   Contractual confidentiality requirements signed by employees.

(3)   Residents' records kept on separate servers.

(4)   Firewalls.

A   (1), (2) and (3) only

B   (1) and (3) only

C   (2), (3) and (4) only

D   (1), (2), (3) and (4)

SPECIALIST COST AND MANAGEMENT ACCOUNTING TECHNIQUES

242 MIDHURST CO (SEPTEMBER/DECEMBER 2020)

Midhurst Co manufactures air conditioning units and is considering an investment in a new unit that will be used in modern office buildings. Advances in technology mean that this unit is more sensitive to changes and variations in temperature and therefore it can regulate airflow and heating more efficiently. Midhurst Co's competitors currently do not have an equivalent product that can offer these features.

Midhurst Co expects to sell 10,000 units over the predicted five-year life cycle of the unit. The finance director has just prepared the initial costings for the unit as follows:

	$000s
Research and development costs	6,200
Design costs	33,450
Marketing costs	177,685
Variable production cost per unit	42
Fixed production cost	98,470
Variable distribution cost per unit	9
Fixed distribution cost	10,300
Variable selling cost per unit	4
Fixed selling cost	7,790
Administration cost	23,450

The finance director plans to use life-cycle costing to measure the profitability of the new product. The chief executive has asked for more information about life-cycle costing, as they are not sure whether it is the right method to use.

The production director has reviewed the costings in detail and suggested a couple of changes. They are enthusiastic about the product and believes that modifications could be made to prolong the product's life but wonders when the best time would be to make changes to the product.

1   **According to the life-cycle costing method, which TWO of the following statements regarding the stages of the life-cycle are true?**

    A   At the introduction stage, further capital expenditure will be needed as production capacity will need to increase to meet demand

    B   The maturity stage occurs when the market has reached 'saturation point' and bought enough of the product

    C   The majority of a product's life-cycle costs are determined by decisions which are made at the design and development stage

    D   The growth stage, when sales will have reached their peak and become stable, will be the most profitable stage

2 **What is the cost per unit for the new air conditioning unit using life-cycle costing (to the nearest $)?**

A $35,740

B $51,847

C $88,390

D $90,735

3 The production director has suggested the following change for the costing of the new unit:

Currently material costs are 20% of the variable production costs per unit. One of the materials used is stainless steel which is budgeted at $2,000 per unit but an alternative corrosion-resistant metal costing 25% less can be used. The production director believes a 15% discount can be negotiated for the remainder of the materials.

What would be the revised material cost per unit (to the nearest whole $)?

$ _____

4 The production director has also asked about the implications for production planning if the company wishes to extend the product's life-cycle.

At what stage of the life-cycle is the new unit most likely to undergo product development?

A   Introduction

B   Growth

C   Maturity

D   Decline

5 The chief executive wants to be briefed on the advantages of using life-cycle costing.

Which of the following statements relating to the advantages of life-cycle costing are correct?

(1)   It draws management's attention to all costs related to a product which other costing methods usually treat as period costs.

(2)   It focuses on measuring a product's costs from concept to withdrawal rather than reviewing costs on a period by period basis.

(3)   It focuses on what consumers are prepared to pay for a product and establishes cost budgets based on an expected selling price.

(4)   It aids understanding of the relationship between decisions at the design stage and the cost of other functions, such as marketing.

A   (2), (3) and (4) only

B   (1), (2) and (4) only

C   (1) and (3) only

D   (1), (2), (3) and (4)

243 DUFF CO (JUNE 2014, ADAPTED)

Duff Co manufactures three products, X, Y and Z and uses cost-plus pricing. Each product uses the same materials and the same type of direct labour, but in different quantities. For many years, the company has been using full absorption costing and absorbing overheads on the basis of direct labour hours. Budgeted production and sales volumes for X, Y and Z for the next year are 20,000 units, 16,000 units and 22,000 units respectively.

The budgeted direct costs of the three products are:

	X	Y	Z
	$ per unit	$ per unit	$ per unit
Direct materials	25	22	28
Direct labour ($12 per hour)	30	36	24
Batch size (units per set-up)	500	800	400
Number of purchase orders per batch	4	5	4
Machine hours per unit	1.5	1.25	1.4

In the next year, Duff Co also expects to incur indirect production costs of $1,377,400, and the company has calculated the Overhead Absorption Rate (OAR) to be $9.70 per direct labour hour.

The indirect production costs of $1,377,400 are analysed as follows:

Cost pools	$	Cost drivers
Machine set up costs	280,000	Number of batches
Material ordering costs	316,000	Number of purchase orders
Machine running costs	420,000	Number of machine hours
General facility costs	361,400	Number of machine hours

1 **What is the full production cost per unit of product Z, using Duff's Co current method of absorption costing?**

   A $71.40 per unit

   B $79.25 per unit

   C $93.10 per unit

   D Cannot be determined without more information

2 **What is the overhead cost per unit for product X, using activity-based costing?**

   A $19.25 per unit

   B $24.64 per unit

   C $26.21 per unit

   D $72.21 per unit

3 Using activity-based costing, total overheads allocated to Product Z amount to $576,583. What is the budgeted full cost production per unit using activity-based costing, for Product Z?

A $65.40 per unit

B $78.21 per unit

C $79.64 per unit

D $83.20 per unit

4 **Which of the following statements about activity-based costing (ABC) in Duff Co are correct?**

(1)   ABC can be applied to all overhead costs, not just production overheads.

(2)   ABC provides a more accurate cost per unit of X, Y or Z, and as a result pricing should be improved.

(3)   ABC recognises that overhead costs are not all related to production and sales volume of X, Y and Z.

(4)   ABC will be of limited benefit if Duff Co's overhead costs are primarily volume related, or if the overheads represent a small proportion of the overall cost.

A   (1) and (2) only

B   (2) and (4) only

C   (1) and (3) only

D   (1), (2), (3) and (4)

5 Using activity-based costing (ABC), the production cost of product X is very similar to the cost calculated using traditional absorption costing, but the cost for product Y is almost $10 less.

Demand for products X and Y is relatively elastic.

Which statements regarding products X and Y are true?

(1)   If the company decides to adopt ABC, the price of product X will change.

(2)   If the company decides to adopt ABC, sales volumes of X are likely to remain unchanged.

(3)   If the company decides to adopt ABC, the price of product Y will go down.

(4)   A reduced selling price is unlikely to give rise to increased sales volumes.

A   (1) and (2) only

B   (2) and (3) only

C   (1) and (4) only

D   (1), (2), (3) and (4)

244   BECKLEY HILL (JUNE 2015)

Beckley Hill (BH) is a private hospital carrying out two types of procedures on patients. Each type of procedure incurs the following direct costs:

	Procedure A	Procedure B
Surgical time and materials	$1,200	$2,640
Anaesthesia time and materials	$800	$1,620

BH currently calculates the overhead cost per procedure by taking the total overhead cost and simply dividing it by the number of procedures, then rounding the cost to the nearest 2 decimal places. Using this method, the total cost is $2,475.85 for Procedure A and $4,735.85 for Procedure B.

Recently, another local hospital has implemented activity-based costing (ABC). This has led the finance director at BH to consider whether this alternative costing technique would bring any benefits to BH. They have obtained an analysis of BH's total overheads for the last year and some additional data, all of which is shown below:

Cost	Cost driver	Costs in $
Administrative costs	Administrative time per procedure	1,870,160
Nursing costs	Length of patient stay	6,215,616
Catering costs	Number of meals	966,976
General facility costs	Length of patient stay	8,553,600
Total overhead costs		**17,606,352**

	Procedure A	Procedure B
Number of procedures	14,600	22,400
Administrative time per procedure (hours)	1	1.5
Length of patient stay per procedure (hours)	24	48
Average no. of meals required per patient	1	4

1   Using the traditional costing system, what is the overhead cost per procedure?

   A $237.93 per procedure

   B $713.78 per procedure

   C $475.85 per procedure

   D $951.70 per procedure

2   Under activity-based costing (ABC), what is the administration cost per hour?

   A $38.80 per hour

   B $50.54 per hour

   C $58.20 per hour

   D $77.60 per hour

3   **Under activity-based costing (ABC), what is the nursing cost per hour?**

A $4.30 per admin hour

B $4.30 per patient hour

C $4.36 per admin hour

D $4.36 per patient hour

4   When using activity-based costing (ABC), the full cost for Procedure A is approximately $2,297 and $4,853 for Procedure B.

Which of the following statements is/are true?

(1)   Using ABC, the allocation of overhead costs would more fairly represent the use of resources driving the overheads.

(2)   The cost of Procedure A goes up using ABC and the cost of Procedure B goes down because the largest proportion of the overhead costs is the nursing and general facility costs.

A   (1) only

B   (2) only

C   Both (1) and (2)

D   Neither (1) nor (2)

5   BH has decided that an activity-based costing (ABC) system is too time consuming and costly to implement.

Which of the following statements is/are true?

(1)   Whilst the comparative costs of Procedures A and B are different under ABC, they are not different enough to justify the implementation of an ABC system.

(2)   A similar allocation of overheads can be achieved simply by using 'patient hours' as a basis to absorb the costs.

A   (1) only

B   (2) only

C   Both (1) and (2)

D   Neither (1) nor (2)

245 ABKABER PLC

Abkaber plc assembles three types of motorcycle at the same factory: the 50cc Sunshine; the 250cc Roadster and the 1000cc Fireball.

Historically, the company has allocated all overhead costs using total direct labour hours, but is now considering introducing Activity Based Costing (ABC). Abkaber plc's accountant has produced the following analysis.

	Annual output (units)	Annual direct labour hours	Selling price ($ per unit)	Raw material cost ($ per unit)
Sunshine	2,000	200,000	4,000	400
Roadster	1,600	220,000	6,000	600
Fireball	400	80,000	8,000	900

The three cost drivers that generate overheads are:

- Deliveries to retailers – the number of deliveries of motorcycles to retail showrooms.
- Set-ups – the number of times the assembly line process is re-set to accommodate a production run of a different type of motorcycle.
- Purchase orders – the number of purchase orders.

The annual cost driver volumes relating to each activity and for each type of motorcycle are as follows:

	Number of deliveries to retailers	Number of set-ups	Number of purchase orders
Sunshine	100	35	400
Roadster	80	40	300
Fireball	70	25	100

The annual overhead costs relating to these activities are as follows:

	$
Deliveries to retailers	2,400,000
Set-up costs	6,000,000
Purchase orders	3,600,000
	————
	12,000,000
	————

All direct labour is paid at $5 per hour. The company holds no inventories.

At a board meeting there was some concern over the introduction of activity based costing.

The finance director argued: 'I very much doubt whether selling the Fireball is viable but I am not convinced that activity based costing would tell us any more than the use of labour hours in assessing the viability of each product.'

The marketing director argued: 'I am in the process of negotiating a major new contract with a motorcycle rental company for the Sunshine model. For such a big order they will not pay our normal prices but we need to at least cover our incremental costs. I am not convinced that activity based costing would achieve this as it merely averages costs for our entire production'.

The managing director argued: 'I believe that activity based costing would be an improvement but it still has its problems. For instance, if we carry out an activity many times surely we get better at it and costs fall rather than remain constant. Similarly, some costs are fixed and do not vary either with labour hours or any other cost driver.'

The chairman argued: 'I cannot see the problem. The overall profit for the company is the same no matter which method of allocating overheads we use. It seems to make no difference to me.'

1 **What is the split of annual overhead costs for each product using the existing method of labour hours to attribute overheads?**

	Sunshine	Roadster	Fireball
A	6,000,000	4,800,000	1,200,000
B	4,800,000	5,280,000	1,920,000
C	4,860,000	4,518,000	2,622,000
D	2,666,667	4,000,000	5,333,333

2 **What level of overheads would be attributed to the Fireball product if Abkaber plc introduced activity based costing?**

   A   1,200,000

   B   1,920,000

   C   2,622,000

   D   5,333,333

3 **Which ONE of the following statements is TRUE about the difference in overhead attribution for the Fireball product (when comparing the existing and new methods) and how it may affect management decisions about this product?**

   A   Both methods are acceptable so management shouldn't be concerned if overhead costs are higher for this product using ABC.

   B   ABC seems to be a more useful method for understanding the costs related to the Fireball, as the low volumes of Fireball sales cause a relatively high amount of set-ups, deliveries and purchase processes

   C   Using ABC is likely to result in a higher profit being recognised for the Fireball product.

   D   The best way to improve the overhead costs for the fireball is to find efficiencies that reduce labour hours on this product.

4   Which of the following statements are true?

(1)   The finance director is correct – ABC will not provide any further information in assessing how viable the Fireball product is, as it's just a different approach to allocating costs.

(2)   The marketing director is correct – ABC can't help with improving our understanding of the incremental costs of a product, as it just averages costs for the entire production.

(3)   The managing director is correct – ABC normally assumes that the cost per activity is constant as the number of times the activity is repeated increases. In practice there may be a learning curve, such that costs per activity are non-linear. As a result, the marginal cost of increasing the number of activities is not the same as the average.

A   (1) and (2)

B   (1) and (3)

C   (2) and (3)

D   (3) only

5   The chairman has stated that it is irrelevant which costing method is used as overall company profit will be unchanged. Which of the following is an advantage of using ABC despite it having no impact on overall company profits?

A   It can allocate costs to specific activities with complete accuracy

B   It is quick and cheap to introduce

C   It is most useful in situations when the overheads are a small proportion of overall costs.

D   It provides a more accurate cost per unit, which helps with management decisions about specific products.

246   HELOT CO (SEPTEMBER 2016)

Helot Co develops and sells computer games. It is well known for launching innovative and interactive role-playing games and its new releases are always eagerly anticipated by the gaming community. Customers value the technical excellence of the games and the durability of the product and packaging.

Helot Co has previously used a traditional absorption costing system and full cost plus pricing to cost and price its products. It has recently recruited a new finance director who believes the company would benefit from using target costing. They are keen to try this method on a new game concept called Spartan, which has been recently approved.

After discussion with the board, the finance director undertook some market research to find out customers' opinions on the new game concept and to assess potential new games offered by competitors. The results were used to establish a target selling price of $45 for Spartan and an estimated total sales volume of 350,000 units. Helot Co wants to achieve a target profit margin of 35%.

The finance director has also begun collecting cost data for the new game and has projected the following:

Production costs per unit	$
Direct material	3.00
Direct labour	2.50
Direct machining	5.05
Set-up	0.45
Inspection and testing	4.30
Total non-production costs	**$000**
Design (salaries and technology)	2,500
Marketing consultants (external)	1,700
Distribution	1,400

1   **Which of the following statements would the finance director have used to explain to Helot Co's board what the benefits were of adopting a target costing approach so early in the game's life-cycle?**

(1)   Costs will be split into material, system, and delivery and disposal categories for improved cost reduction analysis.

(2)   Customer requirements for quality, cost and timescales are more likely to be included in decisions on product development.

(3)   Its key concept is based on how to turn material into sales as quickly as possible in order to maximise net cash.

(4)   The company will focus on designing out costs prior to production, rather than cost control during live production.

A   (1), (2) and (4)

B   (2), (3) and (4)

C   (1) and (3)

D   (2) and (4) only

2   **What is the forecast cost gap for the new game?**

A $2.05

B $0.00

C $13.70

D $29.25

3 The board of Helot Co has asked the finance director to explain what activities can be undertaken to close a cost gap on its computer games.

Which of the following would be appropriate ways for Helot Co to close a cost gap? Place a tick in the boxes in the table below as appropriate.

	Appropriate ways to close a cost gap	Not an appropriate ways to close a cost gap
Buy cheaper, lower grade plastic for the game discs and cases.		
Using standard components wherever possible in production.		
Employ more trainee game designers on lower salaries.		
Use the company's own online gaming websites for marketing.		

4 The direct labour cost per unit has been based on an expected learning rate of 90% but now the finance director has realised that a 95% learning rate should be applied.

Which of the following statements is true?

A   The target cost will decrease and the cost gap will increase

B   The target cost will increase and the cost gap will decrease

C   The target cost will remain the same and the cost gap will increase

D   The target cost will remain the same and the cost gap will decrease

5 Helot Co is thinking about expanding its business and introducing a new computer repair service for customers. The board has asked if target costing could be applied to this service.

Which of the following statements regarding services and the use of target costing within the service sector is true?

A   The purchase of a service transfers ownership to the customer

B   Labour resource usage is high in services relative to material requirements

C   A standard service cannot be produced and so target costing cannot be used

D   Service characteristics include uniformity, perishability and intangibility

247 CHEMICAL FREE CLEAN CO (DECEMBER 2015)

The Chemical Free Clean Co (C Co) provides a range of environmentally-friendly cleaning services to business customers, often providing a specific service to meet a client's needs. Its customers range from large offices and factories to specialist care wards at hospitals, where specialist cleaning equipment must be used and regulations adhered to.

C Co offers both regular cleaning contracts and contracts for one-off jobs. For example, its latest client was a chain of restaurants which employed them to provide an extensive clean of all their business premises after an outbreak of food poisoning.

The cleaning market is very competitive, although there are only a small number of companies providing a chemical free service. C Co has always used cost-plus pricing to determine the prices which it charges to its customers but recently, the cost of the cleaning products C Co uses has increased. This has meant that C Co has had to increase its prices, resulting in the loss of several regular customers to competing service providers.

The finance director at C Co has heard about target costing and is considering whether it could be useful at C Co.

1   **What would be, in the right sequence, the main steps involved in deriving a target cost for C Co?**

     A   Define the service, set a target price, derive the operating profit and calculate a target cost.

     B   Set a target price, derive the total operating profit, calculate a target cost per hour and define the service.

     C   Define the service, derive the operating profit, set a target price and calculate a target cost.

     D   Define the service, derive a target price, calculate a target cost and set the operating profit.

2   **Which TWO of the following statements correctly explain the difficulties faced if target costing is used in a service industry?**

     •   The service can be defined too easily and lacks the necessary complexity.

     •   The service is used at the same time it is produced.

     •   The service is standardised too easily.

     •   Unused labour capacity cannot be stored for use the next day.

3   **Which of the following statements is/are true?**

     (1)   C Co may not be able to get hold of any comparative data available for the one-off jobs, and therefore setting the target cost will be difficult.

     (2)   Some of the work available is very specialist. It may be difficult to establish the market price for a service like this, thus making it difficult to derive a target cost.

     A   (1) only

     B   (2) only

     C   Both (1) and (2)

     D   Neither (1) nor (2)

4   **Which TWO of the following statements are true?**

- Target costing is useful in competitive markets where a company is dominant in their market, like C Co is.

- Target costing is useful in C Co's competitive market in which price increases does lead to loss of customers.

- C Co can ignore the market price for cleaning services and simply pass on cost increases as it has done.

- Target costing would help C Co to focus on the market price of similar services provided by competitors, where this information is available.

5   **Which of the following statement(s) is/are true?**

(1)   If after calculating a target cost C Co finds that a cost gap exists, it will then be forced to examine its internal processes and costs more closely.

(2)   If C Co cannot achieve any reduction in the cost of the cleaning products it uses, it should consider whether it can source cheaper non-chemical products from alternative suppliers.

A   (1) only

B   (2) only

C   Both (1) and (2)

D   Neither (1) nor (2)

248   VOLT CO (MARCH 2019, ADAPTED)

Volt Co generates and sells electricity. It operates two types of power station: nuclear and wind. The costs and output of the two types of power station are detailed below:

Nuclear station

A nuclear station can generate 9,000 gigawatts of electricity in each of its 40 years of useful life. Operating costs are $486m per year. Operating costs include a provision for depreciation of $175m per year to recover the $7,000m cost of building the power station.

Each nuclear station has an estimated decommissioning cost of $12,000m at the end of its life. The decommissioning cost relates to the cost of safely disposing of spent nuclear fuel.

Wind station

A wind station can generate 1,750 gigawatts of electricity per year. It has a life cycle cost of $55,000 per gigawatt and an average operating cost of $40,000 per gigawatt over its 20-year life.

1   **What is the life-cycle cost per gigawatt of the nuclear station (to the nearest $000)?**

A $54,000

B $73,000

C $87,000

D $107,000

2 Which of the following will decrease the total life cycle cost of a nuclear station?

(1)   Increasing the useful life of the station.

(2)   Reducing the decommissioning cost.

A   (1) only

B   (2) only

C   Both (1) and (2)

D   Neither (1) nor (2)

3 How would the disposal cost of spent nuclear fuel be categorised in environmental management accounting (EMA)?

A   A prevention cost

B   A detection cost

C   An internal failure cost

D   An external failure cost

4 If Volt Co sets a price to earn an operating margin of 40% over the life of a wind station, what will be the total lifetime profit per station (to the nearest $m)?

A $35m

B $408m

C $560m

D $933m

5 Which of the following are benefits of life cycle costing for Volt Co?

(1)   It facilitates the designing out of costs at the product development stage.

(2)   It can encourage better control of operating costs over the life cycle.

(3)   It gives a better understanding of the causes of overhead costs.

(4)   It provides useful data for short-term decision-making.

A   (1), (2) and (3)

B   (1) and (2) only

C   (1) and (4)

D   (2), (3) and (4)

249 SHOE CO (JUNE 2016)

Shoe Co, a shoe manufacturer, has developed a new product called the 'Smart Shoe' for children, which has a built-in tracking device. The shoes are expected to have a life cycle of two years, at which point Shoe Co hopes to introduce a new type of Smart Shoe with even more advanced technology. Shoe Co plans to use life cycle costing to work out the total production cost of the Smart Shoe and the total estimated profit for the two-year period. Shoe Co has spent $5.6m developing the Smart Shoe.

The time spent on this development meant that the company missed out on the opportunity of earning an estimated $800,000 contribution from the sale of another product.

The company has applied for and been granted a ten-year patent for the technology, although it must be renewed each year at a cost of $200,000. The costs of the patent application were $500,000, which included $20,000 for the salary costs of Shoe Co's lawyer, who is a permanent employee of the company and was responsible for preparing the application.

The following information relating to the Smart Shoe is also available for the next two years:

Total 'Smart Shoe' Revenue $34.3m

	Year 1	Year 2
Sales volumes (units)	280,000	420,000
Material costs per unit	$16	$14
Labour costs per unit	$8	$7
Total fixed production overheads	$3.8 m	
Selling and distribution costs	$1.5m	

Shoe Co is negotiating with marketing companies with regard to its advertising campaign on another product, 'Smart Boots'. Shoe Co is uncertain as to what the total marketing costs will be each year. However, the following information is available as regards the probabilities of the range of costs which are likely to be incurred:

Year 1		Year 2	
Expected cost ($m)	Probability	Expected cost ($m)	Probability
2.2	0.2	1.8	0.3
2.6	0.5	2.1	0.4
2.9	0.3	2.3	0.3

1   **Which TWO of the following statements about lifecycle costing are true?**

- Lifecycle costing should not be used by Shoe Co, because the material costs per unit differ between the two years of the life of the product.

- Lifecycle costing should not be used by Shoe Co, because the lifecycle of the 'Smart Shoe' is short and the development costs too high.

- Lifecycle costing should be used by Shoe Co because it will provide the true financial cost of producing the shoes.

- A higher price should be charged by Shoe Co from the start, as the product will be unique.

2 What is the total expected profit for Shoe Co on the 'Smart Shoe' for the two-year period? $_____

3 Further research has shown that there will be environmental costs at the end of production of $250,000. Shoe Co is considering how to account for these costs.

Which TWO of the following statements about Environmental Management Accounting are true?

- Cost savings in environmental costs are easily identified.
- Environmental management accounting considers financial costs only.
- Activity-based costing (ABC) can be used to analyse environmental costs.
- Flow cost accounting is a recognised method of accounting for environmental costs.

4 What is the total expected value of the marketing cost for the two years on the 'Smart Boots' range?

A $2.61 m

B $2.07 m

C $4.68 m

D $5.21m

5 Which ONE of the following statements is true, if a decision is made using expected values?

A The risk is minimised for a set level of return

B The risk is minimised irrespective of the level of return

C The return is maximised for a given level of risk

D The return is maximised irrespective of the level of risk

250 SWEET TREATS BAKERY (DECEMBER 2016)

Sweet Treats Bakery makes three types of cake: brownies, muffins and cupcakes. The costs, revenues and demand for each of the three cakes are as follows:

	Brownies	Muffins	Cupcakes
Batch size (units)	40	30	20
Selling price ($ per unit)	1.50	1.40	2.00
Material cost ($ per unit)	0.25	0.15	0.25
Labour cost ($ per unit)	0.40	0.45	0.50
Overheads ($ per unit)	0.15	0.20	0.30
Minimum daily demand (units)	30	20	10
Maximum daily demand (units)	140	90	100

The minimum daily demand is required for a long-term contract with a local café and must be met.

The cakes are made in batches using three sequential processes: weighing, mixing and baking. The products must be produced in their batch sizes but are sold as individual units. Each batch of cakes requires the following amount of time for each process:

	Brownies	Muffins	Cupcakes
Weighing (minutes)	15	15	20
Mixing (minutes)	20	16	12
Baking (minutes)	120	110	120

The baking stage of the process is done in three ovens which can each be used for eight hours a day, a total of 1,440 available minutes. Ovens have a capacity of one batch per bake, regardless of product type.

Sweet Treats Bakery uses throughput accounting and considers all costs, other than material, to be 'factory costs' which do not vary with production.

1   On Monday, in addition to the baking ovens, Sweet Treats Bakery has the following process resources available:

Process	Minutes available
Weighing	240
Mixing	180

Which of the three processes, if any, is a bottleneck activity?

A   Weighing

B   Mixing

C   Baking

D   There is no bottleneck

2   On Wednesday, the mixing process is identified as the bottleneck process. On this day, only 120 minutes in the mixing process are available.

Assuming that Sweet Treats Bakery wants to maximise profit, what is the optimal production plan for Wednesday?

A   80 brownies, 30 muffins and 100 cupcakes

B   0 brownies, 90 muffins and 100 cupcakes

C   120 brownies, 0 muffins and 100 cupcakes

D   40 brownies, 60 muffins and 100 cupcakes

3   Sweet Treats Bakery has done a detailed review of its products, costs and processes and has identified potential actions to improve its throughput accounting ratio (TPAR).

Which of the following statements will improve the throughput accounting ratio (TPAR)? Place a tick in the boxes in the table below as appropriate.

	Will improve the TPAR	Will not improve the TPAR
The café customer will be given a loyalty discount.		
A bulk discount on flour and sugar is available from suppliers.		
There is additional demand for the cupcakes in the market.		
The rent of the premises has been reduced for the next year.		

4   On Friday, due to a local food festival at the weekend, Sweet Treats Bakery is considering increasing its production of cupcakes. These cupcakes can be sold at the festival at the existing selling price.

The company has unlimited capacity for weighing and mixing on Friday but its existing three ovens are already fully utilised. Therefore in order to supply cupcakes to the festival, Sweet Treats Bakery will need to hire another identical oven at a cost of $45 for the day.

How much will profit increase by if the company hires the new oven and produces as many cupcakes as possible?

A $55.00

B $140.00

C $95.00

D $31.00

5   In a previous week, the weighing process was the bottleneck and the resulting throughput accounting ratio (TPAR) for the bakery was 1.45.

Which of the following statements about the TPAR for the previous week is/are true?

(1)   The bakery's operating costs exceeded the total throughput contribution generated from its three products.

(2)   Less idle time in the mixing department would have improved the TPAR.

(3)   Improved efficiency during the weighing process would have improved the TPAR.

A   (3) only

B   (2) only

C   (1) and (2)

D   (1) and (3)

DECISION-MAKING TECHNIQUES

251   SIP CO

Sip Co specialises in refurbishing the inside of yachts and has been asked to quote, on a relevant cost basis, for the refurbishment of a yacht called Bow. The refurbishment will start in one week's time. Sip Co has spent $100 obtaining the following information about the refurbishment:

Materials

The material required will be:

- 20 m^2 of upholstery fabric

- 10 m^2 of teak wood for the flooring.

The cheapest source for the upholstery fabric would be from an overseas supplier at a cost of $85/m^2. Sip Co buys most of its fabric from overseas and pays $400 per month to a shipping company as a retainer and then $7.50/m^2 for each metre transported.

Sip Co has 5m^2 of teak wood in inventory which cost $100/m^2 and could be sold at a 5% discount on original cost. This teak is left from a previous job and is stained dark mahogany. The colour of the stain required for Bow, tan, is lighter and the costs of sanding and staining the teak are:

- sanding $14/m^2

- staining $4.50/m^2

- reset of staining machine, arising after each staining job is completed $80.

To ensure the colour of the teak is consistent, all the teak for one job is stained at the same time, and the staining cost is the same irrespective of the age of the teak. The cost of purchasing new teak is $110/m^2. New teak can be stained the correct colour for Bow with no preparation.

Non-current assets

A new kitchen will be required. This can be purchased for $4,500 and the fitting costs will be $2,000. Alternatively, the existing kitchen can be refurbished. The materials for refurbishment will cost $4,000, and 40 hours of semi-skilled labour will be employed specifically for the refurbishment at a cost of $15/hour. The fitting costs of the refurbished kitchen will be 10% less than a new kitchen.

Labour

100 hours of skilled and 56 hours of unskilled labour will be required for the upholstery and flooring work. Skilled labour is paid the market rate of $25/hour and is currently fully employed on another job, where they earn a contribution of $6/hour. Alternatively new skilled labour could be employed, but the new workers will require training at a cost of $14/hour for the first 10 hours they are working.

Unskilled workers are currently paid $12/hour and each of the 5 workers is guaranteed a minimum wage of $420 per week. Each unskilled employee has enough work allocated to them for the next three weeks to earn $372 per week. The work to be done by the unskilled labour on Bow must be completed within the first week of the project starting and overtime is paid at time and half.

Other costs

It is factory policy to add $2,200 per week to a project, for the duration of the project. This is to cover:

Factory rates	$500
Plant and equipment depreciation	$700
Interest on long term loan to purchase plant and equipment	$400
Profit element	$600

1   What are the costs to be included in the quote for the upholstery fabric and kitchen?

$_____ upholstery fabric

$_____ kitchen

2   What cost should be included in the quote for the teak wood?

A $1,220

B $1,140

C $1,225

D $1,145

3   What cost should be included in the quote for the skilled and unskilled labour?

$_____ skilled labour $_____ unskilled labour

4   Which option correctly classifies these costs? Place a tick in the boxes in the table below as appropriate.

	Committed	Notional
Factory rates		
Depreciation		
Interest		

5   Which TWO of the following statements are true?

- The $100 spent obtaining the cost information should be included in the quote.

- Sip Co should consider the effect of the refurbishment on the tax the company will pay, and include the tax effect in the quote as a relevant cost.

- Opportunity costs arise when a scarce resource, which has an alternative use in the business, is used in a project.

- Relevant costing techniques should be used in cost volume profit analysis.

252 HARE EVENTS (DECEMBER 2016)

Hare Events is a company which specialises in organising sporting events in major cities across Teeland. It has approached the local council of Edglas, a large city in the north of Teeland, to request permission to host a running festival which will include both a full marathon and a half marathon race.

Based on the prices it charges for entry to similar events in other locations, Hare Events has decided on an entry fee of $55 for the full marathon and $30 for the half marathon. It expects that the maximum entries will be 20,000 for the full marathon and 14,000 for the half marathon.

Hare Events has done a full assessment of the likely costs involved. Each runner will receive a race pack on completion of the race which will include a medal, t-shirt, water and chocolate. Water stations will need to be available at every five kilometre (km) point along the race route, stocked with sufficient supplies of water, sports drinks and gels. These costs are considered to be variable as they depend on the number of race entries.

Hare Events will also incur the following fixed costs. It will need to pay a fixed fee to the Edglas council for permits, road closures and support from the local police and medical services. A full risk assessment needs to be undertaken for insurance purposes. A marketing campaign is planned via advertising on running websites, in fitness magazines and at other events Hare Events is organising in Teeland, and the company which Hare Events usually employs to do the race photography has been approached.

The details of these costs are shown below:

	Full marathon	Half marathon
	$	$
Race packs	15.80	10.80
Water stations	2.40	1.20
		$
Council fees		300,000
Risk assessment and insurance		50,000
Marketing		30,000
Photography		5,000

1   If Hare Events decides to host only the full marathon race, what is the margin of safety?

    A   35.0%

    B   47.7%

    C   52.3%

    D   65.0%

2   Assuming that the race entries are sold in a constant sales mix based on the expected race entry numbers, what is the sales revenue Hare Events needs to achieve in order to break even (to the nearest $000)?

   A $385,000

   B $575,000

   C $593,000

   D $597,000

3   Hare Events wishes to achieve a minimum total profit of $500,000 from the running festival.

   What are the number of entries Hare Events will have to sell for each race in order to achieve this level of profit, assuming a constant sales mix based on the expected race entry numbers applies?

   Work to the nearest whole number.

   A   Full marathon: 17,915 entries and half marathon: 12,540 entries

   B   Full marathon: 14,562 entries and half marathon: 18,688 entries

   C   Full marathon: 20,000 entries and half marathon: 8,278 entries

   D   Full marathon: 9,500 entries and half marathon: 6,650 entries

4   Hare Events is also considering including a 10 km race during the running festival. It expects the race will have an entry fee of $20 per competitor and variable costs of $8 per competitor. Fixed costs associated with this race will be $48,000.

   If the selling price per competitor, the variable cost per competitor and the total fixed costs for this 10 km race all increase by 10%, what will happen to the breakeven volume and the breakeven revenue? Place a tick in the boxes in the table below as appropriate.

	Will change	Will not change
Breakeven volume		
Breakeven revenue		

5   **Which of the following statements relating to cost volume profit analysis are true?**

(1)   Production levels and sales levels are assumed to be the same so there is no inventory movement.

(2)   The contribution to sales ratio (C/S ratio) can be used to indicate the relative profitability of different products.

(3)   CVP analysis assumes that fixed costs will change if output either falls or increases significantly.

(4)   Sales prices are recognised to vary at different levels of activity especially if higher volume of sales is needed.

A   (1), (2) and (3)

B   (2), (3) and (4)

C   (1) and (2) only

D   (3) and (4) only

253 CARDIO CO (DECEMBER 2015, ADAPTED)

Cardio Co manufactures four types of fitness equipment: elliptical trainers (E), treadmills (T), cross trainers (C) and rowing machines (R). Cardio Co is considering ceasing to produce elliptical trainers at the end of 20X5.

The budgeted sales prices and volumes for the next year (20X6) are as follows:

	T	C	R	
Selling price	$1,600	$1,800	$1,400	
Units	420	400	380	
Total sales revenue	$672,000	$720,000	$532,000	**$1,924,000**

The standard cost card for each product is shown below:

	T	C	R
Material	$430	$500	$360
Labour	$220	$240	$190
Variable overheads	$110	$120	$95

Labour costs are 60% fixed and 40% variable. General fixed overheads excluding any fixed labour costs are expected to be $55,000 for the next year.

The following multi-product breakeven chart for Cardio Co has correctly been drawn:

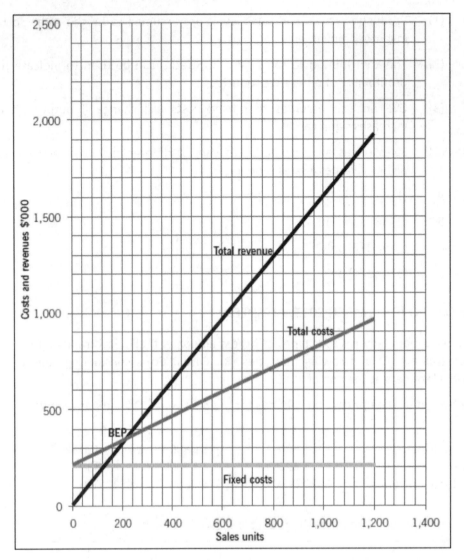

Cardio Co has recently received a request from a customer, Heart Co, to provide a one-off order of fitness machines (T, C and R), in excess of normal budgeted production for 20X6. The order would need to be completed within two weeks.

1 **Which of the following are valid factors to consider in the decision to cease the production of elliptical trainers at the end of 20X5?**

(1) The elliptical trainers made a loss in 20X5.

(2) The elliptical trainers made a positive contribution in the year just passed.

(3) The elliptical trainer market outlook in the long term looks very poor.

(4) Cardio Co also sells treadmills and many elliptical trainers buyers will also buy treadmills.

(5) The business was founded to produce and sell elliptical trainers.

A (3) and (4) only

B (1), (3), (4) and (5)

C (2), (3) and (4)

D None of the above

2 Which of the following statements about relevant costing are true?

(1) Fixed costs are always general in nature and therefore never relevant.

(2) Notional costs are always relevant, as they make the estimate more realistic.

(3) An opportunity cost represents the cost of the best alternative foregone.

(4) Avoidable costs would be saved if an activity did not happen, and therefore are relevant.

A (2) and (4) only

B (3) and (4) only

C (2), (3), and (4)

D (1), (2) and (4)

3 What is the margin of safety in $ revenue for Cardio Co in 20X6?

A $1,172,060

B $1,577,053

C $1,924,000

D $1,993,632

4 What would happen to the breakeven point if the products were sold in order of the most profitable products first?

A The breakeven point would be reached earlier.

B The breakeven point would be reached later.

C The breakeven point would be reached at the same time as in the graph above.

D The breakeven point would never be reached.

5 Which statement correctly describes the treatment of general fixed overheads when preparing the Heart Co quotation?

A The overheads should be excluded because they are a sunk cost.

B The overheads should be excluded because they are not incremental costs.

C The overheads should be included because they relate to production costs.

D The overheads should be included because all expenses should be recovered.

254 CARA CO (MARCH 2019, ADAPTED)

Cara Co makes two products, the Seebach and the Herdorf.

To make a unit of each product the following resources are required:

	Seebach	Herdorf
Materials ($100 per kg)	5 kg	7 kg
Labour hours ($45 per hour)	2 hours	3 hours
Machine hours ($60 per hour)	3 hours	2 hours

Fixed overheads are $300,000 each month.

The contribution per unit made on each product is as follows:

	Seebach	Herdorf
Contribution ($ per unit)	250	315

The maximum demand each month is 4,000 units of Seebach and 3,000 units of Herdorf. The products and materials are perishable and inventories of raw materials or finished goods cannot be stored.

Cara Co has a legally binding obligation to produce a minimum of 2,000 units of Herdorf in each of months 1 and 2. There is no minimum production required in month 3.

The manufacturing manager is planning production volumes and the maximum availability of resources for months 1, 2 and 3 are as follows:

Month	1	2	3
Materials (kg)	34,000	42,000	35,000
Labour (hours)	18,000	12,000	24,000
Machine (hours)	18,000	19,000	12,000

For month 3 the following linear programming graph has been produced:

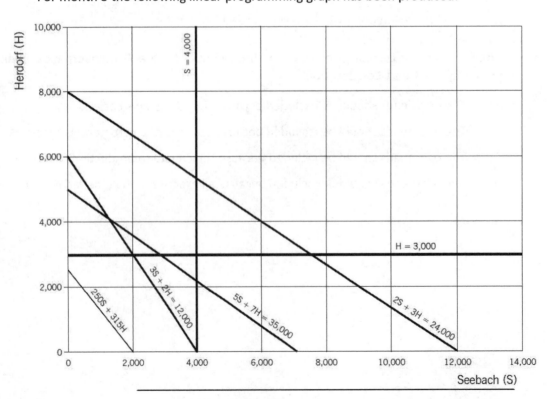

1   **What is/are the limiting factor(s) in month 1?**

    A   Materials, labour hours and machine hours

    B   Materials and machine hours only

    C   Materials only

    D   Labour hours only

2   The production manager has identified that the only limiting factor in month 2 is labour hours.

    What is the production volume for Herdorf for month 2 (to the nearest whole unit)?

    A   0

    B   1,333

    C   2,000

    D   3,000

3   **If the shadow price for month 2 is $125 per labour hour, which of the following statements is/are correct?**

    (1)   The production manager would be willing to pay existing staff a maximum overtime premium of $125 per hour for the next 2,000 hours.

    (2)   The production manager would be willing to pay a maximum of $170 per hour for an additional 2,000 hours of temporary staff time.

    A   (1) only

    B   (2) only

    C   Both (1) and (2)

    D   Neither (1) nor (2)

4   **What is the maximum profit which can be earned in month 3?**

    A $1,080,000

    B $1,380,000

    C $1,445,000

    D $1,145,000

5 **Which of the following interpretations of the linear programming graph produced for month 3 is/are correct?**

(1) All other things being equal, unless demand increases for either product labour will be a slack variable.

(2) If more machine hours were made available in month 3 they would be used initially to make Herdorfs.

A (1) only

B (2) only

C Both (1) and (2)

D Neither (1) nor (2)

255 HOME ELECTRICS CO (MARCH/JUNE 2021)

Home Electrics Co manufactures electrical appliances for domestic use. It is made up of two divisions.

Small Appliances division

Two of the products manufactured by the Small Appliances division are the Blender (Product B) and the Toaster (Product T). The standard cost cards per unit for each of the products is as follows:

	B	T
	$	$
Selling Price	80	120
Direct Materials ($5 per kg)	10	15
Direct Labour ($7 per hour)	21	35
Variable Overheads	12	18
Fixed overheads	8	10
Profit	29	42

In the first quarter of the year the supply of materials was restricted to 2,000 kg per month. This was due to a global shortage.

It is now April and it has been identified that material will continue to be limited to 2,000 kg per month but also labour hours will be restricted to 3,200 hours per month. The management accountant has supplied formulas for the production constraints as follows:

Materials	$2B + 3T = 2000$
Labour	$3B + 5T = 3200$

Large Appliances division

This division also manufactures two products; a Freezer (Product F) which earns a contribution of $150 per unit and a Dishwasher (Product D) which earns a contribution of $200 per unit. Both products use the same resources, several of which are in short supply.

In April only 4,000 labour hours, 2,500 kg of material and 3,200 machine hours will be available. The management accountant has applied linear programming and defined the following constraints:

Materials	4F + 6D = 2500
Labour	10F + 8D = 4000
Machine time	5F + 10D = 3200
Demand for D	250

Labour and machine time have been identified as the binding constraints and an optimum production plan of 240 units of F and 200 units of D has been calculated.

1   **What is the contribution per unit of limiting factor for Product T in the first quarter of the year (to the nearest whole $)?**

$_____

2   **Using simultaneous equations, what is the total contribution to be earned from Products B and T in April?**

A $28,400

B $35,600

C $62,000

D $77,200

3   **Which of the following statements about the use of linear programming to resolve limiting factor problems are true?**

(1)   The linear programming method helps to identify the optimum selling price for a product

(2)   Slack occurs when more than the maximum available of the limited resource is required

A   (1) only

B   (2) only

C   Both (1) and (2)

D   Neither (1) nor (2)

4   **What would be the shadow price of material in the Large Appliances division (to the nearest whole $)?**

$_____

5   **Which of the following statements about the linear programming method in the Large Appliances division are true?**

(1)   Product D has a slack value

(2)   Contribution of $76,000 will be earned from the optimum production plan

(3)   Labour and machine time intersect at the optimum point if shown on a graph

A   (1), (2) and (3)

B   (2) and (3) only

C   (1) and (3) only

D   (2) only

256   ALG CO (JUNE 2015, ADAPTED)

ALG Co is launching a new, innovative product (a computer game) onto the market and is trying to decide on the right launch price for the product.

The product's expected life is three years. Given the high level of costs which have been incurred in developing the product, ALG Co wants to ensure that it sets its price at the right level and has therefore consulted a market research company to help it do this.

The research, which relates to similar but not identical products launched by other companies, has revealed that at a price of $60, annual demand would be expected to be 250,000 units. However, for every $2 increase in selling price, demand would be expected to fall by 2,000 units and for every $2 decrease in selling price, demand would be expected to increase by 2,000 units.

A forecast of the annual production costs which would be incurred by ALG Co in relation to the new product are as follows:

Annual production units	200,000	250,000	300,000	350,000
	$	$	$	$
Direct materials	2,400,000	3,000,000	3,600,000	4,200,000
Direct labour	1,200,000	1,500,000	1,800,000	2,100,000
Overheads	1,400,000	1,550,000	1,700,000	1,850,000

1   **Using the high-low method, what are the total variable cost for an annual demand of 250,000 units?**

A $1,500,000

B $3,000,000

C $4,500,000

D $5,250,000

2   **What are the total fixed overheads?**

A $800,000

B $1,000,000

C $1,850,000

D $6,500,000

3   **If the marginal cost is $21, what is the optimum (profit maximising) selling price for the new product?**

A $150

B $165.50

C $289

D $310

4   The sales director is unconvinced that using an optimum (profit-maximising) selling price is the correct one to charge at the initial launch of the product. They believe that a high price should be charged at launch to take advantage of those customers prepared to pay a higher price for the product.

Which TWO of the following statements are true?

(1)   The sales director is suggesting a market skimming strategy.

(2)   The strategy could be a suitable one for ALG Co as its product is new and different.

(3)   Where products have a long life cycle, this strategy is more likely to be used.

(4)   There is no barrier to entry in the case of ALG Co.

A   (1) and (2)

B   (1) and (3)

C   (3) and (4)

D   (2) and (4)

5   ALG's game is truly unique can only be used in conjunction with another one of the business' products. Students are entitled to a small discount.

Which of the following pricing strategies could be used to price the game?

(1)   Market skimming.

(2)   Complimentary product pricing.

(3)   Penetration pricing.

(4)   Price discrimination.

A   (1) and (3) only

B   (1), (2) and (3)

C   (1), (2) and (4)

D   (2), (3) and (4)

257 JEWEL CO (JUNE 2016, ADAPTED)

Jewel Co is setting up an online business importing and selling jewellery headphones. The cost of each set of headphones varies depending on the number purchased, although they can only be purchased in batches of 1,000 units. It also has to pay import taxes which vary according to the quantity purchased.

Jewel Co has already carried out some market research and identified that sales quantities are expected to vary depending on the price charged. Consequently, the following data has been established for the first month:

Number of batches imported and sold	Average cost per unit, including import taxes ($)	Total fixed costs per month ($)	Expected selling price per unit ($)
1	10.00	10,000	20
2	8.80	10,000	18
3	7.80	12,000	16
4	6.40	12,000	13
5	6.40	14,000	12

Most of Jewel Co's total fixed costs are set-up costs.

Earphones

Jewel Co is also producing luxury earphones and has entered two different new markets. In the USA, it is initially charging low prices so as to gain rapid market share while demand is relatively elastic. In Europe, it is initially charging high prices so as to earn maximum profits while demand is relatively inelastic.

Market research has revealed that the maximum demand for Jewel Co's earphones in the USA is 72,000 units per year, and that demand will reduce by 8,000 units for every $5 that the selling price is increased. Jewel Co has calculated that the profit-maximising level of sales for its earphones, for the coming year, is 32,000 units.

1   How many batches should Jewel Co import and sell (to the nearest whole batch)?
    _____ batches

2   Which of the following statements(s) regarding Jewel Co's fixed costs is/are correct?

    (1)   Jewel Co's fixed costs are stepped.

    (2)   Increasing batch sizes from 1,000 units to 2,000 units would dramatically reduce setup costs and increase profits.

    A   (1) only

    B   (2) only

    C   Both (1) and (2)

    D   Neither (1) nor (2)

3 The following statements have been made about the tabular method used to establish an optimum price:

Which of the following statement(s) regarding Jewel Co's fixed costs is/are correct?

(1) With the tabular method, there must be a consistent relationship between price (P) and demand (Q), as well as a close relationship between demand (Q) and marginal costs (MC).

(2) The tabular method is only suitable for companies operating in a monopoly.

A (1) only

B (2) only

C Both (1) and (2)

D Neither (1) nor (2)

4 **Which price strategy is Jewel Co using in each market?**

A Penetration pricing in the USA and price skimming in Europe

B Price discrimination in the USA and penetration pricing in Europe

C Price skimming in the USA and penetration pricing in Europe

D Price skimming in the USA and price discrimination in Europe

5 **What is the optimum selling price at the profit-maximising level of sales (to the nearest $)? $_____**

258 GAM CO (JUNE 2014)

Gam Co sells electronic equipment and is about to launch a new product onto the market. It needs to prepare its budget for the coming year and is trying to decide whether to launch the product at a price of $30, or $35 per unit. The following information has been obtained from market research:

Price per unit $30		Price per unit $35	
Probability	Sales volume	Probability	Sales volume
0.4	120,000	0.3	108,000
0.5	110,000	0.3	100,000
0.1	140,000	0.4	194,000

The six possible profit outcomes which could arise for Gam Co in the coming year have been correctly tabulated as follows:

Price per unit $30		Price per unit $35	
Sales volume	Profit	Sales volume	Profit
120,000	$930,000	108,000	$1,172,000
110,000	$740,000	100,000	$880,000
140,000	$1,310,000	194,000	$742,000

1   **What is the expected value of profit for the $30 price option?**

    A $117,000

    B $291,000

    C $873,000

    D $1,310,000

2   **What is the expected value of profit for the $35 price option?**

    A $117,000

    B $140,000

    C $912,400

    D $1,172,000

3   **Which is the correct definition of the maximin decision rule?**

    A   Under this rule, the decision-maker is an optimist who selects the alternative which maximises the maximum pay-off achievable.

    B   Under this rule, the decision-maker selects the alternative which maximises the minimum payoff achievable.

    C   Under this rule, the decision-maker selects the alternative which minimises the maximum regret.

    D   Under this rule, the decision-maker selects the alternative which minimises the minimum profit.

4   **Which price should be chosen by management if they use the maximin rule to decide which price should be charged?**

    A $30

    B $35

    C   Any price between $30 and $35

    D   Either $30 or $35, as it makes no difference to the profit

5   **Which price should be chosen by management if they use the maximax rule to decide which price should be charged?**

    A $30

    B $35

    C   Any price between $30 and $35

    D   Either $30 or $35, as it makes no difference to the profit

259 MYLO (SEPTEMBER 2016)

Mylo runs a cafeteria situated on the ground floor of a large corporate office block. Each of the five floors of the building are occupied and there are in total 1,240 employees.

Mylo sells lunches and snacks in the cafeteria. The lunch menu is freshly prepared each morning and Mylo has to decide how many meals to make each day. As the office block is located in the city centre, there are several other places situated around the building where staff can buy their lunch, so the level of demand for lunches in the cafeteria is uncertain.

Mylo has analysed daily sales over the previous six months and established four possible demand levels and their associated probabilities. He has produced the following payoff table to show the daily profits which could be earned from the lunch sales in the cafeteria:

Demand level	Probability	Supply level			
		450	620	775	960
		$	$	$	$
450	0.15	1,170	980	810	740
620	0.30	1,170	1,612	1,395	1,290
775	0.40	1,170	1,612	2,015	1,785
960	0.15	1,170	1,612	2,015	2,496

1   If Mylo adopts a maximin approach to decision-making, which daily supply level will he choose?

   A   450 lunches

   B   620 lunches

   C   775 lunches

   D   960 lunches

2   If Mylo adopts a minimax regret approach to decision-making, which daily supply level will he choose?

   A   450 lunches

   B   620 lunches

   C   775 lunches

   D   960 lunches

3 **Which of the following statements is/are true if Mylo chooses to use expected values to assist in his decision-making regarding the number of lunches to be provided?**

(1) Mylo would be considered to be taking a defensive and conservative approach to his decision.

(2) Expected values will ignore any variability which could occur across the range of possible outcomes.

(3) Expected values will not take into account the likelihood of the different outcomes occurring.

(4) Expected values can be applied by Mylo as he is evaluating a decision which occurs many times over.

A (1), (2) and (3)

B (2) and (4)

C (1) and (3) only

D (4) only

4 The human resources department has offered to undertake some research to help Mylo to predict the number of employees who will require lunch in the cafeteria each day. This information will allow Mylo to prepare an accurate number of lunches each day.

What is the maximum amount which Mylo would be willing to pay for this information (to the nearest whole $)?

A $191

B $359

C $478

D $175

5 Mylo is now considering investing in a speciality coffee machine. He has estimated the following daily results for the new machine:

	$
Sales (650 units)	1,300
Variable costs	(845)
	─────
Contribution	455
Incremental fixed costs	(70)
	─────
Profit	385
	─────

Which of the following statements are true regarding the sensitivity of this investment?

(1)   The investment is more sensitive to a change in sales volume than sales price.

(2)   If variable costs increase by 44% the investment will make a loss.

(3)   The investment's sensitivity to incremental fixed costs is 550%.

(4)   The margin of safety is 84.6%.

A   (1), (2) and (3)

B   (2) and (4)

C   (1), (3) and (4)

D   (3) and (4) only

BUDGETING AND CONTROL

260   LRA (JUNE 2015)

Lesting Regional Authority (LRA) is responsible for the provision of a wide range of services in the Lesting region, which is based in the south of the country 'Alaia'. These services include, amongst other things, responsibility for residents' welfare, schools, housing, hospitals, roads and waste management. Over recent months the Lesting region experienced the hottest temperatures on record, resulting in several forest fires, which caused damage to several schools and some local roads. Unfortunately, these hot temperatures were then followed by flooding, which left a number of residents without homes and saw higher than usual numbers of admissions to hospitals due to the outbreak of disease. These hospitals were full and some patients were treated in tents. Residents have been complaining for some years that a new hospital is needed in the area.

Prior to these events, the LRA was proudly leading the way in a new approach to waste management, with the introduction of its new 'Waste Recycling Scheme.' Two years ago, it began phase 1 of the scheme and half of its residents were issued with different coloured waste bins for different types of waste. The final phase was due to begin in one month's time. The cost of providing the new waste bins is significant but LRA's focus has always been on the long-term savings both to the environment and in terms of reduced waste disposal costs.

The LRA is about to begin preparing its budget for the coming financial year, which starts in one month's time. Over recent years, zero-based budgeting (ZBB) has been introduced at a number of regional authorities in Alaia and, given the demand on resources which LRA faces this year, it is considering whether now would be a good time to introduce it.

1   What are the main steps involved in preparing a zero-based budget?

A   Identifying previous inefficiencies, using adaptative management processes and avoiding wasteful expenditure in planning.

B   Recognising different cost behaviour patterns, planning on a rolling basis and ignoring wasteful expenditure.

C   Analysing the cost of each activity, identifying alternative methods and assessing the consequences of performing the activity at different levels.

D   Updating the budget continually, setting performance standards and controlling performance monthly with the use of variance analysis.

2   Which TWO of the following statements are true?

(1)   Now is a good time to introduce ZBB in LRA.

(2)   The introduction of ZBB in any organisation is relatively straightforward.

(3)   The introduction of ZBB in LRA would be lengthy and costly.

(4)   A conflict situation may arise if ZBB is introduced in LRA.

A   (1) and (2)

B   (1) and (3)

C   (3) and (4)

D   (2) and (4)

3   Which of the following correctly describes a 'decision package' within the context of zero-based budgeting?

A   A method of budgeting that requires each cost element to be specifically justified, as though the activities to which the budget relates were being undertaken for the first time.

B   The decision or choice between making a product in-house or outsourcing and buying in.

C   A method of budgeting based on an activity framework and utilising cost driver data in the budget-setting and variance feedback processes.

D   A list of costs that will not result in an outflow of cash either now or in the future or result in a 'real' cash expenditure.

4   Which ONE of the following statements is true?

A   If any of the activities or operations at LRA are wasteful, ZBB will not be able to identify these and remove them.

B   With the implementation of ZBB, managers may become less motivated as they have had a key role in putting the budget together.

C   ZBB would discourage a more questioning attitude and lead managers to just the status quo.

D   Overall, ZBB at LRA will lead to a more efficient allocation of resources.

5   **Which of the following describe difficulties in assessing performance in not-for-profit organisations?**

   (i)   Benefits and costs are not always easy to quantify.

   (ii)   These organisations often have multiple stakeholders and therefore multiple objectives.

   (iii) These organisations often have unlimited funds and are therefore not motivated to measure performance.

   A   (i) only

   B   (i) and (ii)

   C   (ii) only

   D   (ii) and (iii)

261 BOKCO (JUNE 2015)

Bokco is a manufacturing company. It has a small permanent workforce, but it is also reliant on temporary workers, whom it hires on three-month contracts whenever production requirements increase. All buying of materials is the responsibility of the company's purchasing department. and the company's policy is to hold low levels of raw materials in order to minimise inventory holding costs.

Budgeting is done on spreadsheets and detailed variance reports are produced each month for sales, material costs and labour costs. Departmental managers are then paid a monthly bonus depending on the performance of their department.

Bokco is operating in a fast changing environment and its finance manager thinks the original standard costs are unrealistic. They are considering revising the budget by analysing existing variances into a planning and operational element would help to improve performance.

One month ago, Bokco began production of a new product. The standard cost card for one unit was drawn up to include a cost of $84 for labour, based on seven hours of labour at $12 per hour.

Actual output of the product during the first month of production was 460 units and the actual time taken to manufacture the product totalled 1,860 hours at a total cost of $26,040.

After being presented with some initial variance calculations, the production manager has realised that the standard time per unit of seven hours was the time taken to produce the first unit and that a learning rate of 90% should have been anticipated for the first 1,000 units of production.

The production manager has consequently been criticised by other departmental managers who have said that, 'He has no idea of all the problems this (i.e. the failure to anticipate the learning effect) has caused.'

Bokco uses cost plus pricing to set the selling prices for its products once an initial cost card has been drawn up. Prices are then reviewed on a quarterly basis.

1   **Which TWO of the following statements about using spreadsheets in budgeting are true?**

(1)   Spreadsheets enable managers to consider many different budget options and also carry out sensitivity analysis on the budget figures.

(2)   Minor errors in the spreadsheet cannot affect the validity of the data.

(3)   Spreadsheets are able to take qualitative factors into account.

(4)   The possibility of experimentation with data is so great that it is possible to lose sight of the original intention of the spreadsheet.

A   (1) and (2)

B   (1) and (4)

C   (2) and (3)

D   (3) and (4)

2   **Which TWO of the following sentences about the manipulation issues involved in revising budgets are true?**

(1)   The establishment of ex-post budgets is very difficult. Managers whose performance is reported to be poor using such a budget are unlikely to accept them as performance measures because of the subjectivity in setting such budgets.

(2)   Frequent demands for budget revisions may result in bias.

(3)   The operational variances do not give a fair reflection of the actual results achieved in the actual conditions that existed.

(4)   The analysis does not help in the standard-setting learning process.

A   (1) and (2)

B   (1) and (3)

C   (2) and (3)

D   (3) and (4)

3   **What is the labour efficiency planning variance AFTER taking account of the learning effect?**

Note: The learning index for a 90% learning curve is –0.1520.

A $1,360 F

B $1, 360 A

C $7,104 A

D $23,424 F

4   What is the labour efficiency operational variance AFTER taking account of the learning effect?

Note: The learning index for a 90% learning curve is –0.1520.

A $1,360 F

B $1, 360 A

C $7,104 A

D $23,424 F

5   Which ONE of the following statements about the production manager's failure to anticipate the learning effect is true?

A   There will be no unnecessary extra labour costs.

B   The selling price of the company's products would have been set too low.

C   An adverse material price variance would have arisen.

D   The sales manager's bonus would have still be guaranteed, in spite of the production manager's failure to anticipate the learning effect.

262   CORFE CO (SEPTEMBER 2016)

Corfe Co is a business which manufactures computer laptop batteries and it has developed a new battery which has a longer usage time than batteries currently available in laptops. The selling price of the battery is forecast to be $45.

The maximum production capacity of Corfe Co is 262,500 units. The company's management accountant is currently preparing an annual flexible budget and has collected the following information so far:

Production (units)	185,000	200,000	225,000
	$	$	$
Material costs	740,000	800,000	900,000
Labour costs	1,017,500	1,100,000	1,237,500
Fixed costs	750,000	750,000	750,000

In addition to the above costs, the management accountant estimates that for each increment of 50,000 units produced, one supervisor will need to be employed. A supervisor's annual salary is $35,000.

The production manager does not understand why the flexible budgets have been produced as they have always used a fixed budget previously.

1   Assuming the budgeted figures are correct, what would the flexed total production cost be if production is 80% of maximum capacity?

A $2,735,000

B $2,770,000

C $2,885,000

D $2,920,000

2   The management accountant has said that a machine maintenance cost was not included in the flexible budget but needs to be taken into account.

The new battery will be manufactured on a machine currently owned by Corfe Co which was previously used for a product which has now been discontinued. The management accountant estimates that every 1,000 units will take 14 hours to produce. The annual machine hours and maintenance costs for the machine for the last four years have been as follows:

	Machine time (hours)	Maintenance costs ($000)
Year 1	5,000	850
Year 2	4,400	735
Year 3	4,850	815
Year 4	1,800	450

What is the estimated maintenance cost if production of the battery is 80% of maximum capacity (to the nearest $000)?

A $575,000

B $593,000

C $500,000

D $735,000

3   In the first month of production of the new battery, actual sales were 18,000 units and the sales revenue achieved was $702,000. The budgeted sales units were 17,300.

Based on this information, which of the following statements is true?

A   When the budget is flexed, the sales variance will include both the sales volume and sales price variances.

B   When the budget is flexed, the sales variance will only include the sales volume variance.

C   When the budget is flexed, the sales variance will only include the sales price variance.

D   When the budget is flexed, the sales variance will include the sales mix and quantity variances and the sales price variance.

4   Which of the following statements relating to the preparation of a flexible budget for the new battery are true?

(1)   The budget could be time-consuming to produce as splitting out semi-variable costs may not be straightforward.

(2)   The range of output over which assumptions about how costs will behave could be difficult to determine.

(3)   The flexible budget will give managers more opportunity to include budgetary slack than a fixed budget.

(4)   The budget will encourage all activities and their value to the organisation to be reviewed and assessed.

A   (1) and (2) only

B   (1), (2) and (3)

C   (1) and (4)

D   (2), (3) and (4)

5   The management accountant intends to use a spreadsheet for the flexible budget in order to analyse performance of the new battery.

Which of the following statements are benefits regarding the use of spreadsheets for budgeting?

(1)   The user can change input variables and a new version of the budget can be quickly produced.

(2)   Errors in a formula can be easily traced and data can be difficult to corrupt in a spreadsheet.

(3)   A spreadsheet can take account of qualitative factors to allow decisions to be fully evaluated.

(4)   Managers can carry out sensitivity analysis more easily on a budget model which is held in a spreadsheet.

A   (1), (3) and (4)

B   (1), (2) and (4)

C   (1) and (4) only

D   (2) and (3)

263 BELLAMY CO

Bellamy Co is negotiating with marketing companies with regard to its marketing campaign on its 'Muse' product. Bellamy Co is uncertain as to what the total marketing costs will be each year. However, the following information is available, as the sales manager has provided the data for past marketing expenditure and sales on the 'Muse' product.

The sales manager has plotted both of these variables on a scatter plot with the marketing expenditure from the last 12 quarters on the x-axis, and the associated sales (in $'000) on the y-axis:

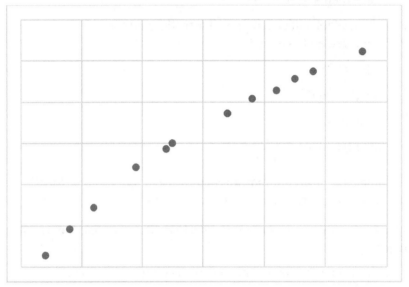

1   Which ONE of the following statements about the above graph is true?

A   The graph shows a positive correlation, which means that low values of sales are associated with low values of marketing expenditure, and high values of sales are associated with high values of marketing expenditure.

B   The graph shows a positive correlation, which means that low values of sales are associated with the high values of marketing expenditure, and high values of sales are associated with low values of marketing expenditure.

C   The graph shows a negative correlation, which means that low values of sales are associated with the low values of marketing expenditure, and high values of sales are associated with high values of marketing expenditure.

D   The graph shows a negative correlation, which means that low values of sales are associated with the high values of marketing expenditure, and high values of sales are associated with low values of marketing expenditure.

2   The linear relationship between marketing spend in thousands of dollars and sales in tens of thousands of dollars was correctly established by the sales manager as $Y = 5 + 2X$.

Which TWO of the following statements are true?

(1)   For every $1,000 spent on marketing, sales revenue increases by $50,000 on average.

(2)   When nothing is spent on marketing, the average sales level is $50,000.

(3)   For every $1,000 spent on marketing, sales revenue increases by $20,000 on average.

(4)   When nothing is spent on marketing, the average sales level is $20,000.

A   (1) and (2)

B   (1) and (4)

C   (2) and (3)

D   (3) and (4)

3   The correlation coefficient between marketing expenditure and sales revenue is calculated to be 0.85

Which of the following statements are true?

A   There is a weak relationship between marketing expenditure and sales revenue.

B   85% of the variation in sales revenue can be explained by the corresponding variation in marketing expenditure.

C   72% of the variation in sales revenue can be explained by the corresponding variation in marketing expenditure.

D   Sales revenue will increase by 85% more than marketing expenditure will increase.

You have been asked to use regression analysis to forecast the impact of future marketing expenditure on sales.

4   **Which TWO of the following are underlying assumptions of forecasts made using regression analysis?**

(1)   A curvilinear relationship exists between the two variables.

(2)   The value of one variable can be predicted or estimated from the value of one other variable.

(3)   A perfect linear relationship between the two variables.

(4)   What has happened in the past will provide a reliable guide to the future.

A   (1) and (2)

B   (1) and (4)

C   (2) and (4)

D   (3) and (4)

5   Which of the following would affect the reliability of a forecast using linear regression?

(1)   The amount of data on which the regression line is based.

(2)   The assumption that the trend line applies outside the range of X values used to establish the line in the first place.

(3)   The assumption that there is a linear relationship between the two variables.

(4)   The coefficient of correlation.

A   (1) and (2) only

B   (3) and (4) only

C   (1), (2), (3) only

D   (1), (2), (3) and (4)

264 OBC (DECEMBER 2015)

The Organic Bread Company (OBC) makes a range of breads for sale direct to the public. The production process begins with workers weighing out ingredients on electronic scales and then placing them in a machine for mixing. A worker then manually removes the dough from the machine and shapes it into loaves by hand, after which the bread is then placed into the oven for baking. All baked loaves are then inspected by OBC's quality inspector before they are packaged up and made ready for sale. Any loaves which fail the inspection are donated to a local food bank. The standard cost card for OBC's 'Mixed Bloomer', one of its most popular loaves, is as follows:

White flour	450 grams at $1.80 per kg	$0.81
Wholegrain flour	150 grams at $2.20 per kg	$0.33
Yeast	10 grams at $20 per kg	$0.20
Total	610 grams	$1.34

Budgeted production of Mixed Bloomers was 1,000 units for the quarter, although actual production was only 950 units. The total actual quantities used and their actual costs were:

	kgs	$ per kg
White flour	408.5	1.90
Wholegrain flour	152.0	2.10
Yeast	10.0	20.00
Total	570.5	

1   What is the total material usage variance for OBC for the last quarter?

A $3.30 favourable

B $20.90 favourable

C $20.90 adverse

D $34.20 favourable

2   **What is the total material mix variance for OBC for the last quarter?**

A $3.30 favourable

B $16.51 favourable

C $16.51 adverse

D $19.77 favourable

3   **What is the total material yield variance for OBC for the last quarter?**

A $3.30 favourable

B $16.51 favourable

C $16.51 adverse

D $19.81 favourable

4   **Which of the following statements below is/are true?**

(1)   An adverse material mix variance may arise because the dough may not be removed completely out of the machine, leaving some dough behind.

(2)   An adverse material yield variance may arise because handmade loaves may be slightly too large, meaning that fewer loaves can be baked.

A   (1) only

B   (2) only

C   Both (1) and (2)

D   Neither (1) nor (2)

5   **Which of the following statement(s) below is/are true?**

(1)   Errors or changes in the mix may cause some loaves to be sub-standard and therefore rejected by the quality inspector.

(2)   The loaves might be baked at the wrong temperature and therefore be rejected by the quality inspector.

A   (1) only

B   (2) only

C   Both (1) and (2)

D   Neither (1) nor (2)

265 VARIANCES – SALES

Fort Co produces and sells three models of family car: a basic model (the Drastic), an upgraded model (the Bomber) and a deluxe model (the Cracker). All of the cars are priced to achieve a 6% mark up on standard cost. For the month of June, Fort Co budgeted to sell 30,000 units of the Drastic and so have 10% market share of the budgeted sales at a price of $10,600 each. Fort Co. actually achieved a 15% share of the market, though the market had actually contracted by 5%.

The following information is available for July.

	Drastic	Bomber	Cracker
Sales units:			
– Budgeted	27,000	15,000	18,000
– Actual	26,000	16,000	14,000
Budgeted sales price	**$10,600**	**$13,250**	**$16,960**

1 **Which option correctly fills the gaps in the paragraph?**

"The difference between the sales quantity and _____ variances is that the standard _____is considered in the former. The difference between standard and actual is _____."

A   volume, mix, ignored

B   price, mix, calculated

C   volume, quantity, ignored

D   price, quantity, calculated

2 **What is the favourable market share and adverse market size variance for the 'Drastic' (to the nearest $)?**

Share $_____ Favourable   Size $_____ Adverse

3 **What is the total adverse sales mix variance for Fort Co (to the nearest $)?**
$_____ Adverse

4 **What is the total adverse sales quantity variance for Fort Co (to the nearest $)?**
$_____ Adverse

5   **Which TWO of the following statements are true?**

(1)   The sales mix variance would not give useful information to the management of Fort Co if the Cracker was a van.

(2)   The sales mix variance will not be affected if the labour efficiency on the Drastic production line increases, all other factors remaining the same.

(3)   The market share variance is a planning variance, not an operational variance.

(4)   If the mix variance was calculated as a physical quantity, the answer would always be zero.

A   (1) and (2)

B   (2) and (3)

C   (3) and (4)

D   (1) and (4)

266   GRAYSHOTT CO (MARCH 2019, ADAPTED)

Marcus manages production and sales of product MN at Grayshott Co. Marcus has been asked to attend a meeting with Grayshott Co's finance director to explain the results for product MN in the last quarter.

Budgeted and actual results for product MN were as follows:

	Budget	Actual
Sales volume (units)	40,000	38,000
	$000	$000
Revenue ($65 per unit)	2,600	2,394
Material (5.2 kg at $4 per kg)	(832)	(836)
Labour (2 hours at $8 per hour)	(640)	(798)
Variable overheads (2 hours at $4 per hour)	(320)	(399)
Fixed overheads	(220)	(220)
Profit	588	141

There was no opening and closing inventory in the last quarter. Grayshott Co operates a marginal costing system.

Marcus is angry about having to attend the meeting as he has no involvement in setting the original budget and he believes that the adverse results are due to the following circumstances which were beyond his control:

(1)   A decision by Grayshott Co's board to increase wages meant that the actual labour rate per hour was 25% higher than budgeted. This decision was made in response to a request by the production department to enable it to meet a large, one-off customer order in the last quarter.

(2)   Due to the closure of a key supplier, Grayshott Co agreed to a contract with an alternative supplier to pay 6% more per kg than the budgeted price for material. The actual cost per kg of material was $4.40.

(3)   Difficult economic conditions meant that market demand for the MN was lower by 10%.

At present Grayshott Co does not operate a system of planning and operational variances and Marcus believes it should do so.

1   **What was the market share variance for product MN for the last quarter?**

    A $40,400 Favourable

    B $80,800 Adverse

    C $29,400 Favourable

    D $38,000 Adverse

2   **What was the adverse materials price planning variance for product MN for the last quarter?**

    A $30,400

    B $76,000

    C $45,600

    D $49,920

3   **What was the labour rate operational variance for product MN for the last quarter?**

    A $159,600 Favourable

    B $159,600 Adverse

    C $160,000 Favourable

    D $160,000 Adverse

4   **Which of the following would explain a labour efficiency planning variance?**

    (1)   A change in employment legislation requiring staff to take longer rest periods.

    (2)   Customers demanding higher quality products leading to a change in product design.

    (3)   The learning effect for labour being estimated incorrectly in the production budget.

    A   (1) and (2) only

    B   (2) and (3) only

    C   (3) only

    D   (1), (2) and (3)

5   **Which of the following statements regarding the problems of introducing a system of planning and operational variances is/are true?**

(1)   Operational managers may argue that variances are due to the original budget being unrealistic.

(2)   Operational managers may seek to blame uncontrollable external factors for the variances.

A   (1) only

B   (2) only

C   Both (1) and (2)

D   Neither (1) nor (2)

267   ROMEO CO (DECEMBER 2016)

Romeo Co is a business which makes and sells fresh pizza from a number of mobile food vans based at several key locations in the city centre. It offers a variety of toppings and dough bases for the pizzas and has a good reputation for providing a speedy service combined with hot, fresh and tasty food to customers.

Each van employs a chef who is responsible for making the pizzas to Romeo Co's recipes and two sales staff who serve the customers. All purchasing is done centrally to enable Romeo Co to negotiate bulk discounts and build relationships with suppliers.

Romeo Co operates a standard costing and variances system and the standard cost card for Romeo Co's basic tomato pizza is as follows:

Ingredient	Weight	Price
	(kg)	($ per kg)
Dough	0.20	7.60
Tomato sauce	0.08	2.50
Cheese	0.12	20.00
Herbs	0.02	8.40
	———	
	0.42	
	———	

In Month 3, Romeo Co produced and sold 90 basic tomato pizzas and actual results were as follows:

Ingredient	Kgs bought and used	Actual cost per kg
Dough	18.9	6.50
Tomato sauce	6.6	2.45
Cheese	14.5	21.00
Herbs	2.0	8.10
	42	

In Month 4, Romeo Co produced and sold 110 basic tomato pizzas. Actual results were as follows:

Ingredient	Kgs bought and used	Actual cost per kg
Dough	21.3	6.60
Tomato sauce	7.5	2.45
Cheese	14.2	20.00
Herbs	2.0	8.50
	45	

In Month 6, 100 basic tomato pizzas were made using a total of 42 kg of ingredients. A new chef at Romeo Co used the expected amount of dough and herbs but used less cheese and more tomato sauce per pizza than the standard. It was noticed that the sales of the basic tomato pizza had declined in the second half of the month.

1   What was the total material price variance for Month 3?

   A $7.22 adverse

   B $7.22 favourable

   C $40.50 favourable

   D $40.50 adverse

2   What was the total materials mix variance for Month 3?

   A $81.02 adverse

   B $41.92 adverse

   C $42.88 adverse

   D $38.14 adverse

3   **What was the materials yield variance for Month 4?**

Note: Calculate all workings to 2 decimal places.

A $12.21 favourable

B $11.63 favourable

C $21.95 adverse

D $9.75 adverse

4   In Month 5, Romeo Co reported a favourable materials mix variance for the basic tomato pizza.

Which of the following statements would explain why this variance has occurred?

A   The proportion of the relatively expensive ingredients used in production was less than the standard.

B   The prices paid for the ingredients used in the mix were lower than the standard prices.

C   Each pizza used less of all the ingredients in actual production than expected.

D   More pizzas were produced than expected given the level of ingredients input.

5   **Based on the above information about Month 6, which of the following statements are correct?**

(1)   The actual cost per pizza in Month 6 was lower than the standard cost per pizza.

(2)   The sales staff should lose their Month 6 bonus because of the reduced sales.

(3)   The value of the ingredients usage variance and the mix variance are the same.

(4)   The new chef will be responsible for the material price, mix and yield variances.

A   (3) and (4)

B   (1) and (2)

C   (1) and (3)

D   (2) and (4)

PERFORMANCE MEASUREMENT AND CONTROL

268 PIND CO

The following information is available for Pind Co, a manufacturing company. You are provided with an extract from the Statement of Profit or Loss:

	$
Operating profit	42,000
Interest charges	(16,000)
	———
Profit before tax	26,000
Taxation	(5,460)
	———
	20,540

Pind Co has an operating profit margin of 15%. You are provided with an extract from its Statement of Financial Position:

	$
Equity and reserves	
Total equity and reserves	420,000
Non-current liabilities	
Loan	150,000
5% Preference shares	40,000
Current liabilities	
Payable	50,000

1   **What are the gearing ratio and interest cover for Pind Co? Place a tick in the boxes in the table below as appropriate.**

	25%	31%	2.625	1.625
Gearing ratio				
Interest cover				

2   **Which TWO of the following statements are correct?**

(1)   A reduction in the tax rate will improve the interest cover ratio.

(2)   If the level of long term debt in Pind Co is reduced, the interest cover and dividend cover ratios will improve.

(3)   If the level of long term debt in Pind Co is reduced, the asset turnover ratio will improve.

(4)   Financial gearing is a measure of risk, but interest cover is a measure of profitability.

A   (1) and (2)

B   (2) and (3)

C   (3) and (4)

D   (1) and (4)

3   Pind Co has a current ratio of 1.5 and a quick ratio of 0.9.

If cash in the bank is used to pay some of the payable, what will be the effect on the current and quick ratios?

	Current ratio	**Quick ratio**
A	Increase	Increase
B	Increase	Decrease
C	Decrease	Increase
D	Decrease	Decrease

4   **If Pind Co has a receivables to cash ratio of 2 : 2.5, what is the receivables collection period (to the nearest whole day)?**   _____ **days**

5   **Which of the following statement(s) is/are true?**

(1)   If the turnover of Pind Co increased by 20%, the asset turnover would increase by 20%.

(2)   If Pind Co has a different depreciation policy to its competitors, the asset turnover ratio will not be comparable.

A   (1) only

B   (2) only

C   Both (1) and (2)

D   Neither (1) nor (2)

Section 3

CONSTRUCTED RESPONSE QUESTIONS – SECTION C

INFORMATION, TECHNOLOGIES AND SYSTEMS FOR ORGANISATIONAL PERFORMANCE

Please note that this syllabus area could be tested as part of section C in the exam. However, whilst the questions in section C may include requirements related to the information systems area of the syllabus, they will not be a full 20 mark questions solely on this syllabus area. Questions 269–272 are therefore not structured in the way you should expect of a real exam question, but are useful for technical practice of this syllabus area.

269 B5 CARS EIS

B5 Cars manufactures motor vehicles for sale to the general public and companies. Several other motor vehicle manufacturers operate within the industry, which is highly competitive: there is a trade association which collects a wide range of information.

B5 Cars has five manufacturing plants and 53 sales outlets in the country in which it operates. Information for the company's executive information system (EIS) is obtained both from internal sources such as the production plants, and also external sources such as customers. Internally-generated information is sent to head office over a wide area network.

Due to the overall escalating cost of the company's EIS, the board has decided to collect only internally-produced information. This decision has been taken against the advice of the chief information officer.

Required:

(a) Suggest and explain reasons why the company's EIS could be becoming expensive to operate. 💻 **(6 marks)**

(b) Discuss the decision of the board to concentrate on internally-produced information. Clearly describe the information sources that will be lost and explain the effects on the company's information systems and its products. 💻 **(14 marks)**

(Total: 20 marks)

270 REES INVESTMENTS

Rees Investments invests money on behalf of its customers. The company guarantees its customers a favourable interest rate in return for long-term investments. Mark Rees started the company five years ago and he was originally the only investment analyst, making all the investment decisions. The company was initially very successful, due to a combination of Rees' expertise and a favourable world economic climate. Specialising in investing in the emerging markets of Asia and Africa, Rees Investments achieved excellent returns on their investments; This allowed them to meet guarantees given to clients as well as funding the expansion of the company itself.

The company has grown and it currently employs 60 staff of whom 12 are investment analysts. However, investment returns have declined and the company is now having problems providing its guaranteed return to investors. Consequently, Mark Rees is reviewing investment procedures and exploring options for returning the company to the profitability it enjoyed in its early years.

Required:

(a)   One of the options Mark Rees is considering is the use of a decision support system to help his investment analysts make appropriate investment decisions.

Briefly describe what is meant by a decision support system and comment on its possible contribution to the investment decisions made by analysts at Rees Investments. 🖥️   **(12 marks)**

(b)   Mark Rees is also considering the development of an expert system.

Required:

Briefly describe what is meant by an expert system and comment on its possible contribution to the investment decisions made by analysts at Rees Investments. 🖥️

(8 marks)

(Total: 20 marks)

271   CDE

 Answer debrief

CDE is a manufacturer of almost 100 hundred different automotive components that are sold in both large and small quantities on a just-in-time (JIT) basis to the major vehicle assemblers. Business is highly competitive and price sensitive. The company is listed on the stock exchange but CDE's share performance has not matched that of its main competitors.

CDE's management accounting system uses a manufacturing resource planning (MRP II) system to control production scheduling, inventory movements and inventory control, and labour and machine utilisation. The accounting department carries out a detailed annual budgeting exercise, determines standard costs for labour and materials, and allocates production overhead on the basis of machine utilisation. Strict accounting controls over labour and material costs are managed by the detailed recording of operator and machine timesheets and raw material movements, and by calculating and investigating all significant variances.

While the information from the MRP II system is useful to management, there is an absence of integrated data about customer requirements and suppliers. Some information is contained within spreadsheets and databases held by the Sales and Purchasing departments respectively. One result of this lack of integration is that inventories are higher than they should be in a JIT environment.

The managers of CDE (representing functional areas of sales, production, purchasing, finance and administration) believe that, while costs are strictly controlled, the cost of the accounting department is excessive and significant savings need to be made, even at the expense of data accuracy. Managers believe that there may not be optimum use of the production capacity to generate profits and cash flow and improve shareholder value. CDE's management wants to carry out sensitivity and other analyses of strategic alternatives, but this is difficult when the existing management accounting system is focused on control rather than on decision support.

Required:

(a) (i) Outline the different types of information system available to manufacturing firms like CDE.

(ii) Recommend with reasons the information system that would be appropriate to CDE's needs. **(8 marks)**

(b) Given the business environment that CDE faces, and the desire of management to reduce the cost of accounting:

(i) Discuss the relevance of the current management accounting system; and

(ii) recommend how the system should be improved. **(12 marks)**

(Total: 20 marks)

> ▶ *Calculate your allowed time, allocate the time to the separate parts...............*

272 THE MG ORGANISATION

The Information Systems strategy within the MG organisation has been developed over a number of years. However, the basic approach has always remained unchanged. An IT budget is agreed by the board each year. The budget is normally 5% to 10% higher than the previous year's to allow for increases in prices and upgrades to computer systems.

Systems are upgraded in accordance with user requirements. Most users see IT systems as tools for recording day-to-day transactions and providing access to accounting and other information as necessary. There is no Enterprise Resource Planning System (ERPS) or Executive Information System (EIS).

The board tends to rely on reports from junior managers to control the business. While these reports generally provide the information requested by the board, they are focused at a tactical level and do not contribute to strategy formulation or implementation.

Required:

(a) Advise the board on how an ERPS and EIS could provide benefits over and above those provided by transaction processing systems. **(12 marks)**

(b) Recommend to the board how it should go about improving its budgetary allocations for IT and how it should evaluate the benefits of ERPS and EIS. **(8 marks)**

(Total: 20 marks)

SPECIALIST COST AND MANAGEMENT ACCOUNTING TECHNIQUES

Please note that this syllabus area will not be tested as part of section C in the exam, however questions 274–278 are included here to allow you to practice some of the key techniques from this syllabus area that could be useful in Section A or B questions.

273 GADGET CO (DECEMBER 2010)

The Gadget Co produces three products, A, B and C, all made from the same material. Until now, it has used traditional absorption costing to allocate overheads to its products. The company is now considering an activity based costing system in the hope that it will improve profitability. Information for the three products for the last year is as follows:

	A	B	C
Production and sales volumes (units)	15,000	12,000	18,000
Selling price per unit	$7.50	$12	$13
Raw material usage (kg) per unit	2	3	4
Direct labour hours per unit	0.1	0.15	0.2
Machine hours per unit	0.5	0.7	0.9
Number of production runs per annum	16	12	8
Number of purchase orders per annum	24	28	42
Number of deliveries to retailers per annum	48	30	62

The price for raw materials remained constant throughout the year at $1.20 per kg. Similarly, the direct labour cost for the whole workforce was $14.80 per hour. The annual overhead costs were as follows:

	$
Machine set up costs	26,550
Machine running costs	66,400
Procurement costs	48,000
Delivery costs	54,320

Required:

(a) Calculate the full cost per unit for products A, B and C under traditional absorption costing, using direct labour hours as the basis for apportionment. ⊞ **(5 marks)**

(b) Calculate the full cost per unit of each product using activity based costing. ⊞ **(9 marks)**

(c) Using your calculation from (a) and (b) above, explain how activity based costing may help The Gadget Co improve the profitability of each product. 🖥 **(6 marks)**

(Total: 20 marks)

274 BRICK BY BRICK (JUNE 2010)

Brick by Brick (BBB) is a building business that provides a range of building services to the public. Recently they have been asked to quote for garage conversions (GC) and extensions to properties (EX) and have found that they are winning fewer GC contracts than expected.

BBB has a policy to price all jobs at budgeted total cost plus 50%. Overheads are currently absorbed on a labour hour basis. BBB thinks that a switch to activity based costing (ABC) to absorb overheads would reduce the cost associated to GC and hence make them more competitive.

You are provided with the following data:

Overhead category	Annual overheads $	Activity driver	Total number of activities per year
Supervisors	90,000	Site visits	500
Planners	70,000	Planning documents	250
Property related	240,000	Labour hours	40,000
Total	400,000		

A typical GC costs $3,500 in materials and takes 300 labour hours to complete. A GC requires only one site visit by a supervisor and needs only one planning document to be raised. The typical EX costs $8,000 in materials and takes 500 hours to complete. An EX requires six site visits and five planning documents. In all cases labour is paid $15 per hour.

Required:

(a) Calculate the cost and quoted price of a GC and of an EX using labour hours to absorb the overheads. ⊞ (5 marks)

(b) Calculate the cost and the quoted price of a GC and of an EX using ABC to absorb the overheads. ⊞ (5 marks)

(c) Assume that the cost of a GC falls by nearly 7% and the price of an EX rises by about 2% as a result of the change to ABC.

Suggest possible pricing strategies for the two products that BBB sells and suggest two reasons other than high prices for the current poor sales of the GC. 💻 (6 marks)

(d) One BBB manager has suggested that only marginal cost should be included in budget cost calculations as this would avoid the need for arbitrary overhead allocations to products.

Briefly discuss this point of view and comment on the implication for the amount of mark-up that would be applied to budget costs when producing quotes for jobs. 💻 (4 marks)

(Total: 20 marks)

275 JOLA PUBLISHING CO (JUNE 2008)

Jola Publishing Co publishes two forms of book.

The company publishes a children's book (CB), which is sold in large quantities to government controlled schools. The book is produced in only four large production runs but goes through frequent government inspections and quality assurance checks.

The paper used is strong, designed to resist the damage that can be caused by the young children it is produced for. The book has only a few words and relies on pictures to convey meaning.

The second book is a comprehensive technical journal (TJ). It is produced in monthly production runs, 12 times a year. The paper used is of relatively poor quality and is not subject to any governmental controls and consequently only a small number of inspections are carried out. The TJ uses far more machine hours than the CB in its production.

The directors are concerned about the performance of the two books and are wondering what the impact would be of a switch to an activity based costing (ABC) approach to accounting for overheads. They currently use absorption costing, based on machine hours for all overhead calculations. They have accurately produced an analysis for the accounting year just completed as follows:

	CB	TJ
	$ per unit	$ per unit
Direct production costs:		
Paper	0.75	0.08
Printing ink	1.45	4.47
Machine costs	1.15	1.95
Overheads	2.30	3.95
Total cost	5.65	10.45
Selling price	9.05	13.85
Margin	3.40	3.40

The main overheads involved are:

Overhead	% of total overhead	Activity driver
Property costs	75.0%	Machine hours
Quality control	23.0%	Number of inspections
Production set up costs	2.0%	Number of set ups

If the overheads above were re-allocated under ABC principles then the results would be that the overhead allocation to CB would be $0.05 higher and the overhead allocated to TJ would be $0.30 lower than previously.

Required:

(a) **Explain why the overhead allocations have changed in the way indicated above.** 🖥
(7 marks)

The directors are keen to introduce ABC for the coming year and have provided the following cost and selling price data:

(1)   The paper used costs $2 per kg for a CB but the TJ paper costs only $1 per kg. The CB uses 400 g of paper for each book, four times as much as the TJ uses.

(2)   Printing ink costs $30 per litre. The CB uses one third of the printing ink of the larger TJ. The TJ uses 150 ml of printing ink per book.

(3)   The CB needs six minutes of machine time to produce each book, whereas the TJ needs 10 minutes per book. The machines cost $12 per hour to run.

(4)   The sales prices are to be $9.30 for the CB and $14.00 for the TJ.

As mentioned above there are three main overheads, the data for these are:

Overhead	Annual cost for the coming year ($)
Property costs	2,160,000
Quality control	668,000
Production set up costs	52,000
Total	2,880,000

The CB will be inspected on 180 occasions next year, whereas the TJ will be inspected just 20 times.

Jola Publishing will produce its annual output of 1,000,000 CBs in four production runs and approximately 10,000 TJs per month in each of 12 production runs.

Required:

(b) **Calculate the cost per unit and the margin for the CB and the TJ using machine hours to absorb the overheads.** ▦
(5 marks)

(c) **Calculate the cost per unit and the margin for the CB and the TJ using activity based costing principles to absorb the overheads.** ▦
(8 marks)

(Total: 20 marks)

276   WARGRIN (DECEMBER 2008)

Wargrin designs, develops and sells many PC games. Games have a short lifecycle lasting around three years only. Performance of the games is measured by reference to the profits made in each of the expected three years of popularity. Wargrin accepts a net profit of 35% of turnover as reasonable. A rate of contribution (sales price less variable cost) of 75% is also considered acceptable.

Wargrin has a large centralised development department which carries out all the design work before it passes the completed game to the sales and distribution department to market and distribute the product.

Wargrin has developed a brand new game called Stealth and this has the following budgeted performance figures.

PM: PERFORMANCE MANAGEMENT

The selling price of Stealth will be a constant $30 per game. Analysis of the costs show that at a volume of 10,000 units a total cost of $130,000 is expected. However at a volume of 14,000 units a total cost of $150,000 is expected. If volumes exceed 15,000 units the fixed costs will increase by 50%.

Stealth's budgeted volumes are as follows:

	Year 1	Year 2	Year 3
Sales volume	8,000 units	16,000 units	4,000 units

In addition, marketing costs for Stealth will be $60,000 in year one and $40,000 in year two. Design and development costs are all incurred before the game is launched and has cost $300,000 for Stealth. These costs are written off to the statement of profit or loss as incurred (i.e. before year 1 above).

Required:

(a) Explain the principles behind lifecycle costing and briefly state why Wargrin in particular should consider these lifecycle principles. 🖥 **(4 marks)**

(b) Produce the budgeted results for the game 'Stealth' and briefly assess the game's expected performance, taking into account the whole lifecycle of the game. ⊞ **(9 marks)**

(c) Explain why incremental budgeting is a common method of budgeting and outline the main problems with such an approach. 🖥 **(7 marks)**

(Total: 20 marks)

277 YAM CO (JUNE 2009)

 Answer debrief

Yam Co is involved in the processing of sheet metal into products A, B and C using three processes, pressing, stretching and rolling. Like many businesses Yam faces tough price competition in what is a mature world market.

The factory has 50 production lines each of which contain the three processes: Raw material for the sheet metal is first pressed then stretched and finally rolled. The processing capacity varies for each process and the factory manager has provided the following data:

	Processing time per metre in hours		
	Product A	Product B	Product C
Pressing	0.50	0.50	0.40
Stretching	0.25	0.40	0.25
Rolling	0.40	0.25	0.25

The factory operates for 18 hours each day for five days per week. It is closed for only two weeks of the year for holidays when maintenance is carried out. On average one hour of labour is needed for each of the 225,000 hours of factory time. Labour is paid $10 per hour.

The raw materials cost per metre is $3.00 for product A, $2.50 for product B and $1.80 for product C. Other factory costs (excluding labour and raw materials) are $18,000,000 per year. Selling prices per metre are $70 for product A, $60 for product B and $27 for product C.

Yam carries very little inventory.

Required:

(a) Identify the bottleneck process and briefly explain why this process is described as a 'bottleneck'.   (3 marks)

(b) Calculate the throughput accounting ratio (TPAR) for each product assuming that the bottleneck process is fully utilised. ▦ (8 marks)

(c) Assuming that the TPAR of product C is less than 1:

(i) Explain how Yam could improve the TPAR of product C. ▭ (4 marks)

(ii) Briefly discuss whether this supports the suggestion to cease the production of product C and briefly outline three other factors that Yam should consider before a cessation decision is taken. ▭ (5 marks)

(Total: 20 marks)

> ▶ *Calculate your allowed time, allocate the time to the separate parts...............*

DECISION MAKING TECHNIQUES

278 ROBBER CO (JUNE 2012)

Robber Co manufactures control panels for burglar alarms, a very profitable product. Every product comes with a one year warranty offering free repairs if any faults arise in this period.

It currently produces and sells 80,000 units per annum, with production of them being restricted by the short supply of labour. Each control panel includes two main components – one key pad and one display screen. At present, Robber Co manufactures both of these components in-house. However, the company is currently considering outsourcing the production of keypads and/or display screens. A newly established company based in Burgistan is keen to secure a place in the market, and has offered to supply the keypads for the equivalent of $4.10 per unit and the display screens for the equivalent of $4.30 per unit. This price has been guaranteed for two years.

The current total annual costs of producing the keypads and the display screens are:

	Keypads	Display screens
Production	80,000 units	80,000 units
	$	$
Direct materials	160	116
Direct labour	40	60
Heat and power costs	64	88
Machine costs	26	30
Depreciation and insurance costs	84	96
Total annual production costs	**374**	**390**

Notes:

1   Materials costs for keypads are expected to increase by 5% in six months' time; materials costs for display screens are only expected to increase by 2%, but with immediate effect.

2   Direct labour costs are purely variable and not expected to change over the next year.

3   Heat and power costs include an apportionment of the general factory overhead for heat and power as well as the costs of heat and power directly used for the production of keypads and display screens. The general apportionment included is calculated using 50% of the direct labour cost for each component and would be incurred irrespective of whether the components are manufactured in-house or not.

4   Machine costs are semi-variable; the variable element relates to set up costs, which are based upon the number of batches made. The keypads' machine has fixed costs of $4,000 per annum and the display screens' machine has fixed costs of $6,000 per annum. Whilst both components are currently made in batches of 500, this would need to change, with immediate effect, to batches of 400.

5   60% of depreciation and insurance costs relate to an apportionment of the general factory depreciation and insurance costs; the remaining 40% is specific to the manufacture of keypads and display screens.

Required:

(a)   Advise Robber Co whether it should continue to manufacture the keypads and display screens in-house or whether it should outsource their manufacture to the supplier in Burgistan, assuming it continues to adopt a policy to limit manufacture and sales to 80,000 control panels in the coming year. ▦   **(8 marks)**

(b)   Robber Co takes 0.5 labour hours to produce a keypad and 0.75 labour hours to produce a display screen. Labour hours are restricted to 100,000 hours and labour is paid at $1 per hour. Robber Co wishes to increase its supply to 100,000 control panels (i.e. 100,000 each of keypads and display screens).

    Advise Robber Co as to how many units of keypads and display panels they should either manufacture and/or outsource in order to minimise their costs. ▦ **(7 marks)**

(c)   Discuss the non-financial factors that Robber Co should consider when making a decision about outsourcing the manufacture of keypads and display screens. ▭
                                                                        (5 marks)

                                                                    (Total: 20 marks)

279 BELLAHOUSTON CO (DECEMBER 2021)

Bellahouston Co manufactures three types of running shoes which it sells to sports clothing retailers: Road which are for running on roads, Spikes which are used for racing on athletics tracks, and Trail which are used for running off-road in rural locations. Each of these products use differing amounts of the same resources. Financial information and the resource requirements related to these products are as follows:

	Road	Spikes	Trail
	$	$	$
Selling price per pair of shoes	60.00	45.00	52.00
Variable costs per pair of shoes:			
Direct material ($5 per metre)	7.50	3.00	6.00
Direct labour ($7 per hour)	7.00	10.50	7.00
Machine hours ($10 per hour)	4.00	2.00	3.00
Fixed overheads absorbed per pair of shoes	4.00	6.00	4.00
Profit per pair of shoes	**37.50**	**23.50**	**32.00**

Fixed overheads are absorbed at a rate of $4 per direct labour hour. Bellahouston Co uses a just-in-time production system.

Demand and resource availability for March

Demand for the three products for the month of March is expected to be:

Road	2,300 pairs
Spikes	1,400 pairs
Trail	1,650 pairs

Bellahouston Co has received a special order from RunWild, which is not included in the demand estimates above. RunWild are a major sports retailer who have an extensive customer base and are known for stocking the most popular brands of sportswear. The order is to supply a maximum of 200 pairs of each type of shoe at a discount of $8.00 on the standard selling price.

RunWild will charge a financial penalty if the order is not fully complete in March. If this first order is successful, RunWild would be keen to enter into a regular supply contract.

Usually Bellahouston Co has sufficient resources to meet production, however during March the maximum availability for the following resources has been identified:

Direct material	7,200 metres
Direct labour	6,900 hours
Machine time	1,815 hours

Demand and resource availability for April

Bellahouston Co predicted that the resource availability in March would continue into April; however, it has been discovered that the availability of direct material and direct labour will be 15% less than in March. The available machine time and demand estimates are unchanged. RunWild would not be placing an order in April.

Required:

(a) (i) Calculate the optimum production plan and the resulting total contribution earned for March, assuming that the order with RunWild is supplied in full. ⊞
(7 marks)

(ii) Calculate the maximum financial penalty Bellahouston Co would be prepared to accept from RunWild, if it does not complete RunWild's order in full. ⊞
(4 marks)

(b) Discuss whether Bellahouston Co should fulfil RunWild's order in full in March. 💻
(4 marks)

(c) Define the variables and formulate the constraints and objective function to be used in a linear programming model to determine the optimum usage of resources in April. 💻
(5 marks)

(Total: 20 marks)

280 CHOCOLATES ARE FOREVER (CAF)

As the exams are tested as CBE, candidates will not have to draw a graph. However, it is good practice to attempt a question such as this as part of a robust revision programme. In the exam, graphs will be part of the question scenario and candidates may be asked to provide further calculation or analysis.

CAF Ltd produces a single large item of confectionary, Product S, which is sold for $12 per unit. You have been provided with the following information about the 'S' for the forthcoming year:

Sales   6,000 units
Variable costs $7 per unit

CAF's overheads are budgeted to amount to $20,000. CAF's Financial Director has asked you to prepare some documents for a presentation to the Board of Directors.

Required:

(a) Calculate, and briefly explain the significance of, CAF'S breakeven point and margin of safety, expressed as a percentage. ⊞
(4 marks)

(b) Based on CAF's information above, construct and explain the purpose of the three following charts:

(1) A breakeven chart

(2) A contribution graph

(3) A profit – volume chart.
(12 marks)

(c) Briefly outline the limitations of breakeven analysis. 💻
(4 marks)

(Total: 20 marks)

281 MANGO LEATHER

As the exams are tested as CBE, candidates will not have to draw a graph. However, it is good practice to attempt a question such as this as part of a robust revision programme. In the exam, graphs will be part of the question scenario and candidates may be asked to provide further calculation or analysis.

Mango has been in the clothing market for the last 3 years and operates in an industry which is very competitive and volatile. Mango's management accountant has heard that break even analysis could be used to assess the risks of the business and helps decision making.

The following information on Mango and its product portfolio is also available – figures are per annum:

Products	Production/sales volume	Selling price (per unit)	Variable cost (excluding material cost) per unit	Material (leather) per unit
		$	$	(Meters)
Bags	1,000	400	150	1
Belts	2,000	125	50	0.25
Shoes	1,500	150	65	0.5
Jackets	3,500	300	125	1.5

Leather is regularly used in the production of all the products above. The company has recently discovered that there is likely to be a shortage of leather on the market for the coming year. Leather used in production is bought from a supplier on a JIT basis for $60 per meter. For now, enough material can be sourced from the supplier to satisfy the production requirement. Fixed cost per annum is $580,000.

Required:

(a) Calculate the break even sales revenue. ⊞ (3 marks)

(b) Draw a profit volume chart by clearly showing all the workings to arrive at the graph. (8 marks)

(c) Explain how the unavailability of leather and the rise in its price affect the profitability and breakeven point of Mango. No calculation is required. 💻 (5 marks)

(d) Explain how breakeven analysis could be used in decision making, and outline the limitations of the technique. 💻 (4 marks)

(Total: 20 marks)

282 BREAKEVEN

C Ltd has presented you with its break-even chart:

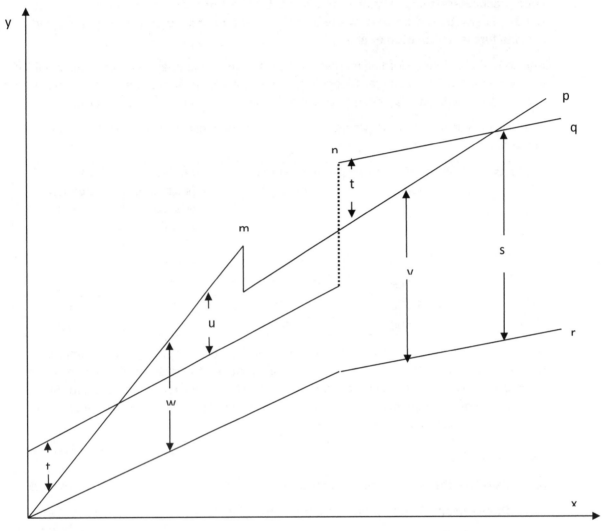

Required:

(a) Identify the components of the breakeven chart labelled *p ,q ,r, s, t, u, v w, x* and *y*. 💻

(10 marks)

(b) Suggest what events are represented at the values of x that are labelled *m* and *n* on the chart. 💻

(5 marks)

(c) Briefly comment on the usefulness of breakeven analysis to senior management of a small company. 💻

(5 marks)

(Total: 20 marks)

283 EC LTD

As the exams are tested as CBE, candidates will not have to draw a graph. However, it is good practice to attempt a question such as this as part of a robust revision programme. In the exam, graphs will be part of the question scenario and candidates may be asked to provide further calculation or analysis.

EC Ltd produces and sells the following two products throughout the year in a constant mix:

	Product X	**Product Y**
Variable cost per $ of sales	$0.45	$0.60
Fixed costs	$1,212,000 per period	

The management of EC has stated that total sales revenue will reach a maximum of $4,000,000, and is generated by the two products in the following proportions:

Product X	**Product Y**
70%	30%

Required:

(a) **Calculate the breakeven sales revenue required per period, based on the sales mix assumed above.** ▦ **(4 marks)**

(b) **Prepare a profit-volume chart of the above situation for the maximum sales revenue. Show on the same chart the effect of a change in the sales mix to product X 50%, product Y 50%, and clearly indicate on the chart the breakeven point for each situation.** **(12 marks)**

(c) **$455,000 of the total fixed costs are attributable to Product X.**

   Calculate the sales revenue required on Product X in order to recover the attributable fixed costs and provide a net contribution of $700,000 towards general fixed costs and profit. ▦ **(4 marks)**

(Total: 20 marks)

284 HEALTH NUTS (SEPTEMBER/DECEMBER 2020)

Health Nuts is a fitness centre, offering 'pay as you go' gym facilities. It has a fully fitted gym with the capacity to accommodate 200 users at one time. It also has 100 car parking spaces and an onsite café, both of which are only for customers using the gym. The fitness centre has shower facilities for customers and Health Nuts provides all customers with a clean towel to use on entry. It is open 360 days a year, from 7:00am until 9:00pm.

Customers pay $8.40 for access to the gym for one hour plus unlimited time in the café. If customers want to use the car park, they have to pay an additional $1 per visit and 80% of visiting customers use the car park. Health Nuts has been monitoring the number of customers attending throughout each day for the month of June, which was considered to be an average month, and for which Health Nuts was open for 30 days. It has determined that the average number of customers per day is 330 with 40 of these customers attending during the time of 9:00am to 5:00pm.

The total costs of the fitness centre for June, **excluding the café**, have also been recorded and analysed as follows:

Fixed costs per month	$48,000
Variable cost per customer	$1.20

On average, half of the customers also used the café in June, with an average spend per customer of $2.20. Of this spend, 60% is related to drinks, which have a profit margin of 60%, and the remainder is related to food items, which have a profit margin of 40%. The specific fixed costs associated with running the café are $3,600 for the month.

Crèche proposal

After reviewing all of the above information, the manager of Health Nuts has put together a proposal to close the café at the fitness centre and convert it into a crèche for children. This would mean that parents could leave their children in the crèche whilst they use the fitness centre between the hours of 9:00am and 5:00pm **only**. The charge for the crèche would be $4 per child, per hour.

Initial research suggests that customers have an average of two children each. The crèche is expected to attract new customers and increase the average number of customers between 9:00am and 5:00pm by 300%. Only these new customers will use the crèche facilities. Car park usage is expected to continue to be 80%. The fixed costs associated with running the crèche are estimated to be $8,000 per month, with a variable cost of $0.50 per child, per hour.

Required:

(a) Calculate both the number of customers Health Nuts needs to break even and the margin of safety as a percentage of the month of June for: ⊞

    (i)   The gym, and   **(3 marks)**

    (ii)   The café.   **(2 marks)**

(b) Explain what each of your calculations in part (a) tells Health Nuts about the performance of the gym and the café. ⊞   **(3 marks)**

(c) Calculate the budgeted total weighted average contribution/sales (C/S) ratio and the budgeted profit per month for Health Nuts if it closes the café and opens a crèche instead. ⊞   **(6 marks)**

(d) Advise Health Nuts, considering both financial and non-financial factors, whether it should replace the café with a crèche, and whether the calculations in part (c) provide enough information to make such a decision. 💻   **(6 marks)**

                                                             (Total: 20 marks)

285 COSMETICS CO (DECEMBER 2010, ADAPTED)

The Cosmetic Co is a company producing a variety of cosmetic creams and lotions. The creams and lotions are sold to a variety of retailers at a price of $23.20 for each jar of face cream and $16.80 for each bottle of body lotion. Each of the products has a variety of ingredients, with the key ones being silk powder, silk amino acids and aloe vera. Six months ago, silk worms were attacked by disease causing a huge reduction in the availability of silk powder and silk amino acids. The Cosmetic Co had to dramatically reduce production and make part of its workforce, which it had trained over a number of years, redundant.

The company now wants to increase production again by ensuring that it uses the limited ingredients available to maximise profits by selling the optimum mix of creams and lotions. Due to the redundancies made earlier in the year, supply of skilled labour is now limited in the short-term to 160 hours (9,600 minutes) per week, although unskilled labour is unlimited. The purchasing manager is confident that they can obtain 5,000 grams of silk powder and 1,600 grams of silk amino acids per week. All other ingredients are unlimited.

The following information is available for the two products:

	Cream	Lotion
Materials required: silk powder (at $2.20 per gram)	3 grams	2 grams
– silk amino acids (at $0.80 per gram)	1 gram	0.5 grams
– aloe vera (at $1.40 per gram)	4 grams	2 grams
Labour required: skilled ($12 per hour)	4 minutes	5 minutes
– unskilled (at $8 per hour)	3 minutes	1.5 minutes

Each jar of cream sold generates a contribution of $9 per unit, whilst each bottle of lotion generates a contribution of $8 per unit. The maximum demand for lotions is 2,000 bottles per week, although demand for creams is unlimited. Fixed costs total $1,800 per week. The company does not keep inventory although if a product is partially complete at the end of one week, its production will be completed in the following week.

The following graph has been accurately drawn:

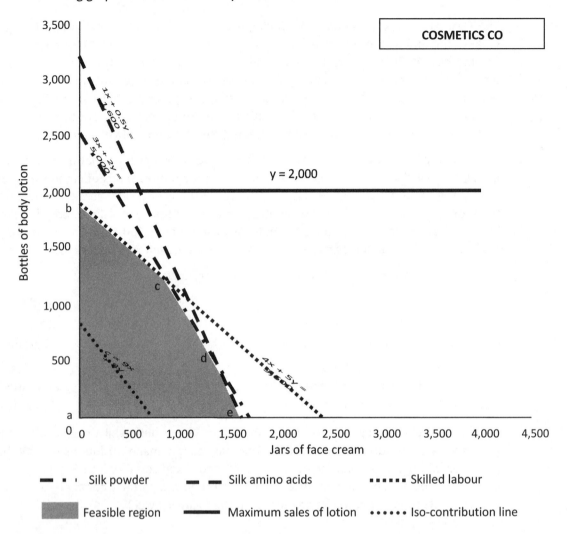

Required:

(a) Calculate the optimum number of each product that the Cosmetics Co should make per week, assuming that it wishes to maximise contribution. Calculate the total contribution per week for the new production plan. All workings MUST be rounded to 2 decimal places. ⊞ (14 marks)

(b) Calculate the shadow price for silk powder and the slack for silk amino acids. All workings MUST be rounded to 2 decimal places. ⊞ (6 marks)

(Total: 20 marks)

286   CUT AND STITCH (JUNE 2010)

Cut and Stitch (CS) make two types of suits using skilled tailors (labour) and a delicate and unique fabric (material). Both the tailors and the fabric are in short supply and so the accountant at CS has correctly produced a linear programming model to help decide the optimal production mix.

The model is as follows:

Variables:

Let W = the number of work suits produced

Let L = the number of lounge suits produced

Constraints

Tailors' time: $7W + 5L \leq 3,500$ (hours) – this is line T on the diagram

Fabric: $2W + 2L \leq 1,200$ (metres) – this is line F on the diagram

Production of work suits: $W \leq 400$ – this is line P on the diagram

Objective is to maximise contribution subject to:

$C = 48W + 40L$

On the diagram provided the accountant has correctly identified OABCD as the feasible region and point B as the optimal point.

Required:

(a)   Find by appropriate calculation the optimal production mix and related maximum contribution that could be earned by CS. ▦   **(4 marks)**

(b)   Calculate the shadow prices of the fabric per metre and the tailor time per hour. ▦

(6 marks)

The tailors have offered to work an extra 500 hours provided that they are paid three times their normal rate of $1.50 per hour at $4.50 per hour.

Required:

(c)   Briefly discuss whether CS should accept the offer of overtime at three times the normal rate. 💻   **(6 marks)**

(d)   Calculate the new optimum production plan if maximum demand for W falls to 200 units. ▦   **(4 marks)**

(Total: 20 marks)

287   CSC CO (SEPTEMBER 2016)

CSC Co is a health food company producing and selling three types of high-energy products: cakes, shakes and cookies, to gyms and health food shops. Shakes are the newest of the three products and were first launched three months ago. Each of the three products has two special ingredients, sourced from a remote part the world. The first of these, Singa, is a super-energising rare type of caffeine. The second, Betta, is derived from an unusual plant believed to have miraculous health benefits.

CSC Co's projected manufacture costs and selling prices for the three products are as follows:

	Cakes	Cookies	Shakes
Per unit	$	$	$
Selling price	5.40	4.90	6.00
Costs:			
Ingredients: Singa ($1.20 per gram)	0.30	0.60	1.20
Ingredients: Betta ($1.50 per gram)	0.75	0.30	1.50
Other ingredients	0.25	0.45	0.90
Labour ($10 per hour)	1.00	1.20	0.80
Variable overheads	0.50	0.60	0.40
	———	———	———
Contribution	2.60	1.75	1.20
	———	———	———

For each of the three products, the expected demand for the next month is 11,200 cakes, 9,800 cookies and 2,500 shakes.

The total fixed costs for the next month are $3,000.

CSC Co has just found out that the supply of Betta is going to be limited to 12,000 grams next month. Prior to this, CSC Co had signed a contract with a leading chain of gyms, Encompass Health, to supply it with 5,000 shakes each month, at a discounted price of $5.80 per shake, starting immediately. The order for the 5,000 shakes is not included in the expected demand levels above.

Required:

(a) **Assuming that CSC Co keeps to its agreement with Encompass Health, calculate the shortage of Betta, the resulting optimum production plan and the total profit for next month.** ▦ **(6 marks)**

One month later, the supply of Betta is still limited and CSC Co is considering whether it should breach its contract with Encompass Health so that it can optimise its profits.

Required:

(b) **Discuss whether CSC Co should breach the agreement with Encompass Health.** 🖳

Note: No further calculations are required. **(4 marks)**

Several months later, the demand for both cakes and cookies has increased significantly to 20,000 and 15,000 units per month respectively. However, CSC Co has lost the contract with Encompass Health and, after suffering from further shortages of supply of Betta, Singa and of its labour force, CSC Co has decided to stop making shakes at all. CSC Co now needs to use linear programming to work out the optimum production plan for cakes and cookies for the coming month. The variable 'x' is being used to represent cakes and the variable 'y' to represent cookies.

The following constraints have been formulated and a graph representing the new production problem has been drawn:

Singa: $0.25x + 0.5y \le 12,000$

Betta: $0.5x + 0.2y \le 12,500$

Labour: $0.1x + 0.12y \le 3,000$

$x \le 20,000$

$y \le 15,000$

$x, y \ge 0$

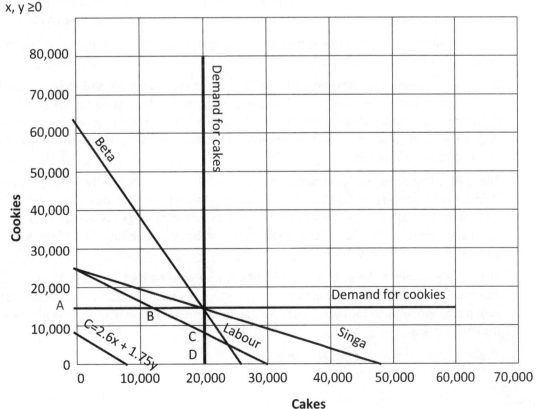

Required:

(c) (i) Explain what the line labelled 'C = 2.6x + 1.75y' on the graph is and what the area represented by the points 0ABCD means.   **(4 marks)**

(ii) Explain how the optimum production plan will be found using the line labelled 'C = 2.6x + 1.75y' and identify the optimum point from the graph.

(2 marks)

(iii) Explain what a slack value is and identify, from the graph, where slack will occur as a result of the optimum production plan.   **(4 marks)**

Note: No calculations are needed for part (c).

(Total: 20 marks)

288 BITS AND PIECES (JUNE 2009)

> ▶ *Answer debrief*

Bits and Pieces (B&P) operates a retail store selling spares and accessories for the car market. The store has previously only opened for six days per week for the 50 working weeks in the year, but B&P is now considering also opening on Sundays.

The sales of the business on Monday through to Saturday averages at $10,000 per day with average gross profit of 70% earned.

B&P expects that the gross profit % earned on a Sunday will be 20 percentage points lower than the average earned on the other days in the week. This is because they plan to offer substantial discounts and promotions on a Sunday to attract customers. Given the price reduction, Sunday sales revenues are expected to be 60% more than the average daily sales revenues for the other days. These Sunday sales estimates are for new customers only, with no allowance being made for those customers that may transfer from other days.

B&P buys all its goods from one supplier. This supplier gives a 5% discount on all purchases if annual spend exceeds $1,000,000.

It has been agreed to pay time and a half to sales assistants that work on Sundays. The normal hourly rate is $20 per hour. In total five sales assistants will be needed for the six hours that the store will be open on a Sunday. They will also be able to take a half-day off (four hours) during the week. Staffing levels will be allowed to reduce slightly during the week to avoid extra costs being incurred.

The staff will have to be supervised by a manager, currently employed by the company and paid an annual salary of $80,000. If the manager works on a Sunday, they will take the equivalent time off during the week when the assistant manager is available to cover for them at no extra cost to B&P. The manager will also be paid a bonus of 1% of the extra sales generated on the Sunday project.

The store will have to be lit at a cost of $30 per hour and heated at a cost of $45 per hour. The heating will come on two hours before the store opens in the 25 'winter' weeks to make sure it is warm enough for customers to come in at opening time. The store is not heated in the other weeks.

The rent of the store amounts to $420,000 annum.

Required:

(a) Calculate whether the Sunday opening incremental revenue exceeds the incremental costs over a year (ignore inventory movements) and on this basis reach a conclusion as to whether Sunday opening is financially justifiable. ⊞ **(12 marks)**

(b) Discuss whether the manager's pay deal (time off and bonus) is likely to motivate him. 💻 **(4 marks)**

(c) Briefly discuss whether offering substantial price discounts and promotions on Sunday is a good suggestion. 💻 **(4 marks)**

(Total: 20 marks)

 Calculate your allowed time, allocate the time to the separate parts..............

---

289 STAY CLEAN (DECEMBER 2009)

Stay Clean manufactures and sells a small range of kitchen equipment. Specifically the product range contains a dishwasher (DW), a washing machine (WM) and a tumble dryer (TD). The TD is of a rather old design and has for some time generated negative contribution. It is widely expected that in one year's time the market for this design of TD will cease, as people switch to a washing machine that can also dry clothes after the washing cycle has completed.

Stay Clean is trying to decide whether or not to cease the production of TD now **or** in 12 months' time when the new combined washing machine/drier will be ready. To help with this decision the following information has been provided:

(1) The normal selling prices, annual sales volumes and total variable costs for the three products are as follows:

	DW	WM	TD
Selling price per unit	$200	$350	$80
Material cost per unit	$70	$100	$50
Labour cost per unit	$50	$80	$40
Contribution per unit	$80	$170	–$10
Annual sales	5,000 units	6,000 units	1,200 units

(2) It is thought that some of the customers that buy a TD also buy a DW and a WM. It is estimated that 5% of the sales of WM and DW will be lost if the TD ceases to be produced.

(3) All the direct labour force currently working on the TD will be made redundant immediately if TD is ceased now. This would cost $6,000 in redundancy payments. If Stay Clean waited for 12 months the existing labour force would be retained and retrained at a cost of $3,500 to enable them to produce the new washing/drying product. Recruitment and training costs of labour in 12 months' time would be $1,200 in the event that redundancy takes place now.

(4)   Stay Clean operates a just in time (JIT) policy and so all material cost would be saved on the TD for 12 months if TD production ceased now. Equally, the material costs relating to the lost sales on the WM and the DW would also be saved. However, the material supplier has a volume based discount scheme in place as follows:

Total annual expenditure ($)	Discount
0 – 600,000	0%
600,001 – 800,000	1%
800,001 – 9 00,000	2%
900,001 – 960,000	3%
960,001 and above	5%

Stay Clean uses this supplier for all its materials for all the products it manufactures. The figures given above in the cost per unit table for material cost per unit are net of any discount Stay Clean already qualifies for.

(5)   The space in the factory currently used for the TD will be sublet for 12 months on a short-term lease contract if production of TD stops now. The income from that contract will be $12,000.

(6)   The supervisor (currently classed as an overhead) supervises the production of all three products spending approximately 20% of their time on the TD production. They would continue to be fully employed if the TD ceases to be produced now.

Required:

(a)   Calculate whether or not it is worthwhile ceasing to produce the TD now rather than waiting 12 months (ignore any adjustment to allow for the time value of money).
(13 marks)

(b)   Explain two pricing strategies that could be used to improve the financial position of the business in the next 12 months assuming that the TD continues to be made in that period.
(4 marks)

(c)   Briefly describe three issues that Stay Clean should consider if it decides to outsource the manufacture of one of its future products.
(3 marks)

(Total: 20 marks)

290   CHOICE OF CONTRACTS

A company in the civil engineering industry with headquarters located 22 miles from London undertakes contracts anywhere in the United Kingdom.

The company has had its tender for a job in north-east England accepted at $288,000 and work is due to begin in March 20X3. However, the company has also been asked to undertake a contract on the south coast of England. The price offered for this contract is $352,000. Both of the contracts cannot be taken simultaneously because of constraints on staff site management personnel and on plant available. An escape clause enables the company to withdraw from the contract in the north-east, provided notice is given before the end of November and an agreed penalty of $28,000 is paid.

The following estimates have been submitted by the company's quantity surveyor:

Cost estimates

	North-east $	South-coast $
Materials:		
In inventory at original cost, Material X	21,600	
In inventory at original cost, Material Y		24,800
Firm orders placed at original cost, Material X	30,400	
Not yet ordered – current cost, Material X	60,000	
Not yet ordered – current cost, Material Z		71,200
Labour – hired locally	86,000	110,000
Site management	34,000	34,000
Staff accommodation and travel for site management	6,800	5,600
Plant on site – depreciation	9,600	12,800
Interest on capital, 8%	5,120	6,400
Total local contract costs	253,520	264,800
Headquarters costs allocated at rate of 5% on total contract costs	12,676	13,240
	266,196	278,040

	North-east $	South-coast $
Contract price	288,000	352,000
Estimated profit	21,804	73,960

(1) X, Y and Z are three building materials. Material X is not in common use and would not realise much money if re-sold; however, it could be used on other contracts but only as a substitute for another material currently quoted at 10% less than the original cost of X. The price of Y, a material in common use, has doubled since it was purchased; its net realisable value if re-sold would be its new price less 15% to cover disposal costs. Alternatively it could be kept for use on other contracts in the following financial year.

(2) With the construction industry not yet recovered from the recent recession, the company is confident that manual labour, both skilled and unskilled, could be hired locally on a sub-contracting basis to meet the needs of each of the contracts.

(3) The plant which would be needed for the south coast contract has been owned for some years and $12,800 is the year's depreciation on a straight-line basis. If the north-east contract is undertaken, less plant will be required but the surplus plant will be hired out for the period of the contract at a rental of $6,000.

(4) It is the company's policy to charge all contracts with notional interest at 8% on estimated working capital involved in contracts. Progress payments would be receivable from the contractee.

(5) Salaries and general costs of operating the small headquarters amount to about $108,000 each year. There are usually ten contracts being supervised at the same time.

(6) Each of the two contracts is expected to last from March 20X3 to February 20X4 which, coincidentally, is the company's financial year.

(7) Site management is treated as a fixed cost.

Required:

As the management accountant to the company present comparative statements to show the net benefit to the company of undertaking the more advantageous of the two contracts.

Explain why you have included, or not, each of the items given in the data in your comparative financial statements. 🖳 (Total: 20 marks)

291 HS EQUATION

HS manufactures components for use in computers. The business operates in a highly competitive market where there are a large number of manufacturers of similar components. HS is considering its pricing strategy for the next 12 weeks for one of its components. The Managing Director seeks your advice to determine the selling price that will maximise the profit to be made during this period.

You have been given the following data:

Market demand

The current selling price of the component is $1,350 and at this price the average weekly demand over the last four weeks has been 8,000 components. An analysis of the market shows that, for every $50 increase in selling price, the demand reduces by 1,000 components per week. Equally, for every $50 reduction in selling price, the demand increases by 1,000 components per week.

Costs

The direct material cost of each component is $270. This price is part of a fixed price contract with the material suppliers and the contract does not expire for another year.

Production labour and conversion costs, together with other overhead costs and the corresponding output volumes, have been collected for the last four weeks and they are as follows:

Week	Output volume (units)	$000
1	9,400	7,000
2	7,600	5,688
3	8,500	6,334
4	7,300	5,446

No significant changes in cost behaviour are expected over the next 12 weeks.

Required:

(a) Calculate the optimum (profit-maximising) selling price of the component for the period. ▦ (14 marks)

(b) Identify and explain three reasons why it may be inappropriate for HS to use this theoretical pricing model in practice. 🖳 (6 marks)

(Total: 20 marks)

292 MKL

Product 'M' is currently being tested by MKL and is to be launched in ten weeks' time. The 'M' is an innovative product which the company believes will change the entire market. The company has decided to use a market skimming approach to pricing this product during its introduction stage.

MKL continually reviews its product range and enhances its existing products by developing new models to satisfy the demands of its customers. The company intends to always have products at each stage of the product life cycle to ensure the company's continued presence in the market.

MKL is currently reviewing its two existing flagship products, Product K and Product L. You have been given the following information:

- Product K was introduced to the market some time ago and is now about to enter the maturity stage of its life cycle. The maturity stage is expected to last for ten weeks. Each unit has a variable cost of $38 and takes 1 standard hour to produce. The Managing Director is unsure which of four possible prices the company should charge during the next ten weeks. The following table shows the results of some market research into the level of weekly demand at alternative prices:

Selling price per unit	$100	$85	$80	$75
Weekly demand (units)	600	800	1,200	1,400

- Product L was introduced to the market two months ago using a penetration pricing policy and is now about to enter its growth stage. This stage is expected to last for 20 weeks. Each unit has a variable cost of $45 and takes 1.25 standard hours to produce. Market research has indicated that there is a linear relationship between its selling price and the number of units demanded, of the form P = a − bx. At a selling price of $100 per unit demand is expected to be 1,000 units per week. For every $10 increase in selling price the weekly demand will reduce by 200 units and for every $10 decrease in selling price the weekly demand will increase by 200 units.

The company currently has a production facility which has a capacity of 2,000 standard hours per week. This facility is being expanded but the extra capacity will not be available for ten weeks.

Required:

(a)   Calculate which of the four selling prices should be charged for product K, in order to maximise its contribution during its maturity stage. ▦   **(5 marks)**

(b)   Following on from your answer above in (a), calculate the selling price of product L during its growth stage. ▦   **(8 marks)**

(c)   Compare and contrast penetration and skimming pricing strategies during the introduction stage, using product M to illustrate your answer. ▭   **(7 marks)**

(Total: 20 marks)

293 SNIFF CO (DECEMBER 2007)

Sniff Limited manufactures and sells its standard perfume by blending a secret formula of aromatic oils with diluted alcohol. The oils are produced by another company following a lengthy process and are very expensive. The standard perfume is highly branded and successfully sold at a price of $39.98 per 100 millilitres (ml).

Sniff Limited is considering processing some of the perfume further by adding a hormone to appeal to members of the opposite sex. The hormone to be added will be different for the male and female perfumes. Adding hormones to perfumes is not universally accepted as a good idea as some people have health concerns. On the other hand, market research carried out suggests that a premium could be charged for perfume that can 'promise' the attraction of a suitor. The market research has cost $3,000.

Data has been prepared for the costs and revenues expected for the following month (a test month) assuming that a part of the company's output will be further processed by adding the hormones.

The output selected for further processing is 1,000 litres, about a tenth of the company's normal monthly output. Of this, 99% is made up of diluted alcohol which costs $20 per litre. The rest is a blend of aromatic oils costing $18,000 per litre. The labour required to produce 1,000 litres of the basic perfume before any further processing is 2,000 hours at a cost of $15 per hour.

Of the output selected for further processing, 200 litres (20%) will be for male customers and 2 litres of hormone costing $7,750 per litre will then be added. The remaining 800 litres (80%) will be for female customers and 8 litres of hormone will be added, costing $12,000 per litre. In both cases the adding of the hormone adds to the overall volume of the product as there is no resulting processing loss.

Sniff Limited has sufficient existing machinery to carry out the test processing.

The new processes will be supervised by one of the more experienced supervisors currently employed by Sniff Limited. Their current annual salary is $35,000 and it is expected that they will spend 10% of their time working on the hormone adding process during the test month. This will be split evenly between the male and female versions of the product.

Extra labour will be required to further process the perfume, with an extra 500 hours for the male version and 700 extra hours for the female version of the hormone-added product. Labour is currently fully employed, making the standard product. New labour with the required skills will not be available at short notice.

Sniff Limited allocates fixed overhead at the rate of $25 per labour hour to all products for the purposes of reporting profits.

The sales prices that could be achieved as a one-off monthly promotion are:

- Male version: $75.00 per 100 ml
- Female version: $59.50 per 100 ml.

Required:

(a) **Outline the financial and other factors that Sniff Limited should consider when making a further processing decision.** 🖥

Note: no calculations are required.   **(5 marks)**

(b) Evaluate whether Sniff Limited should experiment with the hormone adding process using the data provided. Provide a separate assessment and conclusion for the male and the female versions of the product. ▦ **(15 marks)**

(Total: 20 marks)

Note: The original question as written by the examiner had the following additional requirements:

(c) Calculate the selling price per 100 ml for the female version of the product that would ensure further processing would break even in the test month. **(2 marks)**

(d) Sniff Limited is considering outsourcing the production of the standard perfume. Outline the main factors it should consider before making such a decision.

(4 marks)

---

294 FURNIVAL

Furnival has a distillation plant that produces three joint products, P, Q and R, in the proportions 10:5:5. After the split-off point the products can be sold for industrial use or they can be taken to the mixing plant for blending and refining. The latter procedure is normally followed.

For a typical week, in which all the output is processed in the mixing plant, the following statement of profit or loss can be prepared:

	Product P	Product Q	Product R
Sales volume (gallons)	1,000	500	500
Price per gallon ($)	12.50	20	10
Sales revenue ($)	12,500	10,000	5,000
	———	———	———
Joint process cost ($)			
(apportioned using output volume)	5,000	2,500	2,500
Mixing plant cost ($):			
Process costs	3,000	3,000	3,000
Other separable costs	2,000	500	500
	———	———	———
Total costs ($)	10,000	6,000	6,000
	———	———	———
Profit/(loss) ($)	2,500	4,000	(1,000)
	———	———	———

The joint process costs are 25% fixed and 75% variable, whereas the mixing plant costs are 10% fixed and 90% variable and all the 'other separable costs' are variable.

If the products had been sold at the split-off point the selling price per gallon would have been:

Product P	Product Q	Product R
$5.00	$6.00	$1.50

There are only 45 hours available per week in the mixing plant. Typically 30 hours are taken up with the processing of Product P, Q and R (10 hours for each product line) and 15 hours are used for other work that generates (on average) a profit of $200 per hour after being charged with a proportionate share of the plant's costs (including fixed costs). The manager of the mixing plant considers that they could sell all the plant's processing time externally at a price that would provide this rate of profit.

It has been suggested:

(i)   that, since Product R regularly makes a loss, it should be sold off at the split-off point

(ii)   that it might be possible advantageously to change the mix of products achieved in the distillation plant. It is possible to change the output proportions to 7:8:5 at a cost of $1 for each additional gallon of Q produced by the distillation plant.

Required:

Compare the costs and benefits for each of the above proposals. Recommend, for each proposal, whether it should or should not be implemented. 🖥

(Total: 20 marks)

295 RECYC

Recyc plc is a company which reprocesses factory waste in order to extract good quality aluminium. Information concerning its operations is as follows:

(1)   Recyc plc places an advance order each year for chemical X for use in the aluminium extraction process. It will enter into an advance contract for the coming year for chemical X at one of three levels – high, medium or low, which correspond to the requirements of a high, medium or low level of waste available for reprocessing.

(2)   The level of waste available will not be known when the advance order for chemical X is entered into. A set of probabilities have been estimated by management as to the likelihood of the quantity of waste being at a high, medium or low level.

(3)   Where the advance order entered into for chemical X is lower than that required for the level of waste for processing actually received, a discount from the original demand price is allowed by the supplier for the total quantity of chemical X actually required.

(4)   Where the advance order entered into for chemical X is in excess of that required to satisfy the actual level of waste for reprocessing, a penalty payment in excess of the original demand price is payable for the total quantity of chemical X actually required.

A summary of the information relating to the above points is as follows:

			Chemical X costs per kg		
Level of reprocessing	Waste available	Probability	Advance order	Conversion discount	Conversion premium
	000 kg		$	$	$
High	50,000	0.30	1.00		
Medium	38,000	0.50	1.20		
Low	30,000	0.20	1.40		

Chemical X: order conversion:			
Low to medium		0.10	
Medium to high		0.10	
Low to high		0.15	
Medium to low			0.25
High to medium			0.25
High to low			0.60

Aluminium is sold at $0.65 per kg. Variable costs (excluding chemical X costs) are 70% of sales revenue. Aluminium extracted from the waste is 15% of the waste input. Chemical X is added to the reprocessing at the rate of 1 kg per 100 kg of waste.

Required:

(a) **Prepare a summary which shows the budgeted contribution earned by Recyc plc for the coming year for each of nine possible outcomes.** ⊞ **(14 marks)**

(b) **State the contribution for the coming year which corresponds to the use of (i) maximax, and (ii) maximin decision criteria, and comment on the risk preference of management which is indicated by each.** 💻 **(6 marks)**

(Total: 20 marks)

296 TICKET AGENT *Walk in the footsteps of a top tutor*

A ticket agent has an arrangement with a concert hall that holds concerts on 60 nights a year whereby they receive discounts as follows per concert:

For purchase of:	They receive a discount of:
200 tickets	20%
300 tickets	25%
400 tickets	30%
500 tickets or more	40%

Purchases must be in full hundreds. The average price per ticket is $30.

They must decide in advance each year the number of tickets they will purchase. If they have any tickets unsold by the afternoon of the concert they must return them to the box office. If the box office sells any of these they receive 60% of their price.

Their sales records over a few years show that for a concert with extremely popular artistes they can be confident of selling 500 tickets, for one with lesser known artistes 350 tickets, and for one with relatively unknown artistes 200 tickets.

Their records show that 10% of the tickets they return are sold by the box office. (**Note:** these are in addition to any sales made by the ticket agent).

Their administration costs incurred in selling tickets are the same per concert irrespective of the popularity of the artistes.

Sales records show that the frequency of concerts will be:

With popular artistes	45%
With lesser known artistes	30%
With unknown artistes	25%
	———
	100%
	———

Required:

(a) Calculate:

- the expected demand for tickets per concert

- the level of their purchases of tickets per concert that will give them the largest profit over a long period of time and the profit per concert that this level of purchases of tickets will yield. ⊞   **(11 marks)**

(b) Calculate the number of tickets the agent should buy, based on the following criteria:

- Maximin

- Maximax

- Minimax regret. ⊞   **(5 marks)**

(c) Advise the ticket agent, with reference to risk perspectives, how many tickets should be ordered based on the answers to parts (a) and (b). 💻   **(4 marks)**

(Total: 20 marks)

297 SHIFTERS HAULAGE (DECEMBER 2008)

Shifters Haulage (SH) is considering changing some of the vans it uses to transport crates for customers. The new vans come in three sizes; small, medium and large. SH is unsure about which type to buy. The capacity is 100 crates for the small van, 150 for the medium van and 200 for the large van.

Demand for crates varies and can be either 120 or 190 crates per period, with the probability of the higher demand figure being 0.6.

The sale price per crate is $10 and the variable cost $4 per crate for all van sizes subject to the fact that if the capacity of the van is greater than the demand for crates in a period then the variable cost will be lower by 10% to allow for the fact that the vans will be partly empty when transporting crates.

SH is concerned that if the demand for crates exceeds the capacity of the vans then customers will have to be turned away. SH estimates that in this case goodwill of $100 would be charged against profits per period to allow for lost future sales regardless of the number of customers that are turned away.

Depreciation charged would be $200 per period for the small, $300 for the medium and $400 for the large van.

SH has in the past been very aggressive in its decision-making, pressing ahead with rapid growth strategies. However, its managers have recently grown more cautious as the business has become more competitive.

Required:

(a) **Explain the principles behind the maximax, maximin and expected value criteria that are sometimes used to make decisions in uncertain situations.** 🖥 (5 marks)

(b) **Prepare a profits table showing the SIX possible profit figures per period.** ▦
(9 marks)

(c) **Using your profit table from (b) above discuss which type of van SH should buy taking into consideration the possible risk attitudes of the managers.** 🖥 (6 marks)

(Total: 20 marks)

Note: The original question, as written by the examiner, also had the following requirement for six marks:

Describe THREE methods other than those mentioned in (a) above, which businesses can use to analyse and assess the risk that exists in its decision-making.

---

298 AMELIE

Amelie is setting up in business importing French cheeses. She could open up a small shop, a large outlet, or no shop at all if she decides to sell online only (which she won't be able to do for another few years at least.) There will be a 5 year lease on a few shops currently available in the centre of town, and Amelie wants to make the correct decision.

Amelie is also thinking about hiring a consultant to conduct a market research study. If the study is conducted, the results could indicate that the cheese market is either favourable or unfavourable.

Amelie believes there is a 50-50 chance that the market will be favourable, and expects her profits to be as follows if she opens her shop:

	Favourable market	Unfavourable market
Large shop	$60,000	($40,000) loss
Small shop	$30,000	($10,000) loss

The consultant has quoted a charge of $5,000 for the marketing research. They have also hinted that there is a 0.6 probability that the survey will indicate that the cheese market would be favourable.

There is a 0.9 probability that the cheese market will be favourable given a favourable outcome from the study. The consultant warned Amelie that there is only a probability of 0.12 of a favourable market if the marketing research results are not favourable. Amelie has accurately drawn the following decision tree.

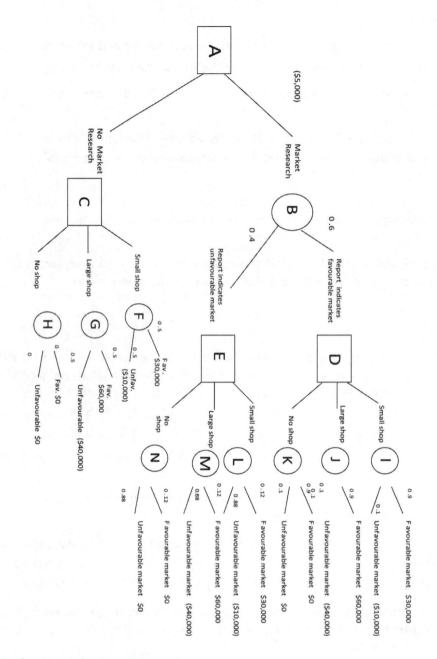

Required:

(a)   Explain why Amelie should hire the market research consultant. 🖥️   (7 marks)

(b)   After discussing the competence of the consultant with another business owner, Amelie now believes that she'd rather contact another market research company which guarantees perfect information concerning the cheese market profitability.

Calculate the value of this perfect information. 🖥️ ▦   (3 marks)

(Total: 10 marks)

299 RY DECISION TREE

As the exams are tested as CBE, candidates will not have to draw a decision tree. However, it is good practice to attempt a question such as this as part of a robust revision programme. In the exam, a decision tree will be part of the question scenario and candidates may be asked to provide further calculations or analysis.

RY Ltd, a transatlantic airline company, has recently launched a low-cost airline company providing flights within Europe. The market is highly competitive and two other low-cost airlines, B Ltd and G Ltd, together hold 98% of the market.

RY Ltd commissioned some market research to help with the pricing decision for one route, London to Paris, which it is thinking of offering. The research identified three possible market states and the likely number of passengers that would be attracted at three price levels on this route.

Ticket price		$80	$90	$100
Market	**Probability**	**Passenger seats**	**Passenger seats**	**Passenger seats**
Pessimistic	0.2	80	60	30
Most likely	0.6	100	90	80
Optimistic	0.2	150	150	120

Airport charges are incurred for each customer and these are expected to be either $5 or $6 per customer depending on the negotiations with the airports involved. The probabilities for the airport charges are 0.6 for an airport charge of $5 per passenger and 0.4 for an airport charge of $6 per customer.

The fixed costs of a flight from London to Paris are $4,422.

Required:

(a)   Draw a decision tree to illustrate the pricing decision faced by RY Ltd.   (8 marks)

(b)   Using the decision tree or otherwise, establish the optimum price that RY Ltd should charge in order to maximise profit. 🖥   (6 marks)

(c)   If RY Ltd knew that there would be a pessimistic market, which price should it charge in order to maximise profit? 🖥   (6 marks)

(Total: 20 marks)

300   TR CO (SEPTEMBER/DECEMBER 2017)

TR Co is a pharmaceutical company which researches, develops and manufactures a wide range of drugs. One of these drugs, 'Parapain', is a pain relief drug used for the treatment of headaches and until last month TR Co had a patent on Parapain which prevented other companies from manufacturing it. The patent has now expired and several competitors have already entered the market with similar versions of Parapain, which are made using the same active ingredients.

TR Co is reviewing its pricing policy in light of the changing market. It has carried out some market research in an attempt to establish an optimum price for Parapain. The research has established that for every $2 decrease in price, demand would be expected to increase by 5,000 batches, with maximum demand for Parapain being one million batches.

Each batch of Parapain is currently made using the following materials:

Material Z:	500 grams at $0.10 per gram
Material Y:	300 grams at $0.50 per gram

Each batch of Parapain requires 20 minutes of machine time to make and the variable running costs for machine time are $6 per hour. The fixed production overhead cost is expected to be $2 per batch for the period, based on a budgeted production level of 250,000 batches.

The skilled workers who have been working on Parapain until now are being moved onto the production of TR Co's new and unique anti-malaria drug which cost millions of dollars to develop. TR Co has obtained a patent for this revolutionary drug and it is expected to save millions of lives. No other similar drug exists and, whilst demand levels are unknown, the launch of the drug is eagerly anticipated all over the world.

Agency staff, who are completely new to the production of Parapain and cost $18 per hour, will be brought in to produce Parapain for the foreseeable future. Experience has shown there will be a significant learning curve involved in making Parapain as it is extremely difficult to handle. The first batch of Parapain made using one of the agency workers took 5 hours to make. However, it is believed that an 80% learning curve exists, in relation to production of the drug, and this will continue until the first 1,000 batches have been completed.

TR Co's management has said that any pricing decisions about Parapain should be based on the time it takes to make the 1,000th batch of the drug.

Note: The learning co-efficient, b = –0.321928

Required

(a)   Calculate the optimum (profit-maximising) selling price for Parapain and the resulting annual profit which TR Co will make from charging this price. ▦

Note: if $P = a - bQ$, then $MR = a - 2bQ$ (12 marks)

(b)   Discuss and recommend whether market penetration or market skimming would be the most suitable pricing strategy for TR Co when launching the new anti-malaria drug. 💻   (8 marks)

(Total: 20 marks)

301   THE ALKA HOTEL (JUNE 2018)

The Alka Hotel is situated in a major city close to many theatres and restaurants.

The Alka Hotel has 25 double bedrooms and it charges guests $180 per room per night, regardless of single or double occupancy. The hotel's variable cost is $60 per occupied room per night.

The Alka Hotel is open for 365 days a year and has a 70% budgeted occupancy rate. Fixed costs are budgeted at $600,000 a year and accrue evenly throughout the year.

During the first quarter (Q1) of the year the room occupancy rates are significantly below the levels expected at other times of the year with the Alka Hotel expecting to sell 900 occupied room nights during Q1. Options to improve profitability are being considered, including closing the hotel for the duration of Q1 or adopting one of two possible projects as follows:

Project 1 – Theatre package

For Q1 only the Alka Hotel management would offer guests a 'theatre package'. Couples who pay for two consecutive nights at a special rate of $67.50 per room night will also receive a pair of theatre tickets for a payment of $100. The theatre tickets are very good value and are the result of long negotiation between the Alka Hotel management and the local theatre. The theatre tickets cost the Alka Hotel $95 a pair. The Alka Hotel's fixed costs specific to this project (marketing and administration) are budgeted at $20,000.

The hotel's management believes that the 'theatre package' will have no effect on their usual Q1 customers, who are all business travellers and who have no interest in theatre tickets, but will still require their usual rooms.

Project 2 – Restaurant

There is scope to extend the Alka Hotel and create enough space to operate a restaurant for the benefit of its guests. The annual costs, revenues and volumes for the combined restaurant and hotel are illustrated in the following graph:

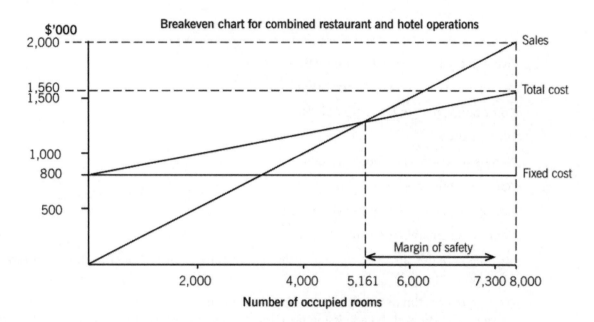

Note: The graph does not include the effect of the 'theatre package' offer.

Required:

(a) Using the current annual budgeted figures, and ignoring the two proposed projects, calculate the breakeven number of occupied room nights and the margin of safety as a percentage. ⊞   (4 marks)

(b) Ignoring the two proposed projects, calculate the budgeted profit or loss for Q1 and explain whether the hotel should close for the duration of Q1. ⊞   (4 marks)

(c) Calculate the breakeven point in sales value of Project 1 and explain whether the hotel should adopt the project. ⊞   (4 marks)

(d) Using the graph, quantify and comment upon the financial effect of Project 2 on the Alka Hotel. ⌨

Note: There are up to four marks available for calculations.   (8 marks)

(Total: 20 marks)

302 BELTON PARK RESORT (MARCH 2019)

Belton Park Resort is a new theme park resort located in the country of Beeland. The resort is made up of a theme park, a hotel and an indoor water park. The resort opened two months ago and is already very popular.

As all theme parks in Beeland are required, by law, to shut down in the colder month of January because of the risk of accidents, Belton Park Resort must decide whether to shut down the whole resort or just the theme park. It could choose to keep open the hotel and/or the water park.

Since Belton Park Resort has not been open for long, there is limited historical data available about costs and revenues. However, based on the last two months, the following average monthly data is available:

Hotel

Number of rooms 120

Average room rate per night $100

Average occupancy rate per month 90%

Average nightly spend on 'extras' per room $20

Contribution margin for 'extras'* 60%

Water park

Number of visitors per month 12,000

Admission price per visitor $21

Average spend on 'extras' per visitor $12

Contribution margin for 'extras'* 60%

*'Extras' includes anything purchased by the customer not included in the room rate or admission price.

Management estimates that, for January, the average room rate per night would need to decrease by 30% and the admission price for the water park by 20%. With such reductions, it is estimated that an occupancy rate of 50% would be achieved for the hotel and that the number of visitors to the water park would be 52% lower than current levels. The average nightly spend on 'extras' per room of $20 at the hotel and $12 per customer at the water park is expected to remain unchanged.

The running costs for the hotel and water park for each of the last two months are as follows:

	Notes	Hotel	Water park
		$	$
Staff costs	1	120,000	75,600
Maintenance costs	2	14,600	6,000
Power costs	3	20,000	18,000
Security costs	4	13,600	8,000
Water costs	5	12,900	12,100

Notes:

(1) **Staff costs**

Permanent staff

Included in the staff costs for the hotel is the salary of $30,000 per annum for the hotel manager and $24,000 per annum for the head chef. These are both permanent members of staff who are paid for the full year regardless of their working hours. The water park employs one permanent member of staff, the manager, on a salary of $24,000 who is also paid for the full year regardless of their working hours.

Temporary staff

The remaining staff costs relate to temporary staff who are only paid for the hours they work. If the hotel stays open in January, half of these staff members will continue to work their current hours because their jobs are largely unaffected by guest occupancy rates. However, the other half of the staff will work proportionately less hours to reflect the 50% occupancy rate in January as opposed to the 90% occupancy rate of the last two months. At the water park, the temporary staff's working hours will fall according to the number of visitors, hence a fall of 52% would be expected for January.

(2) **Maintenance costs**

Maintenance is undertaken by a local company, 'Techworks', which bills Belton Park Resort for all work carried out each month. If the hotel and water park are closed, Techworks will instead be paid a flat fee for the month of $4,000 for the hotel and $2,000 for the water park.

(3) **Power costs**

Electricity

Belton Park Resort pays a fixed monthly charge for electricity of $8,000 for the hotel and $7,000 for the water park, all year round.

Gas

The gas charges relate to heating and include a fixed charge of $2,200 per month for the hotel and $1,500 per month for the water park. The remainder of the gas charges is based solely on usage and would be expected to increase by 50% in January because of the colder weather.

(4)   Security costs

If the hotel and water park close, no changes will be made to the current arrangements for security whilst the premises are empty.

(5)   Water costs

It is estimated that water costs for the hotel would fall to $6,450 for the month if it remains open in January. However, the water costs for the water park would be expected to remain at their current level. If the hotel and water park were closed, all water would be turned off and no charges would arise.

Required:

(a)   Calculate the incremental cash flows, for the month of January (31 days), if Belton Park Resort decides to keep open:

(i)   the hotel

(ii)   the water park.

In each case, state whether it should remain open or should close.

(15 marks)

(b)   Discuss any other factors which Belton Park Resort should consider when making the decision in part (a).

(5 marks)

(Total: 20 marks)

BUDGETING AND CONTROL

303   STATIC CO (DECEMBER 2016)

Static Co is a multinational consumer goods company. Traditionally, the company has used a fixed annual budgeting process in which it sets quarterly sales revenue targets for each of its product lines. Historically, however, if a product line fails to reach its sales revenue target in any of the first three quarters, the company's sales director (SD) and finance director (FD) simply go back and reduce the sales revenue targets for the quarter just ended, to make it look like the target was reached. They then increase the target for the final quarter to include any shortfall in sales from earlier quarters.

During the last financial year ended 31 August 20X6, this practice meant that managers had to heavily discount many of their product lines in the final quarter in order to boost sales volumes and meet the increased targets. Even with the discounts, however, they still did not quite reach the targets. On the basis of the sales targets set at the beginning of that year, the company had also invested $6m in a new production line in January 20X6. However, to date, this new production line still has not been used. As a result of both these factors, Static Co saw a dramatic fall in return on investment from 16% to 8% in the year.

Consequently, the managing director (MD), the FD and the SD have all been dismissed. Two key members of the accounts department are also on sick leave due to stress and are not expected to return for some weeks. A new MD, who is inexperienced in this industry, has been appointed and is in the process of recruiting a new SD and a new FD. The MD has said:

'These mistakes could have been largely avoided if the company had been using rolling budgets, instead of manipulating fixed budgets. From now on, we will be using rolling budgets, updating our budgets on a quarterly basis, with immediate effect.'

The original fixed budget for the year ended 31 August 20X7, for which the first quarter (Q1) has just ended, is shown below:

Budget Y/E 31 August 20X7	Q1	Q2	Q3	Q4	Total
	$000	$000	$000	$000	$000
Revenue	13,425	13,694	13,967	14,247	55,333
Cost of sales	(8,055)	(8,216)	(8,380)	(8,548)	(33,199)
Gross profit	5,370	5,478	5,587	5,699	22,134
Distribution costs	(671)	(685)	(698)	(712)	(2,766)
Administration costs	(2,000)	(2,000)	(2,000)	(2,000)	(8,000)
Operating profit	2,699	2,793	2,889	2,987	11,368

The budget was based on the following assumptions:

(1) Sales volumes would grow by a fixed compound percentage each quarter.

(2) Gross profit margin would remain stable each quarter.

(3) Distribution costs would remain a fixed percentage of revenue each quarter.

(4) Administration costs would be fixed each quarter.

The actual results for the first quarter (Q1) have just been produced and are as follows:

Actual results	Q1
	$000
Revenue	14,096
Cost of sales	(8,740)
Gross profit	5,356
Distribution costs	(705)
Administration costs	(2,020)
Operating profit	2,631

The new MD believes that the difference between the actual and the budgeted sales figures for Q1 is a result of incorrect forecasting of prices, however, they are confident that the four assumptions the fixed budget was based on were correct and that the rolling budget should still be prepared using these assumptions.

Required:

(a)   Prepare Static Co's rolling budget for the next four quarters. ⊞   **(8 marks)**

(b)   Discuss the problems which have occurred at Static Co due to the previous budgeting process and the improvements which might now be seen through the use of realistic rolling budgets. 💻   **(6 marks)**

(c)   Discuss the problems which may be encountered when Static Co tries to implement the new budgeting system. 💻   **(6 marks)**

(Total: 20 marks)

304   YUMI CO (SEPTEMBER 2019)

Yumi Co owns a number of restaurants. It is a well-established company, and its restaurants have gained a favourable reputation for the quality of their meals.

Yumi Co's restaurants are all set in rural locations, where there is limited competition and this enabled them to develop a loyal customer base. Restaurants design their own menus and décor to fit with the requirements of their local market.

Yumi Co has been consistently profitable, however as is the case across the restaurant industry, profit margins are quite low and there is still a constant need for Yumi Co to monitor costs.

One of Yumi Co's restaurants is located in the small town of Cowly. Cowly has recently been the location for the filming of a popular television series and visitor numbers to the town have increased significantly as a result. Yumi Co's restaurant in Cowly has noticed a similar increase in customer numbers.

At the start of the current month a new restaurant opened in Cowly. The manager of Yumi Co's restaurant in Cowly has expressed concerns about the impact this new competitor will have on their ability to achieve profit targets for the rest of the year.

Budgets for all of Yumi Co's restaurants are prepared by the head office. At the start of each year, restaurant managers are given an annual budget, which is split into months. At the end of each month, the manager receives a statement comparing actual monthly performance against budget.

The statement for the Cowly restaurant for the most recent completed month is as follows:

	Actual	Budget	Variance
Number of customers	1,800	1,500	
	$	$	$
Revenue	87,300	75,000	12,300 F
Costs:			
Food and drink	26,100	22,500	3,600 A
Staff wages	38,250	31,500	6,750 A
Heat, light and power	8,100	7,500	600 A
Rent, rates and other overheads	12,600	12,000	600 A
Profit	**2,250**	**1,500**	**750 F**

Notes:

(1)   Rent, rates and other overheads are apportioned to its restaurants by Yumi Co's head office, based on a fixed annual charge.

(2)   All other budgeted costs are treated as variable costs, based on the expected number of customers.

Yumi Co currently adopts an incremental approach to budgeting, with the annual budget figures for each year being based on the previous year's figures. However, a new finance director has recently joined the company, and they have questioned whether this is suitable for all Yumi Co's restaurants.

The new finance director has also suggested that the company should adopt a more participative approach to budgeting.

Required:

(a)   (i)   **Prepare a flexed budget for the Cowly restaurant.** ▦   **(3 marks)**

      (ii) **With reference to your answer from part (i), explain the main weaknesses in the current monthly budget statements issued to the restaurants as a basis for managing performance.** 💻   **(4 marks)**

(b)   **Discuss whether an incremental approach to budgeting is appropriate for Yumi Co.** 💻
                                                                              (6 marks)

(c)   **Define a participative approach to budgeting and explain the potential advantages and disadvantages of introducing this approach at Yumi Co.** 💻   **(7 marks)**

                                                                    (Total: 20 marks)

305   NN

NN Ltd manufactures and markets a range of electronic office equipment. The company currently has a turnover of $40 million per annum. The company has a functional structure and currently operates an incremental budgeting system. The company has a budget committee that is comprised entirely of members of the senior management team. No other personnel are involved in the budget-setting process.

Each member of the senior management team has enjoyed an annual bonus of between 10% and 20% of their annual salary for each of the past five years. The annual bonuses are calculated by comparing the actual costs attributed to a particular function with budgeted costs for that function during the twelve month period ended 31 December in each year.

A new Finance Director, who previously held a senior management position in a 'not for profit' health organisation, has recently been appointed. Whilst employed by the health service organisation, the new Finance Director had been the manager responsible for the implementation of a zero-based budgeting system which proved highly successful.

Required:

(a)   Identify and discuss the factors to be considered when implementing a system of zero-based budgeting within NN Ltd. Include, as part of your discussion, a definition of the existing incremental budgeting system and a zero-based budgeting system. 🖥

(5 marks)

(b)   Identify and discuss the behavioural problems that the management of NN Ltd might encounter in implementing a system of zero-based budgeting, recommending how best to address such problems in order that they are overcome. 🖥   (10 marks)

(c)   Explain how the implementation of a zero-based budgeting system in NN Ltd may differ from the implementation of such a system in a 'not for profit' health organisation. 🖥

(5 marks)

(Total: 20 marks)

306 ZERO BASED BUDGETING (DECEMBER 2010)

Some commentators argue that: 'With continuing pressure to control costs and maintain efficiency, the time has come for all public sector organisations to embrace zero-based budgeting. There is no longer a place for incremental budgeting in any organisation, particularly public sector ones, where zero-based budgeting is far more suitable anyway.'

Required:

(a)   Discuss the particular difficulties encountered when budgeting in public sector organisations compared with budgeting in private sector organisations, drawing comparisons between the two types of organisations. 🖥   (5 marks)

(b)   Explain the terms 'incremental budgeting' and 'zero-based budgeting'. 🖥

(4 marks)

(c)   State the main stages involved in preparing zero-based budgets. 🖥   (3 marks)

(d)   Discuss the view that 'there is no longer a place for incremental budgeting in any organisation, particularly public sector ones,' highlighting any drawbacks of zero-based budgeting that need to be considered. 🖥   (8 marks)

(Total: 20 marks)

307 BIG CHEESE CHAIRS (DECEMBER 2009)

Big Cheese Chairs (BCC) manufactures and sells executive leather chairs. They are considering a new design of massaging chair to launch into the competitive market in which they operate.

They have carried out an investigation in the market and using a target costing system have targeted a competitive selling price of $120 for the chair. BCC wants a margin on selling price of 20% (ignoring any overheads).

The frame and massage mechanism will be bought in for $51 per chair and BCC will upholster it in leather and assemble it ready for despatch.

Leather costs $10 per metre and two metres are needed for a complete chair although 20% of all leather is wasted in the upholstery process.

The upholstery and assembly process will be subject to a learning effect as the workers get used to the new design. BCC estimates that the first chair will take two hours to prepare but this will be subject to a learning rate (LR) of 95%. The learning improvement will stop once 128 chairs have been made and the time for the 128th chair will be the time for all subsequent chairs. The cost of labour is $15 per hour.

The learning formula is shown on the formula sheet and at the 95% learning rate the value of b is –0.074000581.

Required:

(a)   **Calculate the average cost for the first 128 chairs made and identify any cost gap that may be present at that stage.** ▦   **(8 marks)**

(b)   **Assuming that a cost gap for the chair exists suggest four ways in which it could be closed.** ⌨   **(6 marks)**

The production manager denies any claims that a cost gap exists and has stated that the cost of the 128th chair will be low enough to yield the required margin.

(c)   **Calculate the cost of the 128th chair made and state whether the target cost is being achieved on the 128th chair.** ▦   **(6 marks)**

(Total: 20 marks)

308   HENRY COMPANY (DECEMBER 2008)

 Answer debrief

Henry Company (HC) provides skilled labour to the building trade. They have recently been asked by a builder to bid for a kitchen fitting contract for a new development of 600 identical apartments. HC has not worked for this builder before. Cost information for the new contract is as follows:

Labour for the contract is available. HC expects that the first kitchen will take 24 man-hours to fit but thereafter the time taken will be subject to a 95% learning rate. After 200 kitchens are fitted the learning rate will stop and the time taken for the 200th kitchen will be the time taken for all the remaining kitchens. Labour costs $15 per hour.

Overheads are absorbed on a labour hour basis. HC has collected overhead information for the last four months and this is shown below:

	Hours worked	Overhead cost $
Month 1	9,300	115,000
Month 2	9,200	113,600
Month 3	9,400	116,000
Month 4	9,600	116,800

HC normally works around 120,000 labour hours in a year.

HC uses the high low method to analyse overheads.

The learning curve equation is $y = ax^b$, where $b = \log r/\log 2 = -0.074$

Required:

(a)   Describe FIVE factors, other than the cost of labour and overheads mentioned above, that HC should take into consideration in calculating its bid.   **(5 marks)**

(b)   Calculate the total cost including all overheads for HC that it can use as a basis of the bid for the new apartment contract. ▦   **(13 marks)**

(c)   If the second kitchen alone is expected to take 21.6 man-hours to fit demonstrate how the learning rate of 95% has been calculated. ▦   **(2 marks)**

(Total: 20 marks)

> ▶ *Calculate your allowed time, allocate the time to the separate parts...............*

309   MEDICAL TEMP CO (MARCH/JUNE 2021)

This part of the scenario relates to requirements (a) and (b).

Medical Temp Co (MTC) is one of several agencies in Sictopia supplying medical staff, both nurses and doctors, under temporary weekly contracts to local hospitals.

Information regarding the size of the market in Sictopia is as follows:

	Quarter 1	Quarter 2
	$m	$m
Size of national market for supply of temporary nurses	14	18.9
Size of national market for supply of temporary doctors	8	8.2

The increase in the national market for the supply of temporary nurses is due to a shortage of full-time nurses in Sictopia.

All agencies in Sictopia, including MTC, charge a single market rate for the supply of each type of staff $1,000 per week for supplying a nurse and $2,000 per week for supplying a doctor. In quarter 1, MTC held 30% of the market for the supply of temporary nurses, and 40% for the supply of temporary doctors.

MTC uses quarterly rolling budgets. At the end of quarter 1, it prepared aits budgeted revenue figures for quarter 2. It based these budgeted figures on the assumption that the company would continue to maintain the market share it had in quarter 1. IT also assumed that it would maintain its standard contribution margin of 80% for both nurses and doctors.

MTC's actual figures for quarter 2 are as follows:

	Actual
Total revenue from supply of nurses	$5.3m
Total revenue from supply of doctors	$3.6m
Actual contribution margin for both nurses and doctors	75%

This part of the scenario relates to requirement (c).

Cheat Co

The market size and market share variances have also been calculated for quarter 2 of one of MTC's competitors, Cheat Co. These variances are as follows:

	Nurses	Doctors	Total
	$000	$000	$000
Market Size	185 A	724 A	909 A
Market Share	1,065 F	1,043 F	2,108 F

Cheat Co holds the same percentage of each market as MTC. It also uses rolling budgets and prepares its budgeted revenue figures using exactly the same assumptions as MTC. However, when Cheat Co's sales director had to provide the market size figures for quarter 2 to the accounts department, she deliberately reported these figures 30% lower by excluding the market segment relating to maternity units. The accounts department were unaware of this.

Required:

(a) Explain why businesses calculate market size and market share variances. 🖥

(4 marks)

(b) Calculate the total market size (planning) variance and the total market share (operational) variance for MTC for quarter 2. ▦ (10 marks)

(c) Discuss the actions of the sales director at Cheat Co and how this may have impacted on the variances which have been calculated. 🖥

(6 marks)

(Total: 20 marks)

310 VALET CO (JUNE 2014)

Valet Co is a car valeting (cleaning) company. It operates in the country of Strappia, which has been badly affected by the global financial crisis. Petrol and food prices have increased substantially in the last year and the average disposable household income has decreased by 30%. Recent studies have shown that the average car owner keeps their car for five years before replacing it, rather than three years as was previously the case. Figures over recent years also show that car sales in Strappia are declining whilst business for car repairs is on the increase.

Valet Co offers two types of valet – a full valet and a mini valet. A full valet is an extensive clean of the vehicle, inside and out; a mini valet is a more basic clean of the vehicle. Until recently, four similar businesses operated in Valet Co's local area, but one of these closed down three months ago after a serious fire on its premises.

Valet Co charges customers $50 for each full valet and $30 for each mini valet and this price never changes. Their budget and actual figures for the last year were as follows:

	Budget		Actual	
Number of valets				
Full valets	3,600		4,000	
Mini valets	2,000		3,980	
	$	$	$	$
Revenue		240,000		319,400
Variable costs				
Staff wages	(114,000)		(122,000)	
Cleaning materials	(6,200)		(12,400)	
Energy costs	(6,520)		(9,200)	
	———		———	
		(126,720)		(143,600)
		———		———
Contribution		113,280		175,800
Fixed costs				
Rent, rates and depreciation		(36,800)		(36,800)
		———		———
Operating profit		76,480		139,000
		———		———

The budgeted contribution to sales ratios for the two types of valet are 44.6% for full valets and 55% for mini valets.

Required:

(a)   Using the data provided for full valets and mini valets, calculate:

    (i)   The total sales mix contribution variance   **(4 marks)**

    (ii)   The total sales quantity contribution variance. ⊞   **(4 marks)**

(b)   Briefly describe the sales mix contribution variance and the sales quantity contribution variance. 🖥   **(2 marks)**

(c)   Discuss the SALES performance of the business for the period, taking into account your calculations from part (a) AND the information provided in the scenario. 🖥

                                             (10 marks)

                                            (Total: 20 marks)

311 CLEAR CO (MARCH/JULY 2020 SAMPLE EXAM)

Clear Co is an eye treatment specialist, founded in 20X4, which runs five clinics nationwide. It is based in Zeeland, a country in which 20% of the population is over 65 years old, compared to 15% ten years ago.

Clear Co offers two eye treatment procedures: laser treatment and lens treatment. Laser treatment is the less complex of the two procedures. Technology changes rapidly in this industry and as a result 90% of patients now qualify for laser treatment, compared to only 80% five years ago.

The remaining 10% of patients are only able to have lens treatment, of which there are two types: 'refractive lens exchange' (RLE) and 'implantable contact lenses' (ICL). Clear Co started providing RLE, a treatment most effective for patients aged 40 or older, in 20X4 when it was founded. Two years ago, it also began providing ICL, a treatment recommended for patients under the age of 40.

The market for eye treatment procedures in Zeeland is dominated by a few main suppliers, of which Clear Co is one. Until two years ago, Clear Co was the largest supplier but, following the merger of two other companies, it is now the second largest. The merged company, Eos Co, has recently released its financial statements for the year, showing profits which were 10% higher than forecast. Eos Co's press release stated that it has achieved this despite offering reduced prices for the ICL treatment. It has been able to offer reduced prices because of the economies of scale achieved by the merger.

The following information relates to the two types of lens treatments offered by Clear Co for the year just ended:

Lens treatment	RLE		ICL	
	Budget	**Actual**	**Budget**	**Actual**
Number of treatments	3,750	4,130	1,320	960
Selling price per treatment ($)	3,000	2,900	3,650	3,400
Variable cost treatment ($)	600	590	1,150	1,200

Required:

(a) Calculate the following TOTAL variances for Clear Co's lens treatments:

   (i)   the sales mix contribution variance 　　　　　　　　　　　　(4 marks)

   (ii) the sales quantity contribution variance.　　　　　　　　　(4 marks)

(b) Explain what each of the sales mix contribution variance and sales quantity contribution variance measures. 　　　　　　　　　　　　　　　(2 marks)

(c) Using your answer from part (a) and any other relevant calculations, discuss Clear Co's SALES performance for the year just ended.

   Note: There are up to four marks available for additional calculations relevant to SALES performance and six marks available for discussion.　　　(10 marks)

　　　　　　　　　　　　　　　　　　　　　　　　　　　　　(Total: 20 marks)

312   THE SCHOOL UNIFORM COMPANY (MARCH/JUNE 2017)

The School Uniform Company (SU Co) manufactures school uniforms. One of its largest contracts is with the Girls' Private School Trust (GPST), which has 35 schools across the country, all with the same school uniform.

After a recent review of the uniform at the GPST schools, the school's spring/summer dress has been re-designed to incorporate a dropped waistband. Each new dress now requires 2.2 metres of material, which is 10% more material than the previous style of dress required. However, a new material has also been chosen by the GPST which costs only $2.85 per metre which is 5% cheaper than the material used on the previous dresses. In February, the total amount of material used and purchased at this price was 54,560 metres.

The design of the new dresses has meant that a complicated new sewing technique needed to be used. Consequently, all staff required training before they could begin production. The manager of the sewing department expected each of the new dresses to take 10 minutes to make as compared to 8 minutes per dress for the old style. SU Co has 24 staff, each of whom works 160 hours per month and is paid a wage of $12 per hour. All staff worked all of their contracted hours in February on production of the GPST dresses and there was no idle time. No labour rate variance arose in February.

Activity levels for February were as follows:

Budgeted production and sales (units): 30,000

Actual production and sales (units): 24,000

The production manager at SU Co is responsible for all purchasing and production issues which occur.

SU Co uses standard costing and usually, every time a design change takes place, the standard cost card is updated prior to production commencing.

However, the company accountant responsible for updating the standards has been off sick for the last two months. Consequently, the standard cost card for the new dress has not yet been updated.

Required:

(a)   Calculate the material variances in as much detail as the information allows for the month of February. ▦   (7 marks)

(b)   Calculate the labour efficiency variances in as much detail as the information allows for the month of February. ▦   (5 marks)

(c)   Assess the performance of the production manager for the month of February.

(8 marks)

(Total: 20 marks)

313   GLOVE CO (JUNE 2016)

Glove Co makes high quality, hand-made gloves which it sells for an average of $180 per pair. The standard cost of labour for each pair is $42 and the standard labour time for each pair is three hours. In the last quarter, Glove Co had budgeted production of 12,000 pairs, although actual production was 12,600 pairs in order to meet demand. 37,000 hours were used to complete the work and there was no idle time. The total labour cost for the quarter was $531,930.

At the beginning of the last quarter, the design of the gloves was changed slightly. The new design required workers to sew the company's logo on to the back of every glove made and the estimated time to do this was 15 minutes for each pair. However, no-one told the accountant responsible for updating standard costs that the standard time per pair of gloves needed to be changed. Similarly, although all workers were given a 2% pay rise at the beginning of the last quarter, the accountant was not told about this either. Consequently, the standard was not updated to reflect these changes.

When overtime is required, workers are paid 25% more than their usual hourly rate.

Required:

(a)   Calculate the total labour rate and total labour efficiency variances for the last quarter. ▦   **(2 marks)**

(b)   Analyse the above total variances into component parts for planning and operational variances in as much detail as the information allows. ▦   **(6 marks)**

(c)   Assess the performance of the production manager for the last quarter. 💻

                                                                                     (7 marks)

                                                                          (Total: 15 marks)

314   KAPPA CO (SEPTEMBER 2018)

Kappa Co produces Omega, an animal feed made by mixing and heating three ingredients: Alpha, Beta and Gamma. The company uses a standard costing system to monitor its costs.

The standard material cost for 100 kg of Omega is as follows:

Input	Kg	Cost per kg	Cost per 100 kg of Omega
		($)	($)
Alpha	40	2.00	80.00
Beta	60	5.00	300.00
Gamma	20	1.00	20.00
Total	120		400.00

Notes

1   The mixing and heating process is subject to a standard evaporation loss.

2   Alpha, Beta and Gamma are agricultural products and their quality and price varies significantly from year to year. Standard prices are set at the average market price over the last five years. Kappa Co has a purchasing manager who is responsible for pricing and supplier contracts.

3   The standard mix is set by the finance department. The last time this was done was at the product launch which was five years ago. It has not changed since.

Last month 4,600 kg of Omega was produced, using the following inputs:

Input	Kg	Cost per kg $	Total cost $
Alpha	2,200	1.80	3,960
Beta	2,500	6.00	15,000
Gamma	920	1.00	920
Total	5,620		19,880

At the end of each month, the production manager receives a standard cost operating statement from Kappa Co's performance manager. The statement contains material price and usage variances, labour rate and efficiency variances, and overhead expenditure and efficiency variances for the previous month. No commentary on the variances is given and the production manager receives no other feedback on the efficiency of the Omega process.

Required:

(a) Calculate the following variances for the last month:

    (i) the material usage variance for each ingredient and in total   **(4 marks)**

    (ii) the total material mix variance   **(4 marks)**

    (iii) the total material yield variance. ▦   **(3 marks)**

(b) Discuss the problems with the current system of calculating and reporting variances for assessing the performance of the production manager. 💻   **(9 marks)**

                                      (Total: 20 marks)

315 SAFE SOAP CO (DECEMBER 2014)

The Safe Soap Co makes environmentally-friendly soap using three basic ingredients. The standard cost card for one batch of soap for the month of September was as follows:

Material	Kilograms	Price per kilogram ($)
Lye	0.25	10
Coconut oil	0.6	4
Shea butter	0.5	3

The budget for production and sales in September was 120,000 batches. Actual production and sales were 136,000 batches. The actual ingredients used were as follows:

Material	Kilograms
Lye	34,080
Coconut oil	83,232
Shea butter	64,200

Required:

(a) Calculate the total material mix variance and the total material yield variance for September. ▦   **(8 marks)**

(b) In October the materials mix and yield variances were as follows:

Mix: $6,000 adverse

Yield: $10,000 favourable

The production manager is pleased with the results overall, stating:

'At the beginning of September I made some changes to the mix of ingredients used for the soaps. As I expected, the mix variance is adverse in both months because we haven't yet updated our standard cost card but, in both months, the favourable yield variance more than makes up for this. Overall, I think we can be satisfied that the changes made to the product mix are producing good results and now we are able to produce more batches and meet the growing demand for our product.'

The sales manager, however, holds a different view and says:

'I'm not happy with this change in the ingredients mix. I've had to explain to the board why the sales volume variance for October was $22,000 adverse. I've tried to explain that the quality of the soap has declined slightly and some of my customers have realised this and simply aren't happy but no-one seems to be listening. Some customers are even demanding that the price of the soap be reduced and threatening to go elsewhere if the problem isn't sorted out.'

Required:

(i)   **Briefly explain what the adverse materials mix and favourable materials yield variances indicate about production at Safe Soap Co in October.** 🖳

      Note: You are NOT required to discuss revision of standards or operational and planning variances.   **(4 marks)**

(ii)   **Discuss whether the sales manager could be justified in claiming that the change in the materials mix has caused an adverse sales volume variance in October.** 🖳   **(3 marks)**

(c)   **Critically discuss the types of standard used in standard costing and their effect on employee motivation.** 🖳   **(5 marks)**

(Total: 20 marks)

316   ATD (DECEMBER 2013, AMENDED)

Tutorial note

This question is offered for practice on the new syllabus areas of forecasting techniques, but students are not to expect this level of complexity in the exam.

ATD is a medium-sized engineering company providing specialist components for the marine engineering market. The sales manager is currently under pressure from the other departmental managers to explain why the sales revenue forecasts are becoming increasingly unreliable. Errors in the sales manager's forecasts are on production, inventory control, raw materials purchasing and, ultimately, on the profitability of the company itself. They use a 'combination of experience, intuition and guesswork' to produce their sales forecast, but accept that the forecasts are increasingly inaccurate.

Consequently, the sales manager has asked a business analyst to investigate more rigorous, appropriate ways of forecasting. The business analyst has suggested two possible alternatives. The first (summarised in Figure 1) is least squares regression. The second (summarised in Figure 2) is time series analysis. The actual sales figures in both of these examples are for ATD, so the company is currently in quarter 3 – 20X3. However, the business analyst has left the company before completing and explaining either the basis for, or implications of, these two alternative approaches to forecasting.

Figure 1: Least squares analysis

Year/quarter	Quarter Sales ($000)				
	x	y	x^2	xy	y^2
20X0 quarter 1	1	110	1	110	12,100
20X0 quarter 2	2	160	4	320	25,600
20X0 quarter 3	3	155	9	465	24,025
20X0 quarter 4	4	96	16	384	9,216
20X1 quarter 1	5	116	25	580	13,456
20X1 quarter 2	6	160	36	960	25,600
20X1 quarter 3	7	153	49	1,071	23,409
20X1 quarter 4	8	100	64	800	10,000
20X2 quarter 1	9	128	81	1,152	16,384
20X2 quarter 2	10	180	100	1,800	32,400
20X2 quarter 3	11	169	121	1,859	28,561
20X2 quarter 4	12	99	144	1,188	9,801
20X3 quarter 1	13	137	169	1,781	18,769
20X3 quarter 2	14	180	196	2,520	32,400
	1,943	1,015		14,990	281,721
			b		1.84
			a		125.022
			r		0.253

The equation of a straight line is $y = a + bx$

Figure 2: Time series analysis

Quarter	Sales ($000)	Trend	Deviation	Svar (1)	Residual	Sadj (2)
20X0 quarter 1	110					124.70
20X0 quarter 2	160					127.77
20X0 quarter 3	155	131.00	24.00	22.55	1.45	132.45
20X0 quarter 4	96	131.75	−35.75	−40.08	4.33	136.08
20X1 quarter 1	116	131.50	−15.50	−14.70	−0.80	130.70
20X1 quarter 2	160	131.75	28.25	32.23	−3.98	127.77
20X1 quarter 3	153	133.75	19.25	22.55	−3.30	130.45
20X1 quarter 4	100	137.75	−37.75	−40.08	2.33	140.08
20X2 quarter 1	128	142.25	−14.25	−14.70	0.45	142.70
20X2 quarter 2	180	144.13	35.88	32.23	3.64	147.77
20X2 quarter 3	169	145.13	23.88	22.55	1.33	146.45
20X2 quarter 4	99	146.25	−47.25	−40.08	−7.17	139.08
20X3 quarter 1	137					151.70
20X3 quarter 2	180					147.77

		1	2	3	4	
Analysis of seasonal variation				24.00	−35.75	
		−15.50	28.25	19.25	−37.75	
		−14.25	35.88	23.88	−47.25	
Totals		−29.75	64.13	67.13	−120.75	
Average		−14.88	32.06	22.38	−40.25	−0.69
Adjustment		0.17	0.17	0.17	0.17	
Svar (1)		−14.70	32.23	22.55	−40.08	

Note 1: Svar: seasonal variation   **Note 2:** Sadj: seasonally adjusted figures

The analyst has also stated that the trend forecast for 20X3 Q3 will be 151, but has not provided an explanation.

The failure of the company to meet sales targets for quarters 1 and 2 of 20X3 has prompted the Chief Executive Officer (CEO) to put into place a broad cost-cutting policy. They claim that 'our failure to meet sales targets means we must ruthlessly cut costs'. However, many of the departmental managers are critical of such an indiscriminate approach and believe that the measures might be counter-productive.

This cost-cutting has particularly demotivated the production manager and the inventory manager, who both blame the sales director for setting unrealistic targets. The production manager has commented that, 'I am working tirelessly to keep costs down, but my only reward is that I cannot replace one of my best purchasing administrators who left last month'. In general, departmental managers at the company feel 'powerless and undervalued'.

The company currently does not have a formal budgeting process in place. The production manager is sure that such a process, particularly if senior managers were involved in the budget setting process, would help address issues around forecast reliability, the low morale of departmental managers and the seemingly indiscriminate cost-cutting of the CEO.

Required:

(a)   Forecast the sales for 20X3 Q3, using (i) the least squares analysis method and (ii) the times series analysis method.   **(4 marks)**

(b)   Explain both sales forecasting methods and discuss their relative merits for ATD.
                                                                                  (8 marks)

(c)   Analyse how the introduction of a formal budgeting process would benefit ATD.
                                                                                  (8 marks)

(Total: 20 marks)

PERFORMANCE MEASUREMENT AND CONTROL

317   HAMMER (JUNE 2010)

Hammer is a large garden equipment supplier with retail stores throughout Toolland. Many of the products it sells are bought in from outside suppliers but some are currently manufactured by Hammer's own manufacturing division 'Nail'.

The prices (a transfer price) that Nail charges to the retail stores are set by head office and have been the subject of some discussion. The current policy is for Nail to calculate the total variable cost of production and delivery and add 30% for profit. Nail argues that all costs should be taken into consideration, offering to reduce the mark-up on costs to 10% in this case. The retail stores are unhappy with the current pricing policy arguing that it results in prices that are often higher than comparable products available on the market.

Nail has provided the following information to enable a price comparison to be made of the two possible pricing policies for one of its products.

Garden shears

Steel: the shears have 0.4 kg of high quality steel in the final product. The manufacturing process loses 5% of all steel put in. Steel costs $4,000 per tonne (1 tonne = 1,000 kg).

Other materials: Other materials are bought in and have a list price of $3 per kg although Hammer secures a 10% volume discount on all purchases. The shears require 0.1 kg of these materials.

The labour time to produce shears is 0.25 hours per unit and labour costs $10 per hour.

Variable overheads are absorbed at the rate of 150% of labour rates and fixed overheads are 80% of the variable overheads.

Delivery is made by an outsourced distributor that charges Nail $0.50 per garden shear for delivery.

Required:

(a) Calculate the price that Nail would charge for the garden shears under the existing policy of variable cost plus 30%. ⊞ **(6 marks)**

(b) Calculate the increase or decrease in price if the pricing policy switched to total cost plus 10%. ⊞ **(4 marks)**

(c) Discuss whether or not including fixed costs in a transfer price is a sensible policy. 💻 **(4 marks)**

(d) Discuss whether the retail stores should be allowed to buy in from outside suppliers if the prices are cheaper than those charged by Nail. 💻 **(6 marks)**

(Total: 20 marks)

318 MAN CO (JUNE 2016)

A manufacturing company, Man Co, has two divisions: Division L and Division M. Both divisions make a single standardised product. Division L makes component L, which is supplied to both Division M and external customers. Division M makes product M using one unit of component L and other materials. It then sells the completed product M to external customers. To date, Division M has always bought component L from Division L.

The following information is available:

	Component L	Product M
	$	$
Selling price	40	96
Direct materials:		
Component L		(40)
Other	(12)	(17)
Direct labour	(6)	(9)
Variable overheads	(2)	(3)
Selling and distribution costs	(4)	(1)
Contribution per unit before fixed costs	16	26
Annual fixed costs	$500,000	$200,000
Annual external demand (units)	160,000	120,000
Capacity of plant	300,000	130,000

Division L charges the same price for component L to both Division M and external customers. However, it does not incur the selling and distribution costs when transferring internally.

Division M has just been approached by a new supplier who has offered to supply it with component L for $37 per unit. Prior to this offer, the cheapest price which Division M could have bought component L for from outside the group was $42 per unit.

It is head office policy to let the divisions operate autonomously without interference at all.

Required:

(a) Calculate the incremental profit/(loss) per component for the group if Division M accepts the new supplier's offer and recommend how many components Division L should sell to Division M if group profits are to be maximised. ⊞ **(3 marks)**

(b) Using the quantities calculated in (a) and the current transfer price, calculate the total annual profits of each division and the group as a whole. ⊞ **(6 marks)**

(c) Discuss the problems which will arise if the transfer price remains unchanged and advise the divisions on a suitable alternative transfer price for component L. 💻

(6 marks)

(Total: 15 marks)

319 BEST NIGHT CO (MARCH 2019)

Best Night Co operates a chain of 30 hotels across the country of Essland. It prides itself on the comfort of the rooms in its hotels and the quality of service it offers to guests.

The majority of Best Night Co's hotels are located in major cities and have previously been successful in attracting business customers. In recent years, however, the number of business customers has started to decline as a result of tough economic conditions in Essland.

Best Night Co's policy is to set standard prices for the rooms in each of its hotels, with that price reflecting the hotel's location and taking account of competitors' prices. However, hotel managers have the authority to offer discounts to regular customers, and to reduce prices when occupancy rates in their hotel are expected to be low. The average standard price per night, across all the hotels, was $140 in 20X7, compared to $135 in 20X6. In addition to room bookings, the hotels also generate revenue from the additional services available to customers, such as restaurants and bars.

Summary from Best Night Co's management accounts:

	Year ended 30 June 20X7	Year ended 30 June 20X6
	$000	$000
Revenue – Rooms at standard price per night	111,890	104,976
Room discounts or rate reductions given	(16,783)	(11,540)
Other revenue: food, drink	24,270	23,185
Total revenue	119,377	116,621
Operating costs	(95,462)	(92,379)
Operating profit	23,915	24,242

Oher performance information:

	Year ended 30 June 20X7	Year ended 30 June 20X6
	$000	$000
Capital employed (Note 1)	$39.5m	$39.1m
Average occupancy rates (Note 2)	74%	72%
Average customer satisfaction score (Note 3)	4.2	4.5

Note 1: Capital employed is calculated using the depreciated cost of non-current assets at all Best Night Co's hotels.

Note 2: Occupancy rates for the year ended 30 June 20X7 were budgeted to be 72%.

Note 3: Customer satisfaction scores are graded on a scale of 1–5 where '5' represents 'Excellent'. On average, in any given town in Essland, the top 10% of hotels earn a score of 4.5 or above and the top 25% of hotels earn a score of 4.2 or above.

Two themes are becoming increasingly frequent in the comments Best Night Co's customers make alongside the scores:

(1) Repeat customers have said that the standard of service in recent visits has not been as good as in previous visits.

(2) The rooms need redecorating, and the fixtures and fittings need replacing. For example, the beds need new mattresses to improve the level of comfort they provide. Best Night Co had planned a two-year refurbishment programme beginning in 20X7 of all the rooms in each hotel. However, this programme has been put on hold, due to the current economic conditions, and in order to reduce expenditure.

Required:

Using the information provided, discuss Best Night Co's financial and non-financial performance for the year ended 30 June 20X7. Note: There are 5 marks available for calculations and 15 marks available for discussion. 🖥 **(20 marks)**

320 JUMP PERFORMANCE APPRAISAL (JUNE 2010)

Jump has a network of sports clubs which is managed by local managers reporting to the main board. The local managers have a lot of autonomy and are able to vary employment contracts with staff and offer discounts for membership fees and personal training sessions. They also control their own maintenance budget but do not have control over large amounts of capital expenditure.

A local manager's performance and bonus is assessed relative to three targets. For every one of these three targets that is reached in an individual quarter, $400 is added to the manager's bonus, which is paid at the end of the year. The maximum bonus per year is therefore based on 12 targets (three targets in each of the four quarters of the year). Accordingly the maximum bonus that could be earned is 12 × $400 = $4,800, which represents 40% of the basic salary of a local manager. Jump has a 31 March year end.

The performance data for one of the sports clubs for the last four quarters is as follows:

	Qtr to 30 June 20X9	Qtr to 30 Sept 20X9	Qtr to 31 Dec 20X9	Qtr to 31 March 20Y0
Number of members	3,000	3,200	3,300	3,400
Member visits	20,000	24,000	26,000	24,000
Personal training sessions booked	310	325	310	339
Staff days	450	480	470	480
Staff lateness days	20	28	28	20
Days in quarter	90	90	90	90

Agreed targets are:

(1)   Staff must be on time over 95% of the time (no penalty is made when staff are absent from work).

(2)   On average 60% of members must use the clubs' facilities regularly by visiting at least 12 times per quarter.

(3)   On average 10% of members must book a personal training session each quarter.

Required:

(a)   **Calculate the amount of bonus that the manager should expect to be paid for the latest financial year.** ▦   **(6 marks)**

(b)   **Discuss to what extent the targets set are controllable by the local manager (you are required to make a case for both sides of the argument).** 💻   **(9 marks)**

(c)   **Describe two methods as to how a manager with access to the accounting and other records could unethically manipulate the situation so as to gain a greater bonus.** 💻
                                                                           (5 marks)

                                                                    (Total: 20 marks)

321   LENS CO (DECEMBER 2016)

Lens Co manufactures lenses for use by a wide range of commercial customers. The company has two divisions: the Photographic Division (P) and the Optometry Division (O). Each of the divisions is run by a divisional manager who has overall responsibility for all aspects of running their division and the divisions are currently treated as investment centres. Each manager, however, has an authorisation limit of $15,000 per item for capital expenditure and any items costing more than this must first be approved by Head Office.

During the year, Head Office made a decision to sell a large amount of the equipment in Division P and replace it with more technologically advanced equipment. It also decided to close one of Division O's factories in a country deemed to be politically unstable, with the intention of opening a new factory elsewhere in the following year.

Both divisions trade with overseas customers, choosing to provide these customers with 60 days' credit to encourage sales. Due to differences in exchange rates between the time of invoicing the customers and receiving the payment 60 days later, exchange gains and losses often occur.

The cost of capital for Lens Co is 12% per annum.

The following data relates to the year ended 30 November 20X6:

	Division P	Division O
	$000	$000
Revenue	14,000	18,800
Gain on sale of equipment	400	–
	14,400	18,800
Direct labour	(2,400)	(3,500)
Direct materials	(4,800)	(6,500)
Divisional overheads*	(3,800)	(5,200)
Trading profit	3,400	3,600
Exchange gain/(loss)	(200)	460
Exceptional costs for factory closure	–	(1,800)
Allocated Head Office costs	(680)	(1,040)
Net divisional profit	2,520	1,220

* Depreciation on uncontrollable assets included in divisional overheads

	Division P	Division O
	320	460
	Division P	Division O
	$000	$000
Non-current assets controlled by the division	15,400	20,700
Non-current assets controlled by Head Office	3,600	5,200
Inventories	1,800	3,900
Trade receivables	6,200	8,900
Overdraft	500	–
Trade payables	5,100	7,200

To date, managers have always been paid a bonus based on the return on investment (ROI) achieved by their division. However, the company is considering whether residual income would be a better method.

Required:

(a) Calculate the return on investment (ROI) for each division for the year ended 30 November 20X6, ensuring that the basis of the calculation makes it a suitable measure for assessing the DIVISIONAL MANAGERS' performance. ▦ (6 marks)

(b) Explain why you have included or excluded certain items in calculating the ROIs in part (a), stating any assumptions you have made. ▣ (8 marks)

(c) Briefly discuss whether it is appropriate to treat each of the divisions of Lens Co as investment centres. ▣ (2 marks)

(d) Discuss the problems involved in using ROI to measure the managers' performance. ▣ (4 marks)

(Total: 20 marks)

322 ACCOUNTANCY TEACHING CO (DECEMBER 2010)

The Accountancy Teaching Co (AT Co) is a company specialising in the provision of accountancy tuition courses in the private sector. It makes up its accounts to 30 November each year. In the year ending 30 November 20X9, it held 60% of market share. However, over the last twelve months, the accountancy tuition market in general has faced a 20% decline in demand for accountancy training leading to smaller class sizes on courses. In 20X9 and before, AT Co suffered from an ongoing problem with staff retention, which had a knock-on effect on the quality of service provided to students. Following the completion of developments that have been ongoing for some time, in 20Y0 the company was able to offer a far-improved service to students. The developments included:

- A new dedicated 24 hour student helpline
- An interactive website providing instant support to students
- A new training programme for staff
- An electronic student enrolment system
- An electronic marking system for the marking of students' progress tests. The costs of marking electronically were expected to be $4 million less in 20Y0 than marking on paper. Marking expenditure is always included in cost of sales.

Extracts from the management accounts for 20X9 and 20Y0 are shown below:

	20X9		20Y0	
	$000	$000	$000	$000
Turnover		72,025		66,028
Cost of sales		(52,078)		(42,056)
Gross profit		19,947		23,972
Marketing	3,291		4,678	
Property	6,702		6,690	
Staff training	1,287		3,396	
Interactive website running costs	–		3,270	
Student helpline running costs	–		2,872	
Enrolment costs	5,032		960	
Total indirect expenses		(16,312)		(21,866)
Net operating profit		3,635		2,106

On 1 December 20X9, management asked all 'freelance lecturers' to reduce their fees by at least 10% with immediate effect ('freelance lecturers' are not employees of the company but are used to teach students when there are not enough of AT Co's own lecturers to meet tuition needs). All employees were also told that they would not receive a pay rise for at least one year. Total lecture staff costs (including freelance lecturers) were $41.663 million in 20X9 and were included in cost of sales, as is always the case. Freelance lecturer costs represented 35% of these total lecture staff costs. In 20Y0 freelance lecture costs were $12.394 million. No reduction was made to course prices in the year and the mix of trainees studying for the different qualifications remained the same. The same type and number of courses were run in both 20X9 and 20Y0 and the percentage of these courses that was run by freelance lecturers as opposed to employed staff also remained the same.

Due to the nature of the business, non-financial performance indicators are also used to assess performance, as detailed below.

	20X9	20Y0
Percentage of students transferring to AT Co from another training provider	8%	20%
Number of late enrolments due to staff error	297	106
Percentage of students passing exams first time	48%	66%
Labour turnover	32%	10%
Number of student complaints	315	84
Average no. of employees	1,080	1,081

Required:

Assess the performance of the business in 20Y0 using both financial performance indicators calculated from the above information AND the non-financial performance indicators provided. 🖥

Note: Clearly state any assumptions and show all workings clearly. Your answer should be structured around the following main headings: turnover; cost of sales; gross profit; indirect expenses; net operating profit. However, in discussing each of these areas you should also refer to the non-financial performance indicators, where relevant.

(Total: 20 marks)

323 CIM (DECEMBER 2015)

Cardale Industrial Metal Co (CIM Co) is a large supplier of industrial metals. The company is split into two divisions: Division F and Division N. Each division operates separately as an investment centre, with each one having full control over its non-current assets. In addition, both divisions are responsible for their own current assets, controlling their own levels of inventory and cash and having full responsibility for the credit terms granted to customers and the collection of receivables balances. Similarly, each division has full responsibility for its current liabilities and deals directly with its own suppliers.

Each divisional manager is paid a salary of $120,000 per annum plus an annual performance-related bonus, based on the return on investment (ROI) achieved by their division for the year. Each divisional manager is expected to achieve a minimum ROI for their division of 10% per annum. If a manager only meets the 10% target, they are not awarded a bonus. However, for each whole percentage point above 10% which the division achieves for the year, a bonus equivalent to 2% of annual salary is paid, subject to a maximum bonus equivalent to 30% of annual salary.

The following figures relate to the year ended 31 August 20X5:

	Division F $000	Division N $000
Sales	14,500	8,700
Controllable profit	2,645	1,970
Less: apportionment of Head Office costs	(1,265)	(684)
Net profit	1,380	1,286
Non-current assets	9,760	14,980
Inventory, cash and trade receivables	2,480	3,260
Trade payables	2,960	1,400

During the year ending 31 August 20X5, Division N invested $6.8m in new equipment including a technologically advanced cutting machine, which is expected to increase productivity by 8% per annum. Division F has made no investment during the year, although its computer system is badly in need of updating. Division F's manager has said that they have already had to delay payments to suppliers (i.e. accounts payables) because of limited cash and the computer system 'will just have to wait', although the cash balance at Division F is still better than that of Division N.

Required:

(a) **For each division, for the year ended 31 August 20X5:**

(i) **calculate the appropriate closing return on investment (ROI) on which the payment of management bonuses will be based. Briefly justify the figures used in your calculations. Note: There are 3 marks available for calculations and 2 marks available for discussion.** 🖥 **(5 marks)**

(ii) **Based on your calculations in part (i), calculate each manager's bonus for the year ended 31 August 20X5.** ▦ **(3 marks)**

(b) **Discuss whether ROI is providing a fair basis for calculating the managers' bonuses and the problems arising from its use at CIM Co for the year ended 31 August 20X5.** 🖥
(7 marks)

(c) **Briefly discuss the strengths and weaknesses of ROI and RI as methods of assessing the performance of divisions. Explain two further methods of assessment of divisional performance that could be used in addition to ROI or RI.** 🖥 **(5 marks)**

(Total: 20 marks)

324 SPORTS CO (SEPTEMBER/DECEMBER 2017)

Sports Co is a large manufacturing company specialising in the manufacture of a wide range of sports clothing and equipment. The company has two divisions: Clothing (division C) and Equipment (division E). Each division operates with little intervention from Head Office and divisional managers have autonomy to make decisions about long-term investments.

Sports Co measures the performance of its divisions using return on investment (ROI), calculated using controllable profit and average divisional net assets. The target ROI for each of the divisions is 18%. If the divisions meet or exceed this target the divisional managers receive a bonus.

Last year, an investment which was expected to meet the target ROI was rejected by one of the divisional managers because it would have reduced the division's overall ROI. Consequently, Sports Co is considering the introduction of a new performance measure, residual income (RI), in order to discourage this dysfunctional behaviour in the future. Like ROI, this would be calculated using controllable profit and average divisional net assets.

The draft operating statement for the year, prepared by the company's trainee accountant, is shown below:

	Division C	Division E
	$000	$000
Sales revenue	3,800	8,400
Less variable costs	(1,400)	(3,030)
Contribution	**2,400**	**5,370**
Less fixed costs	(945)	(1,420)
Net profit	**1,455**	**3,950**
Opening divisional controllable net assets	13,000	24,000
Closing divisional controllable net assets	9,000	30,000

Notes:

(1)   Included in the fixed costs are depreciation costs of $165,000 and $460,000 for divisions C and E respectively. 30% of the depreciation costs in each division relates to assets controlled but not owned by Head Office. Division E invested $2m in plant and machinery at the beginning of the year, which is included in the net assets figures above, and uses the reducing balance method to depreciate assets. Division C, which uses the straight-line method, made no significant additions to non-current assets. It is the policy of both divisions to charge a full year's depreciation in the year of acquisition.

(2)   Head Office recharges all of its costs to the two divisions. These have been included in the fixed costs and amount to $620,000 for division C and $700,000 for division E.

(3)   Sports Co has a cost of capital of 12%.

Required:

(a)   (i)   Calculate the return on investment (ROI) for each of the two divisions of Sports Co. 🖥   **(6 marks)**

        (ii)   Discuss the performance of the two divisions for the year, including the main reasons why their ROI results differ from each other. Explain the impact the difference in ROI could have on the behaviour of the manager of the worst performing division. 🖥   **(6 marks)**

(b)   (i)   Calculate the residual income (RI) for each of the two divisions of Sports Co and briefly comment on the results of this performance measure. ▦   **(4 marks)**

        (ii)   Explain the advantages and disadvantages of using residual income (RI) to measure divisional performance. 🖥   **(4 marks)**

                                                                                   (Total: 20 marks)

325 THE PORTABLE GARAGE COMPANY (JUNE 2018)

The Portable Garage Co (PGC) is a company specialising in the manufacture and sale of a range of products for motorists. It is split into two divisions: the battery division (Division B) and the adaptor division (Division A). Division B sells one product – portable battery chargers for motorists which can be attached to a car's own battery and used to start up the engine when the car's own battery fails. Division A sells adaptors which are used by customers to charge mobile devices and laptops by attaching them to the car's internal power source.

Recently, Division B has upgraded its portable battery so it can also be used to rapidly charge mobile devices and laptops. The mobile device or laptop must be attached to the battery using a special adaptor which is supplied to the customer with the battery. Division B currently buys the adaptors from Division A, which also sells them externally to other companies.

The following data is available for both divisions:

Division B

Selling price for each portable battery, including adaptor	$180
Costs per battery:	
Adaptor from Division A	$13
Other materials from external suppliers	$45
Labour costs	$35
Annual fixed overheads	$5,460,000
Annual production and sales of portable batteries (units)	150,000
Maximum annual market demand for portable batteries (units)	180,000

Division A

Selling price per adaptor to Division B	$13
Selling price per adaptor to external customers	$15
Costs per adaptor:	
Materials	$3
Labour costs	$4
Annual fixed overheads	$2,200,000
Current annual production capacity and sales of adaptors – both internal and external sales (units)	350,000
Maximum annual external demand for adaptors (units)	200,000

In addition to the materials and labour costs above, Division A incurs a variable cost of $1 per adaptor for all adaptors it sells externally.

Currently, Head Office's purchasing policy only allows Division B to purchase the adaptors from Division A but Division A has refused to sell Division B any more than the current level of adaptors it supplies to it.

The manager of Division B is unhappy. They have a special industry contact who they could buy the adaptors from at exactly the same price charged by Division A if they were given the autonomy to purchase from outside the group.

After discussions with both of the divisional managers and to ensure that the managers are not demotivated, Head Office has now agreed to change the purchasing policy to allow Division B to buy externally, provided that it optimises the profits of the group as a whole.

Required:

(a) Under the current transfer pricing system, prepare a profit statement showing the profit for each of the divisions and for The Portable Garage Co (PGC) as a whole. Your sales and costs figures should be split into external sales and inter-divisional transfers, where appropriate. ⊞ **(9 marks)**

(b) Assuming that the new group purchasing policy will ensure the optimisation of group profits, calculate and discuss the number of adaptors which Division B should buy from Division A and the number of adaptors which Division A should sell to external customers. ⊞ 💻

Note: There are 3 marks available for calculations and 3 marks for discussion. **(6 marks)**

Assume now that no external supplier exists for the adaptors which Division B uses.

(c) Calculate and discuss what the minimum transfer price per unit would be for any additional adaptors supplied above the current level by Division A to Division B so that Division B can meet its maximum annual demand for the new portable batteries.

Note: There are 2 marks available for calculations and 3 marks available for discussion. **(5 marks)**

(Total: 20 marks)

326 CTD

CTD has two divisions – FD and TM. FD is an iron foundry division which produces mouldings that have a limited external market and are also transferred to TM division. TM division uses the mouldings to produce a piece of agricultural equipment called the 'TX' which is sold externally. Each TX requires one moulding. Both divisions produce only one type of product.

The performance of each Divisional Manager is evaluated individually on the basis of the residual income (RI) of his or her division. The company's average annual 12% cost of capital is used to calculate the finance charges. If their own target residual income is achieved, each Divisional Manager is awarded a bonus equal to 5% of his or her residual income. All bonuses are paid out of Head Office profits.

The following budgeted information is available for the forthcoming year:

	TM division TX per unit	FD division Moulding per unit
External selling price ($)	500	80
Variable production cost ($)	*366	40
Fixed production overheads ($)	60	20
	―――	―――
Gross profit ($)	74	20
Variable selling and distribution cost ($)	25	**4
Fixed administration overhead ($)	25	4
	―――	―――
Net profit ($)	24	12
	―――	―――
Normal capacity (units)	15,000	20,000
Maximum production capacity (units)	15,000	25,000
Sales to external customers (units)	15,000	5,000
Capital employed	$1,500,000	$750,000
Target RI	$105,000	$85,000

* The variable production cost of TX includes the cost of an FD moulding.

** External sales only of the mouldings incur a variable selling and distribution cost of $4 per unit.

FD division currently transfers 15,000 mouldings to TM division at a transfer price equal to the total production cost plus 10%. Fixed costs are absorbed on the basis of normal capacity.

Required:

(a) Calculate the bonus each Divisional Manager would receive under the current transfer pricing policy and discuss any implications that the current performance evaluation system may have for each division and for the company as a whole. ▦

(14 marks)

(b) Both Divisional Managers want to achieve their respective residual income targets. Based on the budgeted figures, calculate:

(i) the maximum transfer price per unit that the Divisional Manager of TM division would pay ▦

(ii) the minimum transfer price per unit that the Divisional Manager of FD division would accept. ▦

(6 marks)

(Total: 20 marks)

327 ROTECH (JUNE 2014)

The Rotech group comprises two companies, W Co and C Co.

W Co is a trading company with two divisions: The Design division, which designs wind turbines and supplies the designs to customers under licences and the Gearbox division, which manufactures gearboxes for the car industry.

C Co manufactures components for gearboxes. It sells the components globally and also supplies W Co with components for its Gearbox manufacturing division. The financial results for the two companies for the year ended 31 May 2014 are as follows:

	W Co		C Co
	Design Division	Gearbox Division	
	$000	$000	$000
External sales	14,300	25,535	8,010
Sales to Gearbox division			7,550
			15,560
Cost of sales	(4,900)	(16,200)*	(5,280)
Administration costs	(3,400)	(4,200)	(2,600)
Distribution costs	–	(1,260)	(670)
Operating profit	6,000	3,875	7,010
Capital employed	23,540	32,320	82,975

* Includes cost of components purchased from C Co.

Required:

(a) **Discuss the performance of C Co and each division of W Co, calculating and using the following three performance measures:**

   (i) **Return on capital employed (ROCE)**

   (ii) **Asset turnover**

   (iii) **Operating profit margin.** ▦

   Note: There are 4.5 marks available for calculations and 5.5 marks available for discussion. **(10 marks)**

(b) C Co is currently working to full capacity. The Rotech group's policy is that group companies and divisions must always make internal sales first before selling outside the group. Similarly, purchases must be made from within the group wherever possible. However, the group divisions and companies are allowed to negotiate their own transfer prices without interference from Head Office.

C Co has always charged the same price to the Gearbox division as it does to its external customers. However, after being offered a 5% lower price for similar components from an external supplier, the manager of the Gearbox division feels strongly that the transfer price is too high and should be reduced. C Co currently satisfies 60% of the external demand for its components. Its variable costs represent 40% of revenue.

Required:

Advise, using suitable calculations, the total transfer price or prices at which the components should be supplied to the Gearbox division from C Co. ⊞ 🖳

(10 marks)

(Total: 20 marks)

328 DIVISION A

Division A, which is a part of the ACF Group, manufactures only one type of product, a Bit, which it sells to external customers and also to division C, another member of the group. ACF Group's policy is that divisions have the freedom to set transfer prices and choose their suppliers.

The ACF Group uses residual income (RI) to assess divisional performance and each year it sets each division a target RI. The group's cost of capital is 12% a year.

Division A

Budgeted information for the coming year is:

Maximum capacity	150,000 Bits
External sales	110,000 Bits
External selling price	$35 per Bit
Variable cost	$22 per Bit
Fixed costs	$1,080,000
Capital employed	$3,200,000
Target residual income	$180,000

Division C

Division C has found two other companies willing to supply Bits:

X could supply at $28 per Bit, but only for annual orders in excess of 50,000 Bits. Z could supply at $33 per Bit for any quantity ordered.

Required:

(a) **Division C provisionally requests a quotation for 60,000 Bits from division A for the coming year.**

(i) **Calculate the transfer price per Bit that division A should quote in order to meet its residual income target.** ⊞ (6 marks)

(ii) **Calculate the two prices division A would have to quote to division C, if it became group policy to quote transfer prices based on opportunity costs.** ⊞ (4 marks)

(b) **Discuss, with supporting calculations, the impact of the group's current and proposed policies on the profits of divisions A and C, and on group profit.** 🖳

(10 marks)

(Total: 20 marks)

329 JUNGLE CO (SEPTEMBER 2016)

Jungle Co is a very successful multinational retail company. It has been selling a large range of household and electronic goods for some years. One year ago, it began using new suppliers from the country of Slabak, where labour is very cheap, for many of its household goods. In 20X4, Jungle Co also became a major provider of 'cloud computing' services, investing heavily in cloud technology. These services provide customers with a way of storing and accessing data and programs over the internet rather than on their computers' hard drives.

All Jungle Co customers have the option to sign up for the company's 'Gold' membership service, which provides next day delivery on all orders, in return for an annual service fee of $40. In September 20X5, Jungle Co formed its own logistics company and took over the delivery of all of its parcels, instead of using the services of international delivery companies.

Over the last year, there has been worldwide growth in the electronic goods market of 20%. Average growth rates and gross profit margins for cloud computing service providers have been 50% and 80% respectively in the last year. Jungle Co's prices have remained stable year on year for all sectors of its business, with price competitiveness being crucial to its continuing success as the leading global electronic retailer.

The following information is available for Jungle Co for the last two financial years:

	Notes	31 August 20X6	31 August 20X5
		$000	$000
Revenue	1	94,660	82,320
Cost of sales	2	(54,531)	(51,708)
Gross profit		40,129	30,612
Administration expenses	3	(2,760)	(1,720)
Distribution expenses		(13,420)	(13,180)
Other operating expenses		(140)	(110)
Net profit		23,809	15,602

Notes

1   Breakdown of revenue

	$000	$000
Household goods	38,990	41,160
Electronic goods	41,870	32,640
Cloud computing services	12,400	6,520
Gold membership fees	1,400	2,000
	94,660	82,320

2 Breakdown of cost of sales

	$000	$000
Household goods	23,394	28,812
Electronic goods	26,797	21,216
Cloud computing services	4,240	1,580
Gold membership fees	100	100
	54,531	51,708

3 Administration expenses

Included in these costs are the costs of running the customer service department ($860,000 in 20X5; $1,900,000 in 20X6.) This department deals with customer complaints.

4 Non-financial data

	31 August 20X6	31 August 20X5
Percentage of orders delivered on time	74%	92%
No. of customer complaints	1,400,000	320,000
No. of customers	7,100,000	6,500,000
Percentage of late 'Gold' member deliveries	14.00%	2.00%

Required:

Discuss the financial and non-financial performance of Jungle Co for the year ending 31 August 20X6. Note: There are 7 marks available for calculations and 13 marks available for discussion. 🖳 **(Total: 20 marks)**

330 MEDCOMP (MARCH/JUNE 2021)

Medcomp is a charity based in Ceeland. It provides medical treatment to prevent and cure blindness caused by cataracts, to thousands of people in less developed countries. This disease is relatively easy to cure when treatment is available; but the majority of people who need treatment cannot afford to pay for it. For over 10 years Medcomp has provided free treatment from 12 treatment centres based in fixed locations worldwide.

Medcomp employs a small number of paid permanent staff who consist of medical practitioners, medical administrators and fundraisers; but the majority of its workforce is voluntary The charity has built relationships with several teaching hospitals in Ceeland, from where it recruits newly qualified doctors and nurses. These doctors and nurses volunteer to work unpaid for a year in Medcomp's treatment centres before returning home to work in one of Ceeland's many hospitals. Medcomp believes that using newly qualified medical staff will promote the use of the most effective and up-to-date techniques and procedures.

Financial donations are sourced from large businesses in Ceeland and most of the equipment and other medical supplies needed are donated by hospitals and manufacturers. Thus, it is rare for the treatment centres to run short of supplies.

Medcomp keeps accounts with a year end of 31 August as well as detailed operating data. Data extracts from its management accounts for the current year (20X8) and from 20X7 and 20X6 are as follows:

	20X8	20X7	20X6
Average Size of Donation ($)	600	535	500
Number of Donations	2,850	3,000	2,950
Total Operating Costs ($000s)	1,730	1,550	1,430
New procedures as a percentage of total procedures **(Note)**	20%	5%	5%
Number of treatments performed	5,600	5,000	4,600
Number of successful treatments	4,312	4,300	4,002
Average number of days taken to deliver drugs and equipment to treatment centres	7	7	7

Note: New procedures are procedures which are introduced within the year.

Medcomp is about to introduce a balanced scorecard to help implement its strategy and measure performance. The critical success factors (CSFs), which relate to the four perspectives of the balanced scorecard have been identified as: positive cash flow, innovation, medical effectiveness and functional efficiency.

Required:

(a)   **For each perspective of the balanced scorecard, select the appropriate critical success factor (CSF) which relates to the perspective, suggest ONE key performance indicator (KPI) which will help to measure the CSF and use the KPI to analyse Medcomp's performance from 20X6 to 20X8.** **(16 marks)**

Note: Use the balanced scorecard template provided below to structure your answer.

FINANCIAL	CSF:
	KPI:
	Performance Analysis:
CUSTOMER	CSF:
	KPI:
	Performance Analysis:
INTERNAL BUSINESS PROCESS	CSF:
	KPI:
	Performance Analysis:
LEARNING & GROWTH	CSF:
	KPI:
	Performance Analysis:

(b) Explain the benefits of an organisation using the balanced scorecard to measure performance instead of using solely financial measures 🖥 (4 marks)

(Total: 20 marks)

331 HAMMOCK CO (MARCH/JULY 2020 SAMPLE EXAM)

Hammock Co own and operate a small chain of four luxury vacation resorts. All four resorts are located on islands that enjoy a hot, sunny climate for nine months of the year. Each resort has gourmet restaurants, water sports and spa facilities, as well as sun terraces and pools.

Hammock Co's management currently focus on two distinct stakeholder groups: shareholders and customers, and has two objectives:

(1)   to make a profit long term and

(2)   to create customer loyalty

All operational (non-management) staff at the resorts receive comprehensive training and are employed in secure, long-term contracts, which is unusual in this industry.

Guests who visit the resorts pay one upfront fee and then enjoy unlimited food, drink and use of the resort facilities. When a guest arrives at a resort they are personally greeted by a concierge, offered a drink and cold towel while their luggage is transferred to their luxury room. All rooms are scrupulously clean and contain complimentary drinks, snacks, toiletries, bathrobes and slippers. The rooms are all equipped with appliances, which Hammocks Co's management believe that guests need during their stay, including satellite television, coffee-maker, refrigerator and hairdryer. If a guest requests something that is not available in the room, a call to the reception ensures that it arrives within ten minutes.

An extract from Hammock Co's management accounting data is as follows:

	Budget 20X7	Actual 20X7 (*)	Actual 20X6	Actual 20X6 Competitor 'Loungers'
Average number of guests per week	2,000	1,960	1,940	1,700
Average revenue per week ($)	4,000,000	3,920,000	3,880,000	3,060,000
Average staff costs per week				
– Maintenance ($)	480,000	480,000	470,588	455,000
– Service ($)	960,000	960,000	941,176	800,000
Average weekly spend on repairs ($)	200,000	160,000	196,078	180,000
Ratio of operational staff to guests	1.50	1.53	1.50	1.30
Average rooms available per week **	1,200	1,200	1,200	1,100
Market share %	29	28	29	23

* The actual 20X7 figures are based on the year to date figures (ten weeks)

** Rooms are designed for double occupancy

Note: general inflation is 2% higher in 20X7

Extracts from TripEvent, an influential online customer forum:

'I love Hammock Co; the service and attention to detail is exemplary and the resorts are always pristine. However, their competitor 'Loungers' has full body dryers, ionised water taps and a range of professional haircare equipment in all their rooms.'

'Our third time back to Hammocks Co this year and we continue to be amazed by the wonderful level of service. One thing though is the menus don't seem to have changed from one visit to the next.'

'We booked Hammocks Co on the spur of the moment but then found that we couldn't get a flight. We called Hammocks Co's administrative centre to change our booking to another resort where we could get a flight to and were told that it would not be a problem. However, it took two more calls and three emails to get confirmation and then our credit card was charged twice in error. Of course it was eventually all resolved, the incorrect charge refunded, a complimentary limousine provided to and from the airport and we received the most amazing customer service at the resort, but it was frustrating at the time.'

'When I made my booking I was assured that my bed would be made with the special anti-allergenic bedding which I need for a good night's sleep and that my favourite blend of tea would be available. When I arrived, neither of these requirements were met. To be fair to Hammocks Co though, everything was in order two hours later when I went to bed.'

Required:

(a) Based on the limited information available, discuss the performance of Hammocks Co in light of its two existing objectives. 🖥 **(8 marks)**

(b) (i) Explain TWO advantages of Hammocks Co using the balanced scorecard approach to performance management. 🖥 **(3 marks)**

(ii) Suggest and justify ONE goal and TWO performance measures for each of the TWO perspectives of the balanced scorecard which are not currently addressed by Hammock Co's objectives. 🖥 **(9 marks)**

(Total: 20 marks)

332 THE PEOPLE'S BANK (MARCH/JUNE 2017)

The People's Bank is a bank based in the country of Nawkrei. It has a total of 65 branches across the country and also offers online banking (access to services via computer) and telephone banking (access to customer service agents over the telephone) to its customers. Recently, The People's Bank also began offering its customers a range of mobile banking services, which can be accessed from customers' smartphones and tablet computers. Its customer-base is made up of both private individuals and business customers.

The range of services it offers includes:

- Current accounts
- Savings accounts
- Credit cards
- Business and personal loans
- Mortgages (loans for property purchases).

The People's Bank's vision is to be 'the bank that gives back to its customers' and their purpose is 'to help the people and businesses of Nawkrei to live better lives and achieve their ambitions'. In order to achieve this, the bank's values are stated as:

(1) Putting customers' needs first, which involves anticipating and understanding customers' needs and making products and services accessible to as many customers as possible. The People' Bank has recently invested heavily in IT security to prevent fraud and also invested to make more services accessible to disabled and visually impaired customers.

(2) Making business simple, which involves identifying opportunities to simplify activities and communicating clearly and openly.

(3) Making a difference to the communities they serve, which involves primarily helping the disadvantaged and new homeowners but also supporting small and medium-sized businesses (SMEs) and acting fairly and responsibly at all times.

Extracts from The People's Bank's balanced scorecard are shown below:

Performance measure	20X6 Actual	20X6 Target
Financial perspective		
Return on capital employed (ROCE)	11%	12%
Interest income	$7.5m	$7m
Net interest margin (margin achieved on interest income)	2.4%	2.5%
Amount of new lending to SMEs	$135m	$150m
Customer perspective		
Number of first-time homebuyers given a mortgage by The People's Bank	86,000	80,000
Number of complaints (per 1,000 customers)	1.5	2
Number of talking cashpoints installed for the visually impaired	120	100
Number of wheelchair ramps installed in branches	55	50
Internal processes		
Number of business processes within The People's Bank re-engineered and simplified	110	100
Number of new services made available through 'mobile banking'	2	5
Incidences of fraud on customers' accounts or credit cards (per 1,000 customers)	3	10
Total carbon dioxide emissions (tonnes)	430,000	400,000
Learning and growth		
Number of colleagues trained to provide advice to SMEs	1,300	1,500
Number of hours (paid for by The People's Bank) used to support community projects	1,020,000	1,000,000
Number of trainee positions taken up by candidates from Nawkrei's most disadvantaged areas	1,990	2,000
Number of community organisations supported (either through funding or by volunteers from The People's Bank)	7,250	7,000

Required:

(a) **Explain why the balanced scorecard approach to performance measurement is more useful to measure performance for The People's Bank than a traditional approach using solely financial performance measures.** 🖥 **(4 marks)**

(b) **Using all of the information provided, including The People's Bank's vision and values, discuss the performance of The People's Bank in 20X6. Note: Use each of the four headings of the balanced scorecard to structure your discussion.** 🖥

(16 marks)

(Total: 20 marks)

333 OSC CO (SEPTEMBER 2018)

The One Stop Car Co (OSC Co) offers a range of services for car owners at its 55 service centres across the country. The car maintenance business is extremely competitive in all regions across the country. Each service centre operates autonomously and managers are able to choose how to package up the services they offer. OSC Co's aim is to 'make the task of car maintenance a pleasure and not a chore'.

Its national website states the following:

- Range of service packs available, including express service and full valet
- 'We work whilst you wait' service, with average wait times of only two hours
- Watch our friendly, experienced mechanics producing high quality work
- Freshly made tea and coffee and free internet in our comfortable lounges
- Monthly free prize draw for all customers completing an online feedback form.

Customers initially access the national website, but depending on their location, they are automatically redirected to the website of their nearest service centre so that they can view the offers available at that centre. All bookings are made through the OSC website.

Results for one of the service centres, the Midlands Service Centre (MSC), for the year which has just ended are given below. The column headed 'OSC' shows the average figures for all of OSC Co's 55 service centres:

	Notes	MSC	OSC Average
Sales revenue ($)		760,500	890,365
Gross Profit ($)		304,200	328,146
Number of mechanics: senior	1	7	7.8
Number of mechanics: junior	2	5	5.2
Number of new service packs developed	3	3	2
Number of website hits		14,000	18,260
Total number of jobs booked and completed		9,506	11,870
Number of jobs from repeat customers only		1,500	1,660
Time spent completing jobs (hours)		23,100	24,800
Percentage of customer feedback forms showing score of 9 or 10	4	80%	70%

Notes:

(1)   Mechanics are classified as 'senior' if they have been qualified for more than five years.

(2)   'Junior' mechanics includes both trainee mechanics who are unqualified and mechanics who have been qualified for less than five years.

(3)   The MSC introduced three new service packs during the year:

- free valets for orders over $100

- a safety check costing only $20, instead of the usual $40, for all customers booking a full service

- a $10 air conditioning efficiency check, which usually costs $20, for all customers booking an oil change.

These three new service packs produced revenues of $66,000, $58,000 and $54,000 respectively. Two comparable new service packs developed by other centres produced revenues of $44,000 and $42,000.

(4)   The online feedback form asks customers to rate the centre from 1 to 10, with 10 being the best.

The CEO of OSC Co has recently attended a business seminar and heard about Fitzgerald and Moon's building block model of performance management. The CEO is interested in how the dimensions block could be applied at OSC Co. The dimensions of performance identified in the model are: competitiveness, financial performance, quality of service, flexibility, resource utilisation and innovation.

Required:

(a)   **For each of the dimensions of the building block model, calculate one performance indicator for MSC and one for the OSC average using the data available. Briefly justify your choice of performance indicator and discuss MSC's performance relative to the other OSC service centres.** ⊞ 🖥   **(16 marks)**

(b)   **Explain how the standards and rewards blocks support the dimensions block in Fitzgerald and Moon's building block model.** 🖥   **(4 marks)**

(Total: 20 marks)

334   PUBLIC SECTOR ORGANISATION

A public sector organisation is extending its budgetary control and responsibility accounting system to all departments. One such department concerned with public health and welfare is called 'Homecare'. The department consists of staff who visit elderly 'clients' in their homes to support them with their basic medical and welfare needs.

A monthly cost control report is to be sent to the department manager, a copy of which is also passed to a Director who controls a number of departments. In the system, which is still being refined, the budget was set by the Director and the manager had not been consulted over the budget or the use of the monthly control report.

Shown below is the first month's cost control report for the Homecare department:

Cost Control Report – Homecare Department

Month ending May 20X0

	Budget	Actual	(Overspend)/underspend
Visits	10,000	12,000	(2,000)

	Budget ($)	Actual ($)	$
Department expenses:			
Supervisory salary	2,000	2,125	(125)
Wages (Permanent staff)	2,700	2,400	300
Wages (Casual staff)	1,500	2,500	(1,000)
Office equipment depreciation	500	750	(250)
Repairs to equipment	200	20	180
Travel expenses	1,500	1,800	(300)
Consumables	4,000	6,000	(2,000)
Administration and telephone	1,000	1,200	(200)
Allocated administrative costs	2,000	3,000	(1,000)
	15,400	19,795	(4,395)

In addition to the manager and permanent members of staff, appropriately qualified casual staff are appointed on a week to week basis to cope with fluctuations in demand. Staff use their own transport, and travel expenses are reimbursed. There is a central administration overhead charge over all departments. Consumables consist of materials which are used by staff to care for clients. Administration and telephone are costs of keeping in touch with the staff who often operate from their own homes.

As a result of the report, the Director sent a memo to the manager of the Homecare department pointing out that the department must spend within its funding allocation and that any spending more than 5% above budget on any item would not be tolerated. The Director requested an immediate explanation for the serious overspend.

You work as the assistant to the Directorate Management Accountant. On seeing the way the budget system was developing, they made a note of points they would wish to discuss and develop further, but they were called away before these could be completed.

Required:

Develop and explain the issues concerning the budgetary control and responsibility accounting system which are likely to be raised by the management accountant.

Note: Use the headings in the template provided below to structure your answer

The way the budget was prepared
The implications of a 20% increase in the number of visits

The extent of controllability of costs
The implications of the funding allocation
Social aspects and any other points you think are appropriate

You may include numerical illustrations and comment on specific costs, but you are not required to reproduce the cost control report. Calculations are worth up to 4 marks.

(Total: 20 marks)

335 WOODSIDE CHARITY (JUNE 2007)

Woodside is a local charity dedicated to helping homeless people in a large city. The charity owns and manages a shelter that provides free overnight accommodation for up to 30 people, offers free meals each and every night of the year to homeless people who are unable to buy food, and runs a free advice centre to help homeless people find suitable housing and gain financial aid. Woodside depends entirely on public donations to finance its activities and had a fundraising target for the last year of $700,000. The budget for the last year was based on the following forecast activity levels and expected costs.

Free meals provision: 18,250 meals at $5 per meal

Overnight shelter: 10,000 bed-nights at $30 per night

Advice centre: 3,000 sessions at $20 per session

Campaigning and advertising: $150,000

The budgeted surplus (budgeted fundraising target less budgeted costs) was expected to be used to meet any unexpected costs. Included in the above figures are fixed costs of $5 per night for providing shelter and $5 per advice session representing fixed costs expected to be incurred by administration and maintaining the shelter. The number of free meals provided and the number of beds occupied each night depends on both the weather and the season of the year. The Woodside charity has three full-time staff and a large number of voluntary helpers.

The actual costs for the last year were as follows:

Free meals provision:	20,000 meals at a variable cost of $104,000
Overnight shelter:	8,760 bed-nights at a variable cost of $223,380
Advice centre:	3,500 sessions at a variable cost of $61,600
Campaigning and advertising:	$165,000

The actual costs of the overnight shelter and the advice centre exclude the fixed costs of administration and maintenance, which were $83,000.

The actual amount of funds raised in the last year was $620,000.

Required:

(a) **Prepare an operating statement, reconciling budgeted surplus and actual shortfall and discuss the charity's performance over the last year.** ⊞ **(13 marks)**

(b) **Discuss problems that may arise in the financial management and control of a not-for-profit organisation such as the Woodside charity.** ⌨ **(7 marks)**

(Total: 20 marks)

336 ROBINHOLT UNIVERSITY (SEPT 2019)

Robinholt University is one of the largest and most popular universities in the country of Richpori. It had 27,000 registered students in 20X6, whereas in 20X5, the number of registered students was only 24,000. Robinholt University managed to increase its student numbers in 20X6 by making the entry requirements for students slightly lower than in previous years. All courses at the university last for three years.

Robinholt University has five strategic aims:

(1) To provide education which promotes intellectual initiative and produces confident and ambitious graduates who have reached the highest academic standards to prepare them for success in life and the workplace.

(2) To provide an organised, efficient learning environment with access to cutting edge technology and facilities.

(3) To be a leader in sustainable business practices which protect the environment and support local people.

(4) To provide attractive, innovative conference and event facilities, attracting clients both nationally and internationally.

(5) To be recognised both nationally and internationally for the scope and relevance of their research.

Extracts from the university's statement of profit or loss for the last two years are as follows:

	20X6 $ million	20X5 $ million
Income		
Tuition fees	148.0	135.6
Research grants	3.5	4.5
Conferences and other events	18.0	16.0
Total income	**169.5**	**156.1**
Expenditure		
Academic staff costs	80.8	76.2
Administration staff costs	50.4	48
Premises, facilities and technology costs	7.6	8.4
Event and conference costs	8.3	8.0
Research grants	3.1	4.0
Sustainability and community assistance	1.2	2.4
Total expenditure	**151.4**	**147.0**
Surplus	**18.1**	**9.1**

Every year, final year students complete an external survey run by the National Organisation for Students. In this, they have to agree or disagree with statements made. Extracts from this for the last two years are shown below (the percentage rates show the number of students who agreed with the statements made):

	20X6	20X5
Teaching		
(1) The course is intellectually stimulating and quality of teaching high	83%	86%
Academic support		
(2) I have received good advice and support with my studies from academic staff	82%	86%
Organisation and management		
(3) The course is well organised and its administration is good	81%	90%
Learning resources		
(4) The standard of rooms, facilities and equipment is good	83%	92%
Personal development		
(5) The course has helped me develop as a person	82%	80%
Overall satisfaction		
(6) Overall, I am satisfied with the quality of the course	81%	83%

The 'overall satisfaction' percentage is used by the Education Authority to set the maximum level of tuition fees that a university can charge each year and is seen as the main measure of success both internally and externally.

Other key information

	20X6	20X5
Students graduating with a First Class Honours degree (highest class attainable)	20%	28%
Employers happy with the graduates from Robinholt University	72%	75%
Ratio of students to staff members	40:1	35:1
Staff retention rate	75%	90%

The staff retention rate in 20X5 was consistent with previous years. Data gathered from students who graduated in 20X5 showed that 65% of students found a graduate job within one year of leaving compared to 68% of 20X4's graduates.

In 20X5, Robinholt University won the 'Green Environmental' award for their campuses, which all have extensive recycling facilities. Students were also involved in a local 'Grow to Give' food sharing project that year, which provided thousands of pounds worth of fresh produce to food banks offering food to poorer residents. Due to staff shortages, the university was not involved in this project in 20X6. The recycling bins have also been abandoned because of the cost of using them.

Every year, the University Research Council issues a range of prestigious awards for contributions to research. One of Robinholt University's main competitors in the area won an award in 20X5 for their contribution to some pioneering research on genetics. Robinholt University has yet to win an award for research. However, in 20X5 it did win an 'Innovation' award for its new, innovative conference facilities which have attracted a number of new clients in the last year.

Required:

Using Robinholt University's five strategic aims, assess its performance for 20X6. 🖥 ▦

Note: There are 4 marks available for calculations and 16 marks for discussion. Use the headings in the template provided below to structure your answer.

(1)	To provide education which promotes intellectual initiative and produces confident and ambitious graduates who have reached the highest academic standards to prepare them for success in life and the workplace
(2)	To provide an organised, efficient learning environment with access to cutting edge technology and facilities
(3)	To be a leader in sustainable business practices which protect the environment and support local people
(4)	To provide attractive, innovative conference and event facilities, attracting clients both nationally and internationally
(5)	To be recognised both nationally and internationally for the scope and relevance of their research
Overall satisfaction	

(Total: 20 marks)

337 TONFORD SCHOOL (SEPTEMBER/DECEMBER 2020)

All schools in the country of Ducland are funded by the state and are accountable to the Department of Education (DoE) which oversees educational standards and monitors performance of the schools.

The DoE's objectives, which are also the objectives for all the schools in Ducland, are to:

1   Strive for continuous improvement in performance standards

2   Provide a supportive learning environment, which encourages a high standard of pupil achievement

3   Ensure pupils are prepared for adult life and have the skills and character necessary to contribute to society and the economy

4   Provide all children with access to high quality education, regardless of their location or background.

Summary performance data for each school is accessible via the DoE's website. Parents in Ducland have the right to choose which school their child should attend and many parents use the performance data to help with their selection.

Inspectors from the DoE visit each school in Ducland at the end of every five years. The DoE believes that to gain a better insight into the quality of the teaching and learning environment, inspectors should attend a selection of lessons and speak to some of the pupils.

Tonford School has recently had its inspection visit, and the school's data entry on the DoE's website has been updated following that visit. The revised entry is shown below:

Performance factor	Notes	Tonford School actual (20X7)	National target (20X7)	Tonford School actual (20X2)
Exam results	1	62%	65%	64%
Pupil progress	2	0.4	0.25	0.3
Inspection grade	3, 4	Very Good	Good	Good
Pupil numbers	–	662	n/a	627
Number of teaching staff	5	35	n/a	33

Notes:

(1) The 'exam results' indicator shows the percentage of pupils leaving school with at least five final exams including compulsory subjects of mathematics, science and languages at Grade A-C (the top three grades).

(2) 'Pupil progress' is an indicator of how well pupils have performed in compulsory subjects in their final exams at age 16 compared to their performance in intermediate exams at age 11.

(3) Academic grades are given numerical values, and the 'pupil progress' score is the movement in the average of pupils' grades. Scores typically range between −0.5 and +0.5.

(4) There are six inspection grades: excellent; very good; good; average; poor and very poor.

(5) The inspector's summary report for Tonford School concluded: "There is a very strong sense of community values and citizenship. Pupils appear to have a genuine respect for their teachers, and for one another, despite their diverse backgrounds."

(6) The DoE recommends that the pupil/teacher ratio should be less than 22:1.

Required:

(a) **Explain the problems which not-for-profit organisations face as a result of having multiple objectives.** 🖳   **(4 marks)**

(b) **Assess Tonford School's performance against the objectives set by the DoE, using the performance data published on the DoE's website.** 🖳   **(12 marks)**

Note: Use the four objectives in the template provided below to structure your answer.

Objective 1 – Strive for continuous improvement in performance standards.
Objective 2 – Provide a supportive learning environment, which encourages a high standard of pupil achievement.
Objective 3 – Ensure pupils are prepared for adult life and have the skills and character necessary to contribute to society and the economy.
Objective 4 – Provide all children with access to high quality education, regardless of their location or background.

(c)   Explain the difficulties in assessing performance of schools in Ducland due to the qualitative nature of their objectives. 🖥   **(4 marks)**

(Total: 20 marks)

338 MOBE (JUNE 2015 ADAPTED)

Mobe Co manufactures electronic mobility scooters. The company is split into two divisions: the scooter division (Division S) and the motor division (Division M). Division M supplies electronic motors to both Division S and to external customers. The two divisions run as autonomously as possible, subject to the group's current policy that Division M must make internal sales first before selling outside the group; and that Division S must always buy its motors from Division M. However, this company policy, together with the transfer price which Division M charges Division S, is currently under review.

Details of the two divisions are given below.

Division S

Division S's budget for the coming year shows that 35,000 electronic motors will be needed. An external supplier could supply these to Division S for $800 each.

Division M

Division M has the capacity to produce a total of 60,000 electronic motors per year. Details of Division M's budget which has just been prepared for the forthcoming year, are as follows:

Budgeted sales volumes (units)	60,000
Selling price per unit for external sales of motors	$850
Variable cost per unit for external sales of motors	$770

The variable cost per unit for motors sold to Division S is $30 per unit lower due to cost savings on distribution and packaging.

Maximum external demand for the motors is 30,000 units per year.

Required:

(a) Assuming that the group's current policy could be changed, advise, using suitable calculations, the number of motors which Division M should supply to Division S in order to maximise group profits. Recommend the transfer price or prices at which these internal sales should take place. 🖳 **(10 marks)**

Note: All relevant workings must be shown

(b) Each of Mobe's divisions is managed by a divisional manager who has the power to make all investment decisions within the division. The cost of capital for both divisions is 12%. Historically, investment decisions have been made by calculating the return on investment (ROI) of any opportunities and at present, the return on investment of each division is 16%.

A new manager who has recently been appointed in division S has argued that using residual income to make investment decisions would result in 'better goal congruence' throughout the company.

Each division is currently considering the following separate investments:

	Division S	Division M
Capital required for investment	$82,800	$40,600
Sales generated by investment	$44,600	$21,800
Net profit margin	28%	33%

Required:

(i) Calculate the return on investment for each of the two divisions. ▦ (2 marks)

(ii) Calculate the residual income for each of the two divisions. ▦ (4 marks)

(iii) Comment on the results, taking into consideration the managers views about residual income. 🖳 (4 marks)

(Total: 20 marks)

339 FLAG CO (DECEMBER 2021)

The country of Jayland has two airlines, Flag Co, its national airline, and Budget Co, a recent entrant into the market.

Flag Co

Flag Co was government owned until ten years ago but is now operated as a private company. Its mission is 'to be the airline of choice for long distance travellers'. It charges premium fares and operates routes from Jayland's capital city to the major airports serving the largest cities around the world. Many of its flights have durations greater than 12 hours The majority of its passengers are travelling on business and are prepared to pay high prices, however the demand for business travel is very sensitive to economic conditions. Its fleet of aircraft is regarded as 'ageing' by industry analysts.

Budget Co

Budget Co was founded by a wealthy entrepreneur who invested their personal fortune in the company's equity. Its mission is 'to be the lowest fare airline on any route we serve'. It offers flights to destinations up to three hours travel from Jayland. Its fleet of aircraft are generally less than two years old. Most of its passengers are holiday-makers and the demand for its flights appears to be relatively insensitive to economic conditions.

The following information is available for both companies:

Statement of profit or loss extract for the year end 31 December 20X6	Flag Co	Budget Co
	$m	$m
Total revenue	11,333	6,654
Operating profit	1,239	404
Finance costs	250	50
Other non-operating costs	130	76
Profit before tax	**859**	**278**

Statement of financial position (summarised) for the year end 31 December 20X6	Flag Co	Budget Co
	$m	$m
Non-current assets	11,972	3,177
Current assets **(Note 1)**	3,404	885
Total assets	**15,376**	**4,062**
Total equity	4,598	1,945
Non-current liabilities	5,078	1,001
Current liabilities	5,700	1,116
Total liabilities and shareholders' equity	**15,376**	**4,062**

Note 1: Current assets include inventory of $2.1m and $1.1m respectively.

Other information for year end 31 December 20X6	Flag Co	Budget Co
Aviation fuel litres consumed (millions)	2,434	1,246
Available seat kilometres (millions)	21,423	14,953
Passenger seat kilometres (millions)	14,201	14,206
Operating gearing (contribution/profit before interest and tax)	950%	820%

Required:

(a) **Analyse the financial performance of the two airlines, including reasons for the differences in the two businesses' performance.** 🖥 **(14 marks)**

Note: Use the headings profitability, liquidity and risk to structure your answer. There are up to six marks available for calculations.

(b) **Briefly explain how Fitzgerald and Moon's building block model could be used to manage the performance of a service business.** 🖥 **(6 marks)**

(Total: 20 marks)

Section 4

ANSWERS TO OBJECTIVE TEST QUESTIONS – SECTION A

INFORMATION, TECHNOLOGIES AND SYSTEMS FOR ORGANISATIONAL PERFORMANCE

MANAGING INFORMATION

1   The second and third statements are correct.

A lack of compatibility with existing or other systems is a typical risk or disadvantage of new information system investments. Increased training for staff to become familiar with the system is also considered a disadvantage of a new information system.

2   **B**

An extranet can limit both the amount of information available and the users who have access to it. Giving access to an intranet would open access to more information than the airline would desire to give access to. The internet is more commonly used to give public information to everyone. Emails are unlikely to provide real time information.

3   **A**

A memory stick is much more likely to get mislaid and compromise security than a password protected laptop. It is likely that memory sticks could get lost or that information is left on home computers.

In the context of the scenario all the other options are good practice.

4   **C**

The other statements are not true. Robust security procedures (such as strong passwords) can limit access to a wireless network. Wireless networks can often cover larger distances than wired networks (for example, nurses are likely to be able to access data in rooms where there are no wired access points). There will be no requirement to buy new user devices (although many businesses who switch to wireless technology choose to do so); existing user devices should work with both wired and wireless technology.

But wireless networks can be prone to interference from other devices and networks which can result in them being less stable than wired networks.

5   D

A universal password would apply to everyone and therefore there would be no way to trace the person responsible for printing/transferring or amending the information.

The other three options are common methods for securing the confidentiality of information.

SOURCES OF INFORMATION

6

	Internal	External
Interviewing potential customers		✓
Reading business magazines		✓
Listing employee records from the company's payroll system	✓	
Looking through sales records for the last year	✓	

7

	Internal	External
Number of people clicking on the 'Coming soon' link on the company's website	✓	
How likely one of our customers is to recommend our business to a friend or colleague	✓	
Share prices of different competitors over time		✓
Average household income in Mumbai in 20X0		✓

8   B

(i) is not correct: External information is not usually more reliable than internal information and its sources are usually more difficult to check.

Internal information is produced by the company itself, so managers are aware of limitations in its quality or reliability, whereas this is more difficult to ascertain when dealing with external information.

9   C

Information about machine breakdowns and lost production is most likely to be found in production output reports. The non-current asset register only lists non-current assets, the machine maintenance schedule would not necessarily detail lost production and neither would the purchase ledger account for the supplier that provides replacement machine parts.

10   C

I and II are direct costs of producing and implementing the survey.

11   D

The government figures for RPI or CPI are most reliably to be found in CPI/RPI reports.

12   B

'Acceptable' is not part of the ACCURATE mnemonic.

13   C

The increase in costs is less than $3,700. It is unlikely that cost of preparing the report would be beneficial even if all of the increase was due to increased printing of emails.

14   C

Summarised information is characteristic of strategic reports, as is external information on local competition. Operational reports are likely to be produced frequently (sometimes daily) and contain accurate information on a business' current position.

INFORMATION SYSTEMS AND DATA ANALYTICS

15   C

Strategic reports typically display highly summarised showing overall trends, with options to 'drill down' to obtain detail.

16   B

Statement (1) is not true: strategic planning is concerned with making decisions about the efficient and effective use of future (as well as existing) resources.

17   A

Long-term forecasts are usually associated with strategic planning.

18

	Suited to all levels of management	Not suited to all levels of management
A Management Information System producing management accounts showing margins for individual customers	✓	
An Expert System holding specialist tax information	✓	
An Executive Information System giving access to internal and external information in summarised form, with the option to drill down to a greater level of activity		✓

EIS systems are usually suited to Senior Executives and strategic planning.

19   D

The tracking and summarising of critical strategic information is done by an Executive Information System (EIS).

The other three options are all likely to be potential benefits which would result from the introduction of an ERPS.

20   D

An Expert Systems (ES) emulates the decision-making ability of a human expert, a tax specialist for example. Tax advice software is a classic example of an Expert System installation.

21   B

The report is a typical example of an output from a Management Information System.

22   D

A tax calculator is a typical example of an expert system.

23   D

The first three options are typical characteristics of big data. Vicinity is not normally a word that would be associated with big data.

24   The second and third statements are correct

One of the 'V's' of big data is its velocity – it is created and can change very quickly. Another 'V' is its variety which suggests that it can take multiple forms.

Statement 1 is not correct. Another 'V' that is associated with big data is its veracity – it is often difficult to assess its reliability and accuracy and there is no reason why it should be considered more reliable than other sources of data.

Statement 4 is not correct. Big data does not simply refer to financial numbers nor do the numbers themselves have to be big.

25   D

If organisations analyse big data they can often better understand areas such as customer tastes, potential changes in the market or potential problems in supply chains. If this data is used accurately it can allow the organisation to react in quicker and better ways than rivals and to achieve a competitive advantage.

Option A is not correct. Big data can be useful for any size of organisations. Even the smallest of organisations, can analyse, say, the data contained on their social media feeds.

Options B and C are not correct. Big data refers to any unstructured data, not just data stored or contained on the internet. Many organisations find that they already hold lots of data on customers but it just hasn't been structured yet. This also explains why the data may have been generated internally.

26   A

Using big data allow organisations to react more quickly than rivals in the marketplace giving them a competitive edge. This can be achieved by better tracking of consumer trends as well as the actions of competitors themselves. The actions and changes of competitors can be accounted for by examining data on rivals such as their public announcements and market expectations.

27   The second and third statements are correct

Statement 1 is not correct. One of the criticisms in analysing big data is that it still requires interpretation. This is only of value to the organisation if the analyst also has a deep understanding of the industry.

Statement 4 is not correct. Firstly, analysing all available big data would be almost impossible and certainly very expensive. But it is not all likely to be of use to an organisation. For example, a small accountancy practice would gain little benefit in analysing big data on the potential benefits of future space travel.

28   B

Big data should be used alongside traditional sources of data to make business decisions. There is no reason for traditional sources of data such as economic data, sales trends etc. to be ignored.

The other statements are risks of using big data analytics in making business decisions.

SPECIALIST COST AND MANAGEMENT ACCOUNTING TECHNIQUES

ACTIVITY-BASED COSTING

29   The final two statements are correct.

Modern manufacturing processes tend to be more flexible than traditional systems and have become less rigid. There is also greater levels of employee participation.

The other options are common features of a modern manufacturing environment.

30   The third and fourth statements are correct.

ABC does not affect the prime cost of products. It will however give better details on indirect costs which will be shared between products on a fairer basis (thus impacting on the total production cost of each product and potentially the selling price of each product). This is also likely to make cost control of indirect overheads easier.

31 $71.43

Alpha batches (2,500/500) = 5; therefore inspections required for Alpha (5 × 4) = 20

Zeta batches (8,000/1,000) = 8; therefore inspections required for Zeta (8 × 1) = 8

OAR = $250,000/28 = $8,928.57

Alpha cost/unit = (20 × $8,928.57)/2,500 units = $71.43

32   D

Statement (1) provides a definition of a cost driver. Cost drivers for long-term variable overhead costs will be the volume of a particular activity to which the cost driver relates, so Statement (2) is correct.

Statement (3) is also correct. In traditional absorption costing, standard high-volume products receive a higher amount of overhead costs than with ABC. ABC allows for the unusually high costs of support activities for low-volume products (such as relatively higher set-up costs, order processing costs and so on).

33 $0.50

Cost driver = number of set-ups   Cost pool = $12,000

Total set-ups = 20 (for A) + 4 (for B) = 24   Rate = $12,000/24 = $500 per set-up

Cost for A = $500 × 20 set-ups = $10,000   Per unit=$10,000/20,000 = $0.50

34   A

Statement (2) is not correct. Although the OAR is calculated in the same way as the absorption costing OAR, a separate OAR will be calculated for each cost pool.

35 $0.60

Cost driver = number of set-ups

Cost pool = $84,000

Total set-ups= 20 (for A) + 8 (for B) = 28

Rate =$84,000/28 = 5 $3,000 per set-up

Cost for B = $3,000 × 8 set-ups = $24,000

Per unit = $24,000/40,000 = $0.60.

36 $31.82

$$\text{Overhead absorption rate} = \frac{\text{Total overhead cost}}{\text{Total number of direct labour hours}}$$

$$\text{Overhead absorption rate} = \frac{\$420,000}{66,000 \text{ Direct labour hours}}$$

Overhead absorption rate = $6.36 per labour hour. Alpha uses 5 direct labour hours per unit so will have an overhead cost per unit of 5 hours × $6.36 per hour = $31.82.

37   C

The overhead cost per unit for each unit of product Beta will be the same as product Alpha (see calculations in Q36 above), as both products use the same number of labour hours (5 hours).

38   C

	Volume related	Purchasing related	Set-up related
Costs	$100,000	$145,000	$175,000
Consumption of activities (cost drivers)	66,000 labour hours	160 purchase orders	100 set-ups
Cost per unit of cost driver	$1.5151 per labour hour	$906.25 per purchase order	$1,750 per set-up
Costs per product			
Product Alpha:	6,000 labour hours cost: $9,090.91	75 purchase orders cost: $67,968.75	40 set-ups cost: $70,000
Product Beta:	60,000 labour hours cost: $90,909.09	85 purchase orders cost: $77,031.25	60 set-up cost: $105,000

Total overhead cost for Alpha = $9,090.91 + $67,968.75 + $70,000 = $147,060. Spread over 1,200 units, this represents a cost per unit of $122.55 approx

39   B

Total material budget ((1,000 units × $10) + (2,000 units × $20)) = $50,000 Fixed costs related to material handling = $100,000

OAR = $2/$ of material

Product B = $2 × $20 = $40

Total labour budget ((1,000 units × $5) + (2,000 units × $20) = $45,000 General fixed costs = $180,000

OAR = $4/$ of labour

Product B = $4 × $20 = $80

Total fixed overhead cost per unit of Product B ($40 + $80) = $120.

40   Increase, Increase, Decrease

	Increase	Decrease
Product X	✓	
Product Y	✓	
Product Z		✓

Absorption costing

Since the time per unit is the same for each product, the overheads per unit will also be the same.

$156,000 ÷ 6,000 units = $26

Activity based costing

Number of deliveries for X (1,000/200)	5
Number of deliveries for Y (2,000/400)	5
Number of deliveries for Z (3,000/1,000)	3
Total	**13**

Cost per delivery = $156,000/13 = $12,000

Cost per unit of X = ($12,000/1,000 units) × 5 deliveries = $60

Increase = $60 – $26 = $34.

Cost per unit of Y = ($12,000/2,000 units) × 5 deliveries = $30

Increase = $30 – $26 = $4.

Cost per unit of Z = ($12,000/3,000 units) × 3 deliveries = $12

Decrease = $26 – $12 = $14.

41   B

Total set-ups = Budget production/batch size × set-ups per batch

D (100,000/100 × 3)	3,000
R (100,000/50 × 4)	8,000
P (50,000/25 × 6)	12,000
	23,000

Cost per set-up = $150,000/23,000 = $6.52

Therefore cost per unit of R = $6.52 × 8,000 set-ups/100,000 units = $0.52.

TARGET COSTING

Tutorial note

A technical article 'Target Costing and Lifecycle Costing' has been published on the ACCA website – make sure you read it as part of your revision.

42   D

Answer A is not correct: increasing the selling price is not possible, the industry is competitive so product will not sell effectively at higher prices.

Answer B ('Reduce the expectation gap by reducing the selling price') is not target costing.

Answer C ('Reducing the desired margin on the product') is not possible either: shareholders are demanding and would expect a good return.

43   C

To reduce the acceptable margin would normally require agreement from the owners and altering selling prices in any direction is not valid as the start point of target costing is to find a competing product's price, this cannot be changed.

44 The maximum rate per hour is **$12.40**

	$
Selling price	56.00
Profit (56 × 25/125)	11.20
Target cost	**44.80**
Material cost (16 × 10/8)	20.00
Labour – 2 hours	24.80
Labour rate per hour = 24.80/2	$12.40

45 B

Variance analysis is not relevant to target costing as it is a technique used for cost control at the production phase of the product life cycle. It is a feedback control tool by nature and target costing is feedforward.

Value analysis can be used to identify where small cost reductions can be applied to close a cost gap once production commences.

Functional analysis can be used at the product design stage. It ensures that a cost gap is reached or to ensure that the product design is one which includes only features which customers want.

Activity analysis identifies and describes activities in an organisation and evaluates their impact on operations to assess where improvements can be made.

46 D

Sales revenue 500 units @ $250	$125,000
Return on investment required 15% × $250,000	$37,500
Total cost allowed	$87.500
Target cost per unit	$175

47 D

It is simultaneous as there is no delay between the service being provided by the optician and consumed by the patient.

LIFE-CYCLE COSTING

48 C

Variable production costs ($2.30 × 2,000) + ($1.80 × 5,000) + ($1.20 × 7,000) = $22,000

Variable selling costs ($0.50 × 2,000) + ($0.40 × 5,000) + ($0.40 × 7,000) = $5,800

Fixed production costs = $10,500; Fixed selling costs = $4,700

Administrative costs = $2,100

Total costs = $45,100

Cost per unit = $45,100/14,000 units = $3.22

49   C

OAR for fixed production overheads ($72 million/96 million hours) = $0.75 per hour

Total manufacturing costs (300,000 units × $20) = $6,000,000

Total design, depreciation and decommissioning costs = $1,320,000

Total fixed production overheads (300,000 units × 4 hours × $0.75) = $900,000

Total life-cycle costs = $8,220,000 and life-cycle cost per unit ($8,220,000/300,000 units) = $27.40

50   D

51   Benefits are:

- It provides a true financial cost of a product
- Expensive errors can be avoided in that potentially failing products can be avoided
- Lower costs can be achieved earlier by designing out costs
- Better selling prices can be set.

Note: Shortening the length of a lifecycle is not desirable and decline (for most products) inevitable.

52   A

(1)   This is true, justifying the time and effort of life cycle costing.

(2)   As above.

(3)   This is not true: life cycle costing is not about setting selling prices, it is about linking total revenues to total costs. Even if it were about setting a selling price, the early sales may well be at a loss since it is TOTAL revenues and costs that are considered. Furthermore, the pre-launch costs are sunk at launch and are therefore irrelevant when setting a selling price.

(4)   This is true. The deliberate attempt to maximise profitability is the key to life cycle costing.

53   B

54   A

The original life cycle cost per unit = ($43,000 + (20,000 × $15) + $30,000)/20,000 = $18.65

THROUGHPUT ACCOUNTING

55   C

Overall the cost per unit should reduce, and so the measure for throughput should improve.

A is wrong as the TPAR measures return based on the slowest machine not the fastest. B is wrong since rent has increased so the TPAR will worsen from its current level. D is wrong since we cannot meet demand even at the moment so reducing prices will reduce throughput per unit without any extra sales level benefit.

56

	Product X	Product Y	Product Z
Throughput per unit (selling price – direct material cost)	$20	$30	$1
Machine hours per unit	10	20	2.5
Return per hour (throughput per unit ÷ machine hours per unit)	**$2**	**$1.5**	**$1.6**

As all three products are mutually exclusive, the company would choose to make X as it has the highest throughput return per hour of $2.

Changes to the selling price and material cost of Product X and Product Z will only change the TPAR if the values change enough to mean that the company would prefer to make that product instead of product X. This means the products' return per hour after the changes would need to be more than $2 per hour.

Option 1: return per hour = ($22–$16)/2.5 = $2.4. This would improve the company's TA ratio as now Z would be made instead of X and the TPAR would be higher.

Option 2: return per hour = ($44–$10)/20 = $1.7. This would not improve the company's TA ratio.

Option 3: return per hour = ($20–$15.2)/2.5 = $1.92. This would not improve the company's TA ratio.

Option 4: return per hour = (40–9.5)/20 = $1.525. This would not improve the company's TA ratio.

Of the four possible options, only increasing the selling price of product Z by 10% would give a higher throughput return per hour of $2.40.

	Would improve the company's existing TA ratio?	Would NOT improve the company's existing TA ratio?
Increase the selling price of product Z by 10%	✓	
Increase the selling price of product Y by 10%		✓
Reduce the material cost of product Z by 5%		✓
Reduce the material cost of product Y by 5%		✓

57 $60.00

The first step is to identify the bottleneck.

Process P output is 6 × 8 × 0.9 = 43.2 per hour. Process Q output is 9 × 6 × 0.85 = 45.9 per hour. In the absence of other information, then process P is slower, and so is the bottleneck.

Cloud:

Throughput:	$
Selling price ($20 × 0.85)	17.00
Material cost	5.00
Throughput per unit	12.00
Time in process P (hrs)	0.2
TP per hour	60.00

58   D

As the products are all produced in the same factory the cost per machine hour will be the same across all the products so they can be ranked on their throughput return per machine hour (otherwise they should be ranked ion their throughput accounting ratio).

Product	Production rate per machine hour (units)	Throughput per unit (selling price – material cost) ($)	Throughput per machine hour ($)	Ranking of products
W	200	230	(200 × $230) = 46,000	3rd
X	500	95	(500 × $95) = 47,500	2nd
Y	400	110	(400 × $110) = 44,000	4th
Z	350	140	(350 × $140) = 49,000	1st

The products would be ranked in order: Z, X, W and Y. Product Y would be ranked forth (last).

59   A

Tutorial note

This question tested candidates' knowledge of throughput accounting, and specifically how throughput can be improved. It is also a good example of a question where it's important not to rush – all of the possible answers could improve throughput, depending on what our bottleneck (limiting factor) is – Process 1, 2 or 3. If none of the processes are limited, then increasing demand would improve throughput.

Throughput is determined by the bottleneck resource. Process 2 is the bottleneck as it has insufficient time to meet demand.

The only option to improve Process 2 is to improve the efficiency of the maintenance routine. All the other three options either increase the time available on non-bottleneck resources or increase demand for an increase in supply which cannot be achieved.

60   D

All of these points are true, except D.

Throughput accounting was designed as a performance measurement tool, not a decision-making tool.

One of its advantages is that it will be used by managers to make decisions that have outcomes that are goal congruent with corporate aims. However, it was designed as a performance measurement tool.

61   C

Answers B and D are the same: they are the correct ratio inverted.

Answer A is often referred to as the return per factory hour.

ENVIRONMENTAL ACCOUNTING

Tutorial note

A technical article 'Environmental Management Accounting' has been published on the ACCA website – make sure you read it as part of your revision.

62   B, H

Waste water has been produced which is a failure cost, but it has been cleaned **before** leaving the factory, making it an internal failure cost.

Likewise, waste exhaust gases have been produced, but these have been captured and recycled within the factory.

Environmental prevention costs relate to activities or measure which aim to avoid the pollution or wastage occurring. Insulation of heating pipes in the factory to reduce heat loss and fitting of carbon filters to machine processes to reduce carbon emissions would come under this heading.

Environmental detection costs relate to the costs incurred to test the levels of emissions and wastage to ensure that the organisation is being compliant with internal standards and external regulations. Quality control inspections to monitor pollution levels in water leaving a production process and power usage measuring system to monitor energy consumption within the factory would come under this heading.

External failure costs relate to pollution which has affected the outside environment. Payment of fines for breaching environmental regulations in the industry and public relations costs to remedy reputational damage caused by accidental river pollution would be examples of environmental external failure costs.

63 D

Revised tables:

INPUTS

Description	Comment	Weight (kg)	USD value
Materials		1,000	(50,000)
System costs	Labour, utilities, etc	–	(35,000)
Total			(85,000)

OUTPUTS

Description	Comment	Weight (kg)	USD value
Good output	Expected good output is 76% of input and can be sold for $120 per kg	760	91,200
Waste	Expected waste is 4% of input and must be scrapped at a cost of $10 per kg	40	(400)
Scrap	Expected scrap is 20% of input and can be sold for $15 per kg	200	3,000
Total		1,000	93,800

Revised profit = 93,800 – 85,000 = $8,800

This gives an increase of $2,800

Alternative answer

Impact on profit = extra revenue + cost savings + extra costs

= (60 × 120) + (60 × 10) – 5,000

= $2,800

64 D

Under a system of flow cost accounting material flows are divided into three categories – material, system, and delivery and disposal.

65 Only the first two statements are true.

66 $22,000

Input materials and system costs work out as $80 per kg.

This means that the total input costs to be allocated to waste and scrap = 300 × 80 = (24,000)

Overall net cost of waste and scrap = 3,000 – 1,000 – 24,000 = (22,000)

67 The first and third statements are true.

Manufacturing costs are categorised into material costs, system costs and delivery and disposal costs. After dividing material flows into three categories (material, system and delivery and disposal costs), flow cost accounting calculates the values and costs of each of these three flows. Output costs are allocated between positive products (good finished output) and negative product costs (costs of waste and emissions).

The second statement is not correct: this is a definition of the input/output analysis method of accounting for environmental costs.

The fourth statement is not correct: The aim of flow cost accounting is to reduce the quantity of materials which, as well as having a positive effect on the environment, should have a positive effect on a business' total costs in the long run.

68 **D**

69 **D**

Waste flows are not a category used within flow cost accounting, however, the other three categories are.

70 **B**

Environmental costs can be very long-term, are often not split out in accounting systems and may be hidden. All of this makes accounting for environmental costs difficult. The size of the costs should have no impact on the accountants ability to deal with the costs and is not a valid reason for the difficulties in dealing with environmental costs.

DECISION-MAKING TECHNIQUES

RELEVANT COST ANALYSIS

71 **B**

The original cost is an historic cost and therefore not relevant. There is no intention to replace material X. There are two options for material X, scrap at a value of 50p per kg or use as a replacement for material Y, which would save $4 per kg ($6 – $2). The latter is the preferable option so the relevant cost is $4 per kg for 10 kgs = $40.

72 **C**

Labour is in short supply so there is an opportunity cost. The contribution from Contract Z will still be earned but will be delayed. The relevant cost is therefore the wages earned plus the penalty fee.

($15 × 100) + ($1,000) = $2,500

73 **B**

The material is in regular use by the organisation and so would be replaced if it is used on the special order. The material is readily available at a price of $3.24 per kg.

Therefore the relevant cost of the material is 1,250 kgs × $3.24 = $4,050.

74   C

Since material J is in regular use and is readily available in the market, its relevant cost is the replacement price of $8/kg.

So 2,000 kgs × $8/kg = $16,000

75   A

3,700 kg × $3.80 + 500 kg × $6.30 = $17,210

Tutorial note

The company needs 4,200 kg. It has 3,700 kg in inventory. It will therefore need to buy 500 kg and these can be bought for $6.30 per kg. The tricky bit is the value to the company of the 3,700 kg in inventory. The $4.50 original price is of course a sunk cost and cannot be relevant. The inventory can be sold for $3.20 per kg, so this is its very minimum value.

The inventory is worth $3.20 per kg unless the company has an even better alternative – and there is a better alternative. The company can take the inventory and, by spending $3.70 per kg on it, can turn it into something worth $7.50 per kg. If something will be worth $7.50 if we spend $3.70 on it, then it is at present worth $3.80. This then is the value of the inventory to the company and to fulfil the contract the company will use 3,700 kg of inventory with a value of $3.80 per kg.

76   C

The relevant cash flow is:

Lost disposal proceeds (net)	$10,300
Additional costs of set up	$1,300
Total	$11,600

77   A

The relevant cash flow is:

Extra variable overheads: 450 hours × $4/hr	$1,800
Rent	$1,200
Total	$3,000

Fixed costs are not incremental and idle time would normally mean that the machines are not in use are so are not an incurred cost.

78   D

The options are:

Agency 600 × $9/hr =	$5,400
Internal transfer 600 × (7 + 3) =	$6,000
Hire new $1,200 + (600 × $6/hr)	$4,800

Cleverclogs would select the lower of the costs and so this is the relevant cash flow.

79   D

It could be argued that it is also a sunk cost but the better and more exact description is that it is a committed cost as the cash has not yet been actually paid over.

80   C

81   B

The book value is not relevant as it is a sunk cost. The relevant cost of the paper in inventory is the resale value as that is its next best use. The remaining material required must be bought at the replacement cost of $26.

100 reams @ $10	$1,000
150 reams @ $26	$3,900
	————
	$4,900
	————

COST VOLUME PROFIT ANALYSIS

82   B

Two units of Y and one unit of X would give total contribution of $18. Weighted average contribution per unit = $18/3 units = $6

Sales units to achieve target profit = ($90,000 + $45,000)/$6 = 22,500

83   B

Current breakeven point is: $640,000/40 =	16,000 units
New breakeven point is: $400,000/35 =	11,429 units
Change in level of breakeven is 16,000 – 11,429 =	4,571 units
Current contribution is: $60 – $20 =	$40
New contribution is $60 – $20 – $5 =	$35

Operating gearing reduces with less fixed costs in a business.

84   18,637 units

Number of units required to make target profit = fixed costs + target profit/contribution per unit of P1.

Fixed costs = ($1.2 × 10,000) + ($1 × 12,500) – $2,500 = $22,000.

Contribution per unit of P = $3.20 + $1.20 = $4.40.

($22,000 + $60,000)/$4.40 = 18,637 units rounded up.

85   C

Contribution: $5,000,000 – ($1,400,000 + $400,000) =	$3,200,000
For 20,000 units, that is a contribution of	$160 per unit
Fixed costs amount to $1,600,000 + $1,200,000 =	$2,800,000
BEP units = FC/Unit contribution i.e. $2,800,000/$160 =	17,500

86

Selling price per unit ($36/0.75) =	$48
Contribution per unit $48 – $36 =	$12
Fixed costs	$18,000
Therefore, breakeven point (units) is $18,000/$12 =	1,500

87   D

If budgeted sales increase to 40,000 units, then budgeted profit will increase by $100,000. This is because 10,000 more units will be sold at a contribution per unit of $10. The fixed costs would not be expected to change.

88   D

	Now	Revised
	$	$
Selling price	20	21.60
Variable cost	8	8.416
	12	13.184

Breakeven volume $79,104/$12 = 6,592

$79,104/$13,184 = 6,000

Decrease in breakeven volume = 592/6,592 × 100% = 9%

89   D

The breakeven revenue (BER) = Fixed costs/average CS ratio

BER = $1,400,000/0.2375 (W1) = $5,894,737

(W1)

	Product F $	Product G $	Total $
Budget revenue	6,000,000	2,000,000	8,000,000
Contribution	1,500,000	400,000	1,900,000
C/S	0.25	0.2	
Average C/S			0.2375

90 C

Because the C/S ratio of product G is lower than F the change in mix would reduce the average C/S ratio. As a consequence, the breakeven revenue would increase by an amount but not by the amount of extra sales of product G. This is not relevant.

91 A

The shaded area on the breakeven chart represents loss.

92 B

The fixed costs are at the point where the profit line meets the vertical axis.

93 B

Statement (1) is correct. The line which passes through the origin indicates the sales revenue at various levels of activity. At an activity level of 10,000 units, the sales revenue is $100,000, therefore the selling price is $10 per unit.

Statement (2) is incorrect. The sloping line which intercepts the vertical axis at $30,000 shows the total cost at various levels of activity. The total cost for 10,000 units is $80,000, from which we subtract the $30,000 fixed costs.

Statement (3) is correct. The fixed cost is the cost incurred at zero activity, and is shown as a horizontal line at $30,000.

Statement (4) is incorrect. The profit for 10,000 units is the difference between the sales value $100,000 and the total cost of $80,000, which amounts to $20,000.

94 The second and third statements '3,152 units of sales are required to achieve a profit of $100,000 next month' and 'Monthly fixed costs amount to $136,400' are correct.

Fixed overheads every month amount to $22 fixed overhead per unit × 6,200 units = $136,400

The key to calculating the breakeven point is to determine the contribution per unit.

Contribution per unit = sales price – variable costs

Contribution per unit = $199 – $54 – $50 – $20

Contribution per unit = $75

Breakeven point in units = (Fixed costs/contribution per unit)

Breakeven point in units = $136,400/$75

Breakeven point in units = 1,819 units (and so the first statement is not correct.)

To achieve a profit of $100,000 next month:

Units of sales required = (Fixed costs + target profit)/unit contribution

Units of sales required = ($136,400 + $100,000)/$75

Units of sales required = 3,152

$$\text{Margin of safety expressed as a \%} = \frac{\text{Budgeted sales} - \text{breakeven sales}}{\text{Budgeted sales}} \times 100$$

Margin of safety = (6,200 units – 1,819 units)/6,200 units = 71% (and so the fourth statement is not correct.)

95   The first two statements are correct: point A is the breakeven point if the company's products are sold in order of their C/S ratio, and point B is the breakeven point if the company's products are sold in the budgeted sales mix.

Statement 3 is not correct. Changing the product mix in favour of Product 3, that has a negative contribution and reduces the cumulative profit, would impact negatively on the overall c/s ratio.

Statement 4 is not correct: if all three products are produced, then the company can expect a profit (not revenue) of $350,000.

96   **58.3%**

The breakeven revenue is FC/CS = $1,600,000/0.4 =	$4,000,000
Budget revenue is FC × 6 = $1,600,000 × 6 =	$9,600,000
Margin of safety is = (9,600,000 – 4,000,000)/9,600,000 =	58.3%

LIMITING FACTORS

97   Should be produced, Should not be produced, Should not be produced, Should be produced

	Should be produced	Should not be produced
Product A	✓	
Product B		✓
Product C		✓
Product D	✓	

Product	A	B	C	D
Selling price per unit	$160	$214	$100	$140
Raw material costs	$24	$56	$22	$40
Direct labour cost at $11 per hour	$66	$88	$33	$22
Variable overhead cost	$24	$18	$24	$18
Contribution per unit	$46	$52	$21	$60
	——	——	——	——
Direct labour hours per unit	6	8	3	2
Contribution per labour hour	$7.67	$6.50	$7	$30
	——	——	——	——
Rank	2	4	3	1
Normal monthly hours (total units × hours per unit)	1,800	1,000	720	800

If the strike goes ahead, only 2,160 labour hours will be available. Therefore make all of Product D, then 1,360 hours' worth of Product A (2,160 – 800 hrs).

98   8,000

The optimal production plan will have to be determined by using a simultaneous equations technique.

If the unskilled labour function is multiplied by 3:

Skilled labour: $6X + 4Y \leq 62,000$

Unskilled labour: $6X + 15Y \leq 150,000$

Deducting one from the other, leaves:

$11Y = 88,000$

$Y = 8,000$

99   A

If the values for R and N are substituted into the constraints:

Labour required = $(3 \times 500) + (2 \times 400) = 2,300$ hours which is less than what is available so there is slack.

Machine time required = $(0.5 \times 500) + (0.4 \times 400) = 410$ hours which is exactly what is available and so there is no slack.

100   D

The company maximises contribution by producing Qutwo. Contribution per unit of material is:

$$\frac{\$8.50}{2.5 \text{ kg}} = \$3.40 \text{ and this is the shadow price.}$$

101   C

A shadow price for a scarce resource is its opportunity cost. It is the amount of contribution that would be lost if one unit less of that resource were available. It is similarly the amount of additional contribution that would be earned if one unit more of that resource were available. (This is on the assumption that the scarce resource is available at its normal variable cost.)

102   D

	R	S	T
	$	$	$
Contribution per unit			
$(100 – 15 – 20 – 15)$	50		
$(150 – 30 – 35 – 20)$		65	
$(160 – 25 – 30 – 22)$			83
Direct labour cost per unit	20	35	30
Contribution per $1 of direct labour	2.50	1.85	2.77
Profitability ranking	2nd	3rd	1st

103 B

By definition, a shadow price is the amount by which contribution will increase if an extra kg of material becomes available. 20 × $2.80 = $56.

Tutorial note

In this question, the shadow price is $2.80 per unit, and therefore if 20 kgs of additional material Z becomes available, the increase in contribution would be $56 (20 × $2.80). The answer is therefore B. In the first distractor A, the cost of the material (20 kg × $2) has also been added to the $56. This is because a common mistake made is to add the cost of the material in too.

Similarly, in distractor C, the $40 has been deducted from the $56 leaving a figure of $16. This is because candidates often fail to realise that the shadow price is the amount over and above the normal cost that one would be prepared to pay for an extra unit of scarce material if it becomes available. Therefore, this would lead candidates to think that contribution would only increase by $0.80 ($2.80 − $2) for each extra kg of material Z that becomes available resulting in a total increase in contribution of only $16.

104 A

The slope of the iso-contribution line will be determined by the relative contribution per unit of each product. If it is very flat, the product on the vertical axis must have a higher contribution than the product on the horizontal axis.

105 The first statement is not true: linear programming is only suitable when there are two products.

The second statement is not true: : there needs to be more than one limiting factor, but it is not essential for one of these two to be the level of demand.

The third statement is correct: fixed costs do not change and do not need to be considered.

The fourth statement is correct: a steady state being reached means that variable costs are constant.

106 C

The optimal production plan will have to be determined by using a simultaneous equations technique.

If the Material X function is multiplied by 2:

Material X: 2A + 4B = 16,000

Material Y: 2A + B = 13,000

Deducting one from the other, leaves:

3B = 3,000

B = 1,000

Substituting this into one of the equations:

2A + (4 × 1,000) = 16,000

2A = 12,000

A = 6,000

107 60

If all of the resources have less than or equal to constraints then the feasible region cannot exceed the lowest of the lines on the diagram. This means that the maximum number of units of Product B that can be produced can be no higher than where this line meets the vertical axis which is at 60 units.

108 Only direct labour hours will have a shadow price.

Only resources that meet at the optimal point will have a shadow price. This is at point B, where the direct labour line meets line R. The other constraints lines are above this point and there therefore must be surplus of these resources available. Resources that have a surplus do not have a shadow price.

PRICING DECISIONS

109 C

Not all discrimination is illegal (e.g. the cost of rail travel at peak times). Early adopters normally pay more and maximising sales volume normally means a lower profit.

110 D

Penetration pricing involves setting a low price when a product is first launched in order to obtain strong demand.

It is particularly useful if significant economies of scale can be achieved from a high volume of output and if demand is highly elastic and so would respond well to low prices.

111 C

112 The second and third options are valid. If demand is inelastic or the product life cycle is short, a price skimming approach would be more appropriate.

113 B

114 B

From the formula provided, we can see a = 1,500 and b = –0.01

At the profit maximising point, MR = MC, where MR = a + 2bQ

MR = $1,500 – 0.02Q

MC = $200

Set MR = MC in order to maximise profit, and find profit maximising quantity:

1,500 – 0.02Q = 200

0.02Q = 1,300

Q = 65,000 units

Substitute Q = 65,000 in to the demand equation to find profit maximising price:

P = $1,500 – (0.01 × 65,000)

P = $850

Finally work out the maximum profit:

	$
Revenue ($850 × 65,000)	55,250,000
Variable costs ($200 × 65,000)	(13,000,000)
Fixed costs	(20,000,000)
Maximum total profit	**22,250,000**

115 C

Prime cost + 80% = 12 × (1.8) = $21.6

MC + 60% = 15 × (1.6) = $24.00

TAC + 20% = 21 × (1.2) = $25.20

Net margin would mean 21 × 100/86 = $24.40

116 C

b = –20/1,000 or –0.02

By substitution:

400 = a – 0.02 (5,000)

a = $500

MR = $500 – 0.04Q

MC = $200

Set MR = MC in order to profit maximise thus:

500 – 0.04Q = 200

–0.04 Q = – 300

Q = 7,500

Substitute Q = 7,500 in to the demand equation thus:

P = $500 – 0.02 (7,500)

P = $350

117 The correct options are price skimming, complimentary product pricing and price discrimination. Without brand loyalty or a long shelf life then a strategy of penetration is unlikely to work. Additionally the uniqueness of the product prevents low prices.

118 B

The demand formula is P = a + bQ, with   b = change of price/change of demand quantity

b = –20/500 = –0.04

By substitution:

400 = a –0.04 (5,000)

400 = a – 200

a = 600

Hence: P = 600 – 0.04Q

119 $340

The demand formula is P = a + bQ, with   b = change of price/change of demand quantity

b = –20/500 = –0.04

By substitution:

400 = a –0.04 (5,000)

400 = a – 200

a = 600

Hence: P = 600 – 0.04Q

MR = 600 – 0.08Q

MC = 80

For profit maximisation MR = MC

600 – 0.08Q = 80

Q = –520/–0.08 = 6,500

Again by substitution:

P = 600 – 0.04 (6,500) so P = $340

MAKE-OR-BUY AND OTHER SHORT-TERM DECISIONS

120 The correct items are:

- The variable costs of purchase from the new supplier

- The level of discount available from the new supplier

- The redundancy payments to the supervisor of the product in question

- The materials no longer bought to manufacture the product

121 $4,475

Material A:

Stock – saved disposal costs =	($400)
Bought 300 kg @ $6.25/kg =	1,875
Net cost	$1,475

Material B

Regularly used so replacement cost needed

800 kg @ $3.75/kg	$3,000
Total	$4,475

122 $200

The supervisor is a sunk cost.

123 The correct factors to include are:

> - The market outlook in the long term looks very poor
> - The business also sells pens and many diary buyers will often also buy a pen

The following were NOT to be included:

- The diaries made a loss in the year just passed is a sunk event

- The diaries made a positive contribution in the year just passed is a sunk event

- The budget for next year shows a loss includes fixed costs and these are not relevant

- The business was founded to produce and sell diaries – things change!

124 Before further processing, the sales value of X (10,000 units × $1.20) = $12,000

After further processing:

Sales value of Z (8,000 units × $2.25) = $18,000

Further processing costs ((10,000 units of X × $0.50) + $1,600) = $6,600

This gives a net return of $11,400 which is **$600 less** than the sales value of X.

125 D

Tutorial note

If we manufacture internally, we will incur labour costs of $4.00. Internal manufacture means we couldn't use our labour hours to make 'another item' that would bring us $10 contribution, but that takes twice as long to make as it incurs labour costs of $8.00.

So, this $10 per unit is the 'contribution foregone' but the contribution foregone per labour hour is $10/2 = $5.00. This is part of the relevant cost of manufacturing internally, to which we must add the cost of labour of $4 in our calculations.

	$
Direct material	3.00
Direct labour (W1)	9.00
Variable overhead	1.00
Specific fixed cost	2.50
	15.50

(W1) Relevant cost = Contribution Forgone + Direct labour = $10/2 + $4 = $9

DEALING WITH RISK AND UNCERTAINTY IN DECISION-MAKING

126 A pessimistic buyer would seek to achieve the best results if the worst happens. They would adopt the maximin approach, which involves selecting the alternative that maximises the minimum payoff achievable. The minimum payoffs for each truck are as follows:

Truck A – Minimum $1,400

Truck B – Minimum $1,800

Truck C – Minimum $3,600

Therefore, the 'C' series truck would be chosen.

127 'A' series

This maximises the average daily contribution if the growth rate is forty per cent.

128 'C'

Regret table		Type of truck		
		A Series	**B Series**	**C Series**
		$	$	$
Growth rate	15%	1,200	1,800	0
	30%	3,100	2,600	0
	40%	0	2,100	1,000
Max Regret		3,100	2,600	1,000

129 'C'

Expected value calculations:

A Series: ($2,400 × 0.4) + ($1,400 × 0.25) + ($4,900 × 0.35) = $3,025

B Series: ($1,800 × 0.4) + ($1,900 × 0.25) + ($2,800 × 0.35) = $2,175

C Series: ($3,600 × 0.4) + ($4,500 × 0.25) + ($3,900 × 0.35) = $3,930

130 A

The first two statements are correct. Statement 3 is not correct. Sensitivity analysis only identifies how far a variable needs to change, it does not look at the probability of such a change. Statement 4 is not correct. Sensitivity analysis assumes that changes to variables can be made independently: for example, material prices will change independently of other variables; but it is simulation that allows more than one variable to be changed at a time.

131 True, True, Not True, True

	True	Not true
Simulation models the behaviour of a system.	✓	
Simulation models can be used to study alternative solutions to a problem.	✓	
The equations describing the operating characteristics of the system are known.		✓
A simulation model cannot prescribe what should be done about a problem.	✓	

132 The second and fourth options are correct.

The expected value does not give an indication of the dispersion of the possible outcomes; a standard deviation would need to be calculated, so option 2 is correct.

The expected value is an amalgamation of several possible outcomes and their associated probabilities so it may not correspond to any of the actual possible outcomes, so option 4 is correct.

133 A

New profit figures before salary paid:

Good manager: $180,000 × 1.3 = $234,000 Average manager: $180,000 × 1.2 = $216,000 Poor: $180,000 × 1.1 = $198,000

EV of profits = (0.35 × $234,000) + (0.45 × $216,000) + (0.2 × $198,000) = $81,900 + $97,200 + $39,600 = $218,700

Deduct salary cost and EV with manager = $178,700

Therefore do not employ manager as profits will fall by $1,300.

134 D

Perfect information is certain to be right about the future. Imperfect information may predict wrongly.

135 A

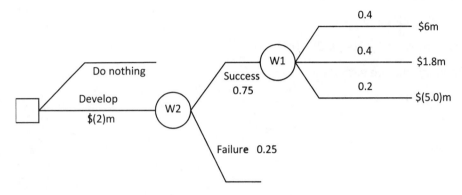

(W1) EV	=	($6m × 0.4) + ($1.8m × 0.4) − ($5m × 0.2)
	=	$2.12m
(W2) EV	=	($2.12m × 0.75) + ($Nil × 0.25)
	=	$1.59m
Net benefit:		$1.59m − $2m = ($0.41m)

136 $600

Without information, the expected profits are:

Product X: $20,000 × 0.2 + $15,000 × 0.5 + $6,000 × 0.3 = $13,300

Product Y: $17,000 × 0.2 + $16,000 × 0.5 + $7,000 × 0.3 = $13,500

So without information, product Y would be selected.

With perfect information, product X would be selected if the market was good, and product Y in the other two cases. The expected value would then be:

$20,000 × 0.2 + $16,000 × 0.5 + $7,000 × 0.3 = $14,100

The expected value of perfect information is therefore $14,100 − $13,500

= $600

137 B

This is an example of sensitivity analysis.

For the project to no longer be worthwhile the expected value would have to fall to $0.

If we make L = the loss made when interest rates fall and restate the expected value calculation we get the following:

EV = (0.3 × 200,000) − (0.7 × L)

If EV falls to zero, (0.3 × 200,000) − 0.7L = 0

Multiplying this out we get:

60,000 − 0.7L = 0

0.7L = 60,000

L = 60,000/0.7

L = 85,714

138 B

Expected value at point A = [(0.60 × 42) − (0.4 × 20)] = $17.2m

Expected value at point B = the higher of (17.2m − 9m) and 15m = 15m

Expected value at point C = [(0.7 × 15m) − (0.3 × 4m)] = $9.3m

The expected value at point D = 9.3m − 5m = $4.3m

139 $506,000

Point B represents a decision point. If the decision is taken to outsource then there is a value of $250,000.

The other decision is to further invest – which appears to have a cost of $40,000. But this then opens up the chance point where there is a 90% chance of making $580,000 and a 10% chance of making $240,000. So this decision to further invest would have an expected value of:

= −40,000 + [(0.90 × 580,000) + (0.1 × 240,000)] = $506,000

Therefore, the decision to further invest is worth more than the outsourcing option. The company would choose to invest and would make $506,000.

140 A

Motivational and measurement research are forms of field research which is considered to be a form of primary research.

BUDGETING AND CONTROL

BUDGETARY SYSTEMS AND TYPES OF BUDGET

141 A

> (2) is wrong – activities drive costs and the aim is to control the causes (drivers) of costs, rather than the costs themselves. This, in turn, will ensure that the costs are better managed, and better understood.

142 B

> (1) is wrong – it would fall under strategic planning.

143 A

144 C

> (1) is wrong, it that would be feedback control. (2) is also wrong, feed-forward control occurs before actual results come through as it is based on forecast results.

145 Incremental budgets are appropriate when applied to stationary costs, the business is stable and for administration costs when the experience of managers is limited.

146 D

> An incremental budget starts with the current period's budget and 'builds' on this to produce the budget for the next period.

147 B

148 A

> Beyond budgeting makes greater use of rolling budgets to create an environment of continuous planning. It also has more local budget setting (rather than a top-down approach), uses a greater number of targets (rather than simply focusing on financial targets) and seeks continuous improvements (rather than standardisation).

149

	E	F	G	
Budgeted number of batches to be produced:	75,000/200	120,000/60	60,000/30	
	= 375	= 2,000	= 2,000	
Machine set-ups per batch:	5	3	9	
Total machine set-ups	1,875	6,000	18,000	**25,875**

Budgeted cost per set-up: $180,000/25,875 = $6.96 per set-up

Therefore the budgeted machine set-up cost per unit of F produced is:

($6.96 × 3)/60 = $0.35 per unit or $6.96 × 6,000/120,000 = **$0.35 per unit**

150 D

151 The third and fourth statements are correct. In beyond budgeting, planning is performed more regularly. Also, as targets become more challenging and more market focused they stretch staff and encourage staff to find better ways to do things, to innovate and improve. They also make the organisation more customer focused by focusing on areas that concern customers such as quality.

Statement 1 is not correct. Because there is less centralised (top-down) budgeting it is much harder to coordinate activities.

Statement 2 is not correct. Beyond budgeting will require the creation and implementation of more performance measures and will require more up-to-date information and more regularly planning. All of this will be difficult and expensive to introduce.

152 A

This is an example of feed-forward control, as the manager is using a forecast to assist in making a future decision.

153 D

A flexible budget controls operational efficiency by producing a realistic budget cost allowance for the actual level of activity achieved. This allows a more meaningful control comparison with the actual results. Statement (i) is therefore correct.

Incremental budgeting uses the current period's results as a base and adjusts this to allow for any known changes, including the cost increases caused by extra planned units of activity. Statement (ii) is therefore incorrect.

In a rolling budget system an extra quarter is added to the end of the budget when the most recent quarter has expired. The remaining budget might be updated at this point. Statement (iii) is therefore incorrect.

154 C

155 ZBB is useful for support expenses as they are discretionary and it can be used to link strategic goals to specific functional areas, so statements 1 and 2 are correct.

156 A

(2) is not correct. ABB can provide useful information for a total quality management programme (TQM) by relating the cost of an activity to the level of service provided and asking the user departments if they feel they are getting a cost-effective service.

QUANTITATIVE TECHNIQUES

157 B

460 – 400 = 60 clients

$40,000 – $36,880 = $3,120

VC per unit = $3,120/60 = $52

Therefore FC = $40,000 – (460 × $52) = $16,080

158 B

	Cumulative average time per unit	No of units	Total time
For first 7 units: y = 6 × 7$^{-0.415}$	2.676	× 7 =	18.72982
For first 6 units: y = 6 × 6$^{-0.415}$	2.8525	× 6 =	17.11472
Time for 7th Assignment			1.6151

Answer 1.62 hours to nearest 0.01 hours

159 D

Using the learning curve model Y = ax^b

Cumulative average time per unit, Y = 50 × 17$^{-0.234}$ = 25.7659 hours per unit

Total time = 27.7659 × 17 units = **438.02 to the nearest 0.01 hours**

160 92%

Batches	Total time	Average time/unit
1	500	500
2		$500 \times r$
4		$500 \times r^2$
8		$500 \times r^3$
16	5,731	$500 \times r^4$

$5{,}731 = 16 \times 500\, r^4$

$5{,}731/(16 \times 500) = r^4$

$r = 0.92$ or 92%

161 $34,400

A high low method analysis will first of all split out the budgeted VC and FC:

	Units	$ Cost
High	1,400	31,600
Low	1,000	30,000
Increment	400	1,600

VC per unit is $1,600/400 = $4/u

Substitution in high:

TC = FC + VC

TC = FC + (1,400 × 4)

31,600 = FC + 5,600

FC = $26,000

For 2,100 units, Fixed costs	= $26,000
VC (2,100 × 4)	= $8,400
Total	= $34,400

162 95%

Units	Total time	Average time/unit
1	100	100
2	190	95

Learning rate is based on the improvement in the average 95/100 = 95%

163 $41,509

Key answer tips

We must work in batches here, where 1 batch = 50 units

Time for the first order:

$Y = ax^b$

$Y = 400 \times 12^{-0.152}$

$Y = 274.17285$ hours

Total time = 3,290.07 hours

Time for first 1,400 units (28 batches)

$Y = ax^b$

$Y = 400 \times 28^{-0.152}$

$Y = 241.04158$ hours

Total time = 6,749.16 hours

Time for second order = 6,749.16 – 3,290.07 = 3,459.09 hours

Cost of second order = 3,459.09 × $12/hr = $41,509.08

164 84.3%

$100r^2 = (100 + 70 + 59 + 55)/4$, giving r = 84.3%

Tutorial note

We could also explain this answer as follows: by the time we have produced two units, we have an average per unit of (100 minutes + 70 minutes)/2 units = 85%. If we were to stop there, the rate of learning would be 85%.

By the time we have got to 4 units, we have an average of (100 minutes + 70 minutes + 59 minutes + 55 minutes)/4 units = 71 minutes. These 71 minutes represent (71/85) = 83.53% of the previous average of 85 minutes.

The overall rate of learning is an average of these two rates of learning, so we have (85% + 83.53%)/2 = 84.265, say 84.3%.

165 9.98 minutes

Using the learning curve model $Y = ax^b$

	Cumulative average minutes	Total minutes
For the 3rd unit	$Y = 22 \times 3^{-0.3219} = 15.45$	$\times 3 = 46.34$
For the 4th unit	$Y = 22 \times 4^{-0.3219} = 14.08$	$\times 4 = 56.32$

Therefore the time for the 4th unit is $56.32 - 46.34 = 9.98$ minutes.

166 D

Year 7, quarter 3 is period 27

Trend sales $= 25,000 + 6,500 (27)$

                $= 200,500$ units

Adjusted for seasonal variations $= 200,500$ units $\times 150\% = 300,750$ units

167 D

The sales revenue 'y' is dependent on the money spent on advertising. The more advertising money is spent, the higher the sales revenue should be. If there is no advertising spend at all, sales revenue can still be forecast at a 'constant' of $150,000.

168 C

'y' total expected overhead costs $= \$127,000 + 18.6 \times 4,600$ labour hours $= \$212,560$

This is calculated using a line of best fit based on 20X5 prices; we need to use an index of 225 for 20X6 when the expected cost index is 225

'y' total expected overhead costs 20X6 $= \$212,560 \times (225/205) = \$233,298$

169 $39,000

Orders $= [100,000 + (30 \times 240)] \times 1.08 = 115,776$

Overhead cost $= \$10,000 + (\$0.25 \times 115,776) = \$38,944$

170 D

Trend $= 9.72 + (5.816 \times 23) = 143.488$

Seasonal factor	+ 6.5
	———
Forecast	149.988
	———

171

	Correct?
89% of the variation in production costs from one month to the next can be explained by corresponding variation in output.	✓
Costs increase as output increases.	
The linear relationship between output and costs is very strong.	✓
An increase of 100% in output is associated with an increase of 89% in costs.	
An increase of 89% in output is associated with an increase of 100% in costs.	

A coefficient of determination between output and production costs, tells us that 89% of the variation in production costs from one month to the next can be explained by corresponding variation in output. It also tells us that the linear relationship between output and costs is very strong. Only a positive correlation can tell us that costs increase as output increases and we cannot assume this from the coefficient of determination.

STANDARD COSTING

172 A

Option B is a current standard, option C is an idea standard and option D is an attainable standard.

173 The first and fourth statements are true.

The second statement is not correct. Standards can include allowances for inefficiencies in operations, through the use of attainable standards.

The third statement is not correct either, standards and budgets are both used for planning and control purposes.

174 C

175 D

176 C

The standard labour rate should be the expected rate/hour, but allowing for standard levels of idle time. For example, if the work force is paid $9 per hour but idle time of 10% is expected, the standard labour rate will be $10 per hour, not $9.

177 C

178 The correct items are: exchange rate movements, increased demand for the material, world oil price rises.

Extra discounts would reduce prices and give a favourable variance. Dividends do not normally count as a cost to a business, and extra supply would normally reduce prices not increase them.

MIX AND YIELD VARIANCES

179 The correct answers are 'Inadequate training of newly recruited staff in the production department', 'Reduced quality materials bought' and 'Change in the production process causing extra losses of materials'.

180 A

A favourable material mix variance is more likely to lead to an adverse material yield variance.

181 C

A planning variance must be caused by an unexpected/unplanned change. If the government unexpectedly increases labour rates then the plan will become outdated and a planning variance will arise.

A planning variance will not always be adverse just because labour rates have increased; there may be no planning variance at all or the planning variance may be favourable if the increase is less than was expected.

A change in production policy by a labour manager is not a planning decision but an operational one.

Whilst the relationship with the variable overhead planning variance may be true, it would not hold for a labour rate planning variance.

182 B

183 $18,000

Original standard hours for actual output = 3 hours × 900 services = 2,700 hours

Revised standard hours for actual output = 3.5 hours × 900 services = 3,150 hours

Variance in hours = 2,700 − 3,150 = 450 adverse

Value of the variance = 450 × $40 = $18,000 adverse

184 A

3,000 units should use 10 kg each (3,000 × 10) = 30,000 kg 3,000 units did use = 29,000 kg

Difference = 1,000 kg favourable

Valued at $6.80 per kg ($68/10 kg)

Variance = $6,800 favourable

185 $72

The planning variance was $40,000 Favourable. This amounts to $2 per hour.

If the revised standard rate per hour was $70 then, for a favourable variance, the original planned rate must have been $2 higher than this.

The original standard rate per hour must have been $72.

186 C

	Material A	Material B	Material C	Total
	kg	kg	kg	kg
Actual input	13,200	7,600	5,600	26,400
Actual input in std proportions				⇓
50:40:20	12,000	9,600	4,800	⇐ 26,400
Difference in quantity	1,200 A	2,000 F	800 A	
× Standard price	× 10	× 5	× 9	
Mix variance	$12,000 A	$10,000 F	$7,200 A	$9,200 A

Key answer tips

An alternative calculation of the mix variance above can be done, using the standard average price per kilogram, as presented below.

Std weighted average price per kg = $\dfrac{(50 \times 10) + (40 \times 5) + (20 \times 9)}{50 + 40 + 20 \text{ kg}}$ = $8/kg

	Material A	Material B	Material C	Total
	kg	kg	kg	kg
Actual input	13,200	7,600	5,600	26,400
Actual input in std proportions				⇓
50:40:20	12,000	9,600	4,800	⇐ 26,400
Difference in quantity	1,200	(2,000)	800	
× Difference in price				
(weighted average std price – Ind. material std price)				
× (8 – 10)	x – 2			
× (8 – 5) × 3		x–3		
× (8 – 9)			x – 1	
Mix variance	$2,400 A	$6,000 A	$800 A	$9,200 A

187 $11.41

	AQAM	AQSM	Difference	Standard	Variance	
	Kgs	Kgs	Kgs	$/kg	$	
Lettuce	62	45.94	−16.06	0.20	−3.21	A
Peppers	81	76.56	−4.44	0.40	−1.78	A
Beetroot	102	122.50	20.50	0.80	16.40	F
	245	245	Material Mix variance		11.41	F

Standard mix:

Lettuce		30	18.75%
Peppers		50	31.25%
Beetroot		80	50%
		160	

188 B

Actual yield	1,500.00
Standard yield	1,531.25
Difference	31.25
Standard cost of a plate	0.09
Yield variance = 31.25 × 0.09 =	2.8125 A
Standard yield is 245,000 × 1/160 =	1,531.25

Standard cost of a plate is:

	Quantity	Price	Cost
	(g)	($)	($)
Lettuce	30	0.0002	0.006
Peppers	50	0.0004	0.020
Beetroot	80	0.0008	0.064
Standard cost:			0.09

189 A

	$
Actual usage in standard proportions	
D = 4,000 litres at $9 per litre	= 36,000
E = 3,500 litres at $5 per litre	= 17,500
F = 2,500 litres at $2 per litre	= 5,000
10,000 litres	58,500
Actual usage in actual proportions	
D = 4,300 litres at $9 per litre	38,700
E = 3,600 litres at $5 per litre	18,000
F = 2,100 litres at $2 per litre	4,200
	60,900

Mix variance is 58,500 − 60,900 = $2,400 Adverse

190 A

The operational labour efficiency variance uses the revised standard time of 12 minutes.

SHSR$\qquad\qquad$ \$

$\dfrac{12}{60} \times 370 \times \$10/hr =$ $\quad$ 740

AHSR $\qquad\qquad\qquad\qquad\qquad$ Efficiency \$60 A

$\qquad$80 hrs × \$10/hr = $\quad$ 800

SALES MIX AND QUANTITY VARIANCES

191 The sales price variance is \$19,800 Adv

AQ × AP = 13,200 × 23.50 =	310,200
AQ × SP = 13,200 × 25.00 =	330,000
Price variance =	19,800 Adv

192 The sales volume variance is \$6,000 Fav

AQ × SC = 13,200 × 5 =	66,000
BQ × SC = 12,000 × 5 =	60,000
Volume variance =	6,000 Fav

193 \$50,000

	Actual mix	Standard mix	Standard contribution from actual mix \$	Standard contribution from standard mix \$
Type A	200,000	150,000	800,000	600,000
Type B	40,000	90,000	200,000	450,000
	240,000	240,000	1,000,000	1,050,000
Difference in contribution			50,000 Adv	

Since Yellow uses MC then the variance should be calculated at standard contribution.

194 \$87,500

Total actual sales	240,000
Total budget sales	220,000
Difference	20,000
Average standard contribution	
((5 × 4) + (3 × 5))/8 = 4.375	\$4.375
Favourable variance is	\$87,500

195

Tutorial note

A sales mix variance indicates the effect on profit of changing the mix of actual sales from the standard mix. Looking a July's budgeted sales levels, we can see that the standard mix of sales is one 'X' for two 'Y's, It means that we expect that every time an 'X' is sold, two units of 'Y' will be sold at the same time. The least profitable unit, 'X', represents a third of the budgeted sales volume.

The actual sales mix is 1'X' for four 'Y's, and is different from the budgeted sales mix. The least profitable unit, 'X', represents a fifth of sales volume. To calculate Jones' sales mix variance, we can use the 'Toolbox' method detailed in your ACCA Performance Management Study Text.

	Actual Quantities, Actual Mix AQAM	Actual Quantities, Standard Mix AQSM	Difference	At standard profit	Variance
Product X	2,000 units	3,333 units	−1,333	$4	($5,332) A
Product Y	8,000 units	6,667 units	1,333	$6	$7,998 F
	10,000 units	**10,000 units**	0		**$2,667 F**

196 A

The sales quantity variance is the difference between the actual sales volume in the standard mix and budgeted sales, valued at the standard profit per unit:

	X	Y	Z	Total
Budgeted sales units, in standard mix	1,000 units (1/6 of total)	2,000 units (1/3 of total)	1,000 units (1/2 of total)	6,000 units
Actual sales volume, in standard mix 1/6; 1/3;1/2	991.67	1,983.33	2,975	5,950
Difference in units	8.33 ADV	16.67 ADV	25 ADV	
Standard profit per unit, as per question	$2	$5	$2	
Variance	$16.67 ADV	$83.34 ADV	$50 ADV	**$150 ADV**

PLANNING AND OPERATIONAL VARIANCES

197 C

Statement 1 is not true: the publication of material price planning variances should not always lead to automatic updates of standard costs. There must be a good reason for deciding that the original standard cost is unrealistic.

Statement 2 is not true either. Although planning variances are not usually the responsibility of operational managers, these variances do need to be investigated by senior management when they are substantial, so that lessons may be learned for the future.

198 D

	Budget units	Actual units	Change
Sales	504,000	532,000	Up 5.55%
Market share	18%	20%	Up 2%
Market size	2,800,000	2,660,000	Down 5%

199 C

	Budget units	Revised units	Actual units	Change
Sales	504,000	478,800	532,000	Up 5.55%
Market share	18%	18%	20%	Up 2%
Market size	2,800,000		2,660,000	Down 5%

Market size variance is $(478,800 - 504,000) \times \$12 = \$302,400$ Adv

200 B

Market share variance compares revised sales volume to actual sales volume.

Revised sales volume (300,000 units × 2%) = 6,000 units Actual sales volume = 5,600 units

Difference = 400 units adverse

Valued at standard contribution of $1,000

Variance = $400,000 adverse

201 C

An operational variance compares revised price to actual price.

20,000 kg should cost $0.40 per kg at the revised price (20,000 kg × $0.40) = $8,000
20,000 kg did cost $0.42 per kg (20,000 kg × $0.42) = $8,400

Variance = $400 adverse

202 A

The material price when flexed is higher than budget whilst the external environment shows that prices are reducing. This indicates that although suppliers lowered their prices, the manager has still overspent which indicates poor performance.

When sales volumes and prices are flexed, it can be seen that the manager has performed better.

203 D

PERFORMANCE ANALYSIS

204 B

The materials mix variance could be affected or influenced by decisions outside the production manager's control, for example the quality of the materials purchased may change the mix.

205 C

PERFORMANCE MEASUREMENT AND CONTROL

PERFORMANCE ANALYSIS IN PRIVATE SECTOR ORGANISATIONS

206 B

(i) and (ii) are financial indicators, and (iv) is a risk indicator.

207 B

208 D

Measuring the budgeted number of quotations actually issued would be monitoring the output and activity of the department but it would not be helpful in improving the department's performance in terms of the accuracy or speed of quotations in the scenario described.

209 'Customer satisfaction ratings' and 'customer retention rates'

'Customer profitability analysis' results belong to the financial quadrant. 'Customer ordering processing times' belongs to the 'Internal business process' quadrant.

210 Innovation and learning perspective

211 D

'Number of returns in the month' is an absolute measure and not appropriate to measure 'quality'. 'Number of faulty goods returned as a percentage of number of orders received in the month' is not a bad measure, but orders may not have been delivered; 'Average customer satisfaction rating where customers were asked a range of questions including quality, delivery and customer service' seems to lack focus as a measure.

212 The correct items are Competitive Performance, Innovation, Financial Performance, Resource utilisation, Flexibility and Quality of Service.

213 A

Co X (2,140/20,000) × 100 = 10.7%

Co Y (2,180/26,000) × 100 = 8.38%

214 C

Company B has a higher asset turnover and is therefore using its assets more efficiently than A. The two companies have the same ROCE and are therefore generating the same profit from every $1 of asset employed. The profit of the two companies is the same but company A has a higher profit margin and is therefore controlling its costs better than company B. The calculations are:

	Co A	Co B
ROCE	20% (10,000/50,000 × 100)	20% (10,000/50,000 × 100)
Profit margin	20% (10,000/50,000 × 100)	5% (10,000/200,000 × 100)
Asset turnover	1 (50,000/50,000)	4 (200,000/50,000)

215 C

Inventory holding period = 44,000/324,500 × 365 days = 49 days

Average inventories/COS × 365

Average inventories = (50,000 + 38,000)/2 = 44,000

Current ratio = 108,000/56,000 = 1.93:1

Current assets: Current liabilities

Current assets = Trade receivables 60,000 + Prepayments 4,000 + Cash in hand 6,000 + Closing inventories 38,000 = 108,000

Current liabilities = Bank overdraft 8,000 + Trade payables 40,000 + Accruals 3,000 + Declared dividends 5,000 = 56,000

216 Accountable, Accountable, Accountable, Not accountable

	Accountable	Not accountable
The generation of revenues	✓	
Transfer prices	✓	
Management of working capital	✓	
Apportioned head office costs		✓

The manager will be accountable for the generation of revenues, transfer prices and management of working capital as they have control over these areas. The manager will not be accountable for the apportioned head office costs as they have no control over those.

217 The first and fourth options are correct. The investment centre manager would have power to make decisions over granting credit to customers and the level of inventory carried. This affects the investment centre's level of working capital, and hence is the responsibility of the investment centre manager.

The second option is not correct: inter-departmental dispute resolution is carried out by head office and should not be the responsibility of the investment centre manager.

The third option is not correct: The manager will not be accountable for the apportioned head office costs as they have no control over those.

218 A

$$Current\ ratio = \frac{Current\ assets}{Current\ liabilities}$$

Current assets include cash, receivables and inventories. The quick ratio (acid test) is similar to the current ratio, but inventory is removed from the current assets due to its poor liquidity in the short term.

$$Acid\ test\ (or\ 'quick')\ ratio = \frac{Current\ assets - Inventory}{Current\ liabilities}$$

Binny's Co sales are all for cash, and therefore its 'Current Assets' figures will not include any receivables.

$$Current\ ratio\ 3.2 = \frac{Cash + Inventory}{Current\ liabilities}$$

$$Current\ ratio\ 3.2 = \frac{Cash\ \$40,000 + Inventory\ \$160,000\ (W1)}{Current\ liabilities\ 62,500\ (W2)}$$

$$Therefore,\ acid\ test\ (or\ 'quick'\ ratio) = \frac{Cash\ \$40,000}{Current\ liabilities\ \$62,500} = 0.64$$

Working 1 – Inventory

$$Cost\ of\ sales = \frac{\$960,000\ annual\ sales \times 100}{150} = \$640,000$$

$$Inventory\ holding\ period\ 90\ days = \frac{Inventory}{Cost\ of\ sales} \times 360$$

$$Inventory = \frac{90\ days \times \$640,000}{360} = \$160,000$$

Working 2 – Current liabilities

$$Current\ ratio\ 3.2 = \frac{\$40,000\ cash + \$160,000\ inventory}{Current\ liabilities}$$

$$So\ current\ liabilities = \frac{\$200,000}{3.2} = \$62,500$$

DIVISIONAL PERFORMANCE AND TRANSFER PRICING

219 B

Increase in variable costs from buying in (2,200 units × $40 ($140 – $100)) = $88,000

Less the specific fixed costs saved if A is shut down = ($10,000)

Decrease in profit = $78,000

220 Would choose to invest, would not choose to invest

	Would choose to invest in the project	Would choose not to invest in the project
Division A	✓	
Division B		✓

Division A: Profit = $14.4 m × 30% = $4.32 m

Imputed interest charge = $32.6 m × 10% = $3.26 m

Residual income = $1.06 m

Division B: Profit = $8.8 m × 24% = $2.112 m

Imputed interest charge = $22.2 m × 10% = $2.22 m

Residual income = $(0.108) m

221 $10.50

Tutorial note

Division A can sell all of its output on the outside market at $12 per unit. Any internal transfer will be at the expense of external sales. However, the external sales also include a packaging cost of $1.50 per unit which is not incurred on an internal transfer and this saving can be passed on to the buying division. Therefore, the correct transfer price from a decision-making point of view is $12 (the market price) – $1.50 (the saving in packaging cost) = $10.50.

222 $830 m

Controllable profit is 1,200 + 90 + 30 + 50 =	$1,370m
Assets at start of year are	$4,500m
Notional interest charges at 12% (4,500 × 0.12)	$540m
Residual Income	$830m

223

$$\text{ROCE} = \frac{\text{Profit before interest and tax}}{\text{Capital employed}} = \frac{500}{2,400} = 20.8\%$$

Capital employed is equity + long-term debt   = 1,500 + 900 = 2,400

or

Total assets less current liabilities   = 3,400 − 1,000 = 2,400

224 C

$236,000

	$000
Profit	500
Imputed interest 11% × 2,400	(264)
	–––––
Residual income	236
	–––––

225 30.4%

ROI = 1,370/4,890 = 28.0%

226 19.8%

Tutorial note

We need to look at how the transactions given affect profits and net assets. With each transaction in turn:

Firstly, a machine with carrying value of $40k was sold for $50k. This will reduce non-current assets by $40k and, as we are told this was a cash transaction, increase cash by $50k – increasing net assets by $10k. As a profit has been made on disposal, it will also increase profits by $10k. Secondly, another machine was purchased for $250k. This will increase non-current assets by $250k, but as this was also a cash transaction, decrease cash by $250k, so no net effect. As no depreciation is charged on either machine there is no further effect. The net effect is therefore +10k to both profit and net assets, so the ROI is ($200k/$1,010k) × 100% = 19.8%.

Revised annual profit = $190,000 + $10,000 profit on the sale of the asset = $200,000

Revised net assets = $1,000,000 − $40,000 carrying value + $50,000 cash − $250,000 cash + $250,000 asset = $1,010,000 ROI = ($200,000/$1,010,000) × 100 = 19.8%

Tutorial note

Do not make the mistake of omitting the profit on disposal from profits and increasing net assets by the $250k machine purchase, but not subtracting the cash.

227 B

Statement (1) is not true: a price above variable costs will generate a positive contribution but will not necessarily cover fixed costs and make a profit, so will not always be accepted.

228 B

Using the opportunity cost approach to transfer pricing, the minimum price charged by the transferring division must be the marginal (variable) cost of producing X + the contribution that is lost from selling however many units of Y could have been made for each X.

'Division A has limited skilled labour' means that skilled labour is a scarce resource. If Division A now has to make X instead of Y, it will lose the contribution it currently makes on Product Y. This contribution is equal to $600 selling price – $200 Material costs – $80 labour costs = $320.

It takes 4 hours to make a Y and 6 hours to make an X. So, every time we (in Division A) make an X, we will not make 1.5Ys because of the shortage of skilled labour. So we lose 1.5 Y × Contribution per unit $320 = $480.

We add to this lost contribution a marginal cost of making an X of $150 (material) + $170 (labour).

Total transfer price = $480 + $150 + $120 = $750

Tutorial note

There is an alternative to approaching this question. You could calculate the contribution per labour hour for Y and then multiplying this by the number of hours X uses. It is the contribution per labour hour that is relevant, because of the fact that it is labour that is in short supply.

Product	Y in $
Selling Price per unit	600
Less Direct Materials (4 kgs)	200
Less Direct Labour (4 hours)	80
Contribution per unit	320
Contribution per labour hour for Y	80

Therefore, if Division A is to be no worse off by selling Product X to Division B instead of Product Y externally, the contribution per labour hour from selling X must also be $80. The opportunity cost is therefore $80 per labour hour.

Since it uses 6 labour hours to make one unit, one unit must generate a contribution (i.e. opportunity cost in this context) of 6 × $80 i.e. $480. To arrive at a minimum transfer price, the marginal cost of producing X must be added. Total variable cost per unit of X = $150 + $270. Therefore, the minimum transfer price is $750.

229 **$12.90**

We must set a price high enough for TM to cover its costs, but not so high that RM cannot make a profit.

For TM, an item sold externally has VC of 60% × $24.00 = $14.40. Of this, $1.50 will not be incurred on an internal transfer so it is not relevant here, VC on internal transfer = $14.40 – $1.50= $12.90. We do not know RM's cost structure, so we leave the price at $12.90; this will ensure that RM is not discouraged from taking an internal transfer when it is profitable to do so.

PERFORMANCE ANALYSIS IN NON-FOR-PROFIT ORGANISATIONS AND THE PUBLIC SECTOR

230 **B**

(1) is not correct: Output does not usually have a market value, and it is therefore more difficult to measure efficiency.

231 Economy, Efficiency, Effectiveness

	Economy	Efficiency	Effectiveness
Target (1)	✓		
Target (2)		✓	
Target (3)			✓

232 **A**

Reducing mortality rates is likely to be a stated objective of the hospital and as such is a measure of output, or effectiveness. Cost per patient is a measure of output related to input i.e. efficiency.

233 **B**

Multiple objectives often conflict and therefore do not ensure goal congruence between stakeholders, therefore Statement 1 is incorrect. This then can lead to the need for compromise between objectives which can be problematic, therefore Statement 2 is correct.

234 **C**

Exam success will be a given objective of a school, so it is a measure of effectiveness.

235 **D**

EXTERNAL CONSIDERATIONS AND THE IMPACT ON PERFORMANCE

236 C

Delaying payments to payables affects cash, not profit. Shortening the useful economic life of a non-current asset would reduce profit, and overstatement of an accrual also reduces profit.

237 D

There is nothing to suggest that imposed standards are more likely to be achieved. Where managers are allowed to participate in the setting of standards, they are usually more motivated and this can lead to more acceptance of these standards.

Managers should be targeted on factors which they can control, and be set targets which are specific to their business area.

It is recognised that ideal standard do not generally motivate, therefore standards are generally set at an achievable level with some stretch built in.

238 A, B and D

It is important to take account of all stakeholders when setting performance targets.

Government policy can have an impact on the internal performance of a business.

239 A

Managers should also have targets which are based on the overall performance of the company and not solely based on their own responsibility centre to aid goal congruence.

Capital investment decisions may be reviewed centrally and judged on the basis of net present value (NPV).

Setting targets involving the overall performance of the company may not be motivating if poorly performing managers are rewarded in the same way as managers who are performing well.

240 C

It is important that performance measures are set to encourage the long term growth of the company. A focus on short term profit could result in risky and dysfunctional behaviour.

The government is also interested in many other aspects including price stability, economic growth and compliance with laws.

Companies have a range of stakeholders, all of which can affect the company and should be considered. Some of these stakeholders are external such as the government, the general public and pressure groups.

Section 5

ANSWERS TO OBJECTIVE TEST CASE STUDY QUESTIONS – SECTION B

INFORMATION, TECHNOLOGIES AND SYSTEMS FOR ORGANISATIONAL PERFORMANCE

MANAGING INFORMATION

241 SILVERSAFE

1   **B**

Tutorial note

Make sure you read the ACCA technical article on information systems at https://www.accaglobal.com/uk/en/student/exam-support-resources/fundamentals-exams-study-resources/f5/technical-articles/info-systems.html, to understand the role of firewalls against hacking, and other controls.

More than preventing hacks, the role of anti-virus software is to prevent, detect, and remove viruses. Anti-virus and firewall software often go together in devices.

Although good practice, daily backups do not prevent systems being hacked, or the data obtained from being used fraudulently.

Rather than stopping access to a system from external users, passwords are usually used to prevent access to files within a system.

2   **B**

An intranet is a private network within an organisation – in the case of Silversafe Co here. The purpose of an intranet is to share information internally.

3   **B**

Statement (i) is not correct: it would not be appropriate for Silversafe employees not directly involved in residents' care to view – let alone alter – all residents' records. Instead, access controls should be in place to ensure that only information required to carry out their duties is made available to employees.

4   D

Statement 3 is not correct: technology (wireless or otherwise) is not intended to provide better understanding of costs – techniques like ABC are.

Statement 4 is correct: It is cheaper to add new users (from future homes) to a wireless network than to install new cabling.

5   D

All statements are correct.

SPECIALIST COST AND MANAGEMENT ACCOUNTING TECHNIQUES

242   MIDHURST CO (SPETEMBER/DECEMBER 2020)

1   A, C

Statements A and C are correct as capital expenditure is likely to increase at the introduction stage and the majority of a product's costs are determined at the outset.

Statement B defines the decline stage of the product lifecycle and Statement D defines the maturity stage.

2   D

To calculate a cost per unit using life-cycle costing, the first step is to calculate the total cost over the full life-cycle of the product.

The total cost of the new product (in $000s) is:

$6,200 + $33,450 + $177,685 + ($42 × 10,000) + $98,470 +($9 × 10,000) + $10,300 + ($4 × 10,000) + $7,790 + $23,450 = **$907,345**

To calculate the cost per unit, divide the total cost by the number of units to be produced over the life-cycle of the product:

$907,345,000/10,000 = **$90,735.**

If A was selected, the variable costs per unit were omitted from the total cost.

If B was selected, the total production cost was used, and all non-production costs were excluded.

If C was selected, the administration costs were excluded.

3 $6,940

Current variable material cost per unit = 20% × $42,000 = $8,400

Revised variable material cost per unit = (85% × ($8,400 – $2,000)) + (75% × $2,000) = **$6,940**

4   C

Normally product development occurs at the maturity phase in order to extend the profitable stage of the life-cycle. This is usually done by adding enhancements or new features.

5   B

Statement 3 is an advantage of target costing and not life-cycle costing.

243 DUFF CO (JUNE 2014, ADAPTED)

1   A

Product	Z
Direct materials	$28.00
Direct labour	$24.00
Overhead ($9.70 × 2 DL hours)	$19.40
Full cost per unit	$71.40

2   B

Full budgeted production cost per unit using activity based costing

Product	X	Y	Z	Total
Budgeted annual production (units)	20,000	16,000	22,000	
Batch size	500	800	400	
Number of batches (i.e. set ups)	**40**	**20**	**55**	**115**
Number of purchase orders per batch	4	5	4	
Total number of orders	**160**	**100**	**220**	**480**
Machine hours per unit	1.5	1.25	1.4	
Total machine hours	**30,000**	**20,000**	**30,800**	**80,800**

Cost driver rates:

Cost per machine set up	$280,000/115 = $2,434.78
Cost per order	$316,000/480 = $658.33
Cost per machine hour	($420,000 + $361,400)/80,800 = $9.67

Allocation of overheads to each product:

Product	X	Y	Z	Total
	$	$	$	
Machine set up costs	**97,391**	48,696	133,913	280,000
Material ordering costs	**105,333**	65,833	144,834	316,000
Machine running and facility costs	**290,100**	193,400	297,836	781,336
Total	**492,824**	307,929	576,583	1,377,336
Number of units produced	**20,000**	16,000	22,000	
Overhead cost per unit	**$24.64**	$19.25	$26.21	

3   B

Total cost per unit:	$ per unit
Direct materials	28
Direct labour	24
Overhead	26.21
ABC cost per unit	78.21

4   D

All statements are correct.

5   B

Statement (1) is not true. When activity based costing is used, the cost for product X is very similar to that cost calculated using full absorption costing. This means that the price for product X is likely to remain unchanged, because cost plus pricing is being used.

Statement (2) is correct. Demand for product X is relatively elastic but since no change in price is expected, sales volumes are likely to remain the same if ABC is introduced.

Statement (3) is correct. The cost for product Y is almost $10 per unit less using ABC. This means that the price of product Y will go down if cost plus pricing is used.

Statement (4) is incorrect. Given that demand for product Y is also elastic, like demand for product X, a reduced selling price is likely to give rise to increased sales volumes.

244   BECKLEY HILL (JUNE 2015)

1   C

	Procedure A	Procedure B
Total cost per procedure, as per question	$2,475.85	$4,735.85
Less: Surgical time and materials (direct cost)	($1,200)	($2,640)
Less: Anaesthesia time and materials (direct cost)	($800)	($1,620)
Overhead cost per procedure	$475.85	$475.85

2   A

$$\text{Administration cost per hour} = \frac{\text{Total admin cost}}{\text{Total number of admin hours}}$$

Administration cost per hour =

$$\frac{\$1,870,160}{(1 \text{ hour} \times 14,600 \text{ procedures 'A'}) + (1.5 \text{ hours} \times 22,400 \text{ procedures 'B'})}$$

Administration cost per hour = $38.80

3   D

Tutorial note

Make sure you use the number of patient hours, not admin hours, to answer this question.

$$\text{Nursing cost per hour} = \frac{\text{Total nursing cost}}{\text{Total number of patient hours}}$$

$$\text{Nursing cost per hour} = \frac{\$6,215,616}{(24 \text{ hours} \times 14,600) + (48 \text{ hours} \times 22,400)}$$

Nursing cost per hour = $4.36 per patient hour

4   A

Only statement (1) is correct. When activity-based costing (ABC) is used, the cost for Procedure A is approximately $2,297 as compared to the approximate $2,476 currently calculated by BH. For Procedure B, the cost using ABC is approximately $4,853 as compared to the approximate current cost of $4,736. Hence, the cost of Procedure A goes down using ABC and the cost of Procedure B goes up. This reflects the fact that the largest proportion of the overhead costs is the nursing and general facility costs. Both of these are driven by the number of patient hours for each procedure. Procedure B has twice as many patient hours as Procedure A.

5   C

Both statements are correct. ABC can be a lot of work to implement, and whilst the comparative costs are different, they are not significantly different. Given that ABC is costly to implement, it may be that a similar allocation in overheads can be achieved simply by using a fairer basis to absorb the costs. If patient hours are used as the basis of absorption instead of simply dividing the overheads by the number of procedures, the costs for Procedures A and B would be $2,296 and $4,853:

$17,606,352/1,425,600 hours = $12.35 per hour.

Therefore absorption cost for A = $1,200 + $800 + (24 × $12.35) = $2,296.

Same calculation for B but with 48 hours instead.

Hence, the same result can be achieved without going to all of the time and expense of using ABC. Therefore BH should not adopt ABC but use this more accurate basis of absorbing overheads instead.

245 ABKABER PLC

1   B

Total overhead cost	= $2,400,000 + $6,000,000 + $3,600,000
	= $12,000,000
Total labour hours	= 200,000 + 220,000 + 80,000
	= 500,000
Overhead absorption rate/labour hour	= $12,000,000/500,000 = $24

	Sunshine	Roadster	Fireball
Direct labour hours	200,000	220,000	80,000
	$	$	$
Overheads ($24/direct labour hour)	**4,800,000**	**5,280,000**	**1,920,000**

2   C

Number of deliveries to retailers	100 + 80 + 70	=	250
Cost driver rate for deliveries	$2,400,000/250	=	$9,600
Number of set-ups	35 + 40 + 25	=	100
Cost driver rate for set-ups	$6,000,000/100	=	$60,000
Number of purchase orders	400 + 300 + 100	=	800
Cost driver rate for purchase orders	$3,600,000/800	=	$4,500

Overheads	**Fireball**
	$
Deliveries ($9,600 × 70)	672,000
Set-ups at ($60,000 × 25)	1,500,000
Purchase orders ($4,500 × 100)	450,000
Total overheads attributed	**2,622,000**

3   B

Both methods are acceptable, but ABC can give more detailed information about the overhead costs per products, so it would be unwise for management to ignore the useful additional information that ABC can provide

Using ABC will give a lower profit to the Fireball as more overheads are attributed to it.

Reducing labour hours would reduce the overheads attributed to the product under the existing method, but is not focussing on what is driving the overheads which is deliveries, set-ups, and purchases processes.

4   D

(1) is false – ABC can provide management with more accurate information as it gives a more accurate cost per unit. This can improve management decisions such as whether the Fireball product is viable.

(2) is false – ABC can help with determining a more accurate incremental cost, however it's accuracy depends on identifying appropriate cost drivers.

(3) is true.

5   D

It is difficult to achieve complete accuracy with ABC as it depends on the accuracy of the cost drivers identified.

ABC is more accurate, but is more expensive and time consuming than traditional methods.

ABC is more useful when overheads are a large proportion of the costs, as accurate attribution of those overheads will have a more significant impact on the cost per product in this instance.

246   HELOT CO (SEPTEMBER 2016)

1   D

Target costing does encourage looking at customer requirements early on so that features valued by customers are included, so Statement 2 is correct. It will also force the company to closely assess the design and is likely to be successful if costs are designed out at this stage rather than later once production has started, so Statement 4 is correct.

Statement 1 explains a benefit of flow cost accounting. Statement 3 explains the concept of throughput accounting.

2   A

Target price is $45 and the profit margin is 35% which results in a target cost of $29.25. The current estimated cost can be calculated as:

Production costs per unit	$
Direct material	3.00
Direct labour	2.50
Direct machining	5.05
Set-up	0.45
Inspection and testing	4.30
Total non-production costs per unit	
Design (salaries and technology) (2,500K ÷ 350K)	7.14
Marketing consultants (1,700K ÷ 350K)	4.86
Distribution (1,400K ÷ 350K)	4.00
Current total cost per unit	**31.30**

$31.30 – $29.25 results in a cost gap of $2.05.

3   **Not appropriate, Appropriate, Not appropriate, Appropriate.**

	An appropriate way to close a cost gap	Not an appropriate way to close a cost gap
Buy cheaper, lower grade plastic for the game discs and cases.		✓
Using standard components wherever possible in production.	✓	
Employ more trainee game designers on lower salaries.		✓
Use the company's own online gaming websites for marketing.	✓	

Using more standardised components and using its own websites for marketing will reduce processing and marketing costs.

Using cheaper materials and trainee designers will reduce costs but could impact the quality and customer perception of the product which would impact the target price.

4   **C**

The change in the learning rate will increase the current estimated cost which will increase the cost gap.

The target cost will be unaffected as this is based on the target selling price and profit margin; neither of which are changing.

5   **B**

Services do use more labour relative to materials.

The other three statements are incorrect as uniformity is not a characteristic of services, there is no transfer of ownership and although it is difficult to standardise a service due to the human influence, target costing can still be used.

Tutorial note

The characteristics of target costing in service industries are frequently highlighted by the examining team as an absolute must-know. Make sure you learn them before attempting the exam.

247 CHEMICAL FREE CLEAN CO (DECEMBER 2015)

1   A

A product or service is developed which is perceived to be needed by customers and therefore will attract adequate sales volumes. A target price is then set based on the customers' perceived value of the product. This will therefore be a market based price. The required target operating profit per unit is then calculated. This may be based on either return on sales or return on investment. The target cost is derived by subtracting the target profit from the target price. If there is a cost gap, attempts will be made to close the gap.

2   The second and fourth statements are correct.

Tutorial note

Make sure you remember the five characteristics of services that make target costing more difficult in service industries: intangibility, simultaneity (in Statement 2 here), heterogeneity, perishability (in statement 4 here) and no transfer of ownership.

3   C

Both statements are correct.

4   B and D

A is not correct: a dominant company will find target costing less useful than a business faced with competitive pressures.

C is not correct either: ignoring the market price in such a competitive market will only lead to C Co's erosion of market share.

5   C

Both statements are correct.

248 VOLT CO (MARCH 2019)

Tutorial note

Make sure you read through the technical article on lifecycle costing published on the ACCA website in the Performance Management (PM) section.

1   C

Nuclear station	$
Operating costs, net of depreciation: ($486 m −$175 m) × 40 years	12,440 m
Building costs	7,000 m
Decommissioning costs	12,000 m
Total costs	$31,440 m
9,000 gigawatts per year × 40 years	360,000 gigawatts
Cost per Gigawatt $31,440m/360,000 gigawatt	$87,333 m

2   B

Statement (1) is not correct: increasing the useful life of the station will decrease the average annual cost. The operating cost will be incurred every year, thus increasing the total life-cycle costs.

Statement (2) is correct. If the decommissioning cost is reduced, this will reduce the total life-cycle costs.

3   C

Environmental internal failure costs are those costs incurred from performing activities that have produced contaminants and waste that have not been discharged into the environment.

We are told that 'the decommissioning cost' is incurred by Volt Co as a result of its activities; It relates to the cost of safely disposing of spent nuclear fuel', and by 'safely' we may deduct that the fuel has not been discharged into the environment, it is being disposed of in a safe manner to ensure that it does not become a cost borne by society as a whole.

4   B

Tutorial note

The total lifecycle cost of $55,000 per gigawatt is split into operating costs ($40,000 per gigawatt) and non-operating costs ($15,000 per gigawatt). An operating margin is calculated after deducting operating costs only.

1,750 Gigawatts per year × 20 years = 35,000 gigawatts in total over the life of the wind station.

		$
Total operating costs over the life of the wind station	35,000 gigawatts × $40,000	(1,400 m)
Operating profit (operating margin)	1,400 × (40/60)	$933.33 m
Less:		
Non-operating costs	35,000 gigawatts × $15,000	($525m)
Lifetime profit		$408.33 m

An alternative debrief, starting from the selling price based on an operating margin of 40%, reads as follows:

		$
Selling price per gigawatt	$40,000/0.60	$66,667 m
Lifetime profit per gigawatt	($66,667 – $55,000)	$11,667 m
Total Lifetime profit	1,750 Gigawatts × $11,667 × 20 years	$408.33 m

5   B

Statements (1) and (2) are benefits of life-cycle costing for Volt Co.

Statement (3) describes a benefit of activity-based costing (ABC), and is not correct: although life-cycle costing tracks the actual costs and revenues attributable to each product from 'cradle to grave' (thereby enabling a product's true profitability to be determined at the end of its economic life), it does not give a better understanding of the actual causes of overhead costs.

Statement 4 describes a benefit of Lifecycle costing, and is not correct either: The objective of LCC is to select the most cost-effective approach, so that the lowest long-term cost of ownership is achieved; but short-term decision making, that focuses on cost control, is not served by the adoption of lifecycle costing.

249 SHOE CO (JUNE 2016)

1   **The third and fourth statements are correct.**

2   **$6,960,000**

Total sales revenue		$34,300,000
Less costs:		
Development and design costs		($5,600,000)
Patent application costs (including $20K)		($500,000)
Patent renewal costs – 2 years		($400,000)
Total material costs	[(280,000 × $16) + (420,000 × $14)]	($10,360,000)
Total labour costs	[(280,000 × $8) + (420,000 × $7)]	($5,180,000)
Fixed production overheads		($3,800,000)
Selling and distribution costs		($1,500,000)
Profit		$6,960,000

3   **The third and fourth statements are correct.**

Statement (1) is not correct: identifying the costs of environment-related activities is difficult. Statement (2) is not correct either: EMA generates and analyses both financial and non-financial information in order to support internal environmental management processes.

4   **C**

Expected marketing cost in year 1: (0.2 × $2.2m) + (0.5 × $2.6m) + (0.3 × $2.9m) = $2.61m

Expected marketing cost year 2: (0.3 × $1.8m) + (0.4 × $2.1m) + (0.3 × $2.3m) = $2.07m

Total expected marketing cost = $4.68m

5   **D**

250 SWEET TREATS BAKERY (DECEMBER 2016)

Tutorial note

The Examiner has reported that performance was weaker in December 2016 on this scenario question, which tested throughput accounting in a situation where resources were scarce. It was interesting that this technique involved an understanding of limiting factor analysis. Understanding is particularly lacking in this area, so make sure you give it the time it deserves in your revision plan.

1   B

Process	Available minutes	Brownies	Muffins	Cupcakes	Total minutes required
Weighing	240	60	45	100	205
Mixing	180	80	48	60	188
Baking	1,440	480	330	600	1,410

The bottleneck is the mixing process as 188 minutes are required to meet maximum demand but there are only 180 minutes available.

Note: Four batches of brownies need to be made in order to have sufficient cakes to meet maximum demand as the cakes must be made in their batch sizes.

2   A

	Brownies	Muffins	Cupcakes
Throughput contribution ($)	50	37.5	35
Mixing minutes	20	16	12
Throughput per mixing minute ($)	2.50	2.34	2.91
Ranking	2	3	1

Optimal production plan:

Fulfil customer order	Number of cakes	Mixing minutes
1 batch of cupcakes	20	12
1 batch of brownies	40	20
1 batch of muffins	30	16
General production (based on ranking)		
4 batches of cupcakes	80	48
1 batch of brownies	40	20

Therefore the bakery should produce 80 brownies, 30 muffins and 100 cupcakes.

3 **Will not improve, Will improve, Will not improve, Will improve.**

	Will improve the TPAR	Will not improve the TPAR
The café customer will be given a loyalty discount.		✓
A bulk discount on flour and sugar is available from suppliers.	✓	
There is additional demand for the cupcakes in the market.		✓
The rent of the premises has been reduced for the next year.	✓	

Reduction in rent and discounts on materials will reduce costs and will improve the TPAR.

Giving a customer a loyalty discount will reduce sales revenue and as a result the TPAR. Demand for cupcakes can increase but it will not impact the TPAR as demand is not the restriction.

4 **C**

Each oven has a capacity of eight hours and each cupcake batch takes two hours, so four extra batches can be made. Extra throughput = four batches × $35 = $140.

Less the hire costs will result in an additional profit of $95

5 **A**

As the TPAR exceeds 1, then the throughout contribution exceeds operating costs, so Statement 1 is false. Less idle time on a non-bottleneck process would not improve the TPAR, so Statement 2 is false.

Improving efficiency during the weighing process would improve the TPAR as any actions to improve throughput on a bottleneck will improve the TPAR, so Statement 3 is true.

DECISION-MAKING TECHNIQUES

251   SIP CO

Tutorial note

There is a lot of information in this question and a lot to do for the marks available. Questions in the exam are unlikely to have this level of detail but the question should still allow you to practice applying your knowledge in these areas.

1   **Upholstery fabric** = $85 × 20 + $7.50 × 20 = **$1,850**

Do not include the retainer as this is paid whether or not the refurbishment goes ahead.

Galley = $4,000 + 40 × $15 + 0.9 × 2,000 = **$6,400**

This is cheaper than the new galley of $6,500

2   **A**

If the teak in inventory is used, the relevant cost is sale proceeds lost plus the cost of sanding – $95 + $14 = $109. This is cheaper than buying new teak. The remaining 5m will need to be bought. All the teak needs staining and the machine resetting.

Relevant cost = 5 × $109 + 5 × $110 + $4.50 × 10 + $80 = $1,220

3   **Skilled labour $2,640   Unskilled labour $648**

The existing skilled labour can be used costing ($25 + $6) × 100 = $3,100

OR new labour can be hired and trained costing $25 × 100 + $14 ×10 = $2,640

Take the cheaper cost.

The unskilled workers are guaranteed work for $420/$12 = 35 hours.

They are currently working $372/$12 = 31 hours. Therefore there are 4 hours per week per worker spare capacity. There are 5 workers therefore 20 hours a week will have no cost, leaving 36 hours to be paid for at time and a half.

36 × $12 × 1.5 = $648

4   **Committed, Notional, Committed**

	Committed	Notional
Factory rates	✓	
Depreciation		✓
Interest	✓	

5   The second and third statements are correct.

252 HARE EVENTS (DECEMBER 2016)

1   B

Total fixed costs = $385,000

Contribution per marathon entry ($55 – $18.20) = $36.80

BEP = 10,462

Margin of safety (20,000 – 10,462)/20,000 = 47.7%

2   C

Weighted average C/S ratio (2 × $36.80) + (1.4 × $18.00)/(2 × $55) + (1.4 × $30) = $98.80/$152 = 65% BER = $385,000/65% = $592,308

3   A

Weighted average C/S ratio = 65%

Revenue to achieve target profit = $885,000/65% = $1,361,538

Marathon ($110/$152) × $1,361,538 = $985,324/$55 = 17,915 entries

Half marathon ($42/$152) × $1,361,538 = $376,214/$30 = 12,540 entries

4   Will not change, Will change.

	Will change	Will not change
Breakeven volume		✓
Breakeven revenue	✓	

Current contribution = $12

Current BEP = $48,000/$12 = 4,000 units

Current BER = $48,000/($12/$20) = $80,000

Revised contribution (($20 × 1.1) – ($8 × 1.1) = $13.20

Revised fixed costs = $48,000 × 1.1 = $52,800

Revised BEP = $52,800/$13.20 = 4,000 units

Revised BER = $52,800/($13.20/$22) = $88,000

The BEP has not changed but the BER has increased by 10%.

5   C

CVP analysis assumes no movement in inventory and the C/S ratio can be used to indicate the relative profitability of different products, so Statements 1 and 2 are correct.

253 CARDIO CO (DECEMBER 2015, ADAPTED)

1   A

Statements (1) and (2) are not valid: 'the elliptical trainers made a loss in 2015' and 'the elliptical trainers made a positive contribution in the year just passed' are sunk events.

Statement (5) is not valid either: businesses evolve and the fact that the business was founded to produce and sell elliptical trainers is irrelevant in this decision.

2 B

Statement (1) is not correct: fixed costs can be incremental to a decision, and in those circumstances would be relevant. Statement (2) is not correct either: notional costs are used to make cost estimates more realistic; however, they are not real cash flows and are not considered to be relevant.

3 B

	T	C	R
	$	$	$
Selling price	1,600	1,800	1,400
Material	(430)	(500)	(360)
Labour 40%	(88)	(96)	(76)
Variable overheads	(110)	($120)	(95)
Contribution	972	1,084	869
Sales units	420	400	380
Total contribution	$408,240	$433,600	$330,220

Total contribution achieved by all three products = $408,240 + $433,600 + $330,220 = $1,172,060

Margin of safety = budgeted sales – breakeven sales

Budgeted sales revenue = $1,924,000

Fixed labour costs = {(420 × $220) + (400 × $240) + (380 × $190)} × 0.6 = $156,360.

Therefore total fixed costs = $156,360 + $55,000 = $211,360.

$$\text{Breakeven sales revenue} = \frac{\text{Fixed costs}}{\text{Weighted average C/S ratio}}$$

$$\text{Breakeven sales revenue} = \frac{\$211,360}{60.92\%}$$

Breakeven sales revenue = $346,947.

Therefore margin of safety = $1,924,000 – $346,947 = $1,577,053.

4 A

If the more profitable products are sold first, this means that the company will cover its fixed costs more quickly. Consequently, the breakeven point will be reached earlier, i.e. fewer sales will need to be made in order to break even. So, the breakeven point will be lower.

5 B

The general fixed overheads should be excluded as they are not incremental, i.e. they are not arising specifically as a result of this order. They are not sunk as they are not past costs.

254 CARA CO (MARCH 2019)

1   **C**

'Materials' is the only limiting factor in Month 1, as more is needed than is available. To satisfy the maximum demand in Month 1 would require:

	4,000 units of 'Seebach'	3,000 units of 'Herdorf'	Total resource needed	Total maximum resource available
Materials	5 kgs per unit × 4,000 units = 20,000 kgs	7 kgs per unit × 3,000 units= 21,000 kgs	41,000 kgs	34,000 kgs
Labour hours	2 hours per unit × 4,000 units = 8,000 hours	3 hours per unit × 3,000 units= 9,000 hours	17,000 hours	18,000 hours
Machine hours	3 hours per unit × 4,000 units = 12,000 hours	2 hours per unit × 3,000 units= 6,000 hours	18,000 hours	18,000 hours

2   **C**

	Seebach	Herdorf
	$	$
Contribution per unit	250	315
Number of labour hours per unit	2	3
Contribution per labour hour:	**125**	**105**
Ranking	1st	2nd

Only the legally binding production of 2,000 units of 'Herdorf' should be honoured in Month 2. It would use up 2,000 × 3 hours = 6,000 hours. The remaining 6,000 hours should be used to produce the top ranking product, the Seebach.

3   **C**

Both statements are correct.

The shadow price is the contribution earned from having one extra unit of limited resource available and is also the extra, on top of the existing cost for that limited resource, which a company would be willing to pay to acquire that extra resource. If the shadow price is $125 per labour hour, it would mean that Cara Co would be willing to pay $125 of overtime premium per hour for the next 2,000 hours. The maximum hourly rate Cara Co would be willing to pay would be ($45 + $125) $170 for an additional 2,000 hours of temporary staff.

4 D

Tutorial note

Although you will not be asked to produce a linear programming graph in the exam, you must be able to read a lot of information from one.

The iso-contribution line can be dragged towards the optimum production point within the feasible region. The optimum point is found at the intersection of the lines 'H=3,000' and '3S + 2H = 12,000'.

This corresponds to a production of 2,000 units of 'Seebach' and 3,000 units of 'Herdorf'.

	Seebach	Herdorf	
	$	$	
Contribution per unit	250	315	
Total number of units as per graph	2,000	3,000	
Total contribution	500,000	945,000	$1,445,000
Fixed costs (monthly)			$300,000

Therefore profit = $1,445,000 – $300,000 = $1,145,000.

5 A

Statement (1) is correct: the line representing the labour constraint '2S + 3H = 24,000' does not delimit the feasible area, and therefore labour is not a scarce resource in Month 3. It can be therefore described as a slack variable.

Statement (2) is not correct: the current number of machine hours satisfies the maximum demand of Herdorfs (3,000 units) and if more machine hours were to become available in Month 3, they should be used to make more of the other product (the Seebach.)

255 HOME ELECTRICS CO (MARCH/JUNE 2021)

1 $17

From the scenario, it is stated that the limiting factor for Product T in the first quarter was direct materials. The calculation is therefore the contribution per kg of direct materials.

Selling Price	$120
Variable Cost ($15+$35+$18)	$(68)
Contribution	$52
Kgs of material required per unit	3 kgs
Contribution per kg of material ($52/3kgs)	**$17.33**

The answer is to be provided to the nearest whole $, therefore $17.

2   B

The constraint equations are given:

Materials   2B + 3T = 2000 (1)
Labour   3B + 5T = 3200 (2)

To solve the simultaneous equations, we must multiply the equations so that we end up with the value of Bs or the value of Ts the same. We could multiply equation (1) by 5 and (2) by 3 to give:

10B + 15T = 10,000 (3)

9B + 15T = 9,600 (4)

Now we can eliminate the Ts by deducting equation (4) from equation (3). This leaves us with

1B = 400.

We can calculate the value of T, by using B = 400 in any of the equations. Using equation (1):

(2 × 400) + 3T = 2,000

800 + 3T = 2,000

3T = 1,200

Therefore, T = 400

Now that we know the quantities of B and T, we can calculate the total contribution.

The contribution of B = ($80 – $10 – $21 – $12) = $37.

The contribution of T = ($120 – $15 – $35 – $18) = $52.

The total contribution is therefore (37 × 400) + (52 × 400) = $35,600.

3   D

The first statement is incorrect. Linear programming identifies the optimum number of units of each product to produce, not the optimum selling price.

The second statement is incorrect. Slack occurs when less of the limited resource is required than is available. When slack occurs, there will be some of the resource left over after production after production of the optimum production pan.

4 $0

There are three constraints for the Large Appliances division (labour hours, material and machine hours). It is stated in the scenario that labour and machine time have been identified as the binding constraints. This suggests that material is NOT a binding constraint, and therefore will have a shadow price of $0. Only binding constraints will have a shadow price.

5   A

(1)   Product D has a slack value. At the optimum solution, the demand for product D is 250, while the output is 200. Product D has unfulfilled demand at the optimum solution, so it has a slack value. This statement is true.

(2)   Contribution of $76,000 will be earned from the optimum production plan. The optimum production plan is to produce 240 units of product F and 200 units of product D. The total contribution will be (240 × $150) + (200 × $200) = $76,000. This statement is true.

(3)   Labour and machine time intersect at the optimum point if shown on a graph. As labour and machine time are the binding constraints, they will be the vertex where the optimum point occurs on a linear programming graph. This statement is true.

256   ALG CO (JUNE 2015, ADAPTED)

1   D

Tutorial note

Make sure you include variable overheads in the calculation of total variable costs per unit.

The total variable cost per unit is made up of direct materials cost per unit, direct labour cost per unit and variable overhead cost per unit is $3.

The variable overheads cost per unit can be calculated using the hi-low method.

$$\text{Variable overheads cost per unit} = \frac{\$1,850,000 \text{ at high level} - \$1,400,000 \text{ at low level}}{\text{high level of units } 350,000 - \text{low level of units } 200,000}$$

Variable overheads cost per unit = $3

Material cost = $2,400,000/200,000 = $12 per unit.

Labour cost = $1,200,000/200,000 = $6 per unit.

Therefore, total variable cost per unit = $21; for 250,000 units, total variable costs = $5,250,000.

2   A

The total variable cost per unit is made up of direct materials cost per unit, direct labour cost per unit and variable overhead cost per unit is $3.

The variable overheads cost per unit can be calculated using the hi-low method.

$$\text{Variable overheads cost per unit} = \frac{\$1,850,000 \text{ at high level} - \$1,400,000 \text{ at low level}}{\text{high level of units } 350,000 - \text{low level of units } 200,000}$$

Variable overheads cost per unit = $3

Fixed costs = $1,400,000 – (200,000 × $3) = $800,000

3 **B**

To find the optimum price, we need to find the demand function.

Demand function is P = a – bx, where P = price and x = quantity.

Therefore, we must find a value for 'a' and 'b' firstly.

b = ΔP/ΔQ = 2/2,000 = 0.001 (ignore the minus sign as it is already reflected in the formula P = a – bx.)

Therefore P = a – 0.001x

Find value for 'a' by substituting in the known price and demand relationship from the question, matching 'p' and 'x' accordingly.

60 = a – (0.001 × 250,000)   60 = a – 250 so 310 = a, therefore P = 310 – 0.001x.

Identify MC: MC = $21

State MR: MR = 310 – 0.002x

Equate MC and MR to find x 21 = 310 – 0.002 × 0.002x = 289 x = 144,500

Substitute x into demand function to find P P = 310 – (0.001 × 144,500)

P = $165.50

4 **A**

If certain conditions exist, the strategy could be a suitable one for ALG Co. The conditions are as follows: – Where a product is new and different, so that customers are prepared to pay high prices in order to gain the perceived status of owning the product early. All we know about ALG Co's product is that it is 'innovative', so it may well meet this condition.

Statement (3) is not correct: where products have a short life cycle this strategy is more likely to be used, because of the need to recover development costs and make a profit quickly. ALG Co's product does only have a three-year life cycle, which does make it fairly short.

Statement (4) is not correct: where barriers to entry exist, which deter other competitors from entering the market; as otherwise, they will be enticed by the high prices being charged. These might include prohibitively high investment costs, patent protection or unusually strong brand loyalty. According to the information we have been given, high development costs were involved in this case, which would be a barrier to entry.

5 **C**

Price skimming, complimentary product pricing and price discrimination would work. without brand loyalty or a long shelf life then a strategy of penetration is unlikely to work. Additionally the uniqueness of the product prevents low prices.

257 JEWEL CO (JUNE 2016, ADAPTED)

1   **4 batches**

Tutorial note

The tabular approach to finding the optimum price Jewel Co should charge is required here. In this exam, pricing questions tend to test the algebraic method (MR=MC), cost-plus and pricing strategies – the tabular method appears less frequently. However, it is impossible to answer this question using the algebraic method, because of the changing fixed costs.

The other trap to avoid here is to calculate the profit per unit for each demand level. This is meaningless for comparison, as it's better to sell 2,000 units for a profit of $1.50 per unit than 1,000 units for a profit of $2 per unit.

Total profit = Total sales revenue – total variable costs – total fixed costs

Batches sold	Total revenue	Total variable costs	Total fixed costs per month	Total profit
		$	$	$
1	1,000 units × $20 = $20,000	1,000 units × $10 = $10,000	10,000	0
2	2,000 units × $18 = $36,000	2,000 units × $8.80 = $17,600	10,000	8,400
3	3,000 units × $16 = $48,000	3,000 units × $7.80 = $23,400	12,000	12,600
4	4,000 units × $13 = $52,000	4,000 units × $6.40 = $25,600	12,000	14,400
5	5,000 units × $12 = $60,000	5,000 units × $6.40 = $32,000	14,000	14,000

The highest total profit is achieved when 4 batches (4,000 units) are sold.

2   **C**

Statement (1) is correct. Jewel Co's fixed costs fit the stepped costs definition – a type of fixed cost that is only fixed within certain levels of activity. Once the upper limit of an activity level is reached then anew higher level of fixed cost becomes relevant.

Statement (2) is also correct. Working on the principle that large cost savings are likely to be found in large cost elements, management's attention should start to focus on how these set-up costs could be reduced. Is there any reason why the headphones units have to be produced in batches of only 1,000? A batch size of 2,000 units would dramatically reduce those set-up costs.

3   B

Statement (1) is not correct. It is the algebraic model that requires a consistent relationship between price (P) and demand (Q), so that a demand equation can be established, usually in the form P = a – bQ. Similarly, there must be a clear relationship between demand and marginal cost, usually satisfied by constant variable cost per unit and constant fixed costs.

Statement (2) is correct. The model is only suitable for companies operating in a monopoly, because any 'optimum' price might become irrelevant if competitors charge significantly lower prices and as Jewel Co is only setting up an online business, it is probably not a monopoly.

4   A

5 $25

When P= 0, demand (Q) = 72,000 units

When P = $5, demand (Q) = (72,000 units – 8,000 units) = 64,000 units.

So, demand (Q) = 72,000 – 5P, where 'P is the selling price in $ (because demand will drop by 8,000 units for every $5 increase in the selling price.)

If the optimum quantity Q = 32,000 units, P = 5/8,000 (72,000 units – 32,000 units) = $25.

258   GAM CO (JUNE 2014)

1   C

Price per unit $30			
Sales volume	Profit	Probability	EV of profit
120,000	$930,000	0.4	$372,000
110,000	$740,000	0.5	$370,000
140,000	$1,310,000	0.1	$131,000
		EV of profit	$873,000

2   C

Price per unit $35			
Sales volume	Profit	Probability	EV of profit
120,000	$1,172,000	0.3	$351,600
110,000	$880,000	0.3	$264,000
140,000	$742,000	0.4	$296,800
		EV of profit	$912,400

3   B

Under the maximin rule, the decision-maker selects the alternative which maximises the minimum payoff achievable.

4   B

Under this rule, the decision-maker selects the alternative which offers the most attractive worst outcome, i.e. the alternative which maximises the minimum profit. In the case of Gam Co, this would be the price of $35 as the lowest profit here is $742,000, as compared to a lowest profit of $740,000 at a price of $30.

5   A

The maximax rule involves selecting the alternative ($30 or $35 selling price) that maximises the maximum payoff available, which in this case is $1,310,000. Therefore, a price per unit of $30 should be selected.

259   MYLO (SEPTEMBER 2016)

1   A

The maximin rule selects the maximum of the minimum outcomes for each supply level. For Mylo the minimum outcomes are:

450 lunches – $1,170

620 lunches – $980

775 lunches – $810

960 lunches – $740

The maximum of these is at a supply level of 450 lunches.

2   D

The minimax regret rule selects the minimum of the maximum regrets.

Demand level	Supply level			
	450	620	775	960
	$	$	$	$
450		190	360	430
620	442	–	217	322
775	845	403	–	230
960	1,326	884	481	–
Max regret	1,326	884	481	430

The minimum of the maximum regrets is $430, so suggests a supply level of 960 lunches.

3   B

Expected values do not take into account the variability which could occur across a range of outcomes; a standard deviation would need to be calculated to assess that, so Statement 2 is correct.

Expected values are particularly useful for repeated decisions where the expected value will be the long-run average, so Statement 4 is correct.

Expected values are associated with risk-neutral decision-makers. A defensive or conservative decision-maker is risk averse, so Statement 1 is incorrect.

Expected values will take into account the likelihood of different outcomes occurring as this is part of the calculation, so Statement 3 is incorrect.

4   A

This requires the calculation of the value of perfect information (VOPI).

Expected value with perfect information = (0.15 × $1,170) + (0.30 × $1,612) + (0.40 × $2,015) + (0.15 × $2,496) = $1,839.50

Expected value without perfect information would be the highest of the expected values for the supply levels = $1,648.25 (at a supply level of 775 lunches).

The value of perfect information is the difference between the expected value with perfect information and the expected value without perfect information = $1,839.50 − $1,648.25 = $191.25, therefore $191 to nearest whole $.

5   D

The investment's sensitivity to fixed costs is 550% ((385/70) × 100), so Statement 3 is correct.

The margin of safety is 84.6%. Budgeted sales are 650 units and BEP sales are 100 units (70/0.7), therefore the margin of safety is 550 units which equates to 84.6% of the budgeted sales, so Statement 4 is therefore correct.

The investment is more sensitive to a change in sales price of 29.6%, so Statement 1 is incorrect.

If variable costs increased by 44%, it would still make a very small profit, so Statement 2 is incorrect.

BUDGETING AND CONTROL

260   LRA (JUNE 2015)

1   C

2   C

Statement (1) is not correct: At present, the LRA finds itself facing particularly difficult circumstances. The fires and the floods have meant that urgent expenditure is now needed on schools, roads and hospitals which would not have been required if these environmental problems had not occurred. Lesting is facing a crisis situation and the main question is therefore whether this is a good time to introduce anything new at the LRA when it already faces so many challenges.

Statement (2) is not correct: the introduction of ZBB in any organisation is difficult at any time because of the fact that the process requires far more skills than, for example, incremental budgeting. Managers would definitely need some specialist training as they simply will not have the skills which they would need in order to construct decision packages. This then would have further implications in terms of time and cost, and, at the moment, both of these are more limited than ever for the LRA.

Statement (3) is correct: with ZBB, the whole budgeting process becomes a lot more cumbersome as it has to be started from scratch. There is a lot of paperwork involved and the whole process of identifying decision packages and determining their costs and benefits is extremely time-consuming. There are often too many decision packages to evaluate and there is frequently insufficient information for them to be ranked. The LRA provides a wide range of services and it is therefore obvious that this would be a really lengthy and costly process to introduce. At the moment, some residents are homeless and several schools have been damaged by fire. How can one rank one as more important than the other when both are equally important for the community?

Statement (4) is correct: ZBB can cause conflict to arise as departments compete for the resources available. Since expenditure is urgently required for schools, roads and hospitals, it is likely that these would be ranked above expenditure on the recycling scheme. In fact, the final phase of the scheme may well be postponed. This is likely to cause conflict between departments as those staff and managers involved in the recycling scheme will be disappointed if the final phase has to be postponed.

3   A

4   D

ZBB will respond to changes in the economic environment since the budget starts from scratch each year and takes into account the environment at that time. This is particularly relevant this year after the fires and the floods. Without ZBB, adequate consideration may not be given to whether the waste management scheme should continue but, if ZBB is used, the scheme will probably be postponed as it is unlikely to rank as high as expenditure needed for schools, housing and hospitals. – If any of the activities or operations at LRA are wasteful, ZBB should be able to identify these and remove them. This is particularly important now when the LRA faces so many demands on its resources. – Managers may become more motivated as they have had a key role in putting the budget together. – It encourages a more questioning attitude rather than just accepting the status quo. – Overall, it leads to a more efficient allocation of resources. – All of the organisations activities and operations are reviewed in depth.

5   B

261 BOKCO (JUNE 2015)

1   B

Statement (2) is not true: a minor error in the design of the model at any point can affect the validity of data throughout the spreadsheet. Even if the spreadsheet is properly designed in the first place, it is very easy to corrupt a model by accidentally inputting data in the wrong place.

Statement (3) is not correct either: spreadsheets cannot take account of qualitative factors that are always, by definition, difficult to quantify.

2   A

Statement (3) is not correct: the operational variances do give a fair reflection of the actual results achieved in the actual conditions that existed. Statement (4) is not correct either: the analysis helps in the standard-setting learning process , which will hopefully result in more useful standards in the future.

3   D

Revised hours for actual production: Cumulative time per hour for 460 units is calculated by using the learning curve formula: $Y = ax^b$

$a = 7$

$x = 460$

$b = -0.1520$ Therefore $y = 7 \times 460^{-0.1520} = 2.7565054$

Therefore revised time for 460 units = 1,268 hours.

Labour efficiency planning variance (Standard hours for actual production − revised hours for actual production) × std rate = ([460 × 7] − 1,268) × $12 = $23,424F

4   C

Labour efficiency operational variance (Revised hours for actual production − actual hours for actual production) × std rate (1,268 − 1,860) × $12 = $7,104A

5   C

Option A is not correct: there **will** be unnecessary extra labour costs. Bokco will have hired too many temporary staff because of the fact that the new product can actually be produced more quickly than originally thought. Given that these staff are hired on three-month contracts, Bokco will presumably have to pay the staff for the full three months even if all of them are not needed.

Option B is therefore not correct either: since Bokco uses cost plus pricing for its products, the price for the product will have been set too high. This means that sales volumes may well have been lower than they otherwise might have been, leading to lost revenue for the company and maybe even failure of the new product launch altogether. This will continue to be the case for the next two months unless the price review is moved forward.

Option C is correct: since production is actually happening more quickly than anticipated, the company may well have run out of raw materials, leading to a stop in production. Idle time is a waste of resources and costs money. If there have been stockouts, the buying department may have incurred additional costs for expedited deliveries or may have been forced to use more expensive suppliers. This would have made the material price variance adverse and negatively affected the buying department's manager bonus.

Option D is not correct: the sales manager will be held responsible for the poorer sales of the product, which will probably be reflected in an adverse sales volume variance. This means that they may lose their bonus through no fault of their own.

262 CORFE CO (SEPTEMBER 2016)

1   D

An 80% activity level is 210,000 units.

Material and labour costs are both variable. Material is $4 per unit and labour is $5.50 per unit. Total variable costs = $9.50 × 210,000 units = $1,995,000

Fixed costs = $750,000

Supervision = $175,000 as five supervisors will be required for a production level of 210,000 units.

Total annual budgeted cost allowance = $1,995,000 + $750,000 + $175,000 = $2,920,000

2   B

Variable cost per hour ($850,000 – $450,000)/(5,000 hours – 1,800 hours) = $125 per hour Fixed cost ($850,000 – (5,000 hours × $125)) = $225,000.

Number of machine hours required for production = 210 batches × 14 hours = 2,940 hours.

Total cost ($225,000 + (2,940 hours × $125)) = $592,500, therefore $593,000 to the nearest $000

3   C

If the budget is flexed, then the effect on sales revenue of the difference between budgeted and actual sales volumes is removed and the variance which is left is the sales price variance.

4   A

Flexible budgeting can be time-consuming to produce as splitting out semi-variable costs could be problematic, so Statement 1 is correct.

Estimating how costs behave over different levels of activity can be difficult to predict, so Statement 2 is correct. A flexible budget will not encourage slack compared to a fixed budget, so Statement 3 is incorrect.

It is a zero-based budget, not a flexible budget, which assesses all activities for their value to the organisation, so Statement 4 is incorrect.

5   C

Spreadsheets can be used to change input variables and new versions of the budgets can be more quickly produced, so Statement 1 is correct.

Sensitivity analysis is also easier to do as variables are more easily changed and manipulated to assess their impact, so Statement 4 is correct.

A common problem of spreadsheets is that it is difficult to trace errors in a spreadsheet and data can be easily corrupted if a cell is changed or data is input in the wrong place, so Statement 2 is incorrect.

Spreadsheets do not show qualitative factors; they show predominantly quantitative data, so Statement 3 is incorrect.

263 BELLAMY CO

1   A

The graph shows a positive correlation, which means that low values of sales are associated with low values of marketing expenditure, and high values of sales are associated with high values of marketing expenditure.

2   C

When there is no marketing expenditure, X = 0, and Y = $5+ (2 × 0) = $5; therefore, sales revenue is $5 × 10,000 = $50,000 on average.

If $1,000 extra is spent on marketing, sales will increase by 20 × $1000 = $20,000. Therefore, the increase in sales revenue when an extra $1,000 is spent on advertising is $20,000 (2 × $10,000).

3   C

Coefficient of determination $r^2 = 0.85^2 = 0.72$

4   C

5   D

All of the stated factors can affect the accuracy of the forecast.

264 OBC (DECEMBER 2015)

1   A

	Actual quantity used	Standard price	Total
White flour	408.50 Kgs	$1.80	$735.30
Wholegrain flour	152 kgs	$2.20	$334.40
Yeast	10 kgs	$20.00	$200.00
Actual quantity at standard price (AQ SP)			**$1,269.70**
Standard quantity at standard price (SQ SP)	950 loaves	$1.34	**$1,273**
Variance			**$3.3 F**

2   C

Ingredient	AQAM (kgs)	AQSM (kgs)	Difference (kgs)	Standard cost ($/kgs)	Variance ($)
White flour	408.50	420.86	12.36 F	1.80	22.25 F
Wholemeal flour	152	140.29	11.71 A	2.20	25.76 A
Yeast	10	9.35	0.65 A	20	13 A
	570.5	570.5			**16.51 A**

Tutorial note

These numbers in the 'Actual Quantity – Standard Mix (AQSM)' column are calculated by taking the actual input in total (that is, 570.5 kgs) from the previous column AQAM, and copying it across to the second column AQSM. Then, work it back in the standard proportions. For example, the standard proportion for 'white flour' is 450 grams out of 610; We take that (450/610) as a proportion and multiply it by the actual total of 570.5 kgs, giving us a standard proportion for white flour, on the actual weight, of (450/610) × 570.5 = 420.89 kgs.

3   D

Tutorial note

There are many ways in which to calculate a yield variance but the easiest is the 'total' method, presented here as the first alternative.

Method 1: the 'Total' method

Actual output (given)	950 loaves
Expected output from actual input	570,500 g/610 g per loaf = 935.25 loaves
Difference	14.75 loaves F
Standard cost per loaf	$1.34
Variance	**$19.77 F**

Method 2: the 'Individual' method:

Ingredient	SQSM (kgs)	AQSM (kgs)	Difference (kgs)	Standard cost ($/kg)	Variance ($)
White flour	427.50	420.86	6.64 F	1.80	11.95 F
Wholemeal flour	142.50	140.29	2.21 F	2.20	4.86 F
Yeast	9.50	9.35	0.15 F	20	3.00 F
	579.5 kgs (*)	570.5 kgs			**19.81 F**

(*) 610 g standard weight per loaf × 950 loaves = 579,500 g or 579.5 kgs

4   B

Statement (1) is not correct: if some mix was left behind, it is the efficiency of turning the inputs into outputs that would be diminished. Therefore, it would be the yield variance that is affected, not the mix variance.

5   C

Both statements are correct: Errors in the quality or proportions of ingredients will make the items sub-standard and therefore rejected by the quality inspector.

When baked at the wrong temperature and therefore be rejected by the quality inspector if they are burnt, or undercooked.

265 VARIANCES – SALES

1 A

"The difference between the sales quantity and **volume** variances is that the standard **mix** is considered in the former. The difference between standard and actual is **ignored**."

2

Profit per unit =	10,600 – (10,600/1.06) = $600
Actual market size =	(30,000/0.1) × 0.95 = 285,000
Sales expected	0.1 × 285,000 = 28,500 units
Actual sales	285,000 × 0.15 = 42,750
So:	
Market size variance	(30,000 – 28,500) × $600 = **$900,000** Adverse
Market share variance	(28,500 – 42,750) × $600 = **$8,550,000** Favourable

3 **$708,000 Adverse**

4 **$2,982,000 Adverse**

Tutorial note

The standard margins (SM) per unit can be calculated as follows:

$10,600 – (10,600/1.06) = $600 (Drastic)   *$13,250 – (10,600/1.06) = $750 (Bomber)*

$16,960 – (10,600/1.06) = $960 (Cracker)

	AQ and AM	Standard Margin	
Drastic	26,000	600	**$41,040,000**
Bomber	16,000	750	
Cracker	14,000	960	
	56,000		**$708,000 Adv**

	AQ and SM	Standard Margin	
Drastic	25,200	600	**$41,748,000**
Bomber	14,000	750	
Cracker	16,800	960	
	56,000		**$2,982,000 Adv**

	SQ and SM	Standard Margin	
Drastic	27,000	600	**$44,730,000**
Bomber	15,000	750	
Cracker	18,000	960	
	60,000		

5 D

266 GRAYSHOTT CO (MARCH 2019)

1 A

Tutorial note

Grayshott operates a marginal costing system and therefore we understand 'standard contribution'(and not standard profit) to be the 'standard margin' here.

In view of the 'difficult economic conditions', we must revise the market demand with a decrease of 10%; this means the revised market demand should be 40,000 units × (1 – 10%), so 36,000 units.

Standard margin (per unit):

	$
Selling price	65.00
Material cost (5.2 kgs × $4 per kg)	(20.80)
Labour (2 hours × $8 per hour)	(16.00)
Variable overheads (2 hours × $4 per hour)	(8.00)
Contribution	20.20

Market share variance: (38,000 units – 36,000 units) × $20.20 = $40,400 favourable

2 C

Tutorial note

We are told here that the actual cost of materials amounted to $4.40 per kilogram. As the total actual expenditure was $836,000, we must have purchased $836,000/$4.40 = 190,000 kilograms of materials.

Original standard price $4 per kilogram of material

Revised standard price $4 × (1 + 6%) = $4.24 per kilogram of material

Based on actual purchases of materials:

190,000 kilograms should have cost 190,000 × $4.00 (old standard) = $760,000

190,000 kilograms should have cost 190,000 × $4.24 (revised standard) = $805,600
Variance = $760,000 – $805,600 = $45,600 Adverse

3 **B**

The budgeted labour rate per hour was, as per question, $8 per hour.

The actual labour rate per hour was 25% higher than the standard of $8 per hour; this means that the actual labour rate per hour was $8 × (1+25%) = $10. This is an adverse operational difference of $2 per hour.

Number of hours worked (based on actual performance) = ($798,000/$10) = 79,800 hours.

79,800 hours × $2.00 per hour adverse = $159,600 adverse.

4 **D**

All statements are correct. Labour efficiency planning variance will occur when the standard hours have to be revised due to factors which are beyond the control of the operational managers. All the factors would require the original standard hours to be revised and would therefore cause a labour efficiency planning variance.

5 **C**

Both statements are correct and are known issues with the introduction of a system of planning and operating variances.

267 ROMEO CO (DECEMBER 2016)

1 **B**

Dough 18.9 kg × ($7.60 – $6.50) = $20.79 favourable

Tomato sauce 6.6 kg × ($2.50 – $2.45) = $0.33 favourable

Cheese 14.5 kg × ($20.00 – $21.00) = $14.50 adverse

Herbs 2 kg × ($8.40 – $8.10) = $0.60 favourable

Total material price variance = $7.22 favourable

2 **D**

	AQSM	AQAM	Diff	Std	Variance
	kg	kg	kg	cost	$
Dough	20	18.9	1.1 F	7.60	8.36 F
Sauce	8	6.6	1.4 F	2.50	3.50 F
Cheese	12	14.5	2.5 A	20.00	50.00 A
Herbs	2	2		8.40	
	42	42			38.14 A

3 **A**

	SQSM	AQSM	Diff	Std	Variance
	kg	kg	kg	cost	$
Dough	22	21.43	0.57 F	7.60	4.33 F
Sauce	8.8	8.57	0.23 F	2.50	0.58 F
Cheese	13.2	12.86	0.34 F	20.00	6.80 F
Herbs	2.2	2.14	0.06 F	8.40	0.50 F
	46.2	45			12.21 F

4   A

A favourable mix variance indicates that a higher proportion of cheaper ingredients were used in production compared to the standard mix.

5   C

The actual cost per pizza will be lower than the standard cost per pizza because expensive cheese has been replaced with cheaper tomato sauce.

The usage variance equals the mix and yield variances. The yield variance will be zero as 100 pizzas used 42 kg, so the mix and usage variances will be the same.

Sales staff should not automatically lose their bonus as the reduced sales could be a result of the change in mix affecting the quality of the pizza and the new chef will only be responsible for the mix and yield variances as they have no control over the purchase costs of ingredients.

PERFORMANCE MEASUREMENT AND CONTROL

268   PIND CO

1   31% and 2.625

	25%	31%	2.625	1.625
Gearing ratio		✓		
Interest cover			✓	

Gearing: 190,000/610,000 = 31%   Interest cover 42,000/16,000 = 2.625

2   B

3   B

4   26 days

Quick ratio = 0.9.

We know payables is $50,000 and therefore, receivables + cash = $45,000.

As receivables : cash is 2 : 2.5, so receivables = $20,000 and hence receivable days are: $(20,000/(42,000/0.15)) \times 365 = 26$ days.

5   C

Current asset turnover = turnover/capital employed = $(42,000/0.15)/610,000 = 0.459$

Increase turnover by 20%: $((42,000/0.15) \times 1.2)/610,000 = 0.551$, which is an increase of 20%.

Section 6

ANSWERS TO CONSTRUCTED RESPONSE QUESTIONS – SECTION C

INFORMATION, TECHNOLOGIES AND SYSTEMS FOR ORGANISATIONAL PERFORMANCE

269   B5 CARS EIS

Key answer tips

This question tests your knowledge of sources of information and the operation of an executive information system (EIS).

In answering the question you need to recognise the costs and benefits associated with information with particular reference to the distinction between internally produced information and that gathered from external sources.

(a)   One of the main reasons why B5 Cars' EIS is becoming expensive to operate is the amount of data which has been, and is being, accumulated. For an EIS to be effective there is a requirement for large amounts of information to be easily accessible – the data should be on-line and as up-to-date as possible. This has disc storage implications which increase over time as the volume of information increases.

The increased costs do not end with disk storage, however. As the system is required to handle larger volumes of data, there are numerous knock-on costs. The larger the database the more processing power required to conduct straightforward operations. Therefore, another increased expense may be a requirement to invest in hardware as the original processor proves inadequate to handle the volume of information within acceptable response times.

Data is obtained from various different external sources; this may be causing a requirement for extra disk storage in excess of the amount required as a result of the normal growth of the databank.

The information requirements of the executives using an EIS may change over time. This means that, however carefully the system was set up originally, there will be costs involved in making changes to the way in which the system is set up. The degree with which maintenance and support costs increase will be dependent to some extent on the original design of the programs and database and to what extent the information requirements alter.

Another area where costs may increase is the network service. As the volume of data increases, particularly if appropriate hardware investment is not made, it is likely that it will take longer to extract the required information. This will result in greater costs of actually using the line. The rental of the line may also have increased.

The EIS uses data collated from various sources. There are potential costs associated with the capture of this data; large amounts of data may need to be manually keyed in which has implications on staffing costs or the cost of hiring an agency to do the work.

(b) Management's decision to concentrate on internally-produced information will have serious implications.

Market information

It is important for companies to be aware of the activities of their competitors. By collecting only internally-produced information the management are getting a restricted picture of what is really taking place. Management need to know how their products measure up to those of their competitors in terms of quality, design etc.

Without external information the information system can hardly be described as an EIS, but would be providing information at an operational level. It is important for organisations to establish their own indicators as a means of measuring their performance, but it is at least as important to set these in context. For example, if a production unit is performing well against its own measures but is failing to perform well in relation to its competitors, management needs to be aware of this and take action to recover the situation.

Without competitor information B5 Cars may find that they are out of line with the rest of the industry. They may find that their competitors are offering free finance, as an example, whereas B5 Cars are offering 'cheap' finance at 7% APR; their main competitors may offer free finance for the first year after purchase. This information is invaluable to B5 Cars to ensure that they remain competitive.

Customer information

One of the sources of information which will be lost will be that relating to customers. This loss will have a damaging impact on the firm; any organisation needs to know about its market, both existing and potential, to survive and grow. Even if an organisation currently enjoys a strong position in its sector of the market it would be short-sighted to assume that this situation would remain without consideration of the ever-changing market. Predicting market behaviour is challenging enough with access to wide-ranging information from external sources; without these tools the task becomes virtually impossible.

The industry

There are many sources of information on specific industries, in this case the motor vehicle industry, which will be lost. Societies established for manufacturers in a particular industry can provide useful information and comparisons about all manufacturers within an industry.

The effect on the company's information system

An EIS needs to afford access to information which is up-to-date and relevant for managers to manage the organisation. The loss of access as described above will, in a very short time, produce the effect that the information available via the EIS is inadequate for effective decision-making. The decisions taken will be short-term and reactive.

The system will cease to be an EIS but will, instead, provide a control mechanism. The kind of information the system will provide will be at an operational level (how many man hours was taken to produce a particular car; how many hours of overtime etc.) rather than providing information to support management decisions.

The effect on the company's products

Without access to external information, B5 Cars will be unaware of technological innovations; as a result their products will lag behind the rest of the industry and their own innovations may not take full advantage of new technological breakthroughs. There is the danger of 'reinventing the wheel' which will leave them behind in terms of technological advances and incur unnecessary research and development costs.

External market information would assist B5 Cars to identify trends in the motor industry, from which they could attempt to create marketing opportunities. Without this information marketing opportunities will be forgone.

The dearth of market information will mean that the organisation cannot accurately position their products in terms of pricing which in turn will affect their profitability. With accurate market information a producer is in a better position to optimise profits by pricing their product at a price low enough to sell, but high enough to ensure maximum profits. The effects on the products identified above will adversely affect the customer's perception thereof.

The Board's decision appears to be misguided which, in the longer-term, may affect the organisation's profitability and future market share.

270 REES INVESTMENTS

Tutorial note

Where possible points should be illustrated using examples relevant to the organisation described in the question.

(a) Decision support systems are software solutions designed to support managers making semi-structured or unstructured decisions. Such systems are best suited to situations where part of the problem is well understood, and hence can be automated, but part is not well understood and the manager will have to use judgement to come to a final decision. Many managers develop simple decision support systems using spreadsheets to provide them with an understanding of the data relevant data.

Decision support systems will usually consist of:

- A large database of information usually drawn from both internal and external sources.

- Problem exploration facilities which allow users to explore different scenarios using what-if and sensitivity analysis.

- Goal seeking and optimisation functions to allow users to determine the values of variables required to achieve a pre-determined or optimal solution.

- Graphical tools to display statistical data.

- In-built statistical, simulation and financial functions to allow users to develop relevant models quickly.

A decision support system could be useful at Rees Investments because the investment decisions are essentially semi-structured or unstructured. Hence a significant part of the problem can be understood from an analysis of data. However, Mark Rees will still be reliant upon his analysts correctly interpreting the information and making appropriate judgements. The decision support system is more likely to be successful if the current investment problems are caused by poor analysis of data rather than by poor judgement or by difficulties due to the worsening economic climate.

(b) An expert system is a software model of the knowledge, facts and reasoning of an acknowledged human expert. The expert system software usually represents knowledge as a set of inter-connected rules. These rules have usually been derived from discussions with experts as well as from observing and recording their decision making behaviour. Experts systems are usually perceived as a specialised form of a decision support system where reasoning is more important than computation. Such systems are particularly appropriate for handling situations where decisions have to be taken on incomplete information.

An expert system usually consists of:

- a knowledge base where the rules and facts are stored

- an inference engine which stores problem solving procedures to perform the reasoning

- a knowledge acquisition facility to allow the expert to enter knowledge and facts

- a knowledge presentation and explanation function to allow users to interrogate the expert system and to have the expert system's decision explained to them.

In the Rees Investments example, it would be possible to use expert system software to build an expert system of the knowledge and expertise of Mark Rees. In this way, less accomplished analysts could use his expertise to help them make their own investment decisions.

This may be particularly attractive to Mark Rees because:

- the company was successful when he used his approach

- he would be reasonably confident that analysts would be using a standard proven approach.

However, it has to be hoped that his approach is still valid in the changed economic environment and that the early success of the company was largely due to his expertise and not the favourable economic climate prevailing at that time.

271   CDE

Key answer tips

There are many types of information system that are available to firms like CDE. It is worth thinking about both parts of (a) together, since you will obviously need to ensure that your recommended system for part (ii) is one that you outline in part (i). Note that there are only 8 marks available in part (a) so this is not an opportunity to write all you know about every system!

In making your recommendation in part (a)(ii) it is critical that you recommend a system that meets the needs of CDE, so your answer should refer to points made in the scenario when justifying your recommendation.

Part (b) of the question commences with a statement about the business environment and the desire to reduce the cost of accounting. These points should be borne in mind throughout your answer, particularly when you come to recommendations in part (ii). You will need to review the scenario again to find precise examples of the current management accounting system (simply look for anything that you will have studied in your earlier management accounting exams!), and then go onto to evaluate these elements.

(a)   (i)   The following types of information system are available to manufacturing firms like CDE:

A **transaction processing system** (TPS) serves the operational level of the organisation. The system records all of the daily routine transactions that take place within the organisation, relating to each particular aspect of operational activities.

Data from the TPS is fed into a **management information system** (MIS). An MIS takes the bulk of data from the TPS and develops it into something useful to management in support of its decision-making responsibility. The MIS is usually computer-based, making use of spreadsheets where 'what if?' analysis can be carried out.

An **enterprise resource planning** (ERP) system is a sophisticated MIS system that covers the whole range of the organisation's activities. It promises the 'seamless integration of all the information flowing through the company'. ERP can be thought of as a development of the MRP II system used currently by CDE. A data warehouse is maintained of inputs from the TPS and MIS systems, from which any required customised report can be produced.

A **strategic enterprise management** (SEM) system assists management in making high-level strategic decisions. Tools such as activity-based management (ABM) and the balanced scorecard are applied to the data in the data warehouse to enable the strategic goals of the organisation to be worked towards.

An **executive information system** (EIS) or **executive support system** (ESS) gives management access to both internal and external data. Managers can access information to monitor the operations of the organisation and to scan general business conditions. The data for an EIS is online and updated in real time to ensure its integrity for decision making at a senior management level.

(ii) CDE is a substantially sized company, listed on the stock exchange, and operating in a highly competitive and fast-moving business. It currently uses an MRP II system to control production scheduling and labour and machine utilisation. This is satisfactory as far as controlling day-to-day operational requirements, but there is an absence of information being collected and presented to management for strategic and decision support purposes.

I recommend that CDE moves towards establishing an EIS system. This will enable managers to integrate the data from the current MRP II system with the known data about customer requirements and available suppliers. Then managers will be able to see an overview of the business as a whole, and can drill down if they wish to see more detail on the contents of any particular figure.

Tutorial note

Other systems could be recommended here and marks will be awarded if reasons are provided. An ERP system would be highly effective at meeting the need for integrated information, the lack of which was mentioned a couple of times in the scenario. Or a SEM system would suit a business such as this in a fast moving, competitive, modern manufacturing environment.

(b) (i) The current management accounting system provides:

- a detailed annual budgeting exercise
- standard costing for labour and materials
- production overhead recovery on the basis of machine hours.

Labour and material costs are analysed from operator and machine timesheets, and variances from standard costs are calculated and investigated.

CDE is therefore carrying out traditional old-fashioned management accounting, whose relevance can be questioned in a fast-moving business environment such as the manufacture of automotive components.

An annual budget is currently drawn up at the beginning of each year and then used for feedforward (planning) and feedback (control) purposes. However, with an uncertain sales mix and in a competitive sales environment, it will be very difficult to draw up an accurate budget. The objective of accuracy may be frustrated, anyway, by managers submitting sales targets that are very low and easy to achieve so that they will not be under any pressure to achieve the budgeted amounts.

Overhead allocation will be difficult to achieve accurately when so many different components are being offered for sale, in both large and small batches. Allocating such overhead on the basis of machine hours is a convenient, but essentially arbitrary, method.

Standard costing is currently carried out for labour and for materials. A standard cost card will be drawn up for each product, suggesting the 'standard' amount of cost of labour and materials that is appropriate. Variances are then calculated between actual amounts and standard amounts. Such traditional standard costing is appropriate in a mass production scenario where competitive advantage is sought by obtaining a low unit cost of production by producing very large production runs. It is much less appropriate in a JIT environment such as at CDE.

In conclusion, the current management accounting system is not altogether relevant to the JIT operations of CDE in the competitive environment in which it operates.

(ii)   The management accounting system should be improved by:

- introducing rolling budgets rather than fixed budgets

- replacing the current detailed standard costing system with a 'lean' management accounting system focused on eliminating waste rather than on building up inventories to reduce the unit cost of production

- moving to an ABC method of overhead allocation rather than recovery on the basis of machine hours worked. This should enable accurate costing and pricing decisions to be taken, which is essential in the price sensitive market in which CDE operates.

CDE currently operates a management accounting system dominated by the costings of its MRP II system. As described in part (a), the move to an EIS system should enable a more holistic view of decision taking by management, concentrating on adding value and satisfying customers rather than on the pursuit of accounting-based cost control.

272   THE MG ORGANISATION

Key answer tips

Part (a) is a straightforward section, requiring you to look at the benefits of two system types over a TPS. Try to include reference to the situation of MG where possible in your answer.

There is a lot to talk about for only 5 marks in part (b) so plan your answer first and ensure that you make the best points only.

(a)   Explanations of system types

A transaction processing system is designed primarily for processing transactions, often within a stand-alone system for a job-specific application. Management reports are produced from such systems, but these are essentially a summary of the transactions that have been processed or provide an analysis of data on the computer master files. The information produced by transaction processing systems is therefore of operational or tactical value, but not strategic value, and it is used to prepare reports for the line management responsible for the particular area of operations.

An ERPS is a commercial software package that integrates information from a variety of sources, both internal and external. The information is both financial and non-financial. An ERP system might capture transaction data from a number of different transaction systems, as well as information from external sources (such as suppliers). This information can then be used to prepare specially-designed reports for management covering a range of different activities, and of strategic as well as tactical value.

Benefits of an ERP system

ERP systems can be used to provide performance data for multi-functional activities, rather than specific transactions, and so can be valuable for activity-based costing, balanced scorecard performance analysis and supply chain management.

ERP systems can provide benefits in excess of transaction processing systems because they provide better-quality strategic management information for senior management. The actual value of any particular ERPS obviously depends on the circumstances of each case, but as a general rule, an information system is beneficial if the expected improvements in management decision-making exceed the cost of providing the system.

Benefits of an EIS

Executive information systems (EIS) as their name suggests, provide information to senior executives within an organisation, from information sources both inside and outside the organisation. They allow executives to monitor the performance of the organisation and scan general business conditions at any time and in 'real time'. They allow executives to obtain summary performance information, and 'drill down' into further detail if required. They can also be used to make 'one-off' file interrogations to obtain information. Crucially, they are easy to use, and an executive does not have to be an IT expert or systems expert to benefit from using an EIS.

An EIS allows senior management to obtain performance information in 'real time' and should therefore help management to improve their control over the organisation. This is a benefit that transaction processing systems are unable to provide.

(b) Budgetary allocations

Budget allocations for IT in the past have been made using an inefficient system. The system has been to allow a 5% to 10% increase in the budget allocation each year to allow for inflation and system upgrades. This approach to budgeting inevitably builds 'slack' into the budget and encourages wasteful spending.

The system is also weak because it appears to be based on the view that the existing IT systems are more or less satisfactory, and will simply need improving or changing with upgrades from time to time. The budgeting process does not appear to consider whether the IT systems remain adequate for the information needs of the organisation.

The appropriate approach should be to consider the information requirements of the organisation and its management, and the benefits that would be obtained from the information. Costs of providing information should be compared with the potential benefits. New IT system developments should also be considered, in terms of costs and benefits. Instead of following an incremental budgeting approach, an activity-based budgeting approach or a zero-based budgeting approach would probably be more effective in constructing a better budget.

> **Tutorial note**
>
> *Although you did not have to use terms like zero-based budgeting, it is good to bring in topics from your earlier studies in this exam.*

Evaluation of benefits

The benefits of an ERPS or EIS are difficult to measure quantitatively. They should provide better management information, and it is important that any new system should be capable of providing the information that management need.

To estimate the benefits of a system, it would be appropriate to consider the improvements in management information that the system would provide (more information, more up-to-date information, more accurate information, and so on) and how this should improve the quality of decision-making within the organisation. If an estimate can be made of how decision-making might improve, it should be possible to make a rough estimate of the potential benefits, for example in terms of revenues, cost savings or profits.

SPECIALIST COST AND MANAGEMENT ACCOUNTING TECHNIQUES

273 GADGET CO (DECEMBER 2010)

(a)   **Cost per unit under full absorption costing**

Total annual overhead costs:	$
Machine set up costs	26,550
Machine running costs	66,400
Procurement costs	48,000
Delivery costs	54,320
	6,900
	195,270

Overhead absorption rate:

	A	B	C	Total
Production volumes	15,000	12,000	18,000	
Labour hours per unit	0.1	0.15	0.2	
Total labour hours	1,500	1,800	3,600	6,900

Therefore, overhead absorption rate = $195,270/6,900 = $28.30 per hour.

Cost per unit

	A	B	C
	$	$	$
Raw materials ($1.20 × 2/3/4 kg)	2.4	3.6	4.8
Direct labour ($14.80 × 0.1/0.15/0.2 hrs)	1.48	2.22	2.96
Overhead ($28.30 × 0.1/0.15/0.2 hrs)	2.83	4.25	5.66
Full cost per unit	6.71	10.07	13.42

(b) **Cost per unit using full absorption costing**

Cost drivers:

Cost pools	$	Cost driver
Machine set up costs	26,550	36 production runs (16 + 12 + 8)
Machine running costs	66,400	32,100 machine hours (7,500 + 8,400 + 16,200)
Procurement costs	48,000	94 purchase orders (24 + 28 + 42)
Delivery costs	54,320	140 deliveries (48 + 30 + 62)
	195,270	

Cost per machine set up	$26,550/36 = $737.50
Cost per machine hour	$66,400/32,100 = $2.0685
Cost per order	$48,000/94 = $510.6383
Cost per delivery	$54,320/140 = $388

Allocation of overheads to each product:

	A	B	C	Total
	$	$	$	$
Machine set up costs	11,800	8,850	5,900	26,550
Machine running costs	15,514	17,375	33,510	66,400
Procurement costs	12,255	14,298	21,447	48,000
Delivery costs	18,624	11,640	24,056	54,320
	58,193	52,163	84,913	195,270
Number of units produced	15,000	12,000	18,000	
	$	$	$	
Overhead cost per unit	3.88	4.35	4.72	

Total cost per unit	A	B	C
Materials	2.4	3.6	4.8
Labour	1.48	2.22	2.96
Overheads	3.88	4.35	4.72
	7.76	10.17	12.48

(c) **Using activity-based costing**

When comparing the full unit costs for each of the products under absorption costing as compared to ABC, the following observations can be made:

Product A

The unit cost for product A is 16% higher under ABC as opposed to traditional absorption costing. Under ABC, it is $7.76 per unit compared to $6.71 under traditional costing. This is particularly significant given that the selling price for product A is $7.50 per unit. This means that when the activities that give rise to the overhead costs for product A are taken into account, product A is actually making a loss. If the company wants to improve profitability it should look to either increase the selling price of product A or somehow reduce the costs. Delivery costs are also high, with 48 deliveries a year being made for product A. Maybe the company could seek further efficiencies here. Also, machine set up costs are higher for product A than for any of the other products, due to the larger number of production runs. The reason for this needs to be identified and, if possible, the number of production runs needs to be reduced.

Product B

The difference between the activity based cost for B as opposed to the traditional cost is quite small, being only $0.10. Since the selling price for B is $12, product B is clearly profitable whichever method of overhead allocation is used. ABC does not really identify any areas for concern here.

Product C

The unit cost for C is 7% lower under ABC when compared to traditional costing. More importantly, while C looks like it is making a loss under traditional costing, ABS tells a different story. The selling price for C is $13 per unit and, under ABC, it costs $12.48 per unit. Under traditional absorption costing, C is making a loss of $0.42 per unit. Identifying the reason for the differences in C, it is apparent that the number of production runs required to produce C is relatively low compared to the volumes produced. This leads to a lower apportionment of the machine set up costs to C than would be given under traditional absorption costing. Similarly, the number of product tests carried out on C is low relative to its volume.

ABC is therefore very useful in identifying that C is actually more profitable than A, because of the reasons identified above. The company needs to look at the efficiency that seems to be achieved with C (low number of production runs less testing) and see whether any changes can be made to A, to bring it more in line with C. Of course, this may not be possible, in which case the company may consider whether it wishes to continue to produce A and whether it could sell higher volumes of C.

Marking scheme

			Marks
(a)	Contribution per unit		
	Overhead absorption rate		2
	Cost for A		1
	Cost for B		1
	Cost for C		1
		Maximum	5
(b)	Cost under ABC		
	Correct cost driver rates		5
	Correct overhead unit cost for A		1
	Correct overhead unit cost for B		1
	Correct overhead unit cost for C		1
	Correct cost per unit under ABC		1
		Maximum	9
(c)	Using ABC to improve profitability		
	One mark per point about the Gadget Co		1
		Maximum	6
Total			20

274 BRICK BY BRICK (JUNE 2010)

(a) Costs and quoted prices for the GC and the EX using labour hours to absorb overheads:

		GC $	EX $
Materials		3,500	8,000
Labour	300 hrs × $15/hr	4,500	
	500 hrs × $15/hr		7,500
Overheads	300 hrs × $10/hr (W1)	3,000	
	500 hrs × $10/hr		5,000
Total cost		11,000	20,500
Quoted price		16,500	30,750

Workings:

(W1) Overhead absorption rate is calculated as $400,000/40,000 hrs = $10/hr

(b) Costs and quoted prices for the GC and the EX using ABC to absorb overheads:

		GC	EX
		$	$
Materials		3,500	8,000
Labour	300 hrs × $15/hr	4,500	
	500 hrs × $15/hr		7,500
Overheads			
– Supervisor	(W2)/(W3)	180	1,080
– Planers	(W2)/(W3)	280	1,400
– Property	(W2)/(W3)	1,800	3,000
Total cost		10,260	20,980
Quoted price		15,390	31,470

(W2)

	Costs	Number of drivers	Cost per driver
Supervisor	90,000	500	180
Planners	70,000	250	280
Property	240,000	40,000	6

(W3)

	Supervisor	Planner	Property
Cost per driver (W2)	$180	$280	$6
GC	180 × 1 = 180	280 × 1 = 280	6 × 300 = 1,800
EX	180 × 6 = 1,080	280 × 5 = 1,400	6 × 500 = 3,000

(c) The pricing policy is a matter for BBB to decide. They could elect to maintain the current 50% mark-up on cost and if they did the price of the GC would fall by around 7% in line with the costs. This should make them more competitive in the market.

They could also reduce the prices by a little less than 7% (say 5%) in order to increase internal margins a little.

It is possible that the issue lies elsewhere. If the quality of the work or the reputation and reliability of the builder is questionable then reducing prices is unlikely to improve sales. It is conceivable that BBB has a good reputation for EX but not for GC, but more likely that a poor reputation would affect all products. Equally poor service levels or lack of flexibility in meeting customer needs may be causing the poor sales performance. These too will not be 'corrected' by merely reducing prices.

It is also possible that the way salesmen discuss or sell their products for the GC is not adequate so that in some way customers are being put off placing the work with BBB.

BBB is in competition and it perhaps needs to reflect this in its pricing more (by 'going rate pricing') and not seek to merely add a mark-up to its costs.

BBB could try to penetrate the market by pricing some jobs cheaply to gain a foothold. Once this has been done the completed EX or GC could be used to market the business to new customers.

The price of the EX would also need consideration. There is no indication of problems in the selling of the EX and so BBB could consider pushing up their prices by around 2% in line with the cost increase. On the figures in my answer the price goes up for a typical extension to $31,470 from $30,750 a rise of $720. This does not seem that significant and so might not lose a significant number of sales.

The reliability and reputation of a builder is probably more important than the price that they charge for a job and so it is possible that the success rate on job quotes may not be that price sensitive.

(d)   Marginal costs are those costs that are incurred as a consequence of the job being undertaken. In this case they would include only the materials and the labour. If overheads are included then this is known as total absorption costing.

Overheads are for many businesses fixed by nature and hence do not vary as the number of jobs changes. In a traditional sense any attempt to allocate costs to products (by way of labour hours for example) would be arbitrary with little true meaning being added to the end result. The overhead absorption rate (OAR) is merely an average of these costs (over labour hours) and is essentially meaningless. This switch (to marginal costing) would also avoid the problem of the uncertainty of budget volume. Budget volume is needed in order to calculate the fixed cost absorption rate.

The marginal cost (MC) is more understandable by managers and indeed customers and a switch away from total absorption cost (TAC) could have benefits in this way. Clearly if overheads are going to be excluded for the cost allocations then they would still have to be covered by way of a bigger margin added to the costs. In the end all costs have to be paid for and covered by the sales in order to show a profit.

A more modern viewpoint is that activity causes costs to exist. For example, it is the existence of the need for site visits that gives rise to the need for a supervisor and therefore, for their costs. If the activities that drive costs are identified, more costs can then be directly traced to products, hence eradicating the need for arbitrary apportionment of many overhead costs. This has the benefit of all costs being covered, rather than the potential shortfall that can arise if marginal cost plus pricing is used.

In the long run businesses have to cover all costs including fixed overheads in order to make a profit, whichever pricing strategy is adopted.

275   JOLA PUBLISHING CO (JUNE 2008)

Key answer tips

Candidates will be expected to understand why overhead allocation differs between activity based costing and traditional absorption costing. The examiner is unlikely to test only the numbers.

(a)   The first thing to point out is that the overhead allocations to the two products have not changed by that much. For example the CB has absorbed only $0.05 more overhead. The reason for such a small change is that the overheads are dominated by property costs (75% of total overhead) and the 'driver' for these remains machine hours once the switch to ABC is made. Thus no difference will result from the switch to ABC in this regard.

The major effect on the cost will be for quality control. It is a major overhead (23% of total) and there is a big difference between the relative number of machine hours for each product and the number of inspections made (the ABC driver). The CB takes less time to produce than the TJ, due to the shortness of the book. It will therefore carry a smaller amount of overhead in this regard. However, given the high degree of government regulation, the CB is subject to 'frequent' inspections whereas the TJ is inspected only rarely. This will mean that under ABC the CB will carry a high proportion of the quality control cost and hence change the relative cost allocations.

The production set up costs are only a small proportion of total cost and would be, therefore, unlikely to cause much of a difference in the cost allocations between the two products. However this hides the very big difference in treatment. The CB is produced in four long production runs, whereas the TJ is produced monthly in 12 production runs. The relative proportions of overhead allocated under the two overhead treatments will be very different. In this case the TJ would carry much more overhead under ABC than under a machine hours basis for overhead absorption.

Tutorial note

Many candidates demonstrated an understanding of this area but failed to get enough depth to score a good mark. There are thirteen minutes available, which should be sufficient time to plan and write up a succinct and relevant answer. Rather than just discussing overheads in general, a good approach would be to review each of the three overhead costs in turn. It should be possible to get two marks for the discussion of each overhead. A general introduction and overall conclusion would gain another two marks.

(b) **Cost per unit calculation using machine hours for overhead absorption**

	CB ($)		**TJ ($)**
Paper (400g at $2/kg)	0.80	(100 g at $1/kg)	0.10
Printing (50 ml at $30/ltr)	1.50	(150 ml at $30/ltr)	4.50
Machine cost (6 mins at $12/hr)	1.20	(10 mins at $12/hr)	2.00
Overheads (6 mins at $24/hr) (W1)	2.40	(10 mins at $24/hr)	4.00
Total cost	5.90		10.60
Sales price	9.30		14.00
Margin	3.40		3.40

Workings:

(W1) Workings for overheads:

Total overhead $2,880,000

Total machine hours (1,000,000 × 6 mins) + (120,000 × 10 mins) = 7,200,000 mins

= 120,000 hours

Cost per hour = $2,880,000 ÷120,000

= $24 per hour

	CB ($)		TJ ($)
Paper (400 g at $2/kg)	0.80	(100 g at $1/kg)	0.10
Printing (50 ml at $30/ltr)	1.50	(150 ml at $30/ltr)	4.50
Machine cost (6 mins at $12/hr)	1.20	(10 mins at $12/hr)	2.00
Overheads (W2)	2.41	(W2)	3.88
	———		———
Total cost	5.91		10.48
Sales price	9.30		14.00
	———		———
Margin	3.39		3.52
	———		———

(c) **Cost per unit calculations under ABC**

(W2) Working for ABC overheads   alternative approach

	Total $	CB $	TJ $	No of drivers	Cost/ driver	CB $	TJ $
Property costs	2,160,000	1,800,000	360,000	120,000	18/hr	1.80	3.00
Quality control	668,000	601,200	66,800	200	3340/ inspection	0.6012	0.56
Production set up	52,000	13,000	39,000	16	3250/ run	0.013	0.325
	———	———	———			———	———
Total	2,880,000	2,414,200	465,800	Cost per unit		2.41	3.88
Production level		1,000,000	120,000			———	———
Cost per unit		2.41	3.88				

The above overheads have been split on the basis of the following activity levels:

	Driver	CB	TJ
Property costs	Machine hours	100,000	20,000
Quality control	Inspections	180	20
Production set up	Set ups	4	12

A cost per driver approach is also acceptable.

Tutorial note

Ensure your answer is well laid out in a logical manner so you get follow-through marks, even if you make a silly error earlier on.

Note: The original question asked for implementation problems. The suggested solution is as follows:

There are many problems with ABC, which, despite its academic superiority, cause issues on its introduction.

- Lack of understanding: ABC is not fully understood by many managers and therefore is not fully accepted as a means of cost control.

- Difficulty in identifying cost drivers: In a practical context, there are frequently difficulties in identifying the appropriate drivers. For example, property costs are often significant and yet a single driver is difficult to find.

- Lack of appropriate accounting records: ABC needs a new set of accounting records, this is often not immediately available and therefore resistance to change is common. The setting up of new cost pools is needed which is time consuming.

	Marking scheme		
			Marks
(a)	Comment on rent and rates		2
	Comment on quality control		2
	Comment on production set up cost		2
	Comment on overall effect		1
			___
		Maximum	**7**
			___
(b)	Paper cost CB		½
	Paper cost TJ		½
	Printing ink cost CB		½
	Printing ink cost TJ		½
	Machine cost CB		½
	Machine cost TJ		½
	Overhead OAR		½
	Overhead cost CB		½
	Overhead cost TJ		½
	Margins		½
			___
		Maximum	**5**
			___
(c)	Split of rent and rates		2
	Split of quality control		2
	Split of production set up cost		2
	Overhead cost per unit CB		½
	Overhead cost per unit TJ		½
	Direct cost as above		1
			___
		Maximum	**8**
			___
Total			**20**
			___

Examiner's comments (extract)

An activity based costing question. As is common with my questions I facilitated a commentary on some calculations already done (in part a) and then followed that up with a requirement to some calculations themselves parts (b) and (c).

In part (a) some candidates misread the requirement and gave text book explanations of the process involved in ABC. This gained very few marks. The old adage of 'answer the question' would have served well here. Vague references to 'activities' without referring to the specific activities in the question gained only a few marks. I wanted candidates to explain why these products costs had changed following the introduction of ABC.

Parts (b) and (c) were extremely well done by many.

Part (d) (i.e. the additional requirement) also produced some good answers. The requirement asked for implementation problems not merely "issues" and so marks were lost through poor focus.

276 WARGRIN (DECEMBER 2008)

(a) Lifecycle costing is a concept which traces all costs to a product over its complete lifecycle, from design through to cessation. It recognises that for many products there are significant costs to be incurred in the early stages of its lifecycle. This is probably very true for Wargrin Limited. The design and development of software is a long and complicated process and it is likely that the costs involved would be very significant.

The profitability of a product can then be assessed taking all costs in to consideration.

It is also likely that adopting lifecycle costing would improve decision-making and cost control. The early development costs would have to be seen in the context of the expected trading results therefore preventing a serious over spend at this stage or under pricing at the launch point.

Key answer tips

Easy marks were available for an explanation of this core costing technique. Common errors included candidates confusing lifecycle costing with the product life cycle and/or a lack of discussion of lifecycle costing within the context of the scenario.

(b) **Budgeted results for game**

	Year 1 ($)	Year 2 ($)	Year 3 ($)	Total ($)
Sales	240,000	480,000	120,000	840,000
Variable cost (W1)	40,000	80,000	20,000	140,000
Fixed cost (W1)	80,000	120,000	80,000	280,000
Marketing cost	60,000	40,000		100,000
Profit	60,000	240,000	20,000	320,000

On the face of it the game will generate profits in each of its three years of life. Games only have a short lifecycle as the game players are likely to become bored of the game and move on to something new.

The pattern of sales follows a classic product lifecycle with poor levels of sales towards the end of the life of the game.

The stealth product has generated $320,000 of profit over its three year life measured on a traditional basis. This represents 40% of turnover – ahead of its target. Indeed it shows a positive net profit in each of its years on existence.

The contribution level is steady at around 83% indicating reasonable control and reliability of the production processes. This figure is better than the stated target.

Considering traditional performance management concepts, Wargrin Limited is likely to be relatively happy with the game's performance.

However, the initial design and development costs were incurred and were significant at $300,000 and are ignored in the annual profit calculations. Taking these into consideration the game only just broke even making a small $20,000 profit. Whether this is enough is debatable, it represents only 2.4% of sales for example. In order to properly assess the performance of a product the whole lifecycle needs to be considered.

Workings

(W1) Split of variable and fixed cost for Stealth

	Volume	Cost $
High	14,000 units	150,000
Low	10,000 units	130,000
Difference	4,000 units	20,000

Variable cost per unit = $20,000/4,000 unit = $5 per unit

Total cost = fixed cost + variable cost

$150,000 = fixed cost + (14,000 × $5)

$150,000 = fixed cost + $70,000

Fixed cost = $80,000 (and $120,000 if volume exceeds 15,000 units in a year.)

Key answer tips

Candidates must be comfortable with the high low method. The examiner is keen to test techniques such as this within the context of a longer calculation question. Good candidates ignored the design and development costs (a sunk cost).

Candidates needed to leave enough time to interpret the calculations and to discuss the expected performance of the game. Almost half of the marks were available for the written points.

(c) Incremental budgeting is a process whereby this year's budget is set by reference to last year's actual results after an adjustment for inflation and other incremental factors. It is commonly used because:

- It is quick to do and a relatively simple process.
- The information is readily available, so very limited quantitative analysis is needed.
- It is appropriate in some circumstances. For example in a stable business the amount of stationery spent in one year is unlikely to be significantly different in the next year, so taking the actual spend in year one and adding a little for inflation should be a reasonable target for the spend in the next year.

There are problems involved with incremental budgeting:

- It builds on wasteful spending. If the actual figures for this year include overspends caused by some form of error then the budget for the next year would potentially include this overspend again.
- It encourages organisations to spend up to the maximum allowed in the knowledge that if they don't do this then they will not have as much to spend in the following year's budget.
- Assessing the amount of the increment can be difficult.
- It is not appropriate in a rapidly changing business.
- Can ignore the true (activity based) drivers of a cost leading to poor budgeting.

277 YAM CO (JUNE 2009)

(a) The output capacity for each process is as follows:

The total processing hours of the factory is given but can be proven as follows:

18 hours × 5 days × 50 weeks × 50 production lines = 225,000 hours.

Given this, the production capacity for pressing must be 225,000 hours/0.5 hours per metre = 450,000 metres. Using this method the production capacity for all processes is as follows:

	Product A	Product B	Product C
Pressing	450,000	450,000	562,500
Stretching	900,000	562,500	900,000
Rolling	562,500	900,000	900,000

The bottleneck is clearly the pressing process which has a lower capacity for each product. The other processes will probably be slowed to ensure smooth processing.

Tutorial note

*Clearly an alternative approach is simply to look at the original table for processing speed and pick out the slowest process. This is pressing. (full marks available for that **explained** observation). This would have been a much more straightforward approach in the exam.*

(b) **TPAR for each product**

	Product A	Product B	Product C
Selling price	70.0	60.0	27.0
Raw materials	3.0	2.5	1.8
Throughput	67.0	57.5	25.2
Throughput per bottleneck hour*	134.0	115.0	63.0
Fixed costs per hour (W1)	90.0	90.0	90.0
TPAR	1.49	1.28	0.7
Working*	67/0.5 = 134	57.5/0.5 = 115	25.2/0.4 = 63

Workings

(W1) **The fixed cost per bottleneck hour can be calculated as follows:**

Total fixed costs are $18,000,000 plus the labour cost. Labour costs $10 per hour for each of the 225,000 processing hours, a cost of $2,250,000.

Total fixed cost is therefore $18,000,000 + $2,250,000 = $20,250,000

Fixed cost per bottleneck hours is $20,250,000/225,000 = $90 per hour

Key answer tips

Calculate the TPAR in three stages:

- Firstly, calculate the throughput per bottleneck hour.
- Secondly, calculate the fixed cost per hour.
- Finally, calculate the TPAR.

Carry forward marks would be awarded if the incorrect bottleneck process was identified in requirement (a).

(c) **(i)** Yam could improve the TPAR of product C in various ways:

Speed up the bottleneck process. By increasing the speed of the bottleneck process the rate of throughput will also increase, generating a greater rate of income for Yam if the extra production can be sold. Automation might be used or a change in the detailed processes. Investment in new machinery can also help here but the cost of that would need to be taken into account.

Increase the selling prices. It can be difficult to increase selling prices in what we are told is a competitive market. Volume of sales could be lost leaving Yam with unsold stock or idle equipment. On the other hand, given the business appears to be selling all it can produce, then a price increase may be possible.

Reduce the material prices. Reducing material prices will increase the net throughput rate. Metal is available from many sources being far from a unique product. Given the industry is mature the suppliers of the raw material could be willing to negotiate on price; this could have volume or quality based conditions attached. Yam will have to be careful to protect its quality levels. Bulk buying increases stock levels and the cost of that would need to be considered.

Reduce the level of fixed costs. The fixed costs should be listed and targets for cost reduction be selected. ABC techniques can help to identify the cost drivers and with management these could be used to reduce activity levels and hence cost. Outsourcing, de-skilling or using alternative suppliers (for stationery for example) are all possible cost reduction methods.

(ii)   A TPAR of less than one indicates that the rate at which product C generates throughput (sales revenue less material cost) is less than the rate at which Yam incurs fixed cost. So on a simple level, producing a product which incurs fixed cost faster than it generates throughput does not seem to make commercial sense. Clearly the TPAR could be improved (using the methods above) before cessation is considered any further.

However, cessation decisions involve consideration of many wider issues (only three required).

Long-term expected net cash flows from the product allowing for the timing of those cash flows (NPV) are an important factor in cessation decisions.

Customer perception could be negative in that they will see a reduction in choice.

Lost related sales: if product C is lost will Yam lose customers that bought it along with another product?

What use could be made of the excess capacity that is created.

Throughput assumes that all costs except raw materials are fixed; this may not necessarily be the case and only avoidable fixed costs need to be taken into account for a cessation decision. If few fixed costs can be avoided then product C is making a contribution that will be lost if the product ceased.

Tutorial note

Note that 11 of the 20 marks in this question are for the written requirements. This is typical of the examiner and therefore it is imperative to practice answering these written requirements.

				Marks
(a)	Identification of bottleneck			1.0
	Explanation			2.0
			Maximum	**3.0**
(b)	Sales prices (per product)			0.5
	Raw material cost (per product)			0.5
	Throughput per bottleneck hour (per product)			0.5
	Fixed costs			1.5
	Fixed cost per hour			0.5
	TPAR (per product)			0.5
			Maximum	**8.0**
(c)	**(i)**	Increase speed of bottleneck		1.0
		Increase selling prices – difficult to do		1.0
		Reduce material prices		1.0
		Reduce level of fixed costs		1.0
			Maximum	**4.0**
	(ii)	Explain a TPAR		2.0
		Long-term cash flows		1.0
		Lost related sales		1.0
		Use of spare capacity		1.0
		Fixed costs		1.0
		Any other reasonable factor e.g. lost contribution		1.0
			Maximum	**5.0**
Total				**20**

Marking scheme

DECISION MAKING TECHNIQUES

278 ROBBER CO (JUNE 2012)

(a)

	Keypads	Display screens
	$	$
Variable costs		
Materials ($160K × 6/12) + ($160K × 1.05 × 6/12)	164,000	
($116K × 1.02)		118,320
Direct labour	40,000	60,000
Machine set-up costs ($26K – 4K) × 500/400	27,500	
($30K – 6K) × 500/400		30,000
	231,500	208,320
Attributable fixed costs		
Heat and power ($64K – $20K)	44,000	
($88K – $30K)		58,000
Fixed machine costs	4,000	6,000
Depreciation and insurance ($84K × 40%)	33,600	
($96K × 40%)		38,400
Total incremental costs of making in-house	313,100	310,720
Cost of buying		
Keypads (80,000 × $4.10)	328,000	
Display screens (80,000 × $4.30)		344,000
Total saving from making	14,900	33,280

Robber Co should therefore make all of the keypads and display screens in-house.

(Note: it has been assumed that the fixed set-up costs only arise if production takes place.)

Alternative method

Relevant costs:

	Keypads	Display screens
	$	$
Direct materials ($160K × 6/12) + ($160K × 1.05 × 6/12)	164,000	
($116K × 1.02)		118,320
Direct labour	40,000	60,000
Heat and power ($64K – (50% × $40K))	44,000	
($88K – (50% × $60K))		58,000
Machine set-up costs:		
Avoidable fixed costs	4,000	6,000
Activity related costs (W1)	27,500	30,000
Avoidable depreciation and insurance ($84K × 40%)	33,600	
($96K × 40%)		38,400
Total incremental costs of making in-house	**313,100**	**310,720**
Relevant cost per unit	3.91	3.88
Cost per unit of buying in	4.10	4.30
Incremental cost of buying in	**0.19**	**0.42**

As each of the components is cheaper to make in-house than to buy in, the company should continue to manufacture keypads and display screens in-house.

(W1) Activity related costs

Current no. of batches produced = 80,000 ÷ 500 = 160.

New no. of batches produced = 80,000 ÷ 400 = 200.

Current cost per batch for keypads = ($26,000 – $4,000) ÷ 160 = $137.5.

Therefore, new activity related batch cost = 200 x $137.5 = $27,500.

Current cost per batch for display screens = ($30,000 – $6,000) ÷ 160 = $150.

Therefore, new activity related batch cost = 200 x $150 = $30,000.

(b) The attributable fixed costs remain unaltered irrespective of the level of production of keypads and display screens, because as soon as one unit of either is made, the costs rise. We know that we will make at least one unit of each component as both are cheaper to make than buy. Therefore, they are an irrelevant common cost.

	Keypads	Display screens
Cost of buying	$4.10	$4.30
Variable cost of making ($231,500 ÷ 80,000)	$2.89	
($208,320 ÷ 80,000)		$2.60
Saving from making per unit	$1.21	$1.70
Labour hours per unit	0.5 hours	0.75 hours
Saving from making per unit of limiting factor	**$2.42**	**$2.27**
Ranking	1	2

Total labour hours available = 100,000

Make maximum keypads, i.e. 100,000, using 50,000 labour hours (100,000 × 0.5 hours)

Make 50,000 ÷ 0.75 display screens, i.e. 66,666 display screens.

Therefore, buy in 33,334 display screens (100,000 – 66,666).

Note 1: It is equally as acceptable to have treated the heat and power costs as variable and include them in the above. It will not have changed the outcome and is an entirely acceptable interpretation of the scenario.

Note 2: If a production run cannot be stopped part way through, then the company would only be able to make 66,400 and would have to buy 33,600, since production takes place in batches of 400 units.

(c)   **Non-financial factors**

The company offering to supply the keypads and display screens is a new company. This would make it extremely risky to rely on it for continuity of supplies. Many new businesses go out of business within the first year of being in business and, without these two crucial components, Robber Co would be unable to meet demand for sales of control panels. Robber Co would need to consider whether there are any other potential suppliers of the components. This would be useful as both a price comparison now and also to establish the level of dependency that would be committed to if this new supplier is used. If the supplier goes out of business, will any other company be able to step in? If so, at what cost?

The supplier has only agreed to these prices for the first two years. After this, it could put up its prices dramatically. By this stage, Robber Co would probably be unable to begin easily making its components in house again, as it would probably have sold off its machinery and committed to larger sales of control panels.

The quality of the components could not be guaranteed. If they turn out to be poor quality, this will give rise to problems in the control panels, leading to future loss of sales and high repair costs under warranties for Robber Co. The fact that the supplier is based overseas increases the risk of quality and continuity of supply, since it has even less control of these than it would if it was a UK supplier.

Robber Co would need to establish how reliable the supplier is with meeting promises for delivery times. This kind of information may be difficult to establish because of the fact that the supplier is a new company. Late delivery could have a serious impact on Robber Co's production and delivery schedule.

Marking scheme		
		Marks
(a) **Incremental cost of buying in**		
Direct materials		1
Direct labour		0.5
Heat and power		1
Set-up costs		3
Depreciation and insurance		1
Total cost of making/cost per unit of making		0.5
Conclusion		1
		___
		8
		___
Alternative method		
Direct materials		1
Direct labour		0.5
Heat and power		1
Avoidable fixed costs		1
Activity related costs		2
Avoidable depreciation and insurance		1
Total relevant cost of manufacturing/cost per unit		0.5
Conclusion		1
		___
		8
		___
(b) **If 100,000 control panels made:**		
Variable cost of making per unit		1
Saving from making		1
Saving per labour hour		1
Ranking		1
Make 100,000 keypads		1
Make 66,666 display screens		1
Buy 33,334 display screens		1
		___
	Maximum	**7**
		___
(c) **Non-financial factors**		
Per factor		1–2
		___
	Maximum	**5**
		___
Total		**20**
		___

279 BELLAHOUSTON CO (DECEMBER 2021)

(a) **(i)** **Identify the limiting factor**

	Road	Spikes	Trail	Total
Direct material/pair	1.5	0.6	1.2	6,930
Direct Labour/pair	1	1.5	1	6,750
Machine time/pair	0.4	0.2	0.3	1,875

Based on the above, machine time is the limiting factor.

Calculate the contribution per unit of limiting factor and rank the products:

	Road	Spikes	Trail
Contribution per pair of shoes ($)	41.50	29.50	36.00
Machine hours required	0.40	0.20	0.30
Contribution per machine hour ($)	103.75	147.50	120.00
Ranking	3	1	2

Prepare the optimum production plan and calculate resultant total contribution earned:

	Machine hours used (1,815 available)	Contribution per pair of shoes ($)	Total contribution ($)
Fulfil customer order:			
200 Road	80	33.50	6,700
200 Spikes	40	21.50	4,300
200 Trail	60	28.00	5,600
	1,635 hours remaining		
Apply ranking:			
1,400 Spikes – 1st	280	29.50	41,300
1,650 Trail – 2nd	495	36.00	59,400
2,150 Road – 3rd	860 (β)	41.50	89,225
			206,525

(ii)   Calculate the profit maximising mix:

	Machine hours used (1,815 available)	Contribution per pair of shoes ($)	Total contribution ($)
Apply ranking for the general sales in March:			
1,400 Spikes	280	29.50	41,300
1,650 Trail	495	36.00	59,400
2,300 Road	920	41.50	95,450
Apply ranking for special order:			
200 Spikes	40	21.50	4,300
200 Trail	60	28.00	5,600
50 Road	20 (β)	33.50	1,675
			207,725

The loss of contribution from fulfilling RunWild's order is $1,200 ($207,725 – $206,525), therefore the maximum financial penalty acceptable would be $1,200.

Alternative approach:

If RunWild's order could only be partially completed, then Bellahouston Co would divert machine hours from making Road shoes for the specific order to making Road shoes for general sale to other retailers. The number of Road shoes for general sale in part (a)(i) fails to meet demand by 150 pairs of shoes and the difference in the contribution earned from making them available for general sale and not to RunWild is $8 per pair. Therefore, the difference in the contribution earned is $1,200 (150 pairs of Road shoes × $8), which would be the maximum financial penalty Bellahouston Co would be willing to accept.

(b)   Although the contribution earned is higher if the order is only partially completed, if Bellahouston Co does not fully complete the order, then RunWild may not enter into a regular supply contract and future sales revenue would therefore be lost. In addition, the customer base and reputation of RunWild will help to market Bellahouston Co's products and increase awareness of their products. This benefit will also be lost if RunWild choose not to order from Bellahouston Co again.

It would also not be good for Bellahouston Co's existing reputation if it becomes known for not fulfilling its obligations. This could make other sports retailers reluctant to order from them. It might also impact the end-customer's perception of their product if they cannot buy Bellahouston Co's running shoes due to a lack of availability.

(c)   **Define the variables:**

R = number of pairs of Road shoes

S = number of pairs of Spikes shoes

T = number of pairs of Trail shoes

Constraints:

Direct material	$1.5R + 0.6S + 1.2T \leq 6,120$
Direct labour	$1R + 1.5S + 1T \leq 5,865$
Machine time	$0.4R + 0.2S + 0.3T \leq 1,815$
Demand	$R \leq 2,300$
	$S \leq 1,400$
	$T \leq 1,650$
Non-negativity	$R, S, T \geq 0$

Objective function:

$C = 41.50R + 29.50S + 36.00T$

ACCA Marking scheme			
			Marks
(a)	(i)	Production plan	7
	(ii)	Financial penalty	4
(b)		Discussion	4
(c)		Linear programming	5
Total			**20**

280   CHOCOLATES ARE FOREVER (CAF)

(a)   The Breakeven point is that number if units produced and sold at which CAF will make no profit or no loss:

$$\text{Breakeven point} = \frac{\text{Fixed costs}}{\text{Contribution per unit}}; \quad \text{Breakeven point} = \frac{\$20,000}{\$12 - 7}$$

Breakeven point = 4,000 units.

The margin of safety expresses the gap between budgeted sales and breakeven sales. It measures by how much CAF needs to fall short of budgeted sales before it starts making a loss:

$$\text{Margin of safety} = \frac{\text{Budgeted sales} - \text{Breakeven sales}}{\text{Budgeted sales}} \times 100\%$$

$$\text{Margin of safety} = \frac{6,000 \text{ units} - 4,000 \text{ units}}{6,000 \text{ units}} \times 100\%; \quad \text{Margin of safety} = 33.33\%$$

(b)   A **breakeven chart** is a graphical representation of the data. It shows the breakeven point when the total cost line and the total revenue line intersect. The total cost line is a total variable cost line sitting on the fixed cost line. The Sales revenue line is also depicted and comes from the origin. (no sales, no revenue). The Margin of Safety can then be read off the chart on the horizontal axis – the difference between the budgeted output and the breakeven output.

A contribution breakeven chart is based on the same principles as a basic breakeven chart, but it shows the variable cost line instead of the fixed cost line.

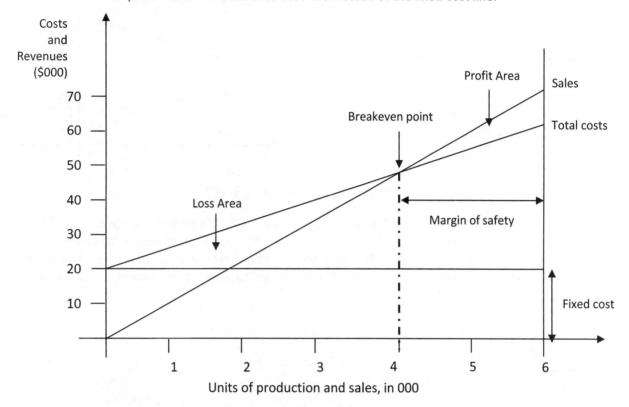

The same lines for total cost and sales revenue are shown so the breakeven point and profit can be read off in the same way as with a conventional chart. However, it is possible also to read the contribution for any level of activity.

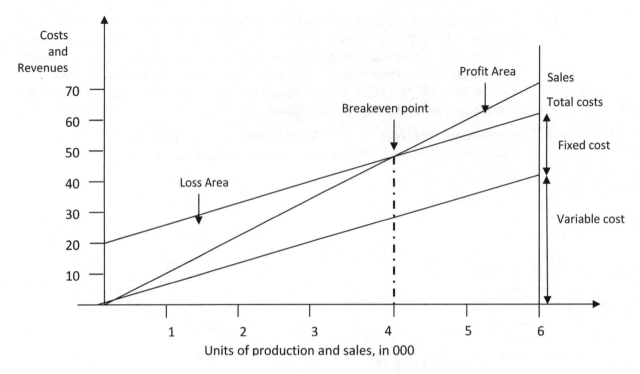

The Profit-Volume chart is an alternative chart, which is simpler, but gives a lot of the same information. By drawing a line between the fixed costs at zero output (where the amount of loss will equal the fixed costs) and the breakeven point – where the profit line crosses the x axis – the chart may be used to work out the expected profit at any level of output.

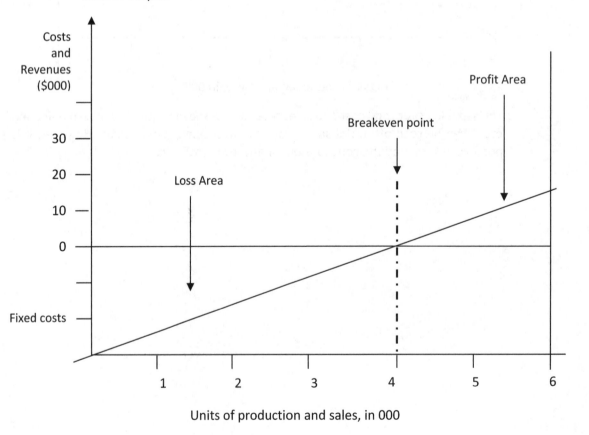

(c) Breakeven calculations and the graphs above involve a number of assumptions; the biggest criticism of CVP analysis is that these assumptions may not be observed in practice. For example:

- Costs behaviour is assumed to be linear, but costs may only be linear within a certain output range. The analysis and its results would change if the variable cost per unit were to change due to economies of scale (that would affect the material cost). Likewise, a learning curve effect could impact on the labour cost per unit.

- In practice, it can sometimes be difficult to separate variable and fixed costs, and the calculations will represent an approximation.

- Revenue is assumed to be linear but CAF, like many companies, may need to cut its unit price to sell more units and/or retain its market share.

- Breakeven analysis assumes that all units produced are sold, i.e. that no inventory is taken into account in calculations.

- Breakeven analysis ignores the effects of tax and inflation.

281 MANGO LEATHER

(a)

$$\text{Breakeven sales revenue} = \frac{\text{Fixed costs}}{\text{Weighted average contribution to sales ratio}}$$

$$\text{Breakeven sales revenue} = \frac{\$580,000}{0.35844 \text{ (W1)}}$$

Breakeven sales revenue = $1,618,123.

(b) Products first need to be ranked according to their contribution to sales ratio:

Products	Selling price (per unit)	Contribution per unit	C/S ratio	Rank
Bags	$400	$190	0.475	2
Belts	$125	$60	0.480	1
Shoes	$150	$55	0.367	3
Jackets	$300	$85	0.283	4

Secondly, cumulative sales and profits need to be established in preparation for the multi-product breakeven chart:

Sales	Cumulative revenue	Contribution (W1)	Cumulative profit or loss
None	$0	$0	$(580,000)
Belts	$250,000	$120,000	$(460,000)
Bags	$650,000	$190,000	$(270,000)
Shoes	$875,000	$82,500	$(187,500)
Jackets	$1,925,000	$297,500	$110,000

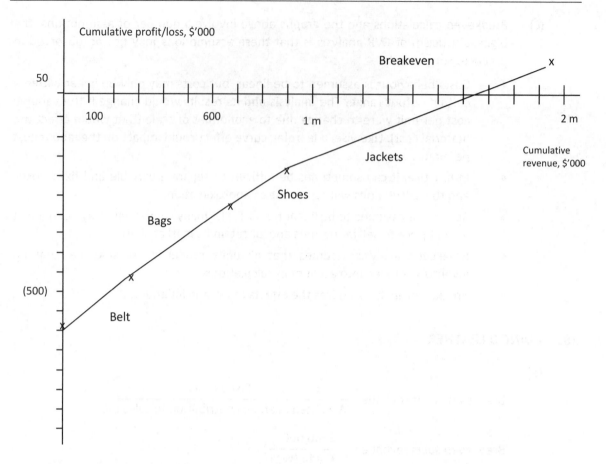

(c) Mango's production process is very dependent on leather. Leather is the only material and represents a third of total variable costs.

An increase of the cost of leather will severely impact on Mango. Any increase will erode contribution margins significantly. A higher material cost will affect contribution by making it lower. This will impact on the breakeven point, as the weighted average C/S ratio calculated in (a) will be lower (assuming that the selling prices, fixed costs and demand remain constant.)

Graphically, the breakeven revenue point will move to the right along the x-axis and the breakeven revenue will increase.

The unavailability of leather will severely disrupt the production process and will affect customer confidence in Mango, although it may encourage the company to look for substitutes and manage its dependency on its unique material a bit better.

(d) The major benefit of using breakeven analysis is that it indicates the lowest amount of activity necessary to prevent losses.

Breakeven analysis aids decision making as it explains the relationship between cost, production volume and returns. It can be extended to show how changes in fixed costs/variable costs relationships or in revenues will affect profit levels and breakeven points.

The following underlying assumptions will limit the precision and reliability of a given cost-volume-profit analysis.

(1)   The behaviour of total cost and total revenue has been reliably determined and is linear over the relevant range.

(2)   All costs can be divided into fixed and variable elements.

(3)   Total fixed costs remain constant over the relevant volume range of the CVP analysis.

(4)   Total variable costs are directly proportional to volume over the relevant range.

(5)   Selling prices are to be unchanged.

(6)   Prices of the factors of production are to be unchanged (for example, material, prices, wage rates).

(7)   Efficiency and productivity are to be unchanged.

(8)   The analysis either covers a single product or assumes that a given sales mix will be maintained as total volume changes.

(9)   Revenue and costs are being compared on a single activity basis (for example, units produced and sold or sales value of production).

(10) Perhaps the most basic assumption of all is that volume is the only relevant factor affecting cost. Of course, other factors also affect costs and sales. Ordinary cost-volume-profit analysis is a crude oversimplification when these factors are unjustifiably ignored.

(11) The volume of production equals the volume of sales, or changes in beginning and ending inventory levels are insignificant in amount.

Working 1 – Weighted average contribution to sales ratio

Products	Sales units	Leather cost at @$60 per metre	Contribution per unit	Total sales	Total contribution
Bags	1,000	$60	$190	$400,000	$190,000
Belts	2,000	$15	$60	$250,000	$120,000
Shoes	1,500	$30	$55	$225,000	$82,500
Jackets	3,500	$90	$85	$1,050,000	$297,500
Total				**$1,925,000**	**$690,000**

$$\text{Weighted average contribution to sales ratio} = \frac{\text{Total contribution}}{\text{Total sales}}$$

$$\text{Weighted average contribution to sales ratio} = \frac{\$690,000}{\$1,925,000}$$

Weighted average contribution to sales ratio = 0.3584 or 35.84%

282 BREAKEVEN

(a) **p**   is the total sales revenue

q   Total cost (Fixed cost + variable cost)

r   Total variable cost

s   Fixed costs at the specific level of activity

t   Total loss at the specific level of activity

u   Total profit at that level of activity

v   Total contribution at the specific level of activity

w   Total contribution at a lower level of activity

x   Level of activity of output sales

y   monetary value of cost and revenue function for level of activity.

(b) At event 'm', the selling price per unit decreases, but it remains constant. P is a straight line, but with a lower gradient above 'm' compared to below 'm'.

At event 'n' there is an increase in fixed costs equal to the dotted line. This is probably due to an increase in capital expenditure in order to expand output beyond this point. Also, at this point, the variable cost per unit declines as reflected by the gradient of the variable cost line. This might be due to more efficient production methods associated with increased investment in capital equipment.

(c) Breakeven analysis is of limited use in a multi-product company, but the analysis can be a useful aid to management of a small single product company. The following are some of the main benefits:

- Breakeven analysis forces management to consider the functional relationship between costs, revenue and activity, and gives an insight to how costs and revenues vary with the level of activity.

- Breakeven analysis forces management to consider the fixed costs at various levels of activity and the selling price that will be required to achieve various levels of output.

283 EC LTD

(a)

$$\text{Breakeven revenue} = \frac{\text{Fixed costs } \$1,212,000}{\text{Average contribution to Sales ratio 50.5\% (W1)}}$$

Breakeven revenue = $2,400,000.

Working 1: Average Contribution to Sales Ratio (on a $100 total sales basis)

	Product X	Product Y	Total
Sales	$70	$30	$100
Contribution	$70 * 0.55 = $38.50	$30 * 0.4 = $12	$50.50

If $50.50 contribution is achieved for every $100 worth of sales

$$\text{Average contribution to Sales ratio} = \frac{\$50.50}{\$100} = 0.505 \text{ or } 50.5\%$$

(b)

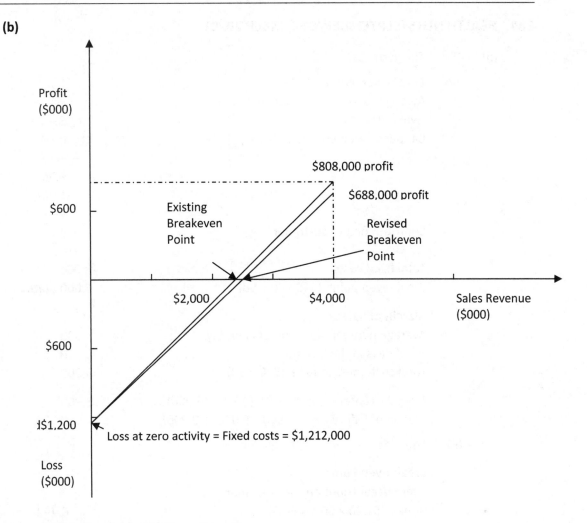

Effect of a change in the sales mix:

	Product X	Product Y	Total
Sales	$50	$50	$100
Contribution	$50 * 0.55 = $27.50	$50 * 0.4 = $20	$47.50

If $47.50 contribution is achieved for every $100 worth of sales,

Average contribution to Sales ratio = 47.50 % and

$$\text{Breakeven revenue} = \frac{\text{Fixed costs } \$1,212,000}{\text{Average contribution to Sales ratio } 47.5\% \text{ (W1)}}$$

Breakeven revenue = $2,551,579.

(c)

$$\text{Sales revenue required} = \frac{\text{Attributable fixed costs } \$455,000 + \$700,000}{\text{X's contribution to Sales ratio } 55\%}$$

Sales revenue required = $2,100,000.

284   HEALTH NUTS (SEPTEMBER/DECEMBER 2020)

(a) (i)   **The gym**

Break-even Point

	$
Average sales revenue per customer	
Gym entry	8.40
Car park expected value (0.8 × $1)	0.80
	9.20
Variable cost	(1.20)
Contribution per customer	**8.00**
Total fixed costs	48,000
Break-even point ($48,000 ÷ $8)	**6,000 units**

Margin of Safety

Average number of customers per day	330
No of days in the month	30
Total customers in June (330 × 30)	**9,900**
Margin of Safety (customers) (9,900 – 6,000)	3,900
Margin of Safety (%) [(9,900 – 6,000) ÷ 9,900]	**39.39%**

(ii)   **The cafe**

Break-even Point

	$
Average contribution per customer	
Drinks ($2.20 × 60% × 60%)	0.792
Food ($2.20 × 40% × 40%)	0.352
	1.144
Total fixed costs	3,600
Break-even point = ($3,600 ÷ $1.144)	**3,147 units**

Margin of Safety

Total customers in June (9,900 ÷ 2)	**4,950**
Margin of Safety (customers) = (4,950 – 3,147)	1,803
Margin of Safety (%) = [(4,950 – 3,147) ÷ 4,950	**36.43%**

(b) The gym needs 6,000 customers per month and the café needs 3,147 customers per month in order to cover its fixed costs.

Each $1 of contribution after this point generates profit.

Whether or not these figures are particularly high can be gauged by comparing them to the expected (or, in this case, actual) customers in one month and this is where the margin of safety is useful. Both the margin of safety for the gym and the café are quite similar, at approximately 39% and 36% respectively. This tells Health Nuts the extent to which it can feel confident about covering its fixed costs and making a profit. In this instance, its margin of safety is such that, even if its customer numbers went down by over one third it could still cover its fixed costs.

(c)

Total sales/contribution from gym

Original number of customers	330
New customers	120
Total customers per day	**450**
Number of days in the month	30
Total customers for the month (450 × 30)	**13,500**
Total sales from gym entry & car park (13,500 × $9.20)	**$124,200**
Total contribution (13,500 × $8)	**$108,000**

Total sales/contribution from crèche

Total customers using the crèche per day	120
Number of days in the month	30
Total customers for the month (120 × 30)	3,600
Total number of children per month (3,600 × 2)	**7,200**
Total sales from crèche (7,200 × $4)	**$28,800**
Total contribution (7,200 × ($4 − $0.5))	**$25,200**
Total sales from gym & crèche	**$153,000**
Total contribution from gym & crèche	**$133,200**
Weighted average C/S ratio ($133,200 ÷ $153,000)	**87.06%**

Budgeted profit per month including crèche	$
Total contribution	133,200
Less: total fixed costs	(56,000)
Budgeted profit	**77,200**

(d)

	$
Total contribution from gym ($8 × 9,900)	79,200
Total contribution from cafe ($1.144 × 4,950)	5,663
Less: total fixed costs (48,000 + 3,600)	(51,600)
Budgeted profit	**31,263**

With the crèche, profit will increase from $33,263 to $77,200 per month, an increase of $43,937. Therefore, from a purely financial point of view, the crèche would seem like a good idea.

However, there are various other factors that need to be taken into account:

Details of how much the conversion from the café to the crèche will cost has not been provided. The investment would need to be appraised using a technique like NPV to assess its financial viability.

The research for the revised customer numbers is only initial. Is this data realistic and can it be relied on? There is no information about how Health Nuts got this research.

The opening of a crèche could put off other customers, who want to exercise in a child-free environment, from using the gym during the day. There is no indication that Health Nuts have taken this into account.

Similarly, closing the café could upset many other customers at all times of day and lead to the loss of their business.

The calculations so far performed are not therefore enough to make this decision.

285   COSMETICS CO (DECEMBER 2010, ADAPTED)

(a)   **Optimum production plan**

Define the variables

Let x = no. of jars of face cream to be produced

Let y = no. of bottles of body lotion to be produced

Let C = contribution

State the objective function

The objective is to maximise contribution, C

$C = 9x + 8y$

State the constraints

Silk powder	$3x + 2y \leq 5,000$
Silk amino acids	$1x + 0.5y \leq 1,600$
Skilled labour	$4x + 5y \leq 9,600$

Non-negativity constraints:

$x, y \geq 0$

Sales constraint:

$y \leq 2,000$

On the graph

Silk powder	$3x + 2y = 5,000$
Silk amino acids	$1x + 0.5y = 1,600$
Skilled labour	$4x + 5y = 9,600$

Solve using iso-contribution line

Using the iso-contribution line, the furthest vertex from the origin is point 'c', the intersection of the constraints for skilled labour and silk powder.

Solving the simultaneous equations for these constraints:

$4x + 5y = 9,600 \times 3$

$3x + 2y = 5,000 \times 4$

$12x + 15y = 28,800$ $12x + 8y = 20,000$

Subtract the second one from the first one $7y = 8,800$, therefore $y = $ **1,257.14**.

If $y = 1,257.14$ and:

$4x + 5y = 9,600$

Then $5 \times 1,257.14 + 4x = 9,600$

Therefore x = 828.58

If $C = 9x + 8y$

$C = \$7,457.22 + \$10,057.12 = \$17,514.34$

(b) **Shadow prices and slack**

The shadow price for silk powder can be found by solving the two simultaneous equations intersecting at point c, whilst adding one more hour to the equation for silk powder.

$4x + 5y = 9,600 \times 3$

$3x + 2y = 5,001 \times 4$

$12x + 15y = 28,800$

$12x + 8y = 20,004$

Subtract the second one from the first one

$7y = 8,796$, therefore $y = 1,256.57$

$3x + (2 \times 1,256.57) = 5,001$.

Therefore $x = 829.29$

$C = (9 \times 829.29) + (8 \times 1,256.57) = \$17,516.17$

Original contribution = $17,514.34

Therefore shadow price for silk powder is $1.83 per gram.

The slack for amino acids can be calculated as follows:

$(828.58 \times 1) + (0.5 \times 1,257.14) = 1,457.15$ grams used.

Available = 1,600 grams.

Therefore slack = 142.85 grams.

	Marking scheme	Marks
(a)	Optimum production plan	
	Defining constraint for silk powder	1
	Defining constraint for amino acids	1
	Defining constraint for labour	1
	Non-negativity constraint	1
	Sales constraint: x	1
	Sales constraint: y	1
	Iso-contribution line worked out	1
	Optimum point identified	2
	Equations solved at optimum point	3
	Total contribution	2
	Maximum	**14**
(b)	Shadow prices and slack	
	Shadow price	4
	Slack	2
	Maximum	**6**
Total		**20**

286 CUT AND STITCH (JUNE 2010)

(a) The optimal production mix can be found by solving the two equations given for F and T.

$7W + 5L = 3,500$

$2W + 2L = 1,200$

Multiplying the second equation by 2.5 produces:

$7W + 5L = 3,500$

$5W + 5L = 3,000$

$2W = 500$

$W = 250$

Substituting W = 250 in the fabric equation produces:

$2 \times 250 + 2L = 1,200$

$2L = 700$

$L = 350$

The optimal solution is when 250 work suits are produced and 350 lounge suits are produced. **The contribution gained is $26,000**:

$C = 48W + 40L$

$C = (48 \times 250) + (40 \times 350)$

$C = 26,000$

(b) The shadow prices can be found by adding one unit to each constraint in turn.

Shadow price of T

$7W + 5L = 3,501$

$2W + 2L = 1,200$

Again multiplying the second equation by 2.5 produces:

$7W + 5L = 3,501$

$5W + 5L = 3,000$

$2W = 501$

$= 250.5$

Substituting W = 250.5 in the fabric equation produces:

$(2 \times 250.5) + 2L = 1,200$

$2L = 1,200 - 501$

$L = 349.5$

Contribution earned at this point would be = $(48 \times 250.5) + (40 \times 349.5) = 26,004$ which is an increase of $4.

Hence the shadow price of T is $4 per hour.

Shadow price of F

$7W + 5L = 3,500$

$2W + 2L = 1,201$

Again multiplying the second equation by 2.5 produces:

$7W + 5L = 3,500.0$

$5W + 5L = 3,002.5$

$2W = 497.5$

$W = 248.75$

Substituting W = 248.75 in the fabric equation produces:

$(2 \times 248.75) + 2L = 1,201$

$2L = 1,201 - 497.5$

$L = 351.75$

Contribution earned at this point would be = $(48 \times 248.75) + (40 \times 351.75) = 26,010$, which is an increase of $10. Hence the shadow price of F is $10 per metre.

(c) The shadow price represents the maximum premium above the normal rate a business should be willing to pay for more of a scarce resource. It is equal to the increased contribution that can be gained from gaining that extra resource.

The shadow price of labour here is $4 per hour. The tailors have offered to work for $4.50 – a premium of $3.00 per hour. At first glance the offer seems to be acceptable.

However, many businesses pay overtime at the rate of time and a half and some negotiation should be possible to create a win/win situation. Equally some consideration should be given to the quality aspect here. If excessive extra hours are worked then tiredness can reduce the quality of the work produced.

(d) If maximum demand for W falls to 200 units, the constraint for W will move left to 200 on the x axis of the graph. The new optimum point will then be at the intersection of:

W = 200 and

2W + 2L = 1,200

Solving these equations simultaneously, if:

W = 200, then (2 × 200) + 2L = 1,200

Therefore L = 400.

So, the new production plan will be to make 400L and 200W

Marking scheme			
			Marks
(a)	Optimal point calculation		3
	Contribution		1
			—
		Maximum	**4**
			—
(b)	For each shadow price		3
			—
		Maximum	**6**
			—
(c)	Rate discussion		3
	Other factors e.g. tiredness, negotiation		3
			—
		Maximum	**6**
			—
(d)	Find optimum point		1
	Solve 2 equations		2
	Conclusion		1
			—
		Maximum	**4**
			—
Total			**20**
			—

287   CSC CO (SEPTEMBER 2016)

Tutorial note

The first part of the question was a typical single limiting factor question, requiring candidates to formulate an optimal production plan and calculate maximum profit. Do not ignore the fact that the company had entered into a contract, and therefore these requirements should be produced first. Secondly there was a requirement to calculate the shortage of material – this was often omitted. Thirdly, many candidates used the dollar value of the limiting material to calculate their production plan, rather than the quantities. These errors didn't seem to come from a lack of understanding, more a lack of care. It's possible that candidates were running short of time by this point, meaning that the requirements and scenarios weren't read properly. This highlights the importance of good time management during the exam – ensuring that some of the more straightforward marks can be obtained.

(a) **(Step 1) Calculate the shortage of Betta for the year**

Total requirements in grams:

Cakes: grams used per cake	0.5
Expected demand	11,200
Total required:	5,600
Cookies: grams used per cookie	0.20
Expected demand	9,800
Total required:	1,960
Shakes: grams used per shake	1
Expected demand	7,500
Total required:	7,500
Overall total required:	**15,060**
Less available:	12,000
Shortage:	**3,060**

(Step 2) Contribution per gram of Betta and ranking

	Cakes	Cookies	Shakes	Shakes (contract)
	$	$	$	$
Contribution per unit	2.60	1.75	1.20	1.00
Grams of Betta per unit	0.5	0.2	1	1
	$	$	$	$
Contribution per gram	5.20	8.75	1.20	1.00
Rank	2	1	3	4

(Step 3) Optimum production plan

Product	Number to be produced	Grams per unit	Total grams per product	Cumulative grams	Contribution per unit	Total contribution
Shakes (contract)	5,000	1	5,000	5,000	1.00	5,000
Cookies	9,800	0.20	1,960	6,960	1.75	17,150
Cakes	10,080	0.5	5,040	12,000	2.60	26,208
Total contribution						48,358
Less fixed costs						(3,000)
Profit						45,358

(b)

Tutorial note

The second part of this question was a discussion about whether the business should breach the contract they have to supply another business. You must not focus purely on the financial factors. Easy marks could be picked up here for realising that breaching a contract will have legal, reputational and ethical issues.

Breach of contract with Encompass Health (EH)

It would be bad for business if CSC Co becomes known as a supplier who cannot be relied on to stick to the terms of its agreements. This could make future potential customers reticent to deal with them.

Even more seriously, there could be legal consequences involved in breaching the contract with EH. This would be costly and also very damaging to CSC Co's reputation.

If CSC Co lets EH down and breaches the contract, EH may refuse to buy from them anymore and future sales revenue would therefore be lost. Just as importantly, these sales to EH are currently helping to increase the marketability of CSC Co's shakes. This will be lost if these sales are no longer made.

Therefore, taking these factors into account, it would not be advisable to breach the contract.

(c)

Tutorial note

You could attempt this part of the question before any other part of Section C – good examination technique especially when under time pressure. Although most candidates are comfortable with the steps involved in linear programming, there is a lack of in-depth understanding of how it works. For example, virtually all candidates could identify the iso-contribution line and feasible region when given on a graph, but few could explain what they meant. Many explained what they were for (finding the optimum point), but not that the iso-contribution line shows all points giving the same contribution, or that the feasible region shows all possible production plans that meet all of the constraints. Similarly, most could define slack in the context of scarce resources, but found it harder to identify slack variables from a completed graph.

(i) This line is what is called the 'iso-contribution line' and it is plotted by finding two corresponding x and y values for the 'objective function'. At any point along this line, the mix of cakes and cookies will provide the same total contribution, 'C'.

Since each cake provides a contribution of $2.60 and each cookie provides a contribution of $1.75, the objective function has been defined as 'C = 2.6x + 1.75y'. This means that the total contribution will be however many cakes are made (represented by 'x') at $2.60 each plus however many cookies are made (represented by 'y') at $1.75 each.

The area 0ABCD is called the 'feasible region'. Any point within this region could be selected and would show a feasible mix of production of cakes and cookies. However, in order to maximise profit, the optimum production mix will be at a point on the edge of the feasible region, not within it.

(ii) The further the iso-contribution line is moved away from the origin, 0, the greater the contribution generated will be. Therefore, a ruler will be laid along the line, making sure it stays at exactly the same angle as the line, and the ruler will then be moved outwards to the furthest vertex (intersection between two constraints) on the feasible region, as represented by either point A, B, C or D. In this case, the optimum point is 'C', the intersection of the 'labour' constraint and the 'demand for cakes' constraint.

(iii) A 'slack' value could arise either in relation to a resource or in relation to production of a product. It means that a resource is not being fully utilised or that there is unfulfilled demand of a product. Since the optimum point is the intersection of the labour and the demand for cakes lines, this means that there will be three slack values. First, there will be a slack value for cookies. This means that there will be unsatisfied demand for cookies since the optimum point does not reach as far as the 'demand for cookies' line on the graph. Also, there will be slack values for Betta and Singa, which means that both of these materials are not actually the binding constraints, such that there will be more material available than is needed.

Marking scheme			
			Marks
(a)	Calculating shortage of Betta		1.5
	Contribution per gram of Betta		1
	Ranking		0.5
	Optimum production plan		2
	Profit		1
		Maximum	6
(b)	Each valid point		1
		Maximum	4
(c)	**(i)**	Identification and explanation of the iso contribution line	2
		Identification and explanation of the feasible region	2
		Maximum	4
	(ii)	explaining how to use line for identification of optimum point	1.5
		Identification of optimum point	0.5
		Maximum	2
	(iii)	Explaining what slack values are	1
		Identifying Betta as slack	1
		Identifying Singa as slack	1
		Identifying slack demand for cookies	1
		Maximum	4
Total			20

288   BITS AND PIECES (JUNE 2009)

(a) The decision to open on Sundays is to be based on incremental revenue and incremental costs:

	Ref	$	$
Incremental revenue	(W1)		800,000
Incremental costs			
Cost of sales	(W2)	335,000	
Staff	(W3)	45,000	
Lighting	(W4)	9,000	
Heating	(W5)	9,000	
Manager's bonus	(W6)	8,000	
Total costs			(406,000)
Net incremental revenue			394,000

Conclusion

On the basis of the above it is clear that the incremental revenue exceeds the incremental costs and therefore it is financially justifiable.

Workings

(W1)   Incremental revenue

Day	Sales	Gross profit	Gross profit	Cost of Sales
	$	%	$	$
Average	10,000	70%		
Sunday (+60% of average)	16,000	50%	8,000	8,000
Annually (50 days)	800,000		400,000	400,000
Current results (300 days)	3,000,000	70.0%	2,100,000	
New results	3,800,000	65.8%	2,500,000	

(W2)   Purchasing and discount on purchasing

Extra purchasing from Sunday trading is $800,000 – $400,000 = $400,000

Current annual purchasing is $18,000 × 50 = $900,000

New annual purchasing is ($900,000 + $400,000) × 0.95 = $1,235,000

Incremental cost is $1,235,000 – $900,000 = $335,000 (a $65,000 discount)

(W3)   Staff costs

Staff costs on a Sunday are 5 staff × 6 hours × $20 per hour × 1.5 = $900 per day
Annual cost is $900 × 50 days = $45,000

(W4)   Lighting costs

Lighting costs are 6 hours × $30 per hour × 50 days = $9,000

(W5)   Heating costs

Heating cost in winter is 8 hours × $45 per hour × 25 days = $9,000

(W6)   Manager's bonus

This is based on the incremental revenue $800,000 × 1% = $8,000 (or $160 per day)

Tutorial note

Only relevant cash flows should be taken into consideration when making this decision, i.e. the future incremental cash flows that occur as a result of Sunday opening. Prepare a summary of the relevant cash flows and reference in workings, where required.

(b) The manager's rewards can be summarised as follows:

Time off

This appears far from generous. The other staff are being paid time and a half and yet the manager does not appear to have this option and also is only being given time off in lieu (TOIL) at normal rates. Some managers may want their time back as TOIL so as to spend time with family or social friends; others may want the cash to spend. One would have thought some flexibility would have been sensible if the manager is to be motivated properly.

Bonus

The bonus can be calculated at $8,000 per annum (W6); on a day worked basis, this is $160 per day. This is less than that being paid to normal staff; at time and a half they earn 6 hours × $20 × 1.5 = $180 per day. It is very unlikely to be enough to keep the presumably better qualified manager happy. Indeed the bonus is dependent on the level of new sales and so there is an element of risk involved for the manager. Generally speaking higher risk for lower returns is far from motivating.

The level of sales could of course be much bigger than is currently predicted. However, given the uplift on normal average daily sales is already +60%, this is unlikely to be significant.

(c) **Discounts and promotion**

When new products or in this case opening times are launched then some form of market stimulant is often necessary. B&P has chosen to offer substantial discounts and promotions. There are various issues here:

Changing buying patterns: It is possible that customers might delay a purchase a day or two in order to buy on a Sunday. This would cost the business since the margin earned on Sunday is predicted to be 20% points lower than on other days.

Complaints: Customers that have already bought an item on another day might complain when they see the same product on sale for much less when they come back in for something else on a Sunday. Businesses need to be strong in this regard in that they have to retain control over their pricing policy. Studies have shown that only a small proportion of people will actually complain in this situation. More might not, though, be caught out twice and hence will change the timing of purchases (as above).

Quality: The price of an item can say something about its quality. Low prices tend to suggest poor quality and vice versa. B&P should be careful so as not to suggest that lower prices do not damage the reputation of the business as regards quality.

		Marks
(a)	Existing total sales	1.0
	New sales	1.0
	Incremental sales	1.0
	Existing purchasing	2.0
	Discount allowed for	1.0
	Incremental Sunday purchasing costs	1.0
	Staff cost	2.0
	Lighting cost	1.0
	Heating cost	1.0
	Manager's bonus	1.0
(b)	Time off at normal rate not time and a half	1.0
	Lack of flexibility	1.0
	Bonus per day worked calculation and comment	1.0
	Risk	1.0
(c)	Changing customer buying pattern	2.0
	Complaints risk	2.0
	Quality link	2.0
		——
	Maximum	4
		——
Total		20
		——

Marking scheme

Examiner's comments (extract)

This question (in the second two parts) required some common business sense. This is sadly lacking in many. The manager's pay deal offered them less money per hour than the staff (on current prediction of incremental sales) and time off on a one to one basis when the staff got time and a half. Most managers would be savvy enough to recognise a poor deal when they saw it. Equally a weekend day is for many a family day and a day off in the week is a poor substitute for that.

The offering of substantial discounts may well encourage sales (a mark earning point). However, surely it is likely that customers could switch from weekday shopping to weekend shopping to save money. Surprisingly few realised this.

Marks gained for part (a) were reasonable with incremental sales, staff costs, and lighting being done correctly by most candidates. For some reason the incremental heating cost was incorrectly calculated by many, with candidates electing to heat the stores all year as opposed to just the winter months as stated in the question.

There were two sunk costs to be excluded (rent and supervisor salary). It is always advisable for a candidate to indicate that the cost is to be excluded rather than simply not mention it at all.

Very few realised that the manager's pay deal was not overly generous both in terms of time off and the amount of cash on offer. Many candidates seemed to think that the mere existence of time off and the offer of money was enough to motivate. The amount of time off and cash was ignored. This is again naive, demonstrating a lack of understanding or experience.

289 STAY CLEAN (DECEMBER 2009)

(a) The relevant costs of the decision to cease the manufacture of the TD are needed:

Cost or Revenue	Working reference	Amount ($)
Lost revenue	Note 1	(96,000)
Saved labour cost	Note 2	48,000
Lost contribution from other products	Note 3	(118,500)
Redundancy and recruitment costs	Note 4	(3,700)
Supplier payments saved	Note 5	88,500
Sublet income		12,000
Supervisor	Note 6	0
		───────
Net cash flow		(69,700)
		───────

Conclusion: It is not worthwhile ceasing to produce the TD now.

Note 1: All sales of the TD will be lost for the next 12 months, this will lose revenue of 1,200 units × $80 = $96,000.

Note 2: All normal labour costs will be saved at 1,200 units × $40 = $48,000.

Note 3: Related product sales will be lost.

This will cost the business 5% × ((5,000u × $150) + (6,000u × $270)) = $118,500 in contribution (material costs are dealt with separately below).

Note 4: If TD is ceased now, then:

Redundancy cost	($6,000)
Retraining saved	$3,500
Recruitment cost	($1,200)
	───────
Total cost	($3,700)
	───────

Note 5: Supplier payments:

	DW ($)	WM ($)	TD ($)	Net cost ($)	Discount level	Gross cost ($)
Current buying cost	350,000	600,000	60,000	1,010,000	5%	1,063,158
Loss of TD			(60,000)	(60,000)	5%	(63,158)
Loss of related sales at cost	(17,500)	(30,000)		(47,500)	5%	(50,000)
New buying cost				921,500	3%	950,000
Difference in net cost				88,500		

Note 6: There will be no saving or cost here as the supervisor will continue to be fully employed.

An alternative approach is possible to the above problem:

Cash flow	Ref	Amount ($)
Lost contribution – TD	Note 7	12,000
Lost contribution – other products	Note 8	(71,000)
Redundancy and recruitment	Note 4 above	(3,700)
Lost discount	Note 9	(19,000)
Sublet income		12,000
Supervisor	Note 6 above	0
		─────
Net cash flow		(69,700)
		─────

Note 7: There will be a saving on the contribution lost on the TD of 1,200 units × $10 per unit = –$12,000

Note 8: The loss of sales of other products will cost a lost contribution of 5% ((5,000 × $80) + (6,000 × $170)) = $71,000

Note 9:

	DW	WM	TD	Total (net)	Discount	Total gross
Current buying cost	350,000	600,000	60,000	1,010,000	5%	1,063,158
Saved cost	(17,500)	(30,000)	(60,000)			
New buying cost	332,500	570,000	0	902,500	5%	950,000
				921,500	3%	950,000
Lost discount				(19,000)		

(b) Complementary pricing

Since the washing machine and the tumble dryer are products that tend to be used together, Stay Clean could link their sales with a complementary price. For example they could offer customers a discount on the second product bought, so if they buy (say) a TD for $80 then they can get a WM for (say) $320. Overall then Stay Clean make a positive contribution of $130 (320 + 80 – 180 – 90).

Product line pricing

All the products tend to be related to each other and used in the utility room or kitchen. Some sales will involve all three products if customers are upgrading their utility room or kitchen for example. A package price could be offered and as long as Stay Clean make a contribution on the overall deal then they will be better off.

(c) Outsourcing requires consideration of a number of issues (only 3 required):

- The cost of manufacture should be compared to cost of buying in from the outsourcer. If the outsourcer can provide the same products cheaper than it is perhaps preferable.

- The reliability of the outsourcer should be assessed. If products are delivered late then the ultimate customer could be disappointed. This could damage the goodwill or brand of the business.

- The quality of work that the outsourcer produces needs to be considered. Cheaper products can often be at the expense of poor quality of materials or assembly.

- The loss of control over the manufacturing process can reduce the flexibility that Stay Clean has over current production. If Stay Clean wanted, say, to change the colour of a product then at present it should be able to do that. Having contracted with an outsourcer this may be more difficult or involve penalties.

290 CHOICE OF CONTRACTS

Note		North East		South Coast	
		$	$	$	$
Contract price			288,000		352,000
(1)	Material X: inventory	19,440			
(2)	Material X: firm orders	27,360			
(3)	Material X: not yet ordered	60,000			
(4)	Material Y			49,600	
(5)	Material Z			71,200	
(6)	Labour	86,000		110,000	
(8)	Staff accommodation and travel	6,800		5,600	
(9)	Penalty clause			28,000	
(10)	Loss of plant hire income			6,000	
			(199,600)		(270,400)
Profit			88,400		81,600

The company should undertake the North-east contract. It is better than the South coast contract by $6,800 ($88,400 – $81,600).

Notes:

(1)   Material X can be used in place of another material which the company uses. The value of material X for this purpose is 90% × $21,600 = $19,440. If the company undertakes the North-east contract it will not be able to obtain this saving. This is an opportunity cost.

(2)   Although the material has not been received yet the company is committed to the purchase. Its treatment is the same therefore as if it was already in inventory. The value is 90% × $30,400 = $27,360.

(3)   The future cost of material X not yet ordered is relevant.

(4)   The original cost of material Y is a sunk cost and is therefore not relevant. If the material was to be sold now its value would be 24,800 × 2 × 85% = $42,160, i.e. twice the purchase price less 15%, however, if the material is kept it can be used on other contracts, thus saving the company from future purchases. The second option is the better. The relevant cost of material Y is 2 × 24,800 = $49,600. If the company uses material Y on the South-coast contract, it will eventually have to buy an extra $49,600 of Y for use on other contracts.

(5)   The future cost of material Z is an incremental cost and is relevant.

(6)   As the labour is to be sub-contracted it is a variable cost and is relevant.

(7) Site management is a fixed cost and will be incurred whichever contract is undertaken (and indeed if neither is undertaken), and is therefore not relevant.

(8) It is assumed that the staff accommodation and travel is specific to the contracts and will only be incurred if the contracts are undertaken.

(9) If the South-coast contract is undertaken the company has to pay a $28,000 penalty for withdrawing from the North-east contract. This is a relevant cost with regard to the South-coast contract.

(10) The depreciation on plant is not a cash flow. It is therefore not relevant. The opportunity cost of lost plant hire is relevant, however.

(11) It is assumed that the notional interest has no cash flow implications.

(12) It is assumed that the HQ costs are not specific to particular contracts.

291 HS EQUATION

(a) p = a − bq where p is price and q is demand for product

When price = $1,350, demand = 8,000 units

When price = $1,400, demand = 7,000 units

So: (1) 1,350 = a − 8,000b and (2) 1,400 = a − 7,000b

so subtracting equation (1) from equation (2), 50 = 1,000b and b = 0.05

and substituting in equation (2):1,400 = a − 0.05 × 7,000 so a = 1,750

so Price = 1,750 − 0.05q and marginal revenue = 1,750 − 0.1q

To find variable production cost per unit, we need to separate fixed and variable costs from the historic cost data. Using the high-low method, dividing the difference in cost for the highest and lowest activity levels by the change in activity.

Variable production cost per unit = $(7,000 − 5,446) × 1,000/(9,400 − 7,300)

= $1,554 × 1,000/2,100

= $740

Direct material cost = $270

Total variable cost = $(270 + 740)

= $1,010

Price is maximised where marginal cost (= variable cost) = marginal revenue

1,010 = 1,750 − 0.1q

q = 7,400 units   and price = 1,750 − 0.05 × 7,400

So optimum price = $1,380

(b)

Tutorial note

*Note that the question only asks for **two** reasons.*

There are a number of reasons why it may be inappropriate for HS to use this model in practice:

- The model depends on the market structure being one in which there is:
    - Perfect competition (which is the closest situation to HS's market)
    - Monopolistic competition
    - Monopoly or
    - Oligopoly

  Whilst the market is highly competitive, it is unlikely that there is perfect competition (in which the action of one company cannot affect the market price).

- The model assumes that costs and demand follow a linear relationship and that there are no step changes in fixed costs. Again this may hold over a small range of volumes but is unlikely to be true for all possible volumes.

- This model can only be used if the company has detailed knowledge of demand and cost curves. It is unlikely that in practice HS would be able to derive accurate cost and demand curves.

292 MKL

(a) The selling price that should be charged for Product K is the one that maximises total contribution, i.e. a price of $75 for a demand of 1,400 units:

Selling price per unit	$100	$85	$80	$75
Variable cost	$38	$38	$38	$38
Unit contribution	$62	$47	$42	$37
Demand units	600 units	800 units	1200 units	1400 units
Total Weekly contribution	**$37,200**	**$37,600**	**$50,400**	**$51,800**

(b) 1,400 units of Product K will use up 1,400 standard hours; in order to utilise all of the spare capacity, we now need to use 600 hours for Product L, for the first 10 weeks.

$\dfrac{600 \text{ hours}}{1.25 \text{ hours}}$ = 480 units will use all the spare capacity.

To maximise profits, the optimum price P will be expressed as P = a – bQ.

Here, a = $100 + ($\dfrac{1,000}{200}$ × $10)

So a = $150 and b = $\dfrac{\$10}{200}$ 0.05

P = $150 – 0.05Q

P = $150 – 0.05 × 480 units

P = $126 for the first 10 weeks.

For the following 10 weeks when the extra capacity becomes available, the optimum price P will be expressed as P = a – bQ and we need to equate MC = MR to maximise profits, with

MR = a – 2bQ.

Profit maximised when MC = MR, i.e. when $45 = a – 2bQ

When $45 = $150 – 0.10Q i.e. when Q =1,050 units and P = $150 – 0.05 × 1,050

P = $97.50

(c)   Skimming

Given that the product is innovative and unlike any current products on the market, then a skimming strategy would seem a very good fit. As the product in new and exciting, charging a high early price would help target the early adopters in the introduction stage. This would also have the advantage of allowing product M to be produced in relatively low volumes, whilst still generating good cashflows to recoup the substantial R&D and launch costs traditionally linked to this kind of products.

Finally, as the market is untested for the product, it allows the firm to start with a high intro price and adjust downwards accordingly.

Penetration pricing

This tactic represents the alternative approach when launching a new product; it involves charging an initial low price to quickly gain market share. It offers the advantage of scaring off potential entrants to the market and may allow the firm to exploit economies of scale. However, given that our product M is differentiated and there will be little, if any, immediate competition, we think the company is right to adopt a skimming strategy for its pricing.

293   SNIFF CO (DECEMBER 2007)

Key answer tips

This is an in-depth question on relevant costing and the further processing decisions.

In part (a) the financial factors may seem obvious, i.e. process further if the profit will increase as a result. However, there are five marks available and so it is not enough to simply make this comment. Consider what will drive profit, e.g. future incremental sales and costs, sales volume. Each of these factors can then be explained briefly.

The main non-financial factor involves the health concerns surrounding the use of the hormones. Ethics is a key motivation of the examiner and so make sure issues such as this are discussed.

In part (b) it is vital that you apply the principles of relevant costing accurately. i.e. you should only include future incremental cash flows:

- Future – Exclude sunk costs such as the market research

- Incremental – The supervisor's salary and fixed costs should be ignored. On the other hand opportunity costs should be included for labour.

(a) Sniff should consider the following factors when making a further processing decision:

Financial factors

- **Incremental revenue.** Sniff should only process the perfume further if the incremental revenues from the new product exceeds the incremental costs of processing the perfume.

- **Incremental costs.** A decision to further process can involve more materials and labour. Care must be taken to only include those costs that change as a result of the decision and therefore sunk costs should be ignored. Sunk costs would include, for example, fixed overheads that would already be incurred by the business before the further process decision was taken. The shortage of labour means that its 'true' cost will be higher and need to be included.

    Also, Sniff should consider both the Direct costs and the indirect costs (although they may not all be easily identifiable) such as:

    (1)   The additional space required

    (2)   Branding costs

    (3)   Patent costs

    (4)   Supervisors' costs.

Other factors

- **Impact on overall sales volumes.** Sniff is selling a 'highly branded' product. Existing customers may well be happy with the existing product. If the further processing changes the existing product too much there could be an impact on sales and loyalty.

- **Impact on reputation.** As is mentioned in the question, adding hormones to a product is not universally popular. Many groups exist around the world that protest against the use of hormones in products. Sniff could be damaged by this association.

- **Potential legal cases** being brought regarding allergic reactions to hormones.

(b)

Tutorial note

There are 27 minutes to answer this requirement and therefore no need to panic. A logical, planned structure is essential. Start by calculating the contribution for 1,000 litres of standard perfume, working through each cost and sales item in turn. Once this is done, set up a separate working for the male and female versions. Calculate the extra costs and revenues of further processing. Take a guess if you are not sure of a particular area and move on. Don't forget to conclude, using the financial and non-financial factors.

Market research is a sunk cost and therefore should be ignored for the purpose of the calculation.

Production costs for 1,000 litres of the standard perfume

		$
Aromatic oils	10 ltrs × $18,000/ltr	180,000
Diluted alcohol	990 ltrs × $20/ltr	19,800
Material cost		199,800
Labour	2,000 hrs × $15/hr	30,000
Total		229,800
Cost per litre		229.80
Sales price per litre		399.80

Lost contribution per hour of labour used on new products

($399,800 − $199,800) ÷ 2,000 hrs = $100/hr

Incremental costs

	Male version		Female version	
		$		$
Hormone	2 ltr × $7,750/ltr	15,500	8 ltr × $12,000/ltr	96,000
Supervisor	Sunk cost	0	Sunk cost	0
Labour	500 hrs × $100/hr	50,000	700 hrs × $100/hr	70,000
Fixed cost	Sunk cost	0	Sunk cost	0
Research	Sunk cost	0	Sunk cost	0
Total		65,500		166,000

Incremental revenues

	Male version		Female version	
		$		$
Standard	200 ltr × $399.80/ltr	79,960	800 ltr × $399.80	319,840
Hormone	202 ltr × $750/ltr	151,500	808 ltr × $595/ltr	480,760
Inc. revenue		71,540		160,920
Benefit/(cost)		6,040		(5,080)

The Male version of the product is worth processing further in that the extra revenue exceeds the extra cost by $6,040.

The Female version of the product is not worth processing further in that the extra cost exceeds the extra revenue by $5,080.

In both cases the numbers appear small. Indeed, the benefit of $6,040 may not be enough to persuade management to take the risk of damaging the brand and the reputation of the business. To put this figure into context: the normal output generates a contribution of $170 per litre and on normal output of about 10,000 litres this represents a monthly contribution of around $1.7m (after allowing for labour costs).

Future production decisions are a different matter. If the product proves popular, however, Sniff might expect a significant increase in overall volumes. If Sniff could exploit this and resolve its current shortage of labour then more contribution could be created. It is worth noting that resolving its labour shortage would substantially reduce the labour cost allocated to the hormone added project. Equally, the prices charged for a one off experimental promotion might be different to the prices that can be secured in the long run.

Note: The original question had parts (c) and (d) as well. The answers to these requirements are as follows:

(c)   The selling price charged would have to cover the incremental costs of $166,000. For 808 litres that would mean the price would have to be $\frac{(\$166,000 + \$319,840)}{808 \text{ ltrs}}$ = $601.29/ltr

or about $60.13 per 100 ml.

This represents an increase of only 1.05% on the price given and so clearly there may be scope for further consideration of this proposal.

(d)   Outsourcing involves consideration of many factors, the main ones being:

Cost. Outsourcing often involves a reduction in the costs of a business. Cost savings can be made if the outsourcer has a lower cost base than, in this case, Sniff. Labour savings are common when outsourcing takes place.

Quality. Sniff would need to be sure that the quality of the perfume would not reduce. The fragrance must not change at all given the product is branded. Equally Sniff should be concerned about the health and safety of its customers since its perfume is 'worn' by its customers.

Confidentiality. We are told that the blend of aromatic oils used in the production process is 'secret. This may not remain so if an outsourcer is employed. Strict confidentiality should be maintained and be made a contractual obligation.

Reliability of supply. Sniff should consider the implications of late delivery on its customers.

Primary Function. Sniff is apparently considering outsourcing its primary function. This is not always advisable as it removes Sniff's reason for existence. It is more common to outsource a secondary function, like payroll processing for example.

Access to expertise. Sniff may find the outsourcer has considerable skills in fragrance manufacturing and hence could benefit from that.

	Marking scheme		*Marks*
(a)	Per factor outlined		1
			—
		Maximum	5
			—
(b)	Hormone costs		2
	Supervisor excluded		1
	Direct labour		3
	Fixed cost allocation excluded		1
	Market research		1
	Incremental revenue		3
	Net benefit		2
	Concluding comment		2
			—
		Maximum	15
			—
Total			20
			—

294 FURNIVAL

Key answer tips

Approach the question one step at a time, applying fundamental decision-making principles.

(a) Identify incremental revenues and incremental costs including opportunity costs.

(b) Ignore fixed costs.

(c) Ignore costs incurred prior to the split off point.

(i) Process R further if incremental revenues are greater than incremental costs.

Incremental revenues

	$
Selling price at split off point (per gallon)	1.50
Selling price after mixing	10.00
	———
Increase per gallon	8.50
∴ Total for 500 gallons $8.50 × 500	$4,250

Incremental costs

Variable costs + Opportunity costs

	$
90% of process costs 0.90 × $3,000	2,700
Other separable costs	500
	———
Total	3,200

Opportunity costs

Mixing hours are limited and scarce. If R is not produced, the 'other work' could earn a contribution – this is foregone by processing R further.

Contribution = Profit + Fixed costs

Product R requires 10 hours work.

	$
Therefore, total profit from other work = $200 × 10 hours =	2,000
Fixed cost element 10% of $3,000 ($30 per hour × 10 hours) =	300
Total contribution	2,300
∴ Total incremental costs $3,200 + $2,300	5,500

Therefore do not process further. R should be sold at the split off point.

Tutorial note

The joint process costs are ignored as they are incurred prior to the separation point.

(ii)

Tutorial note

R is sold at the split off point and production remains at 500 gallons. Therefore, R is not relevant to the decision at hand and it may be ignored.

Consider new output from the distillation plant.

P :	700 gallons
Q :	800 gallons
R :	500 gallons
Production of P falls by (1,000 – 700)	300 gallons
Production of Q increases by (800 – 500)	300 gallons

Joint process costs will not change as total production remains at 2,000 gallons. Relevant costs only arise in the mixing plant.

		Product P		Product Q
Revenue per gallon		$12.50		$20.00
Variable costs:				
Process costs	$\dfrac{\$2,700}{1,000g}$	($2.70)	$\dfrac{\$2,700}{500g}$	($5.40)
Other	$\dfrac{\$2,000}{1,000g}$	($2.00)	$\dfrac{\$500}{500g}$	($1.00)
Contribution per gallon		$7.80		$13.60

Loss in contribution from P = 300 × $7.80 =	($2,340)
Gain in contribution from Q = 300 × $13.60 =	$4,080
Net gain	$1,740
Extra cost of Q = 300 × $1 =	($300)
Total	$1,440

However, this change in output will require additional machine hours:

Production of P: Hours used falls by $\dfrac{10}{1,000} \times 300 = 3$ hours

Production of Q: Hours used rise by $\dfrac{10}{500} \times 300 = 6$ hours

Therefore, additional hours required 3 hours

Thus 3 hours' contribution from 'other work' is forgone.

Contribution per hour from other work = $230 (see earlier).

Lost contribution with new plan = $230 × 3 hours = $690

Overall effect of new plan = $1,440 – $690 = $750 gain

Recommendations – Produce P : Q : R ratio of 7 : 8 : 5 and sell R at the split off point.

295 RECYC

(a) **Payoff table**

		Level of waste		
		High	Medium	Low
Advance	High	962.5	636.5	397.5
order of	Medium	912.5	655.5	442.5
chemical	Low	837.5	617.5	457.5

Workings

(W1)

Advance order of chemical X	Level of waste	Prob.	Contrib. (excl. X) (W2)	Chemical X cost (W3)	Net contribution
			$000	$000	$000
High	High	0.30	1,462.5	500	962.5
	Medium	0.50	1,111.5	475	636.5
	Low	0.20	877.5	480	397.5
Medium	High	0.30	1,462.5	550	912.5
	Medium	0.50	1,111.5	456	655.5
	Low	0.20	877.5	435	442.5
Low	High	0.30	1,462.5	625	837.5
	Medium	0.50	1,111.5	494	617.5
	Low	0.20	877.5	420	457.5

(W2) Waste available

	High	Medium	Low
Aluminium extracted (000 kg)	7,500	5,700	4,500
	$000	$000	$000
Sales revenue (at $0.65 per kg)	4,875.0	3,705.0	2,925.0
Variable cost (at 70%)	3,412.5	2,593.5	2,047.5
Contribution	1,462.5	1,111.5	877.5

(W3) Examples of workings for chemical X cost

- High advance level of order for chemical X and low actual requirement: The price of $1.00 is subject to a penalty of $0.60 per kg. The cost of chemical X is, therefore, 300,000 kg × $1.60 = $480,000.

- Low advance level of order for chemical X and medium actual requirement: The price is subject to a discount of $0.10 per kg. The cost of chemical X is, therefore, 380,000 × $1.30 = $494,000.

(b) Maximax suggests that the decision maker should look for the largest possible profit from all the outcomes. In this case this is a high advance order of chemical X where there is a possibility of a contribution of $962,500. This indicates a risk seeking preference by management. Although it offers the possibility of the highest contribution, there is also a 20% likelihood that the worst outcome of $397,500 will occur.

Maximin suggests that the decision maker should look for the strategy which maximises the minimum possible contribution. In this case this is a low advance order of chemical X where the lowest contribution is $457,500. This is better than the worst possible outcomes from high or medium advance orders of chemical X. This indicates a risk-averse management posture.

296 TICKET AGENT *Walk in the footsteps of a top tutor*

Key answer tips

It would be easy to get absorbed in the detail of this question and to spend too much time trying to perfect the calculations. However, to pass the exam, focus on the easy marks. If mistakes are made in earlier calculations, carry forward marks will be available.

(a) The question specifies that a long-run perspective is being taken so decisions can be made by reference to expected values.

Expected sales demand

> An easy 3 marks are available here.

	Probability	Demand	EV
Popular artistes	0.45	500	225
Lesser known artistes	0.30	350	105
Unknown artistes	0.25	200	50
			———
			380
			———

Expected demand = 380 tickets per concert

> This part is harder but there are 20 minutes available for this requirement and therefore enough time to understand the scenario and to set out clear workings.

Maximising profit

To determine the best decision, the expected profits for each possible order level need to be calculated.

- Payoff table showing profit (W1, W2)

> There are 12 calculations to complete. Show the workings for at least one, so that the marker can follow the approach

Actual sales demand

		200	350	500
	200	1,200	1,200	1,200
Purchase	300	(570)	2,250	2,250
Level	400	(2,040)	2,190	3,600
	500	(2,460)	1,770	6,000

- Expected values

		EV
200 tickets	1,200 × 1	1,200
300 tickets	(570) × 0.25 + 2,250 × 0.75	1,545
400 tickets	(2,040) × 0.25 + 2,190 × 0.3 + 3,600 × 0.45	1,767
500 tickets	(2,460) × 0.25 + 1,770 × 0.3 + 6,000 × 0.45	2,616

> Don't forget to conclude. Another easy mark available.

The optimum purchase level is 500 tickets per concert, which will give an expected profit of $2,616 per concert.

Workings

(W1) The gross profit made per ticket is the discount received on the selling price of $30.

Purchase level	Discount			Profit per ticket sold
200	20%	20% × $30	=	$6.00
300	25%	25% × $30	=	$7.50
400	30%	30% × $30	=	$9.00
500	40%	40% × $30	=	$12.00

(W2) Each net profit calculation consists of up to three elements:

1   the profit on the units sold

2   the cost of the units which are unsold and returned

3   the value of the returns

EV of returns = $30.00 × 60% × 10% = $1.80 per return.

Example calculation:

Buy 300 tickets but can only sell 200 ⇒ Sell 200 tickets and return 100 tickets

> This part is relatively easy.

> This part is harder. Take a guess if unsure and move on.

	$
Sales 200 tickets × 7.50 (W1)	1,500
EV of returns 100 tickets × $1.80	180
	1,680
Cost of returns 100 tickets × $22.50 (25% discount)	(2,250)
	(570)

Tutorial note

An alternative debrief, used by one of our Kaplan tutors using the ACCA's Constructed Response workspace, is presented on the next page.

(a) Payoff Table

	%	200	300	400	500	Best decision
				Purchase level		
	200 0.25	1,200	−570	−2,040	−2,460	1,200
Sales	350 0.3	1,200	2,250	2,190	1,770	2,250
Demand	500 0.45	1,200	2,250	3,600	6,000	6,000
Expected value		1,200	1,545	1,767	2,616	

Workings

Purchased		200	300	300	400	400	400	500	500	500
Direct sales		200	200	300	200	350	400	200	350	500
Remaining tickets		0	100	0	200	50	0	300	150	0
Sales price per ticket		30	30	30	30	30	30	30	30	30
Discount		0.2	0.25	0.25	0.3	0.3	0.3	0.4	0.4	0.4
Cost per ticket		−24	−22.5	−22.5	−21	−21	−21	−18	−18	−18
Direct sales – revenue		6,000	6,000	9,000	6,000	10,500	12,000	6,000	10,500	15,000
Box office sales	10% 18	0	180	0	360	90	0	540	270	0
Ticket cost		−4,800	−6,750	−6,750	−8,400	−8,400	−8,400	−9,000	−9,000	−9,000
Total payoff		1,200	−570	2,250	−2,040	2,190	3,600	−2,460	1,770	6,000

(b)

> **An easy 2 marks.**

Maximax

The agent should order 500 tickets as this gives a maximum possible gain of $6,000 per concert.

Maximin

The agent should buy 200 tickets to maximise the minimum possible pay-off ($1,200).

Minimax regret

A regret table is found by comparing the actual profit with what could have been made given the level of demand that occurred:

> **This is harder. Even if you can't do the calculation, explain what minimax regret is. This will gain 1 easy mark.**

		Actual sales demand		
		200	350	500
	200	0	1,050	4,800
Purchase	300	1,770	0	3,750
Level	400	3,240	60	2,400
	500	3,660	480	0

The agent would thus order 400 tickets as this limits the maximum regret to $3,240.

This level of order would give an average profit of $1,767 per concert.

Tutorial note

An alternative debrief, used by one of our Kaplan tutors using the ACCA's Constructed Response workspace, is presented here.

Regret Table

	Purchase level			
	200	**300**	**400**	**500**
200	0	1,770	3,250	3,660
350	1,050	0	60	480
500	4,800	3,750	2,400	0
Max regret	4,800	3,750	3,240	3,660
			Minimum	

(c) The advice depends on the risk perspective of the agent

> More easy marks available. The advice should be linked back to parts (a) and (b). Points should be separate and succinct.

- If they are willing to take a long term perspective and accept short-term uncertainty, then the expected value calculations in part (a) should be adopted, giving an order of 500 tickets

- If they are an optimist, then the maximax criteria would suggest ordering 500 tickets

- If they are a pessimist, then the maximin criteria would suggest ordering 200 tickets

- If they are a sore loser, then the minimax regret approach would suggest buying 400 tickets.

In reality the agent may be best advised to insist on knowing who the artists are before having to place an order.

297 SHIFTERS HAULAGE (DECEMBER 2008)

(a) Maximax stands for maximising the maximum return an investor might expect. An investor that subscribes to the maximax philosophy would generally select the strategy that could give them the best possible return. They will ignore all other possible returns and only focus on the biggest, hence this type of investor is often accused of being an optimist or a risk-taker.

Maximin stands for maximising the minimum return an investor might expect. This type of investor will focus only on the potential minimum returns and seek to select the strategy that will give the best worst case result. This type of investor could be said to be being cautious or pessimistic in their outlook and a risk-avoider.

Expected value averages all possible returns in a weighted average calculation.

For example if an investor could expect $100 with a 0.3 probability and $300 with a 0.7 probability then on average the return would be:

(0.3 × $100) + (0.7 × $300) = $240

This figure would then be used as a basis of the investment decision. The principle here is that if this decision was repeated again and again then the investor would get the EV as a return. Its use is more questionable for use on one-off decisions.

Key answer tips

Easy marks were available here. This is a core knowledge area and no application of knowledge was required. There will be easy marks for knowledge in each exam.

(b)   Profit calculations

	Small Van	Medium Van	Large Van
Capacity	100	150	200
Low Demand (120)	300 (W1)	468 (W3)	368 (W5)
High Demand (190)	300 (W2)	500 (W4)	816 (W6)

Workings	(W1)	(W2)	(W3)	(W4)	(W5)	(W6)
Sales	1,000	1,000	1,200	1,500	1,200	1,900
VC	(400)	(400)	(480)	(600)	(480)	(760)
Goodwill	(100)	(100)		(100)		
VC adjustment			48		48	76
Depreciation	(200)	(200)	(300)	(300)	(400)	(400)
Profit	300	300	468	500	368	816

Tutorial note

Some candidates were confused about which level of demand should be used. The only levels of demand mentioned were 120 and 190 units and therefore these should have been used. Other candidates were confused about the appropriate adjustments that should have been made for variable costs, goodwill and depreciation.

Profit tables are a key part of risk and uncertainty. The approach to preparing them will always be similar and therefore candidates should practice a number of questions before sitting the exam.

(c)   Which type of van to buy?

This depends on the risk attitude of the investor. If they are optimistic about the future then the maximax criteria would suggest that they choose the large van as this has the potentially greatest profit.

If they are more pessimistic then they would focus on the minimum expected returns and choose the medium van as the worst possible result is $468, which is better than the other options. We are also told that the business managers are becoming more cautious and so a maximin criterion may be preferred by them.

Expected values could be calculated thus:

Small van	$300
Medium van ($468 × 0.4) + ($500 × 0.6) =	$487
Large van ($368 × 0.4) + ($816 × 0.6) =	$637

Given SH is considering replacing a number of vans you could argue that an EV approach has merit (not being a one-off decision – assuming individual booking sizes are independent of each other).

The final decision lies with the managers, but given what we know about their cautiousness a medium sized van would seem the logical choice. The small van could never be the correct choice.

Key answer tips

Good candidates discussed the results for the small, medium and large van in turn. Candidates linked their discussion back to the information provided in the scenario and expanded on the points made in part (a) of the answer.

Note: The original question asked for a discussion of three methods that could be used to analyse and assess the risk in decision making. The suggested answer is given below:

Market research: This can be desk-based (secondary) or field-based (primary). Desk-based is cheap but can lack focus. Field-based research is better in that you can target your customers and your product area but can be time consuming and expensive. The internet is bringing down the cost and speeding up this type of research, email is being used to gather information quickly on the promise of free gifts etc.

Simulation: Computer models can be built to simulate real life scenarios. The model will predict what range of returns an investor could expect from a given decision without having risked any actual cash. The models use random number tables to generate possible values for the uncertainty the business is subject to. Again computer technology is assisting in bringing down the cost of such risk analysis.

Sensitivity analysis: This can be used to assess the range of values that would still give the investor a positive return. The uncertainty may still be there but the affect that it has on the investor's returns will be better understood. Sensitivity calculates the % change required in individual values before a change of decision results. If only a (say) 2% change is required in selling price before losses result an investor may think twice before proceeding. Risk is therefore better understood.

Calculation of worst and best case figures: An investor will often be interested in range. It enables a better understanding of risk. An accountant could calculate the worst case scenario, including poor demand and high costs whilst being sensible about it. They could also calculate best case scenarios including good sales and minimum running costs. This analysis can often reassure an investor. The production of a probability distribution to show an investor the range of possible results is also useful to explain risks involved. A calculation of standard deviation is also possible.

	Marking scheme		
			Marks
(a)	Maximax explanation		2.0
	Maximin explanation		2.0
	Expected value explanation		2.0
			–––––
		Maximum	**5.0**
			–––––
(b)	Small van sales		0.5
	Small van VC		0.5
	Small van goodwill or VC adjustment		1.0
	Small van depreciation		1.0
	Medium van – as above for small van		3.0
	Large van as above for small van		3.0
			–––––
		Maximum	**9.0**
			–––––
(c)	Optimist view		2.0
	Pessimist view		2.0
	Expected value calculation		1.0
	Expected value discussion		1.0
			–––––
		Maximum	**6.0**
			–––––
Total			**20**
			–––––

Examiner's comments (extract)

Part (a) was well done by most. The biggest issue was that some did not mention risk attitudes at all (an optimist would naturally favour maximax for example) this omission meant that 0.5 less marks were scored each time by failing to collect the allocated mark.

Part (b) was also reasonably done by many. There were problems here though:

–   A surprising number of candidates did not seem to understand that if the capacity of a van is 150 and demand is 190 then sales must be restricted to 150. A large number of candidates still put down sales at the 190 level. This indicates a lack of understanding of the question (I assume that they do not read it properly).

–   Many candidates did not include the goodwill adjustment in the profit calculation. This was not entirely unexpected. More than half marks were still available even if this adjustment were ignored.

–   A common mistake was to try and calculate expected sales first and then work out some sort of answer accordingly.

Part (c) was more mixed. I expected that each potential risk attitude be taken in turn and applied to the figures. Where this was done good marks were earned. A surprising number failed to apply themselves to this. Some clearly knew what maximax, maximin and expected value were but could not then apply this knowledge to the question. The step up from F2 is significant and surely an element of application is part of that step.

Part (d) (i.e. the additional requirement) was poorly done by many. Those that had revised the area of risk in decision making did well and scored good marks. Many clearly did not have the knowledge required. Minimax regret was not a valid answer despite what about 50% of candidates thought. Sensitivity, simulation and market research comments all scored good marks.

298 AMELIE

(a) In order to decide whether or not to hire the consultant, expected valued for decision alternatives are calculated, starting on the right hand side of the tree and moving leftwards (backtracking).

At node D:

EV(I) = (0.9 × $30,000) – (0.1 × $10,000) = $26,000

EV(J) = (0.9 × $60,000) – (0.1 × $40,000) = $50,000

EV(K) = (0.9 × $0) – (0.1 × $0) = $0

So, the decision at Node D should be to go for a large shop, as the EV of outcome J is the highest of the three possible decisions I, J and K.

At node E:

EV(L) = (0.12 × $30,000) – (0.88 × $10,000) = ($5,200)

EV(M) = (0.12 × $60,000) – (0.88 × $40,000) = ($28,000)

EV(N) = (0.12 × $0) – (0.88 × $0) = $0

So, the decision at Node E should be not to go for any shop at all, as the EV of outcome N is the only non-loss making option.

At node C:

EV(F) = (0.5 × $30,000) – (0.5 × $10,000) = $10,000

EV(G) = (0.5 × $60,000) – (0.5 × $40,000) = $10,000

EV(H) = (0.5 × $0) – (0.5 × $0) = $0

So, the decision at Node C should be to go for either a small or a large shop, as both offer the same positive EV of a profit.

To decide between hiring a consultant at $5,000 and not hiring a consultant, we need to calculate the EV of profits at node B :

EV(B) = (0.6 × $50,000) + (0.4 × $0) = $30,000

Therefore, profits if a consultant is hired are expected to reach

$30,000 – cost of research $5,000 = $25,000

EV(C) = $10,000, if no market research is undertaken. The expected value of profits is higher if market research is undertaken, therefore Amelie should hire the consultant.

(b) We first need to calculate what the expected value of profits with perfect information would be. If the second consultant predicts a favourable cheese market (0.6 probability), we should opt for a large shop and obtain $60,000 profit. If the consultant predicts an unfavourable market, we should not go for no shop at all (and profits will be nil.)

Therefore EV of profits with perfect information   = 0.6 × $60,000 + (0 × $0)

        = $36,000

Expected profit with imperfect market research information from first consultant

        = $25,000

Value of perfect information   **= $11,000**

299 RY DECISION TREE

(a) and (b)

(b) continued

The optimum price to set is $90. The answer can be calculated from the decision tree (see diagram).

Alternative working:

Expected variable cost per customer; ($5 × 0.6) + ($6 × 0.4) = $5.40

Price	Contribution per customer	Expected demand	Total contribution
$80	$74.60	106 (W1)	$7,907.60
$90	$84.60	96 (W2)	$8,121.60
$100	$94.60	78	$7,378.80

(W1) $(80 \times 0.2) + (100 \times 0.6) + (150 \times 0.2)$ $=$ 106

(W2) $(60 \times 0.2) + (90 \times 0.6) + (150 \times 0.2)$ $=$ 96

(c) Consider the expected contribution for each price alternative if demand is pessimistic

At $80, expected contribution (for pessimistic market) is $5,968

At $90, expected contribution (for pessimistic market) is $5,076

At $100, expected contribution (for pessimistic market) is $2,838.

Note: These figures have been extracted from the decision tree. They could have been calculated without the use of the tree.

Hence a price of $80 should be set.

300 TR CO (SEPTEMBER/DECEMBER 2017)

(a) **Step 1: Establish the demand function**

Tutorial note

This is a fairly technical part (a).

The first skill tested here is the choice of the right pricing method. As students are given information about how changes in price will affect demand, it is the MR = MC method (as opposed to the tabular method) that must be picked.

Students are expected to recognise that information about the learning effect must be taken into account to calculate labour costs and, in turn, establish the 'Marginal Cost' component of their pricing calculations.

Armed with this a sound knowledge of cost behaviour (fixed costs remain fixed!), the step-by-step approach to calculating the optimum price is the perfect example of a tool from the examiner's metaphorical 'toolbox' approach.

b = change in price/change in quantity

b = $2/5,000 units = 0.0004

The maximum demand for Parapain is 1,000,000 units, so where P = 0, Q = 1,000,000, so 'a' is established by substituting these values for P and Q into the demand function:

0 = a – (0.0004 × 1,000,000)

0 = a – 400

Therefore a = 400 and the demand function is therefore: P = 400 – 0. 0004Q

Step 2: Establish the marginal cost

		Total in $
Material Z	500 g × $010	50
Material Y	300 g × $0.50	150
Labour	Working 1	6.6039
Machine running cost	(20/60) × $6.00	2
Total marginal cost per batch		208.6039

Note: Fixed overheads have been ignored as they are not part of the marginal cost.

The marginal cost will now be rounded down to $208.60 per batch.

Working 1: Labour

The labour cost of the 1,000th unit needs to be calculated as follows as this is the basis TR Co will determine the price for Parapain:

Learning curve formula: $Y = aX^b$

'a' is the cost for the first batch: 5 hours × $18 = $90

If X = 1,000 batches and b = –0.321928, then $Y = 90 × 1,000^{-0.321928} = 9.7377411$

Total cost for 1,000 batches = $9,737.7411

If X = 999 batches, then $Y = 90 × 999^{-0.321928} = 9.7408781$

Total cost for 999 batches = $9,731.1372

Therefore the cost of the 1,000 batches ($9,737.7411 – $9,731.1372) = $6.6039

Step 3: Establish the marginal revenue function: MR = a – 2bQ

Equate MC and MR and insert the values for 'a' and 'b' from the demand function in step 1.

208.60 = 400 – (2 × 0.0004 × Q)

Step 4: Solve the MR function to determine optimum quantity, Q

208.60 = 400 – 0.0008Q

0.0008Q = 191.4

Q = 239,250 batches

Step 5: Insert the value of Q from step 4 into the demand function determined in step 1 and calculate the optimum price

P = 400 – (0.0004 × 239,250)

P = $304.30

Step 6: Calculate profit

	Total in $
Revenue (239,250 batches × $304.30)	72,803,775
Variable cost (239,250 batches × $208.60)	(49,907,550)
Fixed costs (250,000 batches × $2)	(500,000)
Profit	22,396,225

(b)   **Market penetration pricing**

Tutorial note

Requirement (b) asked discussions and recommendations; for students wondering where to start, pros and cons of different strategies are a good point to make initially. It is interesting to notice that even if all information pointed towards skimming as the strategy of choice, students would have not maximised marks unless market penetration was mentioned, too.

With penetration pricing, a low price would initially be charged for the anti-malaria drug. The ideology behind this is that the price will make the product accessible to a larger number of buyers and therefore the high sales will compensate for the lower prices being charged. The anti-malaria drug would rapidly become accepted as the only drug worth buying, i.e. it would gain rapid acceptance in the marketplace.

The circumstances which would favour a penetration pricing policy are:

–   Highly elastic demand for the anti-malaria drug, i.e. the lower the price, the higher the demand. There is no evidence that this is the case.

–   If significant economies of scale could be achieved by TR Co so that higher sales volumes would result in sizeable reductions in costs. It cannot be determined if this is the case here.

–   If TR Co was actively trying to discourage new entrants into the market, however in this case, new entrants cannot enter the market anyway due to the patent.

–   If TR Co wished to shorten the initial period of the drug's life-cycle so as to enter the growth and maturity stages quickly but there is no evidence the company wish to do this.

Market skimming pricing

With market skimming, high charges would initially be charged for the anti-malaria drug rather than low prices. This would enable TR Co to take advantage of the unique nature of the product. The most suitable conditions for this strategy are:

–   The product has a short life cycle and high development costs which need to be recovered. There is no information about the drug's life cycle but development costs have been high.

–   Since high prices attract competitors, there needs to be barriers to entry if competitors are to be deterred. In TR Co's case it has a patent for the drug and also the high development costs could act as a barrier.

–   Where high prices in the early stages of a product's life cycle are expected to generate high initial cash flows, this will help TR Co recover the high development costs it has incurred.

Recommendation

Given the unique nature of the drug and the barriers to entry, a market skimming pricing strategy would appear to be the far more suitable pricing strategy. Also, whilst there is demand curve data, it is unknown how reliable this data is, in which case a skimming strategy may be the safer option.

Marking scheme

		Marks
(a)	Demand function	1.5
	Marginal cost/batch	2.5
	Labour 1,000[th] batch	3.5
	Establishing MR function	0.5
	Solve MR to find Q	1.0
	Use demand function and Q to find P	1.0
	Contribution based on P and Q	1.0
	Deduction of fixed costs	0.5
	Profit	0.5
	Maximum	**12**
(b)	Penetration pricing	3
	Skimming pricing	3
	Other relevant comments/recommendation	2
	Maximum	**8**
Total		**20**

301 THE ALKA HOTEL (JUNE 2018)

(a) **Breakeven point (in occupied room nights) = Fixed cost/contribution per room**

$600,000/($180 – $60) = 5,000 occupied room nights

Margin of safety = (Budgeted room occupancy – breakeven room occupancy)/budgeted room occupancy

Total rooms available per annum: 365 days × 25 rooms = 9,125 rooms

Budgeted occupancy level: 9,125 × 70% = 6,387.5 rooms

Margin of safety: (6,387.5 – 5,000)/6,387.5 = 21.72%

(b) **Profit or loss for Q1**

	$
Contribution (900 rooms × $120)	108,000
Fixed costs (($600,000/12) × 3)	(150,000)
Loss	(42,000)

The Alka Hotel should not close in Q1. The fixed costs will still be incurred and closure would result in lost contribution of $108,000. This in turn would result in a decrease in annual profits of $108,000. In addition, the hotel could lose customers at other times of the year, particularly their regular business customers, who may perceive the hotel as being unreliable.

(c) **Contribution/sales ratio of Project 1**

	$
Sales value of two room nights (2 × $67.50)	135
Sales value of a pair of theatre tickets	100
	235
Variable cost of two room nights (2 × $60)	(120)
Variable cost of a pair of theatre tickets	(95)
Contribution	20

C/S ratio (20/235) = 8.51%

Breakeven point in revenue ($20,000/0.0851) = $235,000

Alternatively:

Contribution per theatre package sold = $20

Breakeven point in theatre packages ($20,000/$20) = 1,000

Breakeven point in revenue (1,000 × $235) = $235,000

The unit contribution per theatre package is low and it requires a large number of sales to break even. Each theatre package would require two room nights to be sold which would mean 2,000 room nights needed in Q1 to break even. The available rooms for Q1 are only 2,281.25 (9,125/4) and the Alka Hotel has already sold 900 rooms, so there is insufficient capacity. Based on this, Project 1 is not viable at the quoted prices.

(d) Project 2 will cause the fixed costs of the hotel to rise from $600,000 per annum to $800,000 per annum for the hotel and restaurant combined. This is an annual increase of $200,000.

Revenue per occupied room will rise from $180 to $250 ($2,000,000/8,000 rooms) which reflects the extra guest expenditure in the restaurant.

The total cost predicted at a level of 8,000 occupied rooms is $1,560,000 which means the variable costs must be $760,000 ($1,560,000 – $800,000 fixed costs). This is a variable cost per occupied room of $95 which is an increase of $35. This reflects the variable costs of the restaurant.

As a result of these changes, the breakeven point has increased from 5,000 to 5,161 occupied rooms so the hotel needs to sell more room nights to cover costs.

However, budgeted occupancy is now 7,300 occupied room nights which gives 80% occupancy (7,300/9,125). This gives a margin of safety of 2,139 occupied room nights or 29%. This is an increase on the current position and the hotel's position appears safer. At 7,300 occupied room nights the Alka Hotel's budgeted profit is $331,500 (7,300 × ($250 – $95) –$800,000.

	Marking scheme	Marks
(a)	Contribution	0.5
	BEP	1.0
	Total rooms available	1.0
	Budget occupancy	0.5
	Margin of safety %	1
(b)	Profit/loss	1.5
	Recommendation	0.5
	Explanation	2.0
(c)	C/S ratio	1.0
	BEP $ revenue	0.5
	Recommendation	0.5
	Explanation	2.0
(d)	Calculations	4.0
	Commentary	4.0
Total		**20**

302 BELTON PARK RESORT (MARCH 2019)

(a) **(i)** **Hotel**

Incremental revenue and contribution

Room revenue

Number of rooms	120	
Number of nights	31	
Total room nights	3,720	
Occupancy rate	50%	
Total nights occupied	1,860	
Rate per night	$70	
Total room revenue		$130,200
Extras contribution		
Total nights occupied	1,860	
Contribution per night	$12.00	
Total 'extras' contribution		22,320
Total cash inflows		152,520

Incremental running costs

Staff costs	$120,000	
Less: manager's salary	($2,500)	
Less: chef's salary	($2,000)	
	———	
	$115,500	
50% normal hours		57,750
50% at reduced hours × 50/90		32,083
Maintenance costs:		
If open	$14,600	
If closed	$4,000	
	———	
Incremental cost		10,600
Power costs:		
Electric	$0	
Gas – fixed charge	$0	
Gas – variable ($20,000 – $10,200) × 1.5		14,700
Security		0
Water		6,450
		———
Total cash outflows		**121,583**
		———
Total incremental cash flows		**30,937**
		———

Tutorial note

Note how 'nil' values, such as the one for 'security' in the table above, are listed regardless, so that the marker knows you have understood this cost has no incremental value.

(ii) **Water park**

Incremental revenue and contribution

Visitor revenue		$
Number of visitors	5,760	
Admission cost	$16.80	
Admission revenue		96,768
Extras contribution		
Number of visitors	5,760	
Contribution per visitor	$7.20	
Total contribution		41,472
		———
Total cash inflows		138,240
		———

Incremental running costs

		$
Staff costs		
Manager	$0	
Other staff ($75,600 – $2,000) × 48%		35,238
Maintenance costs:		
If open	$6,000	
If closed	($2,000)	
		$4,000
Incremental cost		
Power costs:		
Electric	$0	
Gas – fixed charge	$0	
Gas – variable ($18,000 – $8,500) × 1.5		14,250
Security		0
Water		12,100
Total cash outflows		**65,678**
Total incremental cash flows		**72,562**

Conclusion: Based on these figures, both of them should stay open because the incremental cash flows are both positive.

(b)

Tutorial note

There are many factors which could have been discussed here and would be given credit.

As regards the estimates calculated, these have been based on very limited data and should be approached with caution. The calculations are based on the first two months' of opening only and, consequently, it is difficult to say how accurate they are likely to be. In addition, the basis of estimating the revised occupancy rates for the hotel, for example, has not been given. If these estimates are too optimistic, the actual results could be far worse.

The figures suggest that both the water park and the hotel should stay open. Given that this is a new business and therefore it is still building up its customer base, this would seem like a wise decision anyway, even if the calculations had shown that the estimated incremental cash flows were not as positive as this.

Similarly, if Belton Park were to close either the hotel or the water park, they would invariably lose some valuable staff who might seek out other jobs after the closure. These staff might not be available again when the hotel and water park reopened in February.

The interdependency of the two sets of projections has not been taken into account in the calculations either. Since the incremental cash flows suggest that both the hotel and the water park should stay open, it is not a big problem. However, if they had shown, for example, that the water park alone should close, the effect that this could have on the number of hotel visitors would also need to be taken into account. Many visitors may be attracted to the hotel because it has a water park.

ACCA Marking scheme				Marks
(a)	**(i)**	Hotel revenue		1.5
		Extras contribution		1
		Staff costs		2.5
		Maintenance cost		1
		Gas variable costs		1
		Water not security		0.5
		Net cash flow		0.5
		Conclusion: hotel		0.5
	(ii)	Admission revenue		1.5
		Extras contribution		1
		Staff costs		0.5
		Maintenance costs		1
		Gas variable costs		1
		Water not security		0.5
		Net cash flow		0.5
		Conclusion: water park		0.5
				———
				15
				———
(b)		Discussion		5
				———
Total				20
				———

BUDGETING AND CONTROL

303 STATIC CO (DECEMBER 2016)

(a) **Workings**

From budgeted figures: need to work out what the compound growth rate is and the distribution costs as a percentage of revenue.

Compound sales growth: $13,694/13,425 or $13,967/13,694 = 2% Distribution costs: $671/$13,425 = 5%

From actual figures: GPM = $5,356/14,096 = 38%

Distribution costs: $705/14,096 = still 5%.

Starting point for revenue now $14,096 but compound growth rate still 2%.

Rolling budget for the 12 months ending 30 November 20X7

	Q2	Q3	Q4	Q1
	$000	$000	$000	$000
Revenue	14,378	14,666	14,959	15,258
Cost of sales	(8,914)	(9,093)	(9,275)	(9,460)
	———	———	———	———
Gross profit	5,464	5,573	5,684	5,798
Distribution costs	(719)	(733)	(748)	(763)
Administration costs	(2,020)	(2,020)	(2,020)	(2,020)
	———	———	———	———
Operating profit	2,725	2,820	2,916	3,015
	———	———	———	———

Tutorial note

The question made it clear that the assumptions of the original budget were accurate but incorrect prices had been used in the first place. This meant that, before the rolling budget could be prepared, the actual gross profit margin (GPM) from the quarter that had just ended needed to be calculated and this percentage then needed to be applied when calculating the cost of sales and gross profit figures for the rolling budget. If you simply calculate the GPM from the original budget and ignore the actual quarter 1 figures, the cost of sales and gross profit figures will be incorrect in their rolling budget.

Another mistake to avoid would be to start the rolling budget with the actual quarter 1 figures that had been given in the question and then only produce three further quarters. This would show a lack of understanding of how rolling budgets work.

(b)   Problems

The use of fixed budgeting has caused serious problems at Static Co. The fact they were using inaccurate sales forecast figures led them to invest in a production line which was not actually needed, even though they knew they were inaccurate. This unnecessary investment cost them $6m and caused the return on investment to halve. Had rolling budgets been used at the time, and used properly, the sales forecasts for the remaining quarters would have been adjusted to reflect a fall in demand and the investment would not have been made.

Presumably, inaccurate sales forecasts would have led the business to get their staffing levels and materials purchases wrong as well. This too will have cost the business money. They were forced to heavily discount their goods in order to try to reach their targets at the end of the year, which was simply unrealistic. It can often be difficult to put prices back up again once they have been discounted. However, the actual results from the first quarter suggest that prices have increased again, which is fortunate.

Improvements

The use of rolling budgets should mean that a downturn in demand is adjusted for in future quarters, rather than sales simply being pushed into the last quarter, which is not a realistic adjustment. Management is forced to reassess the budget regularly and produce up to date information. This means that accurate management decisions can then be made and mistakes like investing in a new production line which is not needed should not happen again. Planning and control will be more accurate.

Tutorial note

Do not make the mistake to simply copy out parts of the scenario without adding any value to them. For example, it was not enough to say that a problem of the previous system was that many product lines had to be heavily discounted in the last quarter. Answers needed to go on and say that this discounting was a problem because it led to reduced sales revenues for the company and made it difficult to subsequently increase prices to their original level in later quarters.

(c) **Problems trying to implement new budgeting system**

The first problem may be trying to obtain the right information needed to update the budget. The FD has been sacked and two other key finance personnel are off work due to stress. This could make it very difficult to obtain information if the department is understaffed and lacking the direction given by the FD. Staff in the finance department may not have the skills to update the budget and roll it forward, having never done it before. Similarly, the sales department is without a SD and they would usually have played a key part in reviewing figures for the sales forecasts. Hence, it may be difficult to obtain reliable sales data.

Even without this staffing issue, obtaining the correct information could be difficult as actually preparing rolling budgets is new for Static Co. Staff will need training. They are only used to preparing fixed budgets, although these have often been revised in the past to move sales into later periods. Staff are not familiar with the process of updating all of their financial information again: reviewing sales demand to realistically reforecast, updating costs, etc. This process takes time and staff may feel resentful about having to do this again so soon after the annual budgeting process which would recently have been undertaken.

The new MD is new to this industry and therefore lacks experience of how it works. Whilst they are confident that the assumptions of the original fixed budget still stand true, they are not in a good position to know that this is in fact the case. The assumptions may be wrong and, if they are, the new rolling budget will be unreliable.

Tutorial note

Make double sure that you read the requirement carefully. On the whole, the problems of implementing rolling budgeting are different from the problems of using rolling budgets on an ongoing basis, apart from the fact that both implementation and ongoing use of rolling budgets are time consuming and therefore expensive. Please carefully review this suggested answer for this part of the question, because answers on exam day were fairly weak here and many opportunities to gain marks were lost.

Marking scheme		Marks
(a) Growth rate		1
Actual distribution cost %		0.5
Actual GPM %		0.5
Use of Q1 actuals		1
Rolling budget: sales		1
COS		1
GPM		0.5
Distribution costs		1
Administration costs		1
Operating profit		0.5
		──
	Maximum	8
		──
(b) Problems and improvements		6
		──
(c) Implementation problems		6
		──
Total		20
		──

PM: PERFORMANCE MANAGEMENT

304 YUMI CO (SEPTEMBER 2019)

(a)   (i)   Flexed budget for Cowly restaurant

	Original budgeted	Flexed budget	Actual	Variance
Number of customers	1,500	1,800	1,800	
	$	$	$	$
Revenue	75,000	90,000	87,300	2,700 A
Food and drink costs	(22,500)	(27,000)	(26,100)	900 F
Staff costs	(31,500)	(37,800)	(38,250)	450 A
Heat, light and power	(7,500)	(9,000)	(8,100)	900 F
Rent, rates and overheads	(12,000)	(12,000)	(12,600)	600 A
Profit	1,500	4,200	2,250	1,950 A

Notes:

Revenue: $75,000/1,500 = $50 per customer: $50 × 1,800 = $90,000

Food and drink: $22,500/1,500 = $15 per customer: $15 × 1,800 = $27,000

Staff costs: $31,500/1,500 = $21 per customer: $21 × 1,800 = $37,800

Heat, light and power: $7,500/1,500 = $5 per customer: $5 × 1,800 = $9,000

(ii) The most significant weakness in the current performance report is that the original budget is not flexed to adjust for the actual numbers of customers served.

The existing report shows that the Cowly restaurant has overspent on all its costs which could be a concern given the importance of cost control in Yumi Co. However, the main reason for the revenue variance and the costs variances is the fact that the number of customers the restaurant served was 20% higher than budgeted (1,800 v 1,500).

If the budget is flexed for the actual number of customers, this allows a more meaningful assessment of the restaurant's performance to be made.

Once the flexed budget is prepared, it can be seen that revenues were actually lower than would have been expected, given the number of customers served with average spend per head being $48.50 instead of $50. Food and drink costs were also less than budget. Taken together with the reduction in average customer spending, this might suggest that some of the items on the menu had been changed since the budget was originally set.

Another weakness in Yumi Co's budgetary control report is the fact that staff costs and heat, light and power costs are assumed to be purely variable costs – dependent on the number of customers. However, although the restaurant may recruit some temporary staff in busy periods, it is likely that at least some of the staff will be permanent, meaning that it would be more appropriate to treat staff costs as semi-variable rather than variable.

Similarly, it seems likely that there will be a significant fixed element within heat, light and power costs, so treating these as wholly variable costs does not seem appropriate.

406   KAPLAN PUBLISHING

(b) Under an incremental budgeting approach, the current year's budget and results are taken as the starting point for preparing the next year's budget. The budget is then adjusted for any expected changes, such as the impact of inflation on costs and prices, and sales growth or decline.

The main advantage of the incremental approach is that it is a relatively straightforward way of preparing a budget, appropriate for organisations which are operating in relatively stable environments. The locations of Yumi Co's restaurants, away from significant competition, suggest that the operating environment is relatively stable, meaning incremental budgeting is appropriate.

Similarly, the fact that Yumi Co appears to have a relatively well-established brand and customer base suggests that using an incremental approach to budgeting future revenues appears reasonable, even if it is difficult to identify some changes which need to be adjusted for in the next year's budget.

However, one of the major disadvantages of incremental budgeting is that it does not provide any incentive to make operations more efficient or economical. If the current year figures include slack or inefficiencies, then using them as the start-point for the next year's figures means that inefficiency is automatically perpetuated into the next year.

Such an approach seems somewhat inconsistent with the focus on cost control within Yumi Co. If the company is worried about its relatively low margins, then an approach to budgeting which challenges costs more critically (such as zero-based budgeting or activity-based budgeting) might be more suitable for helping to drive down costs. For example, the highest cost is staff wages which could be analysed and Yumi Co could investigate making changes to its staffing model to reduce costs and/or improve efficiency.

As mentioned in part (a), whether labour costs and heat, light and power vary proportionately with the number of customers appears debatable. If Yumi Co's incremental budgets ignore the relationship between activities and costs, then ultimately the budgets will provide Yumi Co's management with little relevant information for managing costs. This could become an increasingly important issue if competition in Yumi Co's markets intensifies.

(c) The current budget process is a centralised, top-down process, meaning that the managers from Yumi Co's restaurants do not have any opportunity to influence the budgets for their restaurants.

By contrast, in a participative approach, the managers of each restaurant would be able to influence the figures for their restaurant, rather than having budget targets simply imposed on them. Involving the managers in the budgeting process should help to make the budgets more effective and realistic.

The local managers should have a greater understanding of the environmental factors and operational constraints which will influence the performance of their restaurants. For example, the manager of the Cowly restaurant will have a better understanding of their customers and market conditions and thus provide a greater insight into the potential impact of the new restaurant than a member of the finance team at Yumi Co's head office would have. Similarly, managers are more likely to be committed to achieving a budget if they have been involved in creating it – not least because their involvement in the preparing the budget should help to ensure that they feel the budget figures are realistic. However, involving the restaurant managers in the budgeting process is likely to make it more time-consuming. For example, instead of running their restaurants, managers will have to spend time in meetings with head office staff planning and preparing their budgets. In this respect, it may be more appropriate for Yumi Co to maintain the current, top-down process for restaurants which are operating in a stable environment (and where the insights from local managers will add little value), but introduce a more participative approach for restaurants like Cowly which are facing a period of change.

Another potential disadvantage of participative budgeting is that managers may try to influence the budgets so that their targets can be achieved easily. By doing this, a restaurant's performance, compared to budget, will appear to improve, but this would actually be an illusion. One of the main issues Yumi Co could face in this respect is that, given the range of different locations of its restaurants, it will be difficult for head office staff to know whether individual managers are setting targets which are easy or challenging. If the restaurants were all similar, or in similar locations, it would be easier to compare the figures suggested by individual managers to assess how challenging, or not, they are.

Similarly, managers are more likely to highlight issues which will lead to a reduction in their budget targets, rather than ones which increase their targets. For example, the manager at Cowly has highlighted that the new competitor will make it more difficult for them to achieve budget. However, the manager does not appear to have made a corresponding acknowledgement that the increased numbers of visitors to Cowly could support an increased revenue target. There is a danger that the managers' participation in the budgets could lead to the targets becoming less challenging, which in turn could affect Yumi Co's competitiveness and profitability.

ACCA Marking scheme			
			Marks
(a)	(i)	Flexed budget	
		Revenue	0.5
		Food and drink	0.5
		Staff	0.5
		Heat, light and power	0.5
		Rent and rates	0.5
		Profit	0.5
			―――
			3
			―――
	(ii)	Weaknesses	**4**
(b)		Discussion	**6**
(c)		Definition of participative budgeting	1
		Advantages and disadvantages	6
			―――
			7
			―――
Total			**20**
			―――

305 NN

(a) **The adoption of zero-based budgeting within NN Ltd**

During recent years the management of NN Ltd has used the traditional approach to incremental budgeting. The approach entails the use of the previous year's budget being rolled forward into the next year's budget purely budget.

Zero-based budgeting was developed to overcome the shortcomings of the technique of incremental budgeting. The implementation of a zero-based budgeting would require each manager within NN Ltd to effectively start with a blank sheet of paper and a budget allowance of zero. The managers would be required to defend their budget levels at the beginning of each and every year.

The implementation of a system of zero-based budgeting will require a consideration of the following:

- The need for major input by management
- The fact that it will prove extremely time consuming
- The need for a very high level of data capture and processing
- The subjective judgement inherent in its application
- The fact that it might be perceived as a threat by staff
- Whether its adoption may encourage a greater focus upon the short-term to the detriment of longer-term planning.

(b) The implementation of zero-based budgeting will require a major planning effort by our personnel. It is through the planning process that important guidelines and directions are provided for the development and ranking of the decision packages. Also, the planning process will enable managers to prepare for the uncertainty of the future. Long-range planning allows managers to consider the potential consequences of current decisions over an extended timeframe.

Zero-based budgeting addresses and supports comprehensive planning, shared decision-making, the development and application of strategies and allocation of resources as a way of achieving established goals and objectives. In addition, zero-based budgeting supports the added processes of monitoring and evaluation.

Zero-based budgeting, when properly implemented, has the potential to assist the personnel of an organisation to plan and make decisions about the most efficient and effective ways to use their available resources to achieve their defined mission, goals and objectives.

There is no doubt that the process of zero-based budgeting will consume a great deal more management time than the current system of budgeting does. This will certainly be the case in implementation of the system because managers will need to learn what is required of them. Managers may object that it is too time-consuming to introduce zero-based budgeting, however, it could be introduced on a piece-meal basis. As regards the imposition upon management time, managers may object that they simply do not have the necessary time in order to undertake an in-depth examination of every activity each year. However, if this proves to be the case then we could consider the establishment of a review cycle aimed at ensuring that each activity is reviewed on at least one occasion during every two or three years.

I propose that we hold a series of training seminars for our management to help in the transition to a system of zero-based budgeting. We must also ensure that we 'sell the benefits' that would arise from a successful implementation. A zero-based budgeting system would assist our managers to:

- Develop and/or modify the organisation's mission and goals
- Establish broad policies based on the mission and goals
- Efficiently identify the most desirable programs to be placed in operation
- Allocate the appropriate level of resources to each program
- Monitor and evaluate each program during and at the end of its operation and report the effectiveness of each program.

Thus, as a consequence of the adoption of zero-based budgeting our managers should be able to make decisions on the basis of an improved reporting system.

It is quite possible that zero-based budgeting would help identify and eliminate any budget bias or 'budget slack' that may be present. Budgetary slack is 'a universal behavioural problem' which involves deliberately overstating cost budgets and/or understating revenue budgets to allow some leeway in actual performance. We must acknowledge that in organisations such as ours where reward structures are based on comparisons of actual with budget results, bias can help to influence the amount paid to managers under incentive schemes. However, we should emphasise that if managers are to earn incentives as a consequence of incentive schemes that are based upon a comparison of actual outcomes with budgeted outcomes, then a zero-based budget would provide a fair yardstick for comparison.

It is important to provide reassurance to our managers that we do not intend to operate a system of zero-based budgeting against the backdrop of a blame-culture. This will help to gain their most positive acceptance of the change from a long established work practice that they may perceive afforded them a degree of 'insurance'.

(c)   The finance director is probably aware that the application of zero-based budgeting within NN Ltd might prove most fruitful in the management of discretionary costs where it is difficult to establish standards of efficiency and where such costs can increase rapidly due to the absence of such standards. A large proportion of the total costs incurred by NN Ltd will comprise direct production and service costs where the existence of input: output relationships that can be measured render them more appropriate to traditional budgeting methods utilising standard costs. Since the predominant costs incurred by a not for profit health organisation will be of a discretionary nature, one might conclude that the application of zero-based budgeting techniques is more appropriate for service organisations such as the not for profit health organisation than for a profit-seeking manufacturer of electronic office equipment. A further difference lies in the fact that the ranking of decision packages is likely to prove less problematic within an organisation such as NN Ltd which is only involved in the manufacture and marketing of electronic office equipment. By way of contrast, there is likely to be a much greater number of decision packages of a disparate nature, competing for an allocation of available resources within a not for profit health organisation.

306 ZERO BASED BUDGETING (DECEMBER 2010)

(a) Difficulties in the public sector

In the public sector, the objectives of the organisation are more difficult to define in a quantifiable way than the objectives of a private company. For example, a private company's objectives may be to maximise profit. The meeting of this objective can then be set out in the budget by aiming for a percentage increase in sales and perhaps the cutting of various costs. If, on the other hand, the public sector organisation is a hospital, for example, then the objectives may be largely qualitative, such as ensuring that all outpatients are given an appointment within eight weeks of being referred to the hospital. This is difficult to define in a quantifiable way, and how it is actually achieved is even more difficult to define.

This leads onto the next reason why budgeting is so difficult in public sector organisations. Just as objectives are difficult to define quantifiably, so too are the organisation's outputs. In a private company the output can be measured in terms of sales revenue.

There is a direct relationship between the expenditure that needs to be incurred i.e. needs to be input in order to achieve the desired level of output. In a hospital, on the other hand, it is difficult to define a quantifiable relationship between inputs and outputs. What is more easy to compare is the relationship between how much cash is available for a particular area and how much cash is actually needed. Therefore, budgeting naturally focuses on inputs alone, rather than the relationship between inputs and outputs.

Finally, public sector organisations are always under pressure to show that they are offering good value for money, i.e. providing a service that is economical, efficient and effective. Therefore, they must achieve the desired results with the minimum use of resources. This, in itself, makes the budgeting process more difficult.

(b) Incremental and zero-based budgeting

'Incremental budgeting' is the term used to describe the process whereby a budget is prepared using a previous period's budget or actual performance as a base, with incremental amounts then being added for the new budget period.

'Zero-based budgeting', on the other hand, refers to a budgeting process which starts from a base of zero, with no reference being made to the prior period's budget or performance. Every department function is reviewed comprehensively, with all expenditure requiring approval, rather than just the incremental expenditure requiring approval.

(c) Stages in zero-based budgeting

Zero-based budgeting involves three main stages:

(1) Activities are identified by managers. These activities are then described in what is called a 'decision package'. This decision package is prepared at the base level, representing the minimum level of service or support needed to achieve the organisation's objectives. Further incremental packages may then be prepared to reflect a higher level of service or support.

(2)   Management will then rank all the packages in the order of decreasing benefits to the organisation. This will help management decide what to spend and where to spend it.

(3)   The resources are then allocated based on order of priority up to the spending level.

(d)   No longer a place for incremental budgeting

The view that there is no longer a place for incremental budgeting in any organisation is a rather extreme view. It is known for encouraging slack and wasteful spending, hence the comment that it is particularly unsuitable for public sector organisations, where cash cutbacks are being made. However, to say that there is no place for it at all is to ignore the drawbacks of zero-based budgeting. These should not be ignored as they can make ZBB implausible in some organisations or departments. They are as follows:

- Departmental managers will not have the skills necessary to construct decision packages. They will need training for this and training takes time and money.

- In a large organisation, the number of activities will be so large that the amount of paperwork generated from ZBB will be unmanageable.

- Ranking the packages can be difficult, since many activities cannot be compared on the basis of purely quantitative measures. Qualitative factors need to be incorporated but this is difficult.

- The process of identifying decision packages, determining their purpose, costs and benefits is massively time consuming and therefore costly.

- Since decisions are made at budget time, managers may feel unable to react to changes that occur during the year. This could have a detrimental effect on the business if it fails to react to emerging opportunities and threats.

It could be argued that ZBB is more suitable for public sector than for private sector organisations. This is because, firstly, it is far easier to put activities into decision packages in organisations which undertake set definable activities. Local government, for example, have set activities including the provision of housing, schools and local transport. Secondly, it is far more suited to costs that are discretionary in nature or for support activities. Such costs can be found mostly in not for profit organisations or the public sector, or in the service department of commercial operations.

Since ZBB requires all costs to be justified, it would seem inappropriate to use it for the entire budgeting process in a commercial organisation. Why take so much time and resources justifying costs that must be incurred in order to meet basic production needs? It makes no sense to use such a long-winded process for costs where no discretion can be exercised anyway. Incremental budgeting is, by its nature, quick and easy to do and easily understood. These factors should not be ignored.

In conclusion, whilst ZBB is more suited to public sector organisations, and is more likely to make cost savings in hard times such as these, its drawbacks should not be overlooked.

	Marking scheme		
			Marks
(a)	Explanation		
	Difficulty setting objectives quantifiably		2
	Difficulty in saying how to achieve them		1
	Outputs difficult to measure		2
	No relationship between inputs and outputs		2
	Value for money issue		2
		Maximum	5
(b)	Incremental and zero-based budgeting		
	Explaining 'incremental budgeting'		2
	Explaining 'zero-based budgeting'		2
		Maximum	4
(c)	Stages involved in zero-based budgeting		
	Each stage		1
		Maximum	3
(d)	Discussion		
	Any disadvantage of inc. that supports statement (max. 3)		1
	Incremental budgeting is quick and easy		1
	Any disadvantage of ZBB that refutes statement (max. 3)		1
	Easier to define decision packages in public sector		2
	more appropriate for discretionary costs		2
	Conclusion		1
		Maximum	8
Total			20

307 BIG CHEESE CHAIRS (DECEMBER 2009)

(a) The average cost of the first 128 chairs is as follows:

		$
Frame and massage mechanism		51.00
Leather	2 metres × $10/mtr × 100/80	25.00
Labour	(W1)	20.95
Total		96.95

Target selling price is $120.

Target cost of the chair is therefore $120 × 80% = $96

The cost gap is $96.95 – $96.00 = $0.95 per chair

Workings

(W1) The cost of the labour can be calculated using learning curve principles. The formula can be used or a tabular approach would also give the average cost of 128 chairs. Both methods are acceptable and shown here.

Tabulation:

Cumulative output (units)	Average time per unit (hrs)	Total time (hrs)	Average cost per chair at $15 per hour
1	2		
2	1.9		
4	1.805		
8	1.71475		
16	1.6290125		
32	1.54756188		
64	1.47018378		
128	1.39667459	178.77	20.95

Formula:

$Y = ax^b$

$Y = 2 \times 128^{-0.074000581}$

$Y = 1.396674592$

The average cost per chair is $1.396674592 \times \$15 = \$20.95$

(b) To reduce the cost gap various methods are possible (only four are needed for full marks)

- Re-design the chair to remove unnecessary features and hence cost
- Negotiate with the frame supplier for a better cost. This may be easier as the volume of sales improve as suppliers often are willing to give discounts for bulk buying. Alternatively a different frame supplier could be found that offers a better price. Care would be needed here to maintain the required quality
- Leather can be bought from different suppliers or at a better price also. Reducing the level of waste would save on cost. Even a small reduction in waste rates would remove much of the cost gap that exists
- Improve the rate of learning by better training and supervision
- Employ cheaper labour by reducing the skill level expected. Care would also be needed here not to sacrifice quality or push up waste rates.

(c) The cost of the 128th chair will be:

		$
Frame and massage mechanism		51.00
Leather	2 metres × $10/mtr × 100/80	25.00
Labour	1.29 hours × $15 per hour (W2)	19.35
		———
Total		95.35
		———

Against a target cost of $96 the production manager is correct in their assertion that the required return is now being achieved.

(W2) Using the formula, we need to calculate the cost of the first 127 chairs and deduct that cost from the cost of the first 128 chairs.

$$Y = ax^b$$

$$Y = 2 \times 127^{-0.074000581}$$

$$Y = 1.39748546$$

Total time is $127 \times 1.39748546 = 177.48$ hours

Time for the 128th chair is $178.77 - 177.48 = 1.29$ hours

Marking scheme		
		Marks
(a)	Frame cost	1.0
	Leather cost	2.0
	Labour average time for 128 units	1.0
	Labour total time for 128 units	1.0
	Average cost per chair	1.0
	Target cost	1.0
	Cost gap	1.0
	Maximum	**8.0**
(b)	Per suggestion	1.5
	Maximum	**6.0**
(c)	Frame	0.5
	Leather	0.5
	Average time per unit	2.0
	Total time	1.0
	Time for 128th chair	1.0
	Conclusion	1.0
	Maximum	**6.0**
Total		**20**

308 HENRY COMPANY (DECEMBER 2008)

(a) There are various issues that HC should consider in making the bid. (Only five are required for two marks each.)

Contingency allowance. HC should consider the extent to which its estimates are accurate and hence the degree of uncertainty it is subjected to. It may be sensible to allow for these uncertainties by adding a contingency to the bid.

Competition. HC must consider which other businesses are likely to bid and recognise that the builder may be able to choose between suppliers. Moreover HC has not worked for this builder before and so they will probably find the competition stiff and the lack of reputation a problem.

Inclusion of fixed overhead. In the long run fixed overhead must be covered by sales revenue in order to make a profit. In the short run it is often correctly argued that the level of fixed cost in a business may not be affected by a new contract and therefore could be ignored in bid calculation. HC needs to consider to what extent the fixed costs of its business will change if it wins this new contract. It is these incremental fixed costs that are relevant to a bid calculation.

Materials and loose tools. No allowance has been made for the use of tools and the various fixings (screws etc.) that will be needed to assemble and fit the kitchens. It is possible that most fixings would be provided with the kitchen units but HC should at least consider this.

Supervision of labour. The time given in the question is 24 hours to 'fit' the first kitchen. There seems no allowance for supervision of the labour force. It could of course be included within the overhead figures but no detail is shown.

Idle time. It is common for building works to be delayed by lack of materials for example. The labour time figure needs to reflect this.

Likelihood of repeat business. Some businesses consider it worthwhile to accept a low price for a new contract if it establishes a reputation with a new buyer. HC could offer to do this work cheaper in the hope of more profitable work later on.

The risk of non-payment. HC may decide not to bid at all if it feels that the builder may struggle to pay.

Opportunity costs of alternative work.

Possibility of working in overtime.

Key answer tips

Easy marks were available here for discussing any sensible and relevant factors that should be taken into account. Good candidates related their discussion back to the information provided in the scenario and used short paragraphs to explain each factor, with the aim of scoring one mark for each of the factors explained.

(b) Bid calculations for HC to use as a basis for the apartment contract.

Cost	Hours	Rate per hour	Total
			$
Labour	9,247 (W1)	$15	138,705
Variable overhead	9,247	$8 (W2)	73,976
Fixed overhead	9,247	$4 (W2)	36,988
			_____
Total cost			249,669
			_____

Workings

(W1) Need to calculate the time for the 200th kitchen by taking the total time for the 199 kitchens from the total time for 200 kitchens.

For the 199 Kitchens

Using

$y = ax^b$ OR $y = ax^b$

$y = 24 \times 199^{-0.074}$ $y = (24 \times 15) \times 199^{-0.074}$

$y = 16.22169061$ hours $y = 243.32536$

Total time = 16.22169061×199 Total cost = $48,421.75

Total time = 3,228.12 hours

For the 200 Kitchens

$y = ax^b$ OR $y = ax^b$

$y = 24 \times 200^{-0.074}$ $y = (24 \times 15) \times 200^{-0.074}$

$y = 16.21567465$ hours   Total cost = \$48,647.02

Total time = 16.21567465×200 200th cost = \$225.27

Total time = 3,243.13 hours

The 200th Kitchen took $3,243.13 - 3,228.12 = 15.01$ hours

Total time is therefore:

For first 200	3,243.13 hours
For next 400 (15.01 hours × 400)	6,004.00 hours
Total	9,247.13 hours (9,247 hours)

(W2) The overheads need to be analysed between variable and fixed cost elements.

Taking the highest and lowest figures from the information given:

	Hours	Cost \$
Highest	9,600	116,800
Lowest	9,200	113,600
Difference	400	3,200

Variable cost per hours is \$3,200/400 hours = \$8 per hour

Total cost = variable cost + fixed cost

$116,800 = 9,600 \times 8 +$ fixed cost

Fixed cost = \$40,000 per month

Annual fixed cost = $\$40,000 \times 12 = \$480,000$

Fixed absorption rate is \$480,000/120,000 hours = \$4 per hour

---

Key answer tips

Requirements (b)and (c) Involved learning curve calculations. This is a core knowledge area and candidates who had practised learning curve calculations will have scored well.

(c)   A table is useful to show how the learning rate has been calculated.

Number of Kitchens	Time for Kitchen (hours)	Cumulative time (hours)	Average time (hours)
1	24.00	24.00	24.00
2	21.60	45.60	22.80

The learning rate is calculated by measuring the reduction in the average time per kitchen as cumulative production doubles (in this case from 1 to 2).

The learning rate is therefore 22.80/24.00 or 95%.

	Marking scheme		
			Marks
(a)	1 mark for each description	**Maximum**	5
(b)	Average time for the 199th kitchen		1.0
	Total time for 199 kitchens		1.0
	Average time for the 200th kitchen		1.0
	Total time for 200 kitchens		1.0
	200th kitchen time		1.0
	Cost for the first 200		1.0
	Cost for the next 400		1.0
	Variable cost per hour		2.0
	Fixed cost per month		1.0
	Fixed cost per hour		1.0
	Cost for variable overhead		1.0
	Cost for fixed overhead		1.0
		Maximum	13
(c)	Average time per unit and explanation		2
Total			20

Examiner's comments (extract)

Part (a) was not done well by many. All that was required was sensible ideas about figures that might have to be included in the bid (without calculations). The marking scheme was generously applied and marks were given if candidates included factors relating whether or not to bid instead of factors concerning the amount of the bid. Some marks were also given for a more theoretical approach (opportunity costs should be allowed for...). Despite this the average mark struggled to reach half marks. Perhaps candidates were looking for something more difficult than is there or grasping at the text book hoping for a text book answer to fit.

Part (b) was well done by many candidates despite it being a fairly demanding aspect of learning curves (the steady state).

Part (c) was reasonably attempted by most.

309 MEDICAL TEMP CO (MARCH/JUNE 2021)

(a) The market size and market share variances are a breakdown of the sales volume variance. The sales volume variance shows the effect on profit of the actual sales level being different from the budgeted sales level. However, without considering how the market itself has changed, it is difficult to draw conclusions about performance from the sales volume variance. Therefore, the sales volume variance is broken down into its two components. By doing this, it is possible to assess the extent to which changes in profit are as a result of:

(i) A change in the size of the market as a whole, which is beyond the control of the sales manager; and

(ii) A change in the share of the market which the company holds, which is deemed to be within the control of the sales manager.

Consequently, the variances become far more meaningful for performance management as businesses can identify external and internal factors which can influence the results and what was controllable and uncontrollable.

(b) **Quarter 2 original budgeted sales volumes and contribution**

	Nurses	Doctors
National Q1 sales volume (no. of weekly contracts)	14,000	4,000
Percentage of market	30%	40%
Budgeted Sales Volume	4,200	1,600
	$000	$000
Budgeted Revenue for MTC	4,200	3,200
Standard Contribution	80%	80%
Budgeted Standard Contribution	3,360	2,560

Quarter 2 revised budgeted sales volumes and contribution

	Nurses	Doctors
National Q2 sales volume (no. of weekly contracts)	18,900	4,100
Percentage of market	30%	40%
Budgeted Sales Volume	5,670	1,640
	$000	$000
Budgeted Revenue for MTC	5,670	3,280
Standard Contribution	80%	80%
Budgeted Standard Contribution	4,536	2,624

Quarter 2 Actual Results

	Nurses	Doctors
	$000	$000
Actual Revenue in quarter 2	5,300	3,600
Standard Contribution	80%	80%
Budgeted Standard Contribution	4,240	2,880

Market size variance (planning)

(Budgeted vs revised contribution)

	Nurses		Doctors		Total	
	$000		$000		$000	
Budget contribution for MTC	3,360		2,560			
Revised budget contribution for MTC	4,536		2,624			
Variance	**1,176**	F	**64**	F	**1,240**	F

Market share variance (operational)

(Revised contribution vs actual)

	Nurses		Doctors		Total	
	$000		$000		$000	
Revised budget contribution for MTC	4,536		2,624			
Actual sales volume at standard contribution	4,240		2,880			
Variance	(296)	A	256	F	(40)	A

(c) The sales director at Cheat Co has deliberately manipulated the market size figures to make the market for doctors and nurses look smaller. Now, instead of being the actual market size of 18,900 weekly contracts ($18.9m/$1,000) and 4,100 weekly contracts ($8.2m/$2,000), they will be much lower at 13,230 and 2,870 respectively. This means that the revised budgeted sales volume figures used to calculate Cheat Co's variances were far lower. This behaviour is unethical and may well lead to the sales director getting a bonus which they do not deserve.

As a consequence of this, the market size variances are highly adverse, so it looks like Cheat Co's original budgets are very wrong. The sales director will not care about this since they will not be held accountable for that variance; instead they will be responsible for the favourable market share variance of over $2m. This makes the sales director's performance look really good, but the reality is that it only looks this high because the budgeted sales figures include revenue for maternity units and the revised budgeted figures do not. This does not reflect the sales director's real performance for the quarter.

ACCA marking scheme		
		Marks
(a)	Market size and share variances are breakdown of sales volume variance/need to consider change in size of market	1
	Description of market size/market share variances/reference to controllability	3
		4
(b)	Original budget (1 mark each doctors and nurses)	2
	Revised budget (1 mark each doctors and nurses)	2
	Actual sales volume at standard contribution (0·5 each doctors and nurses)	1
	Market size variance – doctors	1
	Market size variance – nurses	1
	Total market size variance	0.5
	Market share variance – doctors	1
	Market share variance – nurses	1
	Total market share variance	0.5
		10
(c)	Discussion – up to 2 for each well discussed point. Must address both parts of the requirement	6
Total		20

310 VALET CO (JUNE 2014)

(a) **Variances**

(i) **The sales mix contribution variance**

Calculated as (actual sales quantity – actual sales quantity in budgeted proportions) × standard contribution per unit.

Standard contributions per valet:

Full = $50 × 44.6% = $22.30 per valet

Mini = $30 × 55% = $16.50 per valet

Actual sales quantity in budgeted proportions (ASQBP):

Full: 7,980 × (3,600/5,600) = 5,130

Mini: 7,980 × (2,000/5,600) = 2,850

Valet type	AQAM	AQBM	Difference	Standard contribution $	Variance $
Full	4,000	5,130	(1,130)	22.30	25,199 A
Mini	3,980	2,850	1,130	16.50	18,645 F
					6,554 A

(ii) **The sales quantity contribution variance**

Calculated as (actual sales quantity in budgeted proportions – budgeted sales quantity) × standard contribution per unit.

Valet type	AQBM	BQBM	Difference	Standard contribution $	Variance $
Full	5,130	3,600	1,530	22.30	34,119 F
Mini	2,850	2,000	850	16.50	14,025 F
					48,144 F

(b) **Description**

The sales mix contribution variance measures the effect on profit of changing the mix of actual sales from the standard mix. The sales quantity contribution variance measures the effect on profit of selling a different total quantity from the budgeted total quantity.

(c) **Sales performance of the business**

The sales performance of the business has been very good over the last year, as shown by the favourable sales quantity variance of $48,144. Overall, total sales revenue is 33% higher than budgeted (($319,400 – $240,000)/$240,000). This is because of a higher total number of valets being performed. When you look at where the difference in sales quantity actually is, you can see from the data provided in the question that it is the number of mini valets which is substantially higher. This number is 99% ((3,980 – 2,000)/2,000) higher than budgeted, whereas the number of full valets is only 11% ((4,000 – 3,600)/3,600) higher. Even 11% is still positive, however.

The fact that the number of mini valets is so much higher combined with the fact that they generate a lower contribution per unit than the full valet led to an adverse sales mix variance of $6,554 in the year. This cannot be looked at in isolation as a sign of poor performance; it is simply reflective of the changes which have occurred in Strappia. We are told that disposable incomes in Strappia have decreased by 30% over the last year.

This means that people have less money to spend on non-essential expenditure such as car valeting. Consequently, they are opting for the cheaper mini valet rather than the more expensive full valet. At the same time, we are also told that people are keeping their cars for an average of five years now as opposed to three years. This may be leading them to take more care of them and get them valeted regularly because they know that the car has to be kept for a longer period. Thus, the total quantity of valets is higher than budgeted, particularly the mini valets. Also, there is now one less competitor for Valet Co than there was a year ago, so Valet Co may have gained some of the old competitor's business. Together, all of these factors would explain the higher number of total valets being performed and in particular, of the less expensive type of valet.

Note: Other valid points will be given full credit.

311 CLEAR CO (MARCH/JULY 2020 SAMPLE EXAM)

Tutorial note

Previous question practice should hopefully help students identify that the first thing to calculate (in a separate working, for example) is the budgeted (=standard) contribution per type of lens treatment. It amounts to $2,400 per RLE treatment and $2,500 per ICL treatment.

(a) **Variance calculations**

	RLE	ICL	Total
AQAM	4,130	960	5,090
AQBM	3,764.79	1,325.21	5,090
BQBM	3,750	1,320	5,070
Standard contribution (W1)	$2,400	$2,500	
Mix variance	$876,504 F	$913,025 A	$36,521 A
Quantity variance	$35,496 F	$13,025 F	$48,521 F

Alternative quantity variance calculation:

Total contribution ($)	12,300,000
Budgeted total sales quantity	5,070
Weighted average contribution ($)	2,426.04
Quantity variance ($)	48,521F

(W1) Standard contribution

	RLE	ICL
	$	$
Selling price	3,000	3,650
Variable costs	600	1,150
	2,400	2,500

(b) The sales mix contribution variance measures the effect on contribution of changing the mix of actual sales from the budgeted sales mix.

The sales quantity contribution variance measures the effect on contribution of selling a different total quantity from the budgeted total quantity.

(c) Possible additional calculations

Actual compared to budgeted revenue	RLE	ICL	Total	
	$	$	$	
Actual sales revenue	11,977,000	3,264,000	15,241,000	
Budgeted sales revenue	11,250,000	4,818,000	16,068,000	
Difference in revenue	**727,000**	**–1,554,000**	**–827,000**	
Percentage terms	**6.46%**	**–32.25%**	**–5.15%**	
Sales volume variance (AQ–BQ) × standard contribution	$ **912,000 F**	$ **900,000 A**	$ **12,000 F**	
Selling price variance (AP–SP) × AQ	**413,000 A**	**240,000 A**	**653,000 A**	
Total sales variance (AP – standard variable costs) × AQ	9,499,000	2,160,000	11,659,000	Actually received
Budgeted units × standard contribution	9,000,000	3,300,000	12,300,000	Expect to receive
	499,000 F	**1,140,000 A**	**641,000 A**	

Sales performance

When comparing budgeted revenues to actual revenues, it can be seen that ICL has under-performed this year, with revenues being 32.25% lower than budgeted. This is a result of both lower sales volumes and a lower selling price for ICL, which has resulted in an adverse sales volume variance of $900,000 and an adverse sales price variance of $240,000. The main reason for this is probably the merger that took place during the year, which resulted in Clear Co's now biggest competitor subsequently reducing prices for ICL and presumably capturing a bigger slice of the market as a result. Even though Clear Co's actual price for ICL was $250 less than budgeted, its sales volumes still fell by 27% so it was apparently unable to match the competition.

Looking at the mix of sales between RLE and ICL at Clear Co, there is an adverse mix variance of $36,521. This is because, whilst the sales of ICL were lower than budgeted, the sales of RLE were higher than budgeted. Since RLE has a lower standard contribution than ICL, this produced an adverse mix variance. This shift in sales mix could be partly attributable to the fact that the RLE procedure is for people aged over 40 and there is an increasingly ageing population in Zeeland. Clear Co has had to lower its price to take these sales of RLE but again, this is probably due to increased pressure to reduce prices resulting from the merger.

Another factor which it is not possible to quantify from the information provided, but which will invariably have had an impact on sales of lens treatments overall, is the increased availability of laser treatments to customers. Given that 90% of customers are now eligible for the less complex laser treatment, this side of the business may well have grown at Clear Co.

Overall, the sales volume variance is favourable for Clear Co because of the increased sales of RLE. However, to achieve this, prices have been reduced, resulting in a significant adverse sales price variance of $653,000. These results are disappointing and Clear Co may have to rethink its strategy moving forwards.

ACCA Marking scheme			
			Marks
(a)	(i)	Calculation of sales mix contribution variance	4
	(ii)	Calculation of sales quantity contribution variance	4
(b)		Explanation of what sales mix contribution variance measures	1
		Explanation of what sales quantity contribution variance measures	1
(c)		Calculations	4
		Discussion of sales performance	6
Total			**20**

312   THE SCHOOL UNIFORM COMPANY (MARCH/JUNE 2017)

Tutorial note

In the first requirement it is clear that we need to know material variances. The question is not specific however, and we don't know which variances are required – this is one of the key skills that are being tested. There are several variances we might be able to calculate here – the "basic" price and usage variances and the more advanced planning and operational variances or mix and yield.

Reading the scenario very carefully, and being on the lookout for information about both standard and actual usage and prices for material, will help. The second paragraph provides information – firstly that the design has changed, and now requires more material than previously – the standard cost card will need to be revised to allow for this, and any usage variance should be analysed between the planning variance caused by the change in design, and the operational variance which we can use to assess the production manager. Secondly, a new material is being used, which is cheaper than the previous material. It is worth noting here that the new material was chosen by GPST – a customer of SU, therefore this decision was not made by the production manager. This is crucial for two reasons – firstly this cannot be used to assess the production manager's performance for part (c) and secondly an uncontrollable change from the original standard means that we should split our materials price variance into planning and operational components – the 5% reduction in price constitutes the planning variance.

In answering parts (a) and (b), it's essential to know the variances calculations. Avoid the pitfall in the exam: there are 12 marks available in total – for 6 variances – materials price (planning and operational), materials usage (planning and operational) and labour efficiency (planning and operational). Calculating just the 3 basic variances would not score a passing mark.

(a) SP (standard price per metre: $2.85/0.95) $3.00

SQ (standard quantity per dress: 2.2 metres/1.1) 2 metres

From scenario the revised price per metre (RP) is $2.85, the actual price per metre (AP) is $2.85 and the revised quantity per dress (RQ) is 2.2 metres.

SQAP (standard quantity for actual production: 2 metres × 24,000) 48,000 metres
RQAP (revised quantity for actual production: 2.2 metres × 24,000) 52,800 metres.

From the scenario the actual production level (AP) is 24,000 dresses and actual quantity of material bought and used (AQ) is 54,560 metres.

Material price variances

Planning variance (SP – RP) × AQ: ($3.00 – $2.85) × 54,560	8,184F
Operational variance (RP – AP) × AQ: ($2.85 – $2.85) × 54,560	0
Total price variance	8,184 F

Material usage variances

Planning variance (SQAP – RQAP) × SP: (48,000 – 52,800) × $3.00	14,400 A
Operational variance (RQAP – AQ) × SP: (52,800 – 54,560) × $3.00	5,280 A
Total usage variance	19,680 A
Total material variance	11,496 A

Tutorial note

The most common error when calculating variances of this type is to use budgeted production to calculate standard usage. For example, taking the basic materials usage variance –many candidates write this as the difference between the actual quantity of material at the standard price, and the standard quantity of material at the standard price. It is the SQ that causes the problems – it means the standard (expected) quantity of material to make ACTUAL production.

So in our case, actual production was 24,000 units – the original standard amount per unit was 2m, so SQ would be 2m*24,000 = 48,000m. Similarly, the revised standard quantity would be 2.2*24,000 = 52,800m. You would never use the budgeted quantity to calculate standard usage, as you're comparing it to the actual quantity of material used to make ACTUAL production.

> **Tutorial note:** *These variances could have been calculated using the alternative approach as below:*
>
> **Material price variances**
>
> **Planning variance**
>
> *(AP × RQ) × (SP − RP): 24,000 × 2.2 metres × ($3.00 − $2.85)*   7,920 F
>
> **Operational variance**
>
> *(RP − AP) × AQ: 54,560 metres × ($2.85 − $2.85)*

Material usage variances

Planning variance

(SQ − RQ) × AP × SP: 24,000 × (2 metres − 2.2 metres) × $3.00   14,400 A

Operational variance

((AP × RQ) − AQ) × RP: 24,000 × 2.2 metres − 54,560 × $2.85   5,016 A

Total material variance   11,496 A

(b)   AH (actual hours worked and paid): 24 × 160 hours   3,840 hours

SHAP (standard hours for actual production): (24,000 × 8)/60   3,200 hours RHAP

(revised hours for actual production): (24,000 × 10)/60   4,000 hours

From the scenario the standard rate per hour (SR) is $12, the standard time per dress is eight minutes and the revised time per dress is 10 minutes.

Labour efficiency variances

Planning variance (SHAP − RHAP) × SR: (3,200 − 4,000) × $12   9,600 A

Operational variance (RHAP − AH) × SR: (4,000 − 3,840) × $12   1,920 F

Total labour efficiency variance   7,680 A

Tutorial note

We know we will need details about labour time to calculate our efficiency variance. Again, the change in design has had an effect on time taken – the new design will take 2 minutes longer to make. Again, this will cause a planning variance – the original standard will need to be revised to allow for this extra time, as the production manager should not be criticised for the change in design, which was not their decision. We are also told that there was no idle time, ruling out any idle time variances.

Next we are given budgeted and actual production. Actual production levels are essential in working out variances, as they compare actual figures to the flexed budget (based on actual production). The budgeted production figure is less important here, although it could be noted that actual production was 20% under budget, which may have a knock-on effect on profits.

(c)

Tutorial note

In the final paragraph, we are told that the production manager is responsible for purchasing and production issues. This means that they can be have some control over the materials price variance, as well as materials usage and labour efficiency variances, so we can use these to assess their performance.

The production manager did not have any control over the change in the design of the dress as this change was requested by the client. Similarly, it was not their fault that the company accountant responsible for updating standard costs was off sick and therefore unable to update the standards. Therefore, the production manager should be judged only by those variances over which they have control, which are the operational variances.

Materials

No operational variance arose in relation to materials price, since the actual price paid was the same as the revised price. A planning variance of $8,184F does arise but the production manager cannot take the credit for this, as the material chosen by GPST for the new dresses just happens to be cheaper. As regards usage, an adverse variance of $5,280 arose. This suggests that, even with the revised quantity of material being taken into account, staff still used more than 2.2 metres on average to produce each dress. This is probably because they had to learn a new sewing technique and they probably made some mistakes, resulting in some wastage. The manager is responsible for this as it may have been caused by insufficient training. However, the labour efficiency variances below shed some more light on this.

Tutorial note

It was much easier to score well on part (c) if you had already determined what was controllable and what was not. Easy marks could be gained here for explaining that the materials usage was due to the change in design, and therefore not controllable, and the materials price planning variance was due to GPST's decision to change the material – again, not controllable. You could then look at the operational variances and, based on whether they were adverse or favourable, decide whether the production manager had performed well or not.

Labour

Tutorial note

Easy marks could be gained here for explaining that labour efficiency planning variances were due to the change in design, and therefore not controllable, You could then look at the operational variances and, based on whether they were adverse or favourable, decide whether the production manager had performed well or not.

Remember that in many cases the variances have some interconnectivity. For example here, the operational labour efficiency variance was favourable, showing that the workers worked faster than expected. However the operational material usage variance was adverse, meaning that more material was used to make the actual production of 24,000 dresses than expected. This could have been because the workers were rushing, and therefore more material was wasted. Identifying possible cause and effect relationships like this will lead to a lot of credit being given.

The labour efficiency operational variance was favourable, which suggests good performance by the production manager. Staff took less than the expected revised 10 minutes per dress. However, when looked at in combination with the material usage operational variance above, it could be inferred that staff may have rushed a little and consequently used more material than necessary.

Tutorial note

When assessing performance it is also useful to give a conclusion. This should be in line with your previous findings – using total operational variance here would be a useful yardstick.

When both of the operational variances are looked at together, the adverse materials usage $5,280 far outweighs the favourable labour efficiency variance of $1,920. Consequently, it could be concluded that, overall, the manager's performance was somewhat disappointing.

ACCA Marking scheme		Marks
(a)	Standard price	1
	Standard quantity	0.5
	SQAP	0.5
	RQAP	0.5
	Price planning variance	1.5
	Usage planning variance	1.5
	Usage op variance	1.5
	Maximum	**7**
(b)	Actual hours	1
	SHAP	0.5
	RHAP	0.5
	Planning variance	1.5
	Operating variance	1.5
	Maximum	**5**
(c)	Controllability	1
	Variances/performance	6
	Other/conclusion	1
	Maximum	**8**
Total		**20**

313 GLOVE CO (JUNE 2016)

(a) Basic variances

Tutorial note

A fundamental mistake to avoid here is to use the labour rate per unit ($42) rather than the labour rate per hour ($42 per unit/3 hours per unit = $14 per labour hour). Using $42 by mistake would lead to very large labour variances and ring alarm bells for the candidate.

Labour rate variance

Standard cost of labour per hour = $42/3 = $14 per hour.

Labour rate variance = (actual hours paid × actual rate) – (actual hours paid × std rate)

Actual hours paid × actual rate = $531,930.

Actual hours paid × std rate = 37,000 × $14 = $518,000.

Therefore rate variance = $531,930 – $518,000 = $13,930 A.

Labour efficiency variance

Labour efficiency variance = (actual production in std hours – actual hours worked) × std rate [(12,600 × 3) – 37,000] × $14 = $11,200 F.

(b) Planning and operational variances

Labour rate planning variance

(Revised rate – std rate) × actual hours paid = [$14.00 – ($14.00 × 1.02)] × 37,000 = $10,360 A.

Labour rate operational variance

Revised rate × actual hours paid = $14.28 × 37,000 = $528,360. Actual cost = $531,930.

Variance = $3,570 A.

Labour efficiency planning variance

(Standard hours for actual production – revised hours for actual production) × std rate Revised hours for each pair of gloves = 3.25 hours.

[37,800 – (12,600 × 3.25)] × $14 = $44,100 A.

Labour efficiency operational variance

(Revised hours for actual production – actual hours for actual production) × std rate (40,950 – 37,000) × $14 = $55,300 F.

(c)   Analysis of performance

Tutorial note

Most students are aware that uncontrollable factors are not to be used to assess performance, and will score marks in the exam for saying so. But in order to bag even more marks, identifying WHY things happened, and what they mean, is essential. A good understanding of the variances helps here. For example, if we have an adverse operational labour rate variance, what does this mean? It means that our hourly rate was higher than expected, after adjusting for the uncontrollable factors. Why would this be – look for help in the scenario. An overtime rate is mentioned – this would explain a higher hourly rate. Explaining reasons for variances or movements will score many more marks than bland comments such as 'the variance is adverse which is bad.' This doesn't assess the performance of the production manager.

At a first glance, performance looks mixed because the total labour rate variance is adverse and the total labour efficiency variance is favourable. However, the operational and planning variances provide a lot more detail on how these variances have occurred.

The production manager should only be held accountable for variances which they can control. This means that they should only be held accountable for the operational variances. When these operational variances are looked at it can be seen that the labour rate operational variance is $3,570 A. This means that the production manager did have to pay for some overtime in order to meet demand but the majority of the total labour rate variance is driven by the failure to update the standard for the pay rise that was applied at the start of the last quarter. The overtime rate would also have been impacted by that pay increase.

Then, when the labour efficiency operational variance is looked at, it is actually $55,300 F. This shows that the production manager has managed their department well with workers completing production more quickly than would have been expected when the new design change is taken into account. The total operating variances are therefore $51,730 F and so overall performance is good.

The adverse planning variances of $10,360 and $44,100 do not reflect on the performance of the production manager and can therefore be ignored here.

		Marks
(a)	Basic variances	
	Each variance	1
		—
	Maximum	2
		—
(b)	Operational and planning variance	
	Labour rate planning	1.5
	Labour rate operational	1.5
	Labour efficiency planning	1.5
	Labour efficiency operational	1.5
		—
	Maximum	6
		—
(c)	Performance	
	Only operational variances	1
	Adverse op. variance	2
	Failure to update the standard	1
	Overtime rate impacted	1
	Favourable efficiency variance	2
	Good overall	1
		—
	Maximum	7
		—
Total		15
		—

Marking scheme

314 KAPPA CO (SEPTEMBER 2018)

(a) **(i)** **Usage variance**

	Should use	Did use	Difference	Std cost/kg	Variance
	kg	kg	kg	$	$
Alpha	1,840	2,200	360 A	2.00	720 A
Beta	2,760	2,500	260 F	5.00	1,300 F
Gamma	920	920		1.00	
	———	———			———
	5,520	5,620			580 F
	———	———			———

(ii) **Mix variance**

	AQSM	AQAM	Difference	Std cost/kg	Variance
	kg	kg	kg	$	$
Alpha	1,873.33	2,200	326.67 A	2.00	653.34 A
Beta	2,810.00	2,500	310.00 F	5.00	1,550.00 F
Gamma	936.67	920	16.67 F	1.00	16.67 F
	———	———			———
	5,620	5,620			913.33 F
	———	———			———

(iii) **Yield variance**

	SQSM	AQSM	Difference	Std cost/kg	Variance
	kg	kg	kg	$	$
Alpha	1,840	1,873.33	33.33 A	2.00	66.66 A
Beta	2,760	2,810.00	50.00 A	5.00	250.00 A
Gamma	920	936.67	16.67 A	1.00	16.67 A
	5,520	5,620			333.33 A

Alternative solution

5,620 kg input should produce 4,683.33 kg of Omega

5,620 kg input did produce 4,600 kg of Omega

Difference = 83.33 kg × $4 per kg ($400/100 kg) = $333.32 A

(b) The raw material price variances included in the report are probably outside the production manager's control, and are more the responsibility of the purchasing manager. Furthermore, the production manager has no participation in setting the standard mix. Holding managers accountable for variances they cannot control is demotivating.

There appears to be no use of planning variances. Prices and quality of the three materials are volatile and using ex ante prices and usage standards can give a distorted view of mix and yield variances. Failing to isolate non-controllable planning variances can be demotivating.

The standard mix for the product has not changed in five years despite changes in the quality and price of ingredients. It can also lead the production manager to attempt control action based on variances which are calculated based on standards which are out of date.

As Kappa Co does not currently give feedback or commentary, a true picture is lacking as to the production manager's performance. There is also no follow up on the variances calculated. As Kappa Co does not appear to place much importance on the variances, the production manager will not be motivated to control costs and could become complacent which could adversely impact Kappa Co overall.

This can be illustrated by looking at the overall usage variance reported which shows a $580 favourable variance, so the production manager could assume good performance. However, if the usage variance is considered in more detail, through the mix and yield calculations, it can be seen that it was driven by a change in the mix. There is a direct relationship between the materials mix variance and the materials yield variance and by using a mix of materials which was different from standard, it has resulted in a saving of $913.33; however, it has led to a significantly lower yield than Kappa Co would have got had the standard mix of materials been adhered to. Also changing the mix could impact quality and as a result sales and there is no information about this.

ACCA marking scheme			
			Marks
(a)	**(i)**	Alpha usage variance	1
		Beta usage variance	1
		Gamma usage variance	1
		Total usage variance	1
			4
	(ii)	AQSM figures	1.5
		Variance quantities	0.5
		Variance in $	1.5
		Total mix variance	0.5
			4
	(iii)	SQSM or $4,683.33 kg (depending on method used)	1
		Variance quantity or 83.33 kg (depending on method used)	0.5
		Variance in $ or calculation of $4 (depending on method used)	1
		Total yield variance	0.5
			3
(b)		Controllability issues	5
		Other relevant points relating to performance	4
			9
Total			**20**

315 SAFE SOAP CO (DECEMBER 2014)

(a) Variance calculations

Mix variance

Total kg of materials per standard batch = 0.25 + 0.6 + 0.5 = 1.35 kg

Therefore standard quantity to produce 136,000 batches = 136,000 × 1.35 kg = 183,600 kg

Actual total kg of materials used to produce 136,000 batches = 34,080 + 83,232 + 64,200 = 181,512 kg

Material	Actual quantity standard mix in kgs	Actual quantity actual mix in kgs	Variance in kgs	Standard cost per kg in $	Variance $
Lye	181,512 × 0.25/1.35 = 33,613.33	34,080	(466.67)	10	(4,666.70)
Coconut oil	181,512 × 0.6/1.35 = 80,672	83,232	(2,560.00)	4	(10,240.00)
Shea butter	181,512 × 0.5/1.35 = 67,226.67	64,200	3,026.67	3	9,080.01
	181,512	181,512			(5,826.69) A

Yield variance

Material	Standard quantity standard mix in kgs	Actual quantity standard mix in kgs	Variance in kgs	Standard cost per kg in $	Variance $
Lye	0.25 × 136,000 = 34,000	33,613.33	386.67	10	3,866.70
Coconut oil	0.6 × 136,000 = 81,600	80,672	928	4	3,712
Shea butter	0.5 × 136,000 = 68,000	67,226.67	773.33	3	2,319.99
	————	————			————
	183,600	181,512			9,898.69 F
	————	————			————

(b) **(i)** A materials mix variance will occur when the actual mix of materials used in production is different from the standard mix. So, it is inputs which are being considered. Since the total mix variance is adverse for the Safe Soap Co, this means that the actual mix used in September and October was more expensive than the standard mix.

A material yield variance arises because the output which was achieved is different from the output which would have been expected from the inputs. So, whereas the mix variance focuses on inputs, the yield variance focuses on outputs. In both September and October, the yield variance was favourable, meaning that the inputs produced a higher level of output than one would have expected.

(ii) Whilst the mix and yield variances provide Safe Soap Co with a certain level of information, they do not necessarily explain any quality issues which arise because of the change in mix. The consequences of the change may well have an impact on sales volumes. In Safe Soap Co's case, the sales volume variance is adverse, meaning that sales volumes have fallen in October. It is not known whether they also fell in September but it would be usual for the effects on sales of the change in mix to be slightly delayed, in this case by one month, given that it is only once the customers start receiving the slightly altered soap that they may start expressing their dissatisfaction with the product.

There may also be other reasons for the adverse sales volume variance but given the customer complaints which have been received, the sales manager's views should be taken on board.

(c) The **theory of motivation** suggests that having a clearly defined target results in better performance than having no target at all, that targets need to be accepted by the staff involved, and that more demanding targets increase motivation provided they remain accepted. It is against this background that basic, ideal, current and attainable standards can be discussed.

A **basic standard** is one that remains unchanged for several years and is used to show trends over time. Basic standards may become increasingly easy to achieve as time passes and hence, being undemanding, may have a negative impact on motivation. Standards that are easy to achieve will give employees little to aim at.

Ideal standards represent the outcome that can be achieved under perfect operating conditions, with no wastage, inefficiency or machine breakdowns. Since perfect operating conditions are unlikely to occur for any significant period, ideal standards will be very demanding and are unlikely to be accepted as targets by the staff involved as they are unlikely to be achieved. Using ideal standards as targets is therefore likely to have a negative effect on employee motivation.

Current standards are based on current operating conditions and incorporate current levels of wastage, inefficiency and machine breakdown. If used as targets, current standards will not improve performance beyond its current level and their impact on motivation will be a neutral one or a negative one since employees may feel unmotivated due to the lack of challenge.

Attainable standards are those that can be achieved if operating conditions conform to the best that can be practically achieved in terms of material use, efficiency and machine performance. Attainable standards are likely to be more demanding than current standards and so will have a positive effect on employee motivation, provided that employees accept them as achievable.

316 ATD (DECEMBER 2013, AMENDED)

(a) (i) **Least squares**

From the data presented in Figure 1 the line of best fit is: y = 125.022 + 1.84x

This equation can be used to predict a value for the next quarter (2013 quarter 3 is quarter 15):

y = 125.022 + 1.84 × (15)

y = 152.62 or $152,620.

(ii) **Time series analysis**

Based on a trend value of 151, the predicted value for quarter 3 of 2013 would be 173.55, that is 151 + 22.55.

The value of 22.55 is the seasonal variation for third quarters.

Tutorial note

We could also state here that we moved from 124.70 (x = 1) to 147.77 (x =14) in 13 steps, so the average increase was 1.77 per step. This can help calculate a trend line for x = 15 as 147.77 + 1.77 = 149.54.

A totally different approach and answer that would still harvest a mark in the exam.

(b) The **least square analysis** of the sales data defines the equation of a straight line that 'best' fits the data by minimising the squares of deviations of actual values from the mean. In least squares analysis, one set of data is defined as the independent variable (x – in this case, time) and the other set of data, sales, is defined as y – the dependent variable.

The positive value of b suggests that the overall sales trend is upwards.

The correlation coefficient 'r' shows the strength of the statistical relationship between the two variables. In Figure 1 the value of r is 0.253, which suggests that the two variables are weakly connected. The coefficient of determination (r2) shows that 6.4% of the variation in sales (y) is due to the passage of time (x). Low coefficients of correlation (and determination) are usual when data is widely scattered around the mean and/or are related in a non-linear fashion. Both these factors might be applicable here, particularly due to the pattern caused by large seasonal variations.

At ATD, linear regression appears to be of little practical use. The predicted value for 2013 quarter 3 appears too low (it is lower than all actual quarter 3 figures to date and much lower than the previous quarter 3 figure of 169). The technique might be more useful if the annual data was plotted (hence eliminating the seasonal variation) or to identify alternative variables which better explained the seasonal variation and to calculate a correlation coefficient between these and the sales data.

Time series analysis uses a moving average to define a trend. In Figure 2, the moving average has been calculated on a quarterly basis, which seems appropriate as this is how the data has been presented. The trend line is calculated from the average of the first two quarters (for example, quarters 1–4 and quarters 2–5) to allow the trend to be centralised against an actual sales value. The difference between the actual values and the trend line is also averaged to produce a seasonal variation. Any difference left between the actual sales value and the seasonally adjusted trend is defined as a residual variation. Figure 2 also shows the seasonally adjusted trend values.

Forecasting future values is achieved by extrapolating the trend line and then adding or subtracting the seasonal variation. There is no agreed way of extrapolating the trend. A scatter graph could be drawn and a trend line drawn by hand. Alternatively, a least square regression of the trend values could be performed to define a line of best fit. Using a 'best guess' approach, a trend value of 149 might be hypothesised for quarter 1 of 2013, giving a predicted value of 134.3 (149 – 14.7), just below the actual recorded value of 137. Predicted values would also be calculated for subsequent quarters. For example, based on a (hand drawn) trend value of 151, the predicted value for quarter 3 of 2013 would be 173.55 (151 + 22.55), which subjectively seems much more realistic than the 152.55 suggested by the least squares analysis.

The moving average method also explicitly defines the significant seasonal variations for this product and so reflects these in the predicted values, meaning that production capacity, inventory levels and resource purchase requirements are sensitive to the fluctuating demand. The high residual variation in 2012 quarter 4 probably needs some investigation. It is possible that demand is falling faster than might be expected and this will have important consequences for estimated sales figures.

One of the problems of both techniques is that forecasts are based on past data. Sudden changes in the market will not be immediately reflected in the forecasts. Thus there may still be a role for the sales manager to use their experience, intuition and judgement to amend the forecasts produced by the statistical analysis.

Finally, of the two approaches presented here, time series analysis seems the most appropriate technique for sales forecasting at ATD.

(c) Budgets should allow proper, realistic targets to be set not only for sales but also for functions where there is clear accountability (such as production management and inventory management). Targets need to be rigorous and achievable. They also need to be connected to clear organisational demarcation where targets are under the control of a manager who has responsibility for that target. Thus budgeting should improve forecasting through requiring a rigorous and collectively responsible process. Flexing the budget would allow the performance of parts of the organisation to be assessed in the context of missed sales targets. For example, an analysis might reveal that the production manager has reduced target raw material costs even though lower sales volumes mean that overall revenue targets have not been met. At present, the production manager is frustrated because they feel that they are working 'tirelessly to keep costs down, but my only reward is that I cannot replace one of my best purchasing administrators who left last month'. However, we only have their assertion about their ability to keep costs down. With a flexed budget, the business can actually see if they have effectively controlled costs. Flexed budgets and their associated variances provide an important insight into how different functions or departments (and their managers) are actually performing.

There is also significant evidence to suggest that departmental managers will be motivated if they are required to strive to achieve targets that they themselves have helped set, fostering a sense of ownership and commitment. This would help address the managers' feelings of powerlessness and the sense that they are undervalued. Their morale should improve as they see their experience and opinions valued. Benefits should also accrue for the organisation as a whole. As knowledge from different departments is pooled, understanding, target setting and co-ordination should be improved due to the number of different departments involved in budget setting.

Because budgets include planning, feedback and control elements, they offer important insights into how an organisation should react to failed sales targets. The response of the CEO has been to take general measures which appear, on the face of it, to offer immediate savings, but have an unpredictable effect. Such indiscriminate measures as a ban on business travel, cancelled marketing initiatives and a complete freeze on recruitment may be legitimate responses, but without a budget, it is not really possible to assess their effectiveness. A proper variance analysis might suggest better reactions, and indeed if reduced sales targets are compensated for in some way by reduced raw material and labour costs, then the overall performance might not warrant, in the short term, such an extreme response. The organisation needs to respond to variances and exercise proper controls, revising plans (and budgets) if necessary. The suggested measures may be counter-productive. For example, banning business travel might prevent the production manager from travelling to a supplier where they would be able to negotiate reduced material costs. Cancelled marketing initiatives might further affect the capability of the organisation to meet sales targets and a complete freeze of recruitment may affect the organisation's effectiveness and its capacity to deliver products on time and to the required quality.

Thus a formal budgeting process would allow ATD to address three particular areas of concern. The ability of the organisation to make realistic forecasts, the poor morale of departmental managers and the appropriateness of the organisation's response to its failure to hit predicted sales targets.

PERFORMANCE MEASUREMENT AND CONTROL

317 HAMMER (JUNE 2010)

(a) **Price under existing policy**

	$
Steel (0.4/0.95 × $4.00)	1.68
Other materials ($3.00 × 0.9 × 0.1)	0.27
Labour (0.25 × $10)	2.50
Variable overhead (0.25 × $15)	3.75
Delivery	0.50
	―――
Total variable cost	8.70
Mark-up 30%	2.61
	―――
Transfer price	11.31
	―――

(b) The only difference would be to add the fixed costs and adjust the mark-up %.

	$
Existing total variable cost	8.70
Extra fixed cost (0.25 × $15 × 0.8)	3.00
	―――
Total cost	11.70
Mark-up 10%	1.17
	―――
Transfer price	12.87
	―――

The price difference is therefore 12.87 − 11.31 = $1.56 per unit

(c) As far as the manufacturer is concerned, including fixed costs in the transfer price will have the advantage of covering all the costs incurred. In theory this should guarantee a profit for the division (assuming the fixed overhead absorption calculations are accurate). In essence the manufacturer is reducing the risk in their division.

The accounting for fixed costs is notoriously difficult with many approaches possible. Including fixed costs in the transfer price invites manipulation of overhead treatment.

One of the main problems with this strategy is that a fixed cost of the business is being turned into a variable cost in the hands of the seller (in our case the stores). This can lead to poor decision-making for the group since, although fixed costs would normally be ignored in a decision (as unavoidable), they would be relevant to the seller because they are part of their variable buy in price.

(d) **Degree of autonomy allowed to the stores in buying policy**

If the stores are allowed too much freedom in buying policy Hammer could lose control of its business. Brand could be damaged if each store bought a different supplier's shears (or other products). On the other hand, flexibility is increased and profits could be made for the business by entrepreneurial store managers exploiting locally found bargains. However, the current market price for shears may only be temporary (sale or special offer) and therefore not really representative of their true market 'value'. If this is the case, then any long-term decision to allow retail stores to buy shears from external suppliers (rather than from Nail) would be wrong.

The question of comparability is also important. Products are rarely 'identical' and consequently, price differences are to be expected. The stores could buy a slightly inferior product (claiming it is comparable) in the hope of a better margin. This could seriously damage Hammer's brand.

Motivation is also a factor here, however. Individual managers like a little freedom within which to operate. If they are forced to buy what they see as an inferior product (internally) at high prices it is likely to de-motivate. Also with greater autonomy, the performance of the stores will be easier to assess as the store managers will have control over greater elements of their business.

	Marking scheme		
			Marks
(a)	Steel		1
	Other material		1
	Labour		1
	Variable overhead		1
	Delivery		1
	Mark-up		1
		Maximum	6
(b)	Fixed cost		2
	Mark-up		2
		Maximum	4
(c)	Covers all cost		1
	Risk		1
	Fixed cost accounting		1
	Converts a FC to VC		2
		Maximum	4
(d)	Market price may be temporary		1
	Brand		1
	Profitability		1
	Flexibility		1
	Control		1
	Motivation		1
	Performance assessment		1
	Comparability		1
		Maximum	6
Total			20

318 MAN CO (JUNE 2016)

(a)   Maximising group profit

Division L has enough capacity to supply both Division M and its external customers with component L. Therefore, incremental cost of Division M buying externally is as follows:

Cost per unit of component L when bought from external supplier: $37 Cost per unit for Division L of making component L: $20.

Therefore incremental cost to group of each unit of component L being bought in by Division M rather than transferred internally: $17 ($37 – 20).

From the group's point of view, the most profitable course of action is therefore that all 120,000 units of component L should be transferred internally.

(b)   Calculating total group profit

Total group profits will be as follows:

Division L:

Contribution earned per transferred component = $40 – $20 = $20 Profit earned per component sold externally = $40 – $24 = $16.

	$
120,000 × $20	2,400,000
160,000 × $16	2,560,000
	4,960,000
Less fixed costs	(500,000)
Profit	4,460,000

Division M:

Profit earned per component sold externally = $27 – $1 = $26

	$
120,000 × $26	3,120,000
Less fixed costs	(200,000)
Profit	2,920,000
Total profit	7,380,000

(c)   Problems with current transfer price and suggested alternative

The problem is that the current transfer price of $40 per unit is now too high. Whilst this has not been a problem before since external suppliers were charging $42 per unit, it is a problem now that Division M has been offered component L for $37 per unit. If Division M now acts in its own interests rather than the interests of the group as a whole, it will buy component L from the external supplier rather than from Division L. This will mean that the profits of the group will fall substantially and Division L will have significant unused capacity.

Consequently, Division L needs to reduce its price. The current price does not reflect the fact that there are no selling and distribution costs associated with transferring internally, i.e. the cost of selling internally is $4 less for Division L than selling externally. So, it could reduce the price to $36 and still make the same profit on these sales as on its external sales. This would therefore be the suggested transfer price so that Division M is still saving $1 per unit compared to the external price. A transfer price of $37 would also presumably be acceptable to Division M since this is the same as the external supplier is offering.

Marking scheme		Marks
(a) Maximising group profits		
Calculating incremental cost per unit		2
Recommendation		1
	Maximum	**3**
(b) Profit		
Profit of L		3
Profit of M		2
Total profit		1
	Maximum	**6**
(c) Discussion		
Transfer price is too high		2
Division M will not buy		1
Profits for group will fall		1
S/D costs should mean lower TP anyway		2
Suggested transfer price		1
	Maximum	**6**
Total		**15**

319 BEST NIGHT CO (MARCH 2019)

Performance for year ended 30 June 20X7

Gross room revenue – Best Night's 'gross' room revenue based on standard room rates has increased by 6.6% in 20X7, which reflects the higher occupancy rates (74% v 72%) and the increase in standard room rates ($140 v $135 per night).

However, this gives a rather misleading impression of how well the hotels have performed in the year to 20X7.

Revenue after discounts – Revenue from room sales, adjusted for discounts or rate reductions offered, has actually only increased 1.8%, and that reflects the significant 45% increase in discounts or reductions offered:

	20X7	20X6	% change
	$000	$000	
Standard revenue	111,890	104,976	6.6%
Discounts/reductions	16,783	11,540	45.4%
Room revenue net of discounts	95,107	95,107	1.8%

Faced with the declining number of business customers, and consequently the prospect of lower occupancy rates, managers may have decided to offer lower room rates to try to retain as many of their existing business customers as possible, or to try to attract additional leisure customers.

Although occupancy rates increased by 2.8% (from 72% to 74% which now exceeds the budgeted level), revenue, net of discounts, only increased by 1.8%. This means that revenue per room per night after discounts in 20X7 was lower than in 20X6, despite the standard rate being higher ($140 v $135).

In the context of tough market conditions, the decision to increase the standard room rate for 20X7 appears rather optimistic. Although the hotel managers have managed to achieve occupancy rates higher than budget, they have only managed to do so by reducing room rates.

Additional revenue – One of the potential benefits of increased occupancy rates, even if guests are paying less per room per night, is that they will generate additional revenue from food and drink sales. This appears to be the case because additional revenues have increased by approximately 5%.

Total revenue – In total, revenue (net of discounts) has increased 2.4% in 20X7 v 20X6. Given the tough competitive environment, Best Night Co could view any increase in revenues as positive. Moreover, provided the revenue achieved from selling the room is greater than the variable cost of providing it, then increasing occupancy levels should increase the hotels' contribution to profit.

Operating profit – However, despite the increase in revenue, operating profits have fallen by $0.3m (1.3%) between 20X7 and 20X6, due to a sizeable increase in operating costs. There is no detail about Best Night Co's operating costs, for example, the split between fixed and variable costs. However, in an increasingly competitive market, cost control is likely to be very important. As such, the $3 million (3.3%) increase in operating costs between 20X6 and 20X7 is potentially a cause for concern, and the reasons for the increase should be investigated further. However, when looking to reduce costs, it will be very important to do so in a way which does not compromise customer satisfaction. More generally, Best Night Co needs to avoid cutting expenditure in areas which will have a detrimental impact on customer satisfaction ratings, for example, not replacing mattresses even though they are becoming uncomfortable to sleep on.

Operating profit margin – The increase in costs has also led to a fall in operating profit margin from 20.8% to 20.0%. It is perhaps more instructive to look at the margin based on standard room rates per night, thereby reflecting the impact of the discounts offered as well as the increase in costs. On this basis, the margin falls slightly more: from 18.9% to 17.6%.

	20X7	20X6
	$000	$000
Total revenue	119,377	116,621
Discounts offered	16,783	11,430
Gross revenue	136,160	128,051
Operating profit	23,915	4,242
Operating profit margin	17.6%	18.9%

ROCE – This reduced profitability is also reflected in the company's return on capital employed which has fallen slightly from 62% ($24.2m/$39.1m) to 60.5% ($23.9m/$39.5m). This suggests that the value which Best Night Co is generating from its assets is falling. The decline in ROCE could be a particular concern given the relative lack of capital investment in the hotels recently. Capital investment will increase the cost of Best Night Co's non-current assets, thereby reducing ROCE for any given level of profit.

Customer satisfaction scores

Although the reduction in profitability should be a concern for Best Night Co, the reduction in customer satisfaction scores should potentially be seen as a greater cause for concern. The scores suggest that, in the space of one year, Best Night Co hotels have gone from being in the top 10% of hotels to only just being in the top 25%. This is a significant decline in one year, and one which Best Night Co cannot afford to continue.

Best Night Co prides itself on the comfort of its rooms and the level of service it offers its guests. Both of these factors are likely to be important considerations for people when considering whether or not to stay in a Best Night Co hotel. Therefore, falling customer satisfactions levels could be seen as an indication that fewer existing customers will stay at a Best Night Co hotel in future – thereby threatening occupancy rates, and prices, in future.

Moreover, the scores suggest that the decision to defer the refurbishment programme is likely to have a detrimental impact on future performance.

ACCA marking scheme	
	Marks
Calculations	5
Revenue	4
Operating profit	2
ROCE	2
Customer satisfaction	3
Other valid point	4
	—
Total	**20**
	—

320 JUMP PERFORMANCE APPRAISAL (JUNE 2010)

(a) Bonus calculation:

	Qtr to 30 June 20X9	Qtr to 30 September 20X9	Qtr to 31 December 20X9	Qtr to 31 March 20Y0	Bonus; hits'
Staff on time?					
On-time %	430/450 = 95.5%	452/480 = 94.2%	442/470 = 94.0%	460/480 = 95.8%	
Bonus earned?	Yes	No	No	Yes	2
Members visits					
Target visits	60% × 3,000 × 12 = 21,600	60% × 3,200 × 12 = 23,040	60% × 3,300 × 12 = 23,760	60% × 3,400 × 12 = 24,480	
Actual visits	20,000	24,000	26,000	24,000	
Bonus earned?	No	Yes	Yes	No	2
Personal training					
Target	10% × 3,000 = 300	10% × 3,200 = 320	10% × 3,300 = 330	10% × 3,400 = 340	
Actual sessions	310	325	310	339	
Bonus earned	Yes	Yes	No	No	2
Total					6

The bonus earned by the manager would be 6 × $400 = $2,400, which is 50% of the total bonus available.

(b) An important principle of any target based bonus system is that the targets must be based on controllable aspects of the manager's role.

Staff on time

The way in which a manager manages staff can have a big bearing on whether or not an individual staff member is keen to work and arrive on time. We are told that the local manager has the power to vary employment contracts so the manager should be able to agree acceptable shift patterns with staff and reward them for compliance. In this respect the lateness of staff is controllable by the manager.

On the other hand an individual staff member may be subject to home pressures or problems with public or other transport meaning that even they cannot control the time of arrival at work on some days. The manager cannot control these events either. If this problem became regular for a member of staff then the local manager could vary the contract of employment accordingly.

Overall, lateness to work is controllable by the local manager.

Member use of facilities

The local manager controls the staff and hence the level of customer service. Good quality customer services would probably encourage members to use the facilities more often. Equally, by maintaining the club to a high standard then the local manager can remove another potential reason for a member not to use the facilities regularly.

On the other hand customers are influenced by many factors outside of the club. Their state of health or their own work pressures can prevent members being able to come to the club.

Overall, the local manager can only partly control the number of member visits.

Personal training sessions

Again, the local manager controls the level of customer service and the standard of maintenance in the personal training department. The manager also has control over prices so, if the bookings fall, they are able to reduce price or make special offers to encourage use of the facilities.

On the other hand, personal training sessions may be seen as a luxury by customers and in times of financial difficulty they are expendable by them. Personal training sessions are often available from other sources and competition can force down the sales of the club. The manager can respond to that by improving services. They cannot, however, make significant investment in improving the facilities without board approval.

Overall, the local manager can only partly control the number of personal training sessions booked.

(c)   There are a variety of methods that the performance data can be manipulated:

Cut off

The unethical manager could record visits in a different period than was actually the case. For example in quarter three the target for personal training sessions was not met by 20 sessions. This was probably obvious to the manager in the last few days of that quarter. They could have therefore recorded some sessions as having taken place in the next quarter. Indeed, only one session would have to be moved in this way in order for the manager to meet the target in the final quarter and gain another $400 of bonus.

Reduce prices to below economic levels to encourage use

The targets that the manager is subject to are mainly volume driven. A reduction in prices would harm profitability but would not damage the manager's bonus potential. More sessions are bound to follow if the price is set low enough.

(Other ideas would be acceptable including advising staff to take the day off if they were going to be late. This would damage service levels admittedly, but would potentially gain a bonus for lateness.)

Marking scheme			
			Marks
(a)	Per target		2
		Maximum	6
(b)	For each target – supporting controllability		1.5
	For each target – denying controllability		1.5
	Target		9
(c)	For each idea of manipulation up to		2.5
		Maximum	5
Total			20

321 LENS CO (DECEMBER 2016)

(a) **Return on investment**

Controllable profit

	Division P	Division O
	$000	$000
Revenue	14,000	18,800
Direct labour	(2,400)	(3,500)
Direct materials	(4,800)	(6,500)
Divisional overheads excl. uncontrollable depreciation	(3,480)	(4,740)
Exchange gain/(loss)	(200)	460
Net divisional profit	3,120	4,520

Net assets controlled by the divisions

	Division P	Division O
	$000	$000
Non-current assets controlled by division	15,400	20,700
Inventories	1,800	3,900
Trade receivables	6,200	8,900
Overdraft	(500)	–
Trade payables	(5,100)	(7,200)
Net controllable assets	17,800	26,300

ROI for Division P

Controllable profit/controllable assets

= $3,120/$17,800

= 17.53%.

ROI for Division O

$4,520/$26,300 = 17.19%

Tutorial note

*'A basis ... suitable for measuring the divisional managers' performance' means that calculations should have been based on controllable profit. Whilst most items affecting profit were either clearly controllable or uncontrollable, the exchange rate gain/loss could have been argued either way, provided that the explanation in part (b) was sufficient. Similarly, the assets figure used for the calculation should have only included **controllable** assets.*

(b) The ROIs in part (a) have been calculated by applying the principle of 'controllability'. This principle states that managers should only be held accountable for areas which they can control. This means that, when calculating 'profit' for the purposes of calculating ROI, the only revenues and costs included should be controllable by the manager. Similarly, when calculating 'net assets' for the ROI calculation, only assets which the divisional managers can control should be included.

Applying the principles of controllability, treatment of certain costs is explained below:

Gain on sale of equipment

This has been excluded from the profit figure as the decision to dispose of a large amount of equipment in division P was taken by Head Office. The divisional manager had no control over this decision.

Divisional overheads

The depreciation on HO controlled assets has been excluded when calculating profit for ROI purposes. Again, this is because divisional managers do not control some of the assets.

Exchange gains/losses

These have been left in when arriving at a profit figure for ROI purposes. This is because the scenario states that the divisions choose to give the overseas customers 60 days' credit and it is this delay between the point of sale and the point of payment which gives rise to the exchange gain or loss. The managers make the choice to deal with these customers so they have control here.

Exceptional cost of factory closure

The effect of this has been removed from the 'profit' calculation as this decision was made by Head Office, not the manager of division O. It was therefore beyond the manager's control and its effect should be excluded.

Allocated Head Office costs

These have been excluded when calculating profit as the divisional managers have no control over these and should not be held accountable for them.

Non-current assets controlled by Head Office

These have been excluded from the 'net assets' calculation as these assets are not under the control of the divisional managers.

Tutorial note

Given the use of the verb 'explain' and the fact that this part was worth 8 marks, many of the items needed more explanation than simply saying that they were 'controllable' or 'uncontrollable'. It needed to be explained why they were controllable or uncontrollable. Do not lose easy marks with answers that are repetitive and too brief. You must always be careful to interpret the instruction and be guided by the marks available in determining how much they need to write.

(c)   Investment centres

An investment centre is a type of responsibility centre in which managers have responsibility for not only sales prices, volume and costs but also for investment in working capital and non-current assets. Both divisions do have responsibility for working capital; that is clear from the scenario. However, they only have responsibility over some of the assets. In the circumstances, it could be argued that it is correct to treat them as investment centres provided that appropriate adjustments are made when using ROI to assess their performance.

On the other hand, however, managers are only able to sign off $15,000 of capital expenditure, which is a relatively small amount, suggesting that treatment as an investment centre is not appropriate. Bringing the divisions under Head Office control may even be beneficial as then exchange rate risk can be managed more closely.

Tutorial note

In order to answer a requirement of this nature, it is necessary to state what an investment centre is and then very briefly discuss whether this seems to be the case for the divisions in question.

(d)   Problems of using ROI

The main disadvantage of using ROI is that the percentage increases as assets get older. This is because the carrying value of the assets decreases as a result of higher accumulated depreciation, hence capital employed falls. This, in turn, can lead managers to hold onto ageing assets rather than replace them, especially where their bonuses are linked to ROI. It may be that division P's manager would not have made the same decision which Head Office made to invest in the more advanced technology for this reason.

Another disadvantage is that ROI is based on accounting profits, which are subjective, rather than cash flows. It is therefore open to manipulation.

Additionally, it does not take into account the cost of capital. It merely looks at profits relative to capital employed without taking into account the cost of the capital which has been invested. It is therefore not consistent with maximising returns to investors.

Tutorial note

The trap to avoid here is spending too long discussing the problems of using residual income, which was not asked for. This wasted time and therefore their potential to earn marks elsewhere.

Marking scheme			
			Marks
(a)	Calculation of controllable profit		2
	Calculation of controllable assets		2
	ROI		2
			───
		Maximum	**6**
			───
(b)	Explanation about controllability		2
	Inclusion/exclusion explanations		6
			───
		Maximum	**8**
			───
(c)	Description of investment centre		1
	Application to Lens Co		1
			───
		Maximum	**2**
			───
(d)	Problems with using ROI		4
Total			20
			───

322 ACCOUNTANCY TEACHING CO (DECEMBER 2010)

Turnover has decreased from $72.025 million in 20X9 to $66.028 million in 20Y0, a fall of 8.3%. However, this must be assessed by taking into account the change in market conditions, since there has been a 20% decline in demand for accountancy training. Given this 20% decline in the market place, AT Co's turnover would have been expected to fall to $57.62m if it had kept in line with market conditions. Comparing AT Co's actual turnover to this, it's actual turnover is 14.6% higher than expected. As such, AT Co has performed fairly well, given market conditions.

It can also be seen from the non-financial performance indicators that 20% of students in 20Y0 are students who have transferred over from alternative training providers. It is likely that they have transferred over because they have heard about the improved service that AT Co is providing. Hence, they are most likely the reason for the increased market share that AT Co has managed to secure in 20Y0.

Cost of sales

Cost of sales has decreased by 19.2% in 20Y0. This must be considered in relation to the decrease in turnover as well. In 20X9, cost of sales represented 72.3% of turnover and in 20Y0 this figure was 63.7%. This is quite a substantial decrease. The reasons for it can be ascertained by, firstly, looking at the freelance staff costs.

In 20X9, the freelance costs were $14.582m. Given that a minimum 10% reduction in fees had been requested to freelance lecturers and the number of courses run by them was the same year on year, the expected cost for freelance lecturers in 20Y0 was $13.124m. The actual costs were $12.394m. These show that a fee reduction of 15% was actually achieved. This can be seen as a successful reduction in costs.

The expected cost of sales for 20Y0 before any cost cuts, was $47.738m assuming a consistent ratio of cost of sales to turnover. The actual cost of sales was only $42.056m, $5.682m lower. Since freelance lecturer costs fell by $2.188m, this means that other costs of sale fell by the remaining $3.494m. Staff costs are a substantial amount of this balance but since there was a pay freeze and the average number of employees hardly changed from year to year, the decreased costs are unlikely to be related to staff costs. The decrease is therefore most probably attributable to the introduction of online marking. AT Co expected the online marking system to cut costs by $4m, but it is probable that the online marking did not save as much as possible, hence the $3.494m fall. Alternatively, the saved marking costs may have been partially counteracted by an increase in some other cost included in cost of sales.

Gross profit

As a result of the above, the gross profit margin has increased in 20Y0 from 27.7% to 36.3%. This is a big increase and reflects very well on management.

Indirect expenses

- Marketing costs: These have increased by 42.1% in 20Y0. Although this is quite significant, given all the improvements that AT Co has made to the service it is providing, it is very important that potential students are made aware of exactly what the company now offers. The increase in marketing costs has been rewarded with higher student numbers relative to the competition in 20Y0 and these will hopefully continue increasing next year, since many of the benefits of marketing won't be felt until the next year anyway. The increase should therefore be viewed as essential expenditure rather than a cost that needs to be reduced.

- Property costs: These have largely stayed the same in both years.

- Staff training: These costs have increased dramatically by over $2 million, a 163.9% increase. However, AT Co had identified that it had a problem with staff retention, which was leading to a lower quality service being provided to students. Also, due to the introduction of the interactive website, the electronic enrolment system and the online marking system, staff would have needed training on these areas. If AT Co had not spent this money on essential training, the quality of service would have deteriorated further and more staff would have left as they became increasingly dissatisfied with their jobs. Again, therefore, this should be seen as essential expenditure.

- Given that the number of student complaints has fallen dramatically in 20Y0 to 84 from 315, the staff training appears to have improved the quality of service being provided to students.

- Interactive website and the student helpline: These costs are all new this year and result from an attempt to improve the quality of service being provided and, presumably, improve pass rates. Therefore, given the increase in the pass rate for first time passes from 48% to 66% it can be said that these developments have probably contributed to this. Also, they have probably played a part in attracting new students, hence improving turnover.

- Enrolment costs have fallen dramatically by 80.9%. This huge reduction is a result of the new electronic system being introduced. This system can certainly be seen as a success, as not only has it dramatically reduced costs but it has also reduced the number of late enrolments from 297 to 106.

Net operating profit

This has fallen from $3.635m to $2.106m. On the face of it, this looks disappointing but it has to be remembered that AT Co has been operating in a difficult market in 20Y0. It could easily have been looking at a large loss. Going forward, staff training costs will hopefully decrease. Also, market share may increase further as word of mouth spreads about improved results and service at AT Co. This may, in turn, lead to a need for less advertising and therefore lower marketing costs.

It is also apparent that AT Co has provided the student website free of charge when really, it should have been charging a fee for this. The costs of running it are too high for the service to be provided free of charge and this has had a negative impact on net operating profit.

Note: Students would not have been expected to write all this in the time available.

Workings (Note: All workings are in $000)

(1)   Turnover

Decrease in turnover = $72,025 – $66,028/$72,025 = 8.3%.

Expected 20Y0 turnover given 20% decline in market = $72,025 × 80% = $57,620 Actual 20Y0 turnover CF expected = $66,028 – $57,620/$57,620 = 14.6% higher.

(2)   Cost of sales

Decrease in cost of sales = $42,056 – $52,078/$52,078 = 19.2%.

Cost of sales as percentage of turnover: 20X9 = $52,078/$72,025 = 72.3% 20Y0 = $42,056/$66,028 = 63.7%.

Freelance staff costs: in 20X9 = $41,663 × 35% = $14,582 Expected cost for 20Y0 = $14,582 × 90% = $13,124 Actual 20Y0 cost = $12,394.

$12,394 – $14,582 = $2,188 decrease $2,188/$14,582 = 15% decrease in freelancer costs.

Expected cost of sales for 20Y0, before costs cuts, = $66,028 × 72.3% = $47,738.

Actual cost of sales = $42,056.

Difference = $5,682, of which $2,188 relates to freelancer savings and $3,494 relates to other savings.

(3)   Gross profit margin

20X9: $19,947/$72,025 = 27.7%

20Y0: $23,972/$66,028 = 36.3%

(4)   Increase in marketing costs = $4,678 – $3,291/$3,291 = 42.1%

(5)   Increase in staff training costs = $3,396 – $1,287/$1,287 = 163.9%

(6)   Decrease in enrolment costs = $960 – 5,032/5,032 = 80.9%

(7)   Net operating profit

Decreased from $3,635 to $2,106. This is fall of 1,529/3,635 = 42.1%

Marking scheme	
	Marks
Turnover	
8.3% decrease	0.5
Actual t/o 14.6% higher	0.5
Performed well CF market conditions	1
Transfer of students	1
Max. turnover	**3**
Cost of sales	
19.2% decrease	0.5
63.7% of turnover	0.5
15% fee reduction from freelance staff	2
Other costs of sale fell by $3.555m	2
Online marking did not save as much as planned	1
Max. COS	**5**
Gross profit – numbers and comment	1
Indirect expenses:	
Marketing costs	
42.1% increase	0.5
Increase necessary to reap benefits of developments	1
Benefits may take more than one year to be felt	0.5
Property costs – stayed the same	0.5
Staff training	
163.9% increase	0.5
Necessary for staff retention	1
Necessary to train staff on new website etc.	1
Without training, staff would have left	1
Less student complaints	1
Interactive website and student helpline	
Attracted new students	1
Increase in pass rate	1
Enrolment costs	
Fall of 80.9%	0.5
Result of electronic system being introduced	1
Reduced number of late enrolments	1
Max. Indirect expenses	**9**
Net operating profit	
Fallen to $2.106	0.5
Difficult market	1
Staff training costs should decrease in future	1
Future increase in market share	1
Lower advertising cost in future	1
Charge for website	1
Max. net operating profit	**3**
Total	**20**

323 CIM (DECEMBER 2015)

(a)   (i)   **Division F**

Controllable profit = $2,645k.

Total assets less trade payables = $9,760k + $2,480k – $2,960k = $9,280k.

ROI = 28.5%.

Division N

Controllable profit = $1,970k.

Total assets less trade payables = $14,980k + $3,260k – $1,400k = $16,840k.

ROI = 11.7%.

In both calculations controllable profit has been used to reflect profit, rather than net profit. This is because the managers do not have any control over the Head Office costs and responsibility accounting deems that managers should only be held responsible for costs which they control. The same principle is being applied in the choice of assets figures being used. The current assets and current liabilities figures have been taken into account in the calculation because of the fact that the managers have full control over both of these.

(ii)   **Bonus**

Bonus to be paid for each percentage point = $120,000 × 2% = $2,400.

Maximum bonus = $120,000 × 0.3 = $36,000.

Division F: ROI = 28.5% = 18 whole percentage points above minimum ROI of 10%.

18 × $2,400 = $43,200.

Therefore manager will be paid the maximum bonus of $36,000.

Division N: ROI = 11.7% = 1 whole percentage point above minimum.

Therefore bonus = $2,400.

(b)   **Discussion**

The manager of Division N will be paid a far smaller bonus than the manager of Division F. This is because of the large asset base on which the ROI figure has been calculated. Total assets of Division N are almost double the total assets of Division F. This is largely attributable to the fact that Division N invested $6.8m in new equipment during the year. If this investment had not been made, net assets would have been only $10.04m and the ROI for Division N would have been 19.62%. This would have led to the payment of a $21,600 bonus (9 × $2,400) rather than the $2,400 bonus. Consequently, Division N's manager is being penalised for making decisions which are in the best interests of their division. It is very surprising that they did decide to invest, given that they knew that they would receive a lower bonus as a result. they have acted totally in the best interests of the company. Division F's manager, on the other hand, has benefitted from the fact that they have made no investment even though it is badly needed. This is an example of sub-optimal decision making.

Division F's trade payables figure is much higher than Division N's. This also plays a part in reducing the net assets figure on which the ROI has been based. Division F's trade payables are over double those of Division N. In part, one would expect this because sales are over 50% higher (no purchases figure is given). However, it is clear that it is also because of low cash levels at Division F. The fact that the manager of Division F is then being rewarded for this, even though relationships with suppliers may be adversely affected, is again an example of sub-optimal decision making.

If the controllable profit margin is calculated, it is 18.24% for Division F and 22.64% for Division N. Therefore, if capital employed is ignored, it can be seen that Division N is performing better. ROI is simply making the division's performance look worse because of its investment in assets. Division N's manager is likely to feel extremely demotivated by their comparatively small bonus and, in the future, they may choose to postpone investment in order to increase their bonus. Managers not investing in new equipment and technology will mean that the company will not keep up with industry changes and affect its overall future competitiveness.

To summarise, the use of ROI is leading to sub-optimal decision making and a lack of goal congruence, as what is good for the managers is not good for the company and vice versa. Luckily, the manager at Division N still appears to be acting for the benefit of the company but the other manager is not. The fact that one manager is receiving a much bigger bonus than the other is totally unfair here and may lead to conflict in the long run. This is not good for the company, particularly if there comes a time when the divisions need to work together.

(c)   ROI is expressed as a percentage and is more easily understood by non-financial managers.

ROI can be used to compare performance between different sized divisions or companies.

It is not necessary to know the cost of capital in order to calculate ROI.

ROI may lead to dysfunctional decisions. For instance, if a division has a very high ROI of say, 40%, and is considering a project with an ROI of 30%, which is still well above the cost of capital of say 10%, then the project should be accepted as it provides a return well in excess of the cost of capital. The division may quite possibly reject the project, however, as when added to its existing operations it will reduce the ROI from 40%.

Using residual income as a performance measure should ensure that divisions make decisions which are in the best interests of the group as a whole and should eliminate the problem outlined in the previous paragraph.

Different divisions can use different rates to reflect different risk when calculating residual income.

Residual income is not useful for comparing divisions of different sizes.

Both residual income and ROI improve as the age of the assets increase and both provide an incentive to hang onto aged possibly inefficient machines.

Other methods of assessment that could be used in addition to ROI or RI include:

*   expected value added is similar to residual income except that, instead of using book values for profit and capital employed, the figures are adjusted to reflect the true economic value of the profit and of the capital employed

*   the Balanced Scorecard, which still looks at financial performance, perhaps using residual income or ROI, but also encompasses three other perspectives: the customer perspective, the internal business process perspective, and the learning and innovation perspective.

324 SPORTS CO (SEPTEMBER/DECEMBER 2017)

(a)   (i)

Tutorial note

In (a) (i), calculating the ROI should have been very straightforward indeed for the well prepared candidate. The areas to watch out for, or pitfalls to avoid, centred around the controllability of some of the fixed costs. The skill tested here is the ability to adjust profit calculations by discarding uncontrollable fixed costs.

Return on investment = controllable profit/average divisional net assets

Controllable profit

	C	E
	$000	$000
Net profit	1,455	3,950
Add back depreciation on non-controllable assets	49.5	138
Add back Head Office costs	620	700
Controllable profit	2,124.50	4,788

Average divisional net assets

	C	E
	$000	$000
Opening assets	13,000	24,000
Closing assets	9,000	30,000
Average assets	11,000	27,000
ROI	19.3%	17.7%

(ii)

Tutorial note

The discursive aspects of questions very often drive candidates to focus on the irrelevant or the unnecessary. In here, once the ROI difference between the divisions had been established, time should be spent establishing the impact of that difference as part of the discussion.

Other narrative marks worth harvesting centred around behavioural considerations such as how a demotivated manager would be tempted to try and manipulate figures by not investing and thereby improving ROI artificially.

Whilst Division C has exceeded the target ROI, Division E has not. If controllable profit in relation to revenue is considered, Division C's margin is 56% compared to Division E's margin of 57%, so Division E is actually performing slightly better.

However, Division E has a larger asset base than Division C too, hence the fact that Division C has a higher ROI.

Since Division E appears to be a much larger division and is involved in sports equipment manufacturing, then it could be expected to have more assets. Division E's assets have gone up partly because it made substantial additions to plant and machinery. This means that as well as increasing the average assets figure, the additions will have been depreciated during the year, thus leading to lower profits. This may potentially have had a large impact on profits since Division E uses the reducing balance method of depreciation, meaning that more depreciation is charged in the early years.

Based on the ROI results, the manager of Division C will get a bonus and the manager of Division E will not. This will have a negative impact on the motivation level of the manager of Division E and may discourage them from making future investments, unless a change in the performance measure used is adopted.

(b) **(i)**

	C	E
	$000	$000
Controllable profit	2,124.50	4,788
Less: imputed charge on assets at 12%	(1,320)	(3,240)
Residual income	804.50	1,548

From the residual income results, it can clearly be seen that both divisions have performed well, with healthy RI figures of between $0.8m and $1.55m. The cost of capital of Sports Co is significantly lower than the target return on investment which the company seeks, making the residual income figure show a more positive position.

(ii)

Tutorial note

Don't simply state the pros and cons of the RI measure – explain in as much detail as necessary. A tip to candidates: the use of the word 'because' often helps to grasp the last remaining marks. For example, simply stating that 'RI reduces dysfunctional decision making' is not enough; explaining that 'RI reduces dysfunctional decision making because it uses the whole company's cost of capital, so positive RI projects for the company would also be accepted by the division' is more likely to maximise marks.

Advantages

The use of RI should encourage managers to make new investments, if the investment adds to the RI figure. A new investment can add to RI but reduce ROI and in such a situation measuring performance with RI would not result in the dysfunctional behaviour which has already been seen at Sports Co. Instead, RI will lead to decisions which are in the best interests of the company as a whole being made.

RI reduces dysfunctional decision making **because** it uses the whole company's cost of capital, so positive RI projects for the company would also be accepted by the division.

Since an imputed interest charge is deducted from profits when measuring the performance of the division, managers are made more aware of the cost of assets under their control. This is a benefit as it can discourage wasteful spending.

Alternative costs of capital can be applied to divisions and investments to account for different levels of risk. This can allow more informed decision-making.

Disadvantages

RI does not facilitate comparisons between divisions since the RI is driven by the size of divisions and their investments. This can clearly be seen in Sports Co where the RI of Division E is almost twice that of Division C, which will be related to Division E being a much larger division.

RI is also based on accounting measures of profit and capital employed which may be subject to manipulation so as, for example, to obtain a bonus payment. In this way it suffers from the same problems as ROI.

Marking scheme			
			Marks
(a)	**(i)**	Net profit	1
		Add back depreciation	1
		Add back HO costs	1
		Controllable profits	1
		Average assets	1
		ROI	1
			—
		Maximum	6
			—
	(ii)	Discussion	6
			—
(b)	**(i)**	Controllable profit	1
		Imputed interest	1
		RI	1
		Comment	1
			—
		Maximum	4
			—
	(ii)	Maximum	4
			—
Total			20
			—

325   THE PORTABLE GARAGE COMPANY (JUNE 2018)

Tutorial note

Check out this link to an excellent technical article on Transfer Pricing from the ACCA website:

https://www.accaglobal.com/my/en/student/exam-support-resources/fundamentals-exams-study-resources/f5/technical-articles/trans-pricing.html.

(a)   Profit statement for current position:

	Division B $000	Division A $000	PGC Co $000
Sales revenue:			
External sales (150,000 × $180/200,000 × $15)	27,000	3,000	30,000
Internal transferred sales (150,000 × $13)		1,950	
Total revenue	27,000	4,950	30,000
Variable costs:			
External material costs	6,750	1,050	7,800
Internal transferred costs	1,950		
Labour costs	5,250	1,400	6,650
Other costs of external sales		200	200
Total variable costs	13,950	2,650	14,650
Contribution	13,050	2,300	15,350
Less fixed costs	5,460	2,200	7,660
Profit	7,590	100	7,690

(b)   If Division B can buy adaptors from outside the group at $13 per unit, then the optimum position is for Division A to sell as many adaptors as possible to external customers at $15 each and then sell the remainder to Division B at a price to be agreed between them.

This would mean that Division A continues to sell Division B 150,000 adaptors but Division B then buys the remaining 30,000 adaptors from an external supplier. This is because the contribution per unit for Division A's external sales is $7 ($15 – $3 – $4 – $1). This means that for every external sale it loses, it forfeits $7 for the group. However, the incremental cost for the group of Division B buying adaptors from outside the group is only $6 ($13 external cost less the $7 cost of making them in-house). So, it makes sense for Division A to satisfy its external sales first before selling internally.

(c)   In order for Division A to supply Division B with 180,000 adaptors, it would have to reduce its external sales from 200,000 units to 170,000. This is because it only has enough spare capacity to supply Division B with 150,000 units at present after it has supplied adaptors to its external customers.

The minimum transfer price in situations where there is no spare capacity is marginal cost plus opportunity cost. In this case, contribution is lost by not selling 30,000 units to the external customers. As the marginal cost for Division A's internal sales is $7 ($4 + $3) and the contribution per unit for external sales is $7 per unit ($15 – $3 – $4 – $1), the transfer price for the additional 30,000 units would need to be $14.

ACCA marking scheme		
		Marks
(a)	External sales – A/B	1
	Internal sales – A	0.5
	External materials – A/B	1
	Internal costs – B	0.5
	Labour costs – A/B	1
	Other costs – A	1
	Fixed costs	0.5
	Profit – A/B	1
	PGC Co figures	2.5
		⎯⎯
	Maximum	**9**
		⎯⎯
(b)	External cont of $7 – A	1
	Incremental cost of $6	1
	External sales first – A	1
	150,000 from A/30,000 externally	1
	Approach	2
		⎯⎯
	Maximum	**6**
		⎯⎯
(c)	Minimum transfer price (marginal cost + opportunity cost)	1
	Opportunity cost – lost contribution $7	1
	Add marginal cost for transfer price of $14	1
	Approach	2
		⎯⎯
	Maximum	**5**
		⎯⎯
Total		**20**
		⎯⎯

326 CTD

(a) The current transfer price is ($40 + $20)) × 1.1 = $66.

		FD		TM	
		$000	$000	$000	$000
Internal sales	15,000 × $66		990		
External sales	5,000 × $80		400		
	15,000 × $500				7,500
			1,390		7,500
Production – variable costs	20,000 × $40	(800)			
	15,000 × $366			(5,490)	
Selling/distribution – variable costs	5,000 × $4	(20)			
	15,000 × $25			(375)	
			(820)		(5,865)
			570		1,635
Production overheads	20,000 × $20	(400)			
	15,000 × $60			(900)	
Administration overheads	20,000 × $4	(80)			
	15,000 × $25			(375)	
Net profit			90		360
Interest charge	$750,000\$1,500,000 × 12%		(90)		(180)
Residual income (RI)			0		180
Target RI			85		105
Bonus	$180,000 × 5%		0		9

Implications of the current reward system

While the TM manager has received a bonus and presumably will be pleased about it, the FD manager has received nothing. This will not be very motivating and may lead to problems within the division as a whole, such as inefficiency, staff turnover and unreliability. Since the TM division relies so completely on the FD division, this situation is clearly unacceptable.

Key answer tips

The calculations involved in this question are very straightforward, but don't be deceived – the real thrust of this question is to make sure that you both understand the principles of different transfer pricing methods, and can apply them to a situation.

(b) **(i)** In order to achieve a 5% bonus, the manager of TM division will be willing to accept a decrease in residual income of $(180,000 – 105,000) = $75,000. This is an increase in transfer price of the 15,000 units transferred of $75,000/15,000 = $5. Thus the transfer price would rise to $66 + $5 = $71.

(ii) In order to achieve a 5% bonus, the manager of FD division will want an increase in residual income of $85,000. This is an increase in transfer price of the 15,000 units transferred of $85,000/15,000 = $5.67. Thus the transfer price would have to rise to $66 + $5.67 = $71.67.

327 ROTECH (JUNE 2014)

(a) **Ratios**

(i) **ROCE = operating profit/capital employed × 100%**

		$000	ROCE
W Co	Design Division	6,000/23,540	25.49%
	Gearbox division	3,875/32,320	11.99%
C Co		7,010/82,975	8.45%

(ii) **Asset turnover = sales/capital employed × 100%**

		$000	Asset turnover
W Co	Design Division	14,300/23,540	0.61
	Gearbox division	25,535/32,320	0.79
C Co		15,560/82,975	0.19

(iii) **Operating profit margin = operating profit/sales × 100%**

		$000	Operating profit
W Co	Design Division	6,000/14,300	41.96%
	Gearbox division	3,875/25,535	15.18%
C Co		7,010/15,560	45.05%

Both companies and both divisions within W Co are clearly profitable. In terms of what the different ratios tell us, ROCE tells us the return which a company is making from its capital.

The Design division of W Co is making the highest return at over 25%, more than twice that of the Gearbox division and nearly three times that of C Co. This is because the nature of a design business is such that profits are largely derived from the people making the designs rather than from the assets. Certain assets will obviously be necessary in order to produce the designs but it is the employees who are mostly responsible for generating profit.

The Gearbox division and C Co's ROCE are fairly similar compared to the Design division, although when comparing the two in isolation, the Gearbox division's ROCE is actually over three percentage points higher than C Co's (11.99% compared to 8.45%).

This is because C Co has a substantially larger asset base than the Gearbox division. From the asset turnover ratio, it can be seen that the Gearbox division's assets generate a very high proportion of sales per $ of assets (79%) compared to C Co (19%).

This is partly because the Gearbox division buys its components in from C Co and therefore does not need to have the large asset base which C Co has in order to make the components. When the unit profitability of those sales is considered by looking at the operating profit margin, C Co's unit profitability is much higher than the Gearbox division (45% operating profit margin as compared to 15%).

The Design division, like the Gearbox division, is also using its assets well to generate sales (asset turnover of 61%) but then, like C Co, its unit profitability is high too (42% operating profit margin.) This is why, when the two ratios (operating profit margin and asset turnover) are combined to make ROCE, the Design division comes out top overall – because it has both high unit profitability and generates sales at a high level compared to its asset base.

It should be noted that any comparisons between such different types of business are of limited use. It would be more useful to have prior year figures for comparison and/or industry averages for similar businesses. This would make performance review much more meaningful.

(b) Transfer prices

From C Co's perspective

C Co transfers components to the Gearbox division at the same price as it sells components to the external market. However, if C Co were not making internal sales then, given that it already satisfies 60% of external demand, it would not be able to sell all of its current production to the external market.

External sales are $8,010,000, therefore unsatisfied external demand is ([$8,010,000/0.6] – $8,010,000) = $5,340,000. From C Co's perspective, of the current internal sales of $7,550,000, $5,340,000 could be sold externally if they were not sold to the Gearbox division.

Therefore, in order for C Co not to be any worse off from selling internally, these sales should be made at the current price of $5,340,000, less any reduction in costs which C Co saves from not having to sell outside the group (perhaps lower administrative and distribution costs). As regards the remaining internal sales of $2,210,000 ($7,550,000 – $5,340,000), C Co effectively has spare capacity to meet these sales.

Therefore, the minimum transfer price should be the marginal cost of producing these goods. Given that variable costs represent 40% of revenue, this means that the marginal cost for these sales is $884,000. This is therefore the minimum price which C Co should charge for these sales. In total, therefore, C Co will want to charge at least $6,224,000 for its sales to the Gearbox division.

From the Gearbox division's perspective

The Gearbox division will not want to pay more for the components than it could purchase them for externally. Given that it can purchase them all for 95% of the current price, this means a maximum purchase price of $7,172,500.

Overall

Taking into account all of the above, the transfer price for the sales should be somewhere between $6,224,000 and $7,172,500.

328 DIVISION A

Key answer tips

This is a demanding question linking transfer prices to performance targets. As with all transfer pricing questions the key aspects of discussion are linking transfer prices to managerial performance.

(a) **(i)** Profit required by division A to meet RI target:

	$
Cost of capital $3.2m @ 12%	384,000
Target RI	180,000
	————
Target profit	564,000
Add fixed costs	1,080,000
	————
Target contribution	1,644,000
	————
Contribution earned from external sales 90,000 @ ($35 – $22)	1,170,000
Contribution required from internal sales	474,000
Contribution per bit on internal sales ($474,000/60,000)	$7.90
Transfer price to division C $22.00 + $7.90	$29.90

(ii) The two transfer prices based on opportunity costs:

40,000 units (150,000 – 110,000) at the marginal cost of $22.00

20,000 units (110,000 – 90,000) at the external selling price of $35.00

(b) Where divisional managers are given total autonomy to purchase units at the cheapest price and where divisional performance is assessed on a measure based on profit, sub-optimal behaviour could occur i.e. divisional managers could make decisions that may not be in the overall interests of the group.

Impact of group's current transfer pricing policy

Division C's objective is to maximise its RI in order to achieve its target RI. It will therefore endeavour to find the cheapest source of supply for Bits. As C requires 60,000 Bits and X is willing to supply them at $28 each, C would prefer to buy them from X rather than division A. However this will not benefit the group, as division A will be unable to utilise its spare capacity of 40,000 Bits. The effect on the group's profit will be as follows:

	$
Additional payment by division C 60,000 Bits@ ($28 – $22)	(360,000)
Gain in contribution by Division A 20,000 Bits @ $13	260,000
	————
Net loss to group	(100,000)
	————

Impact of group's proposed transfer pricing policy

If division A were to set transfer prices based on opportunity costs the effect on its divisional profit would be as follows:

	$
Reduction in profit 40,000 Bits @ ($29.90 – $22.00)	(316,000)
Increase in profit 20,000 Bits @ ($35 – $29.90)	102,000
Net loss to division	(214,000)

Division C has the following two purchase options:

	$
Purchase from division A 40,000 Bits @ $22	880,000
Purchase from Z 20,000 Bits @ $33	660,000
Total cost of Bits	1,540,000
Or: Purchase 60,000 from X 60,000 Bits @ $28	1,680,000

As division C will opt to source the Bits from the cheapest supplier(s) it will choose to purchase 40,000 Bits from division A at $22 per Bit and the remaining 20,000 Bits from Z at $33 per Bit. This also benefits the group, as there is no opportunity cost to division A on the 40,000 units transferred to division C.

When marginal cost is used as the transfer price division C will make the correct decision and the group will maximise profits. However division A would suffer. This can be overcome by changing the way it measures the performance of its divisions – rather than using a single profit-based measure it needs to introduce a variety of quantitative and qualitative measures.

329 JUNGLE CO (SEPTEMBER 2016)

Tutorial note

The key with these questions is to identify 'cause and effect' relationships. Marks will be awarded for explaining WHY something has changed, along with how it might affect other aspects of the business. The most common mistake made by candidates was not applying the above. Most candidates were comfortable calculating percentage movement, but added no value to their calculations. Points such as "Cost of sales have decreased by 18%. This is a good performance." were common, but apart from the calculation scored no marks. Answers which looked into why cost of sales might have decreased, or what impact that might have had, scored many more marks. In this case, the decrease in cost of sales could partly be put down to a fall in revenue, but the main point is that the scenario explains how the company changed to a cheaper supplier – this would have a direct effect on their cost of sales. Even better answers would discuss how the rise in customer complaints may have been caused by the poor quality of these supplies. Another common error was to offer the business advice. The requirement clearly stated "discuss the performance," and marks could not be given for advice. It is really important to read the requirement carefully and answer the question being asked.

Sales volumes

Since prices have remained stable year on year, it can be assumed that changes to revenue are as a result of increases or decreases in sales volumes. Overall, revenue has increased by 15%, which is a substantial increase. In order to understand what has happened in the business, it is necessary to consider sales by looking at each of the different categories.

Household goods

Although this was the largest category of sales for Jungle Co last year, this year it has decreased by 5% and has now been overtaken by electronic goods. The company changed suppliers for many of its household goods during the year, buying them instead from a country where labour was cheap. It may be that this has affected the quality of the goods, thus leading to decreased demand.

Electronic goods

Unlike household goods, demand for electronic goods from Jungle Co has increased dramatically by 28%. This is now Jungle Co's leading revenue generator. This is partly due to the fact that the electronic goods market has grown by 20% worldwide. However, Jungle Co has even outperformed this, meaning that it has secured a larger segment of the market.

Cloud computing service

This area of Jungle Co's business is growing rapidly, with the company seeing a 90% increase in this revenue stream in the last year. Once again, the company has outperformed the market, where the average growth rate is only 50%, suggesting that the investment in the cloud technology was worthwhile.

Gold membership fees

This area of the business is relatively small but has shrunk further, with a decrease in revenue of 30%. This may be because customers are dissatisfied with the service that they are receiving. The number of late deliveries for Gold members has increased from 2% to 14% since Jungle Co began using its own logistics company. This has probably been at least partly responsible for the massive increase in the number of customer complaints.

Gross profit margins

Overall, the company's gross profit margin (GPM) has increased from 37% to 42%. Whilst the GPM for electronic goods has only increased by 1 percentage point, the margin for household goods has increased by 10 percentage points. This is therefore largely responsible for the increase in overall GPM. This has presumably occurred because Jungle Co is now sourcing these products from new, cheaper suppliers.

Gold membership fees constitute only a small part of Jungle Co's income, so their 2 percentage point fall in GPM has had little impact on the overall increase in GPM. Cloud computing services, on the other hand, now make up over $12m of Jungle Co's sales revenue. For some reason, the GPM on these sales has fallen from 76% to 66%. This is now 14 percentage points less than the market average gross profit margin of 80%. More information is needed to establish why this has happened. It has prevented the overall increase in GPM being higher than it otherwise would have been.

Administration expenses/customer complaints

Tutorial note

When it comes to the discussion, use the calculations to guide you to the key areas to focus on. If administrative expenses have increased by 0.2%, don't waste any time worrying about why – it's not significant.

Administration expenses have increased by 60% from $1.72m to $2.76m. This is a substantial increase. The costs of the customer service department are in here.

Given the number of late deliveries increase from 2% to 14%, and the corresponding increase in customer complaints from 5% to 20% of customers, the number of complaints has actually increased by 338% in absolute terms. Therefore, it is not surprising that the administration costs have increased. As well as being concerned about the impact on profit of this increase of over $1m, Jungle Co should be extremely worried about the effect on its reputation. Bad publicity about reliable delivery could affect future business.

Distribution costs

Despite an increase in sales volumes of 15%, distribution expenses have increased by less than 2 percentage points. They have gone down from $0.16 to $0.14 per $ of revenue. Although this means that Jungle Co has been successful in terms of saving costs, as discussed above, the damage which late deliveries are doing to the business cannot be ignored. The company needs to urgently address the issue of late deliveries.

Net profit margin

This has increased from 19% to 25%. This means that, all in all, Jungle Co has had a successful year, with net profit having increased from $15.6m to $23.8m. However, the business must address its delivery issues if its success is to continue.

Gross profit margins	31 August 20X6	31 August 20X5
Household goods	40.00%	30.00%
Electronic goods	36.00%	35.00%
Cloud computing services	65.81%	75.77%
Gold membership fees	92.86%	95.00%
Overall	42.39%	37.19%
Net profit margin	25.15%	18.95%

Increase/decrease in revenue	
Household goods	−5.27%
Electronic goods	28.28%
Cloud computing services	90.18%
Gold membership fees	−30.00%
Total revenue increase	14.99%

Increase/decrease in cost of sales

Household goods	−18.80%
Electronic goods	26.31%
Cloud computing services	168.35%
Gold membership fees	0.00%
Total cost of sales increase	5.46%

Increase in administration expenses	60.47%
Increase in distribution expenses	1.82%
Increase in other operating expenses	27.27%
Increase in costs of customer service department	120.93%
([$1,900,000 − $860,000]/$860,000)	

	31 August 20X6	31 August 20X5
Customer complaints as % customers	19.72%	4.92%
Delivery cost per $ of revenue	$0.14	$0.16

Marking scheme	
	Marks
Sales volumes (up to 2 marks per revenue stream)	8
COS and gross margins	5
Administration expenses/customer complaints	3
Distribution costs/late deliveries	2
Net profit margin	2
	—
Total	**20**
	—

330 MEDCOMP (MARCH/JUNE 2021)

(a)

FINANCIAL	**CSF:** The critical success factor identified for this perspective is most likely to be positive cash flow.
	KPI: The most appropriate performance indicator is total donations less operating costs.
	Performance Analysis: Total donations in 20X7 and 20X6 are $1 and $1 respectively and when the operating costs are deducted, the net cash flows are $55,000 and $45,000 respectively. This shows that for the current year Medcomp is not achieving a positive cash flow.
	However, this is a relatively small cash deficit for the year and does not suggest that the charity has any real problems. The size of the donations has risen considerably over the years and the number of businesses donating has fallen. This could indicate that the fundraisers have focused their efforts on a smaller number of more affluent businesses.
CUSTOMER	**CSF:** The critical success factor identified for this perspective is most likely to be medical effectiveness.
	KPI: The best performance indicator for this perspective is the percentage of successful treatments.

	Performance Analysis: For the years 20X8, 20X7 and 20X6 these are 77%, 86% and 87% respectively. As treatment for cataracts is a relatively simple procedure, a high success rate would be expected but the results in 20X8 show a significant deterioration. The reasons for the recent fall in effectiveness could be the result of factors outside the control of Medcomp, such as variations in the disease or the advanced condition of the disease when presented. However, it could be also linked to the lack of efficiency of the new treatments.
INTERNAL BUSINESS PROCESS	**CSF:** The critical success factor identified for this perspective is most likely to be functional efficiency.
	KPI: The performance indicator for this perspective could be: 'average number of days to deliver drugs and equipment to treatment centres'.
	Performance Analysis: This has remained at seven days since 20X6 and in some ways this can be expected as the 12 treatment centres have been at the same location for many years and the logistics of the delivery well established. It should be noted that this measure is an average lead time and will also vary on location. However, as Medcomp rarely experiences shortages at the treatment centres, it can be surmised that transport costs are managed as efficiently as possible and this means an average seven-day lead time.
LEARNING & GROWTH	**CSF:** The critical success factor identified for this perspective is most likely to be innovation.
	KPI: The performance indicator for this perspective is the new procedures as a percentage of total procedures from the table.
	Performance Analysis: It is clear that Medcomp has made several changes to the existing protocol in 20X8. One in five procedures administered are new and have been introduced within the past 12 months. This is a clear improvement on 20X7 and 20X6 as the CSF is for new treatments. However, the new treatments have not improved the efficiency of the treatment, as evidenced by the percentage of successful treatments, and this will need to be monitored.

(b) The benefits to an organisation of using the balanced scorecard to assess performance instead of relying solely on financial measures are as follows:

Not all organisations have profit or financial return as the main objective. In an altruistic not-for-profit charity such as Medcomp, the objectives are based on delivering a service which can be measured in benefit to people who are unable to pay for the service. Therefore, it is necessary to have measures which are not purely financial to reflect the different emphasis of the mission and supporting objectives.

Financial performance indicators are 'lagging' indicators. This means that the events and decisions which caused these indicators occurred long ago. The balanced scorecard includes 'leading' indicators. For example, the learning and growth perspective may encourage spending on training or techniques which will depress profits or increase costs in the short term, but will have much greater benefits in the future.

The balanced scorecard helps to align key performance measures with strategy at all levels. This means that all employees will be able to link their individual goals to those of the organisation as a whole. The benefit of this is that it ensures that what gets measured is important to the organisation.

Financial measures used in isolation are relatively easy to manipulate in the short term. For example, a high return on investment figure may be considered an indicator of good performance whereas it may have been caused by a manager delaying the purchase of a necessary asset. The balanced scorecard provided a range of indicators which makes this type of manipulation more difficult to conceal.

ACCA Marking scheme		
		Marks
(a)	Identification of CSF for each perspective (0·5 each)	2
	Identification of KPI for each perspective (1 each)	4
	Analysis of performance using the KPIs (max 4 for any perspective)	10
		___
		16
		___
(b)	Benefits of balanced scorecard – up to 2 for each well discussed point	4
Total		**20**

331 HAMMOCK CO (MARCH/JULY 2020 SAMPLE EXAM)

(a) To make a profit long-term

In order to make a profit the long term revenues need to be higher than the long term costs.

The weekly revenue per guest is $2,000 in the 20X7 budget, the 20X7 actual results and the 20X6 actual results which is not in line with inflation. This means that revenues per guest are falling in real terms.

However, all staff costs have increased by 2% which is caused by inflation.

Overall this means that the profit per guest, based on the limited figures available is falling.

The repair costs, allowing for inflation have been set at the same level as 20X6. The actual for 20X7 appears to be better than budget, but as repairs are likely to be incurred on an ad hoc basis, this does not necessarily indicate an improvement. The 20X6 repair costs are higher than the competitor's but it is difficult to compare because Hammocks Co have more rooms so we are not comparing like with like. On a repair per room basis Hammocks has slightly lower cost at $163 per room compared to the competition's $164 per room.

Due to the secure long-term contracts which Hammocks Co offers its staff, staff costs are fixed costs in the management accounts. This means that in order to be profitable, these costs need to be covered by the contribution per guest. Although there is not the data to calculate the contribution per guest per week, the higher level of guest occupancy level in 20X7 (both budgeted and actual) is a positive indication. Hammocks' occupancy level per room was 81% compared to the competitor's 77% (all based on double occupancy) indicating that performance is good.

To create customer loyalty

There are a number of indicators to show that Hammocks Co have created a loyal customer base.

Firstly, compared to their main competitor Hammocks Co receive more revenue, charge a higher price per guest per week and have better occupancy rates. This indicates good customer satisfaction.

Secondly the ratio of staff to guest is higher than the competition; 1.5 compared to 1.3 in 20X6 (actual in 20X7 is slightly higher due to a lower occupancy rate than budgeted and the fact that staff numbers are fixed). As this is a seasonal business this is may simply be a blip.

Finally, the comments on TripEvent are very positive about the level of service and standard of cleanliness and maintenance. However it should be noted that the entire customer experience is not positive. Complaints like the administrative errors and unchanging menus could be a warning sign of possible erosion of customer loyalty.

(b) (i) A balanced scorecard approach to performance management is important to Hammocks Co because it will provide management with a set of information which covers all relevant areas of business performance. At present Hammocks Co considers performance from a financial and customer perspective. These perspectives are important but they do not allow a wide enough consideration of all of the factors that should be considered in this business.

Introducing the balanced scorecard will:

- Ensure that all internal systems and processes support the customer and financial objectives. For example, in decision-making there is little point in buying a new IT system that does not either improve customer experience or reduce processing costs.

- Encourage full integration between all departments. Errors in invoicing or sending specific requirements are system or internal process errors. While a customer might not choose a holiday resort for its excellent administration, they may refuse to use a company again if they receive poor service. Thus neglecting one aspect of the scorecard can impact on customer satisfaction and longer term financial performance.

- Make sure important elements are assessed and expected performance levels quantified and/or qualified. This this means that performance can be measured, explained, compared and where necessary, control action can be taken. The errors that occur at Hammocks Co are spoiling the company's reputation, but there is no evidence that any action is being taken.

(Note: Only TWO were required)

(ii) **Internal business process**

Goal: To have an effective and efficient administration.

The feedback on TripEvent indicates that the only guest complaints relate to administrative issues prior to the guest arrival and not operational issues at the resort. In fact the actions of the resort staff with the speedy resolution of bedding issues and the organising of a complimentary transfer seems to have diverted trouble. Therefore measures need to be focused on the weaker area which is the administration.

Measures:

1   Number of times that a guest request is not received at resort prior to their arrival/number of requests made.

     This will measure the number of times the guest experience is not seamless from booking to arrival.

2   Average number of corrections to booking due to an administrative error.

     This measures inefficient use of staff time and potentially increased customer frustration.

Innovation and Learning

Goal: To match leading competitor's facilities

The comment on TripEvent shows that even loyal customers are noticing that rivals are including more innovative facilities at their resorts. Although the true strength of Hammocks Co lies in the quality of the service it is important that the facilities' appliances and service offerings are updated to compare favourably with that of its rivals.

Measures:

1   Number of in-room appliances offered by rivals but not by Hammocks Co.

     The measure will ensure that Hammocks Co consider what is included within the guest rooms by comparing to external factors.

2   Number of new items offered on the menu each month.

     This should ensure that the chefs consider the latest trends in fine dining and do not ever appear stagnant from the point of view of the customer.

ACCA Marking scheme			
			Marks
(a)	Discuss the performance of Hammocks		8
(b)	(i)	Two advantages of using the Balanced Scorecard	3
	(ii)	One goal, two performance measures for:	
		– Internal business processes	4.5
		– Innovation and growth	4.5
Total			20

332   THE PEOPLE'S BANK (MARCH/JUNE 2017)

(a)

Tutorial note

Part (a) asks why the balanced scorecard would be more useful to the People's Bank than using solely financial performance measures. Although there are only four marks available, it highlights some candidates' weakness in not being able to use the information in the scenario to help them answer the question.

It is easy to identify the generic point that the balanced scorecard gives a more rounded view by looking at a wider range of performance measures (financial and non-financial) as well as internal and external factors. However, the scenario gives us more help and shows us how important these non-financial factors are to the bank – the 3 values given highlight this. If their performance was assessed purely on profit they would never strive to meet those values, or looking at it another way they might be judged to have failed by spending money on improving customer accessibility or simplifying their processes.

The balanced scorecard approach looks not only at the financial performance but also non-financial performance. In order to maintain a competitive edge, organisations have to be very aware of the changing needs of their customers.

In the case of The People's Bank, this has involved identifying specific categories of customers which have particular needs, like SMEs in a commercial context, or like the disabled or visually impaired in a non-commercial context. This permits these needs to be addressed. The People's Bank has a vision and strategy which goes far beyond just making money. They want to help the community and disadvantaged people and give something back to customers also. Hence, by using the balanced scorecard, performance measures which address whether the Bank is being successful in pursuing their vision can be incorporated.

In addition, from a purely business perspective, if employees and customers are valued and internal processes are efficient, an organisation should have more chance of achieving long-term success anyway. So, even putting aside the social objectives The People's Bank has, the balanced scorecard can be useful to The People's Bank to measure these other aspects of future success too.

(b)

Tutorial note

Part (b) was a more traditional performance assessment question. Exam technique was crucial here. The note in the requirement says to use each of the four headings of the balanced scorecard to structure your answer. Ignoring this makes it much harder to score well on this question, as it would be harder to see how their points corresponded to the perspectives of the balanced scorecard. Use the headings suggested (which were given in the scenario). Similarly, the requirement specifically asked candidates to use the bank's vision and values to assess performance. Therefore, a sensible approach would be to take each perspective, use the performance measures given and details in the scenario to see how they link to the bank's vision and values.

The performance of the bank will be considered under each of the headings used in the balanced scorecard:

Financial perspective

The People's Bank has had a year of mixed success when looking at the extent to which it has met its financial targets. Its return on capital employed (ROCE) shows how efficiently it has used its assets to generate profit for the business. The target for the year was 12% but it has only achieved an 11% return. The People's Bank's interest income, however, was in fact $0.5m higher than its target, which is good. This may have been achieved by offering slightly better interest rates to customers than competing banks, as the interest margin The People's Bank achieved is slightly lower than target. The most likely reason for the under target ROCE is therefore probably the investment which The People's Bank has made in IT security and facilities for the disabled and visually impaired. Whilst this may have reduced ROCE, this investment is essentially a good idea as it helps The People's Bank pursue its vision and will keep customers happy. It will also, in the case of the IT security investment, prevent the bank and its customers from losing money from fraud in the future.

The other performance measure, the amount of new lending to SMEs, is a little bit disappointing, given The People's Bank's stated value of making a difference to communities. The failure to meet this target may well be linked to the fact that an insufficient number of staff were trained to provide advice to SMEs and consequently, fewer of them may have been successful in securing additional finance.

Tutorial note

The other key skill in these questions is to identify linkages between measures – cause and effect relationships. For example on the Financial perspective we can see that new lending to SMEs was significantly (10%) down on target. The first point you should make is that this is not in line with the bank's third value – to support SMEs. This alone will be given credit, and similar points should be made for each heading, however even more credit can be given if you go on to say that the drop in new lending to SMEs is due to the fact that fewer colleagues have been trained to provide advice to SMEs under learning and growth.

Customer perspective

With regard to its customers, The People's Bank has performed well in the year. It has exceeded its target to provide mortgages to new homeowners by 6,000. This is helping The People's Bank pursue its vision of helping new homeowners. It has also managed to beat the target for customer complaints such that there are only 1.5 complaints for every 1,000 customers, well below the target of 2. This may be as a result of improved processes at the bank or improved security. It is not clear what the precise reason is but it is definitely good for The People's Bank's reputation.

The bank has also exceeded both of its targets to help the disabled and visually impaired, which is good for its reputation and its stated value of making services more accessible.

Internal processes

The number of processes simplified within the bank has exceeded the target, which is good, and the success of which may well be reflected in the lower customer complaints levels. Similarly, the investment to improve IT systems has been a success, with only three incidences of fraud per 1,000 customers compared to the target of 10. However, perhaps because of the focus on this part of the business, only two new services have been made available via mobile banking, instead of the target of five, which is disappointing. Similarly, it is possible that some of the new systems have prevented the business from keeping its CO_2 emissions to their target level.

Learning and growth

The People's Bank has succeeded in helping the community, exceeding both of its targets relating to hours of paid volunteer work and number of community organisations supported by volunteers or funding. These additional costs could have contributed to the fact that the bank did not quite meet its target for ROCE. However, the bank has not quite met its targets for helping small businesses and helping the disadvantaged.

As mentioned earlier, the shortfall in training of employees to give advice to SMEs may have had an impact on The People's Bank's failure to meet its target lending to SMEs. As regards the percentage of trainee positions, the target was only just missed and this may well have been because the number of candidates applying from these areas was not as high as planned and the bank has no control over this.

Tutorial note

Finally, a long discussion question like this should finish with a brief, overall conclusion. This should be in line with your findings – sometimes it will be very clear that performance has been good or bad, otherwise you might have to say something like "with the exception of the financial perspective, The People's Bank has performed well in meeting its vision."

Overall, the bank has had a fairly successful year, meeting many of its targets. However, it still has some work to do in order to meet its stated values and continue to pursue its vision.

333 OSC CO (SEPTEMBER 2018)

(a) Competitiveness

	MSC	OSC Average
Percentage of website hits converted into orders		
(9,506/14,000) × 100	67.9%	
(11,870/18,260) × 100		65%

This ratio indicates whether MSC's services are attractive compared to its competitors, which is important if it is going to survive in such a competitive market.

It has performed substantially better than other OSC service centres on average, having converted 67.9% of website hits into jobs, compared to the 65% converted by other service centres. This is a good result.

Financial performance

	MSC	OSC Average
Gross profit margin		
($304,200/$760,500) × 100	40%	
($328,146/$890,365) × 100		36.9%

Gross profit margin is the preferred measure for financial performance from the data presented. It shows the percentage of revenue which exceeds the cost of goods sold.

MSC's gross profit margin is almost 3 percentage points higher than the average, which is a good result. This could be partly because they did relatively well on their new service pack sales (note 4) but it is also likely to be because their ratio of senior mechanics to junior mechanics is lower than the average, and junior mechanics will invariably be paid less than senior ones.

Quality of service

	MSC	OSC Average
Percentage of jobs from repeat customers		
(1,500/9,506) × 100	15.78%	
(1,660/11,870) × 100		13.98%

Quality is a key element of MSC's service to customers and if it is poor, customers will not return.

Again, MSC has outperformed the other service centres on average by 1.8 percentage points. This could be because it has a higher ratio of senior mechanics to junior mechanics than other service centres, so the quality of work is probably better, hence the higher level of repeat customers.

Flexibility

	MSC	OSC Average
Time taken per job		
(23,100/9,506)	2.43 hours	
(24,800/11,870)		2.09 hours

The time taken to complete each job is important as many customers will use MSC because they can sit and wait for the work to be done, rather than having to hire a rental car for the day, for example.

The comparison shows that MSC takes longer to complete a job than the OSC average. This is not really a good thing and is probably because they have slightly less experienced staff on the whole, but it could also be that they do a more thorough job than other service centres. Given the fact that they have a higher level of return customers than the average and they are graded 9 or 10 by their customers (10 percentage points higher than the average), this is presumably not viewed negatively by customers.

Resource utilisation

	MSC	OSC Average
Sales per mechanic		
$760,500/12	$63,375	
$890,365/13		$68,490

The key resource in a service company is its staff and so these indicators measure how this resource is being utilised.

MSC's utilisation of its staff is lower than that of the other service centres by $5,115 per mechanic. This clearly ties in with the fact that the average time to complete a job is longer at MSC than other service centres. However, given that they use a slightly less experienced staff on average than other centres and the fact that their gross margin is higher than average, this should not be viewed too negatively.

Innovation

	MSC	OSC Average
Percentage revenue generated from new service packs		
[($66,000 + $58,000 + $54,000)/$760,500]	23.4%	
[($44,000 + $42,000)/$890,365]		9.66%

MSC wants to offer a wide variety of service packs to its customers and needs to be innovative in packaging services up.

The 23.4% indicates that MSC is indeed innovative in their approach to their customers' needs, offering an innovative mix of services. MSC has really outperformed other service centres on this front, generating a far larger part of its revenue by the introduction of new service packs, which must have attracted customers. This is a really strong performance.

(b) The standards block sets the target for the performance indicators chosen for each of the dimensions. The targets must meet three criteria – they must be achievable, fair and encourage employees to take ownership. If the targets set do not meet these criteria, then the performance of the organisation could suffer.

The rewards block ensures that employees are motivated to achieve the standards. It also considers the properties of good reward schemes which are that they should be clear, motivating and based on controllable factors.

If standards and rewards are set appropriately, the staff will be engaged and motivated and it is then more likely that the goals, i.e. dimensions, of the organisation will be achieved.

ACCA Marking scheme		*Marks*
(a)	Calculations	6
	Justification of PI	3
	Discussion of performance under the dimensions	7
(b)	Explanation	4

Total		**20**

334 PUBLIC SECTOR ORGANISATION

Budget preparation

It would be in line with the principles of modern management if the department manager was encouraged to participate more in setting the budget. In this way, they would be more likely to show commitment to the organisational goals in general and the budget in particular. They are closer to the activity for which the budget is prepared, and so the relevance and accuracy of the budget should be improved. This involvement should extend also to discussion of the form and frequency of the reporting which is to take place for their department.

Activity volume

Overall actual costs ($19,795) have exceeded budgeted costs ($15,400) by $4,395, which is 28.5% higher than budget. On the face of it, this seems like a poor performance against budget. However, there are some important considerations to consider in relation to the number of visits.

The volume of visits undertaken is 20% greater than that budgeted. It is inappropriate to compare the actual costs of visiting 12,000 clients with a budget for 10,000 clients. Costs such as wages, travel expenses and consumables are likely to be variable, or have a variable element, and so would be expected to be higher than the fixed budget in these circumstances.

One way to deal with this is to adjust, or flex, the budget to acknowledge the cost implications of the higher number of visits, or to be aware of it when making any comparison. If a factor of 1.20 is applied to the overall wages budget for permanent and casual staff (i.e. on the assumption that it is a variable cost), the flexed budget $5,040 [($2,700 + 1,500) × 1.2] is greater than the actual cost of ($2,400 + $2,500) = $4,900. Taking a similar approach to travel expenses and consumables expenses:

- actual travel expenses are exactly in line with the flexed budget (1,500 × 1.20) = $1,800, but

- the consumables costs of $6,000 seem to be highly overspent compared to the flexed budget (4,000 × 1.2) = $4,800

To circulate a report as originally constructed seems to highlight and publicise some invalid comparisons from which inappropriate conclusions may be drawn. It is recommended that for cost control purposes, a report is prepared which compares actual spending with a flexed budget based on the actual activity. This would require an estimate of the variable, fixed and semi-variable nature of the cost items.

Controllability

It is possible to question whether all the costs shown need to feature in the report. For example, the allocated administrative costs and equipment depreciation are book entries that do not directly affect the department and are not likely to be controllable by employees of the department. There are, therefore, adverse variances on the report contributing to the overall overspend that are not the responsibility of the departmental manager. Allocated administrative costs are 50% higher than budget and account for ($1,000 ÷ $4,395) = 22.7% of the overspend (based on the fixed budget). The difference between actual and budgeted cost of administration serves no useful purpose in this report, because the manager can take no action to influence this directly. The only justification to include this is if the manager can bring about some pressure to reduce this spending by someone else.

It may be unwise to adopt the guide of a 5% deviation to judge variances. The key is whether a cost is out of control and can be corrected by managerial action. Also, 5% of some values can be significant whilst on others 5% of the total cost might be of little consequence.

Funding allocation

The Director is correct in pointing out that 'the department must live within its funding allocation'. However, it is not like a commercial organisation where more output can result in more revenue and hence more money to spend. Increased funding will only be achieved if this organisation and the department is allocated more funds as a result of national or local government decisions to support an increase in services.

It would be appropriate for the funding allocation to be compared with the flexible budget (based on actual activity) to encourage the managers to be aware of and live within the budget allocation. Ways can always be found to spend more money, and so authority structures must be in place to ensure that requests to spend have been budgeted and appropriately funded. Hence the organisational arrangements which authorised the increased visits would be examined.

The nature of the activity for which the budget is being developed should not be lost sight of. It is more complex to deal with budget decisions related to the welfare needs of society than those for a typical manufacturing firm. There are no clear input-output relationships in the former, and hence it is difficult to judge what is justifiable spending for the department compared with other departments and public sector organisations.

Social and other aspects

One possible outcome from discussion over the appropriate form of report would be the use of non-financial measures. The total staff hours worked, client satisfaction and size of the potential client population are all examples of extensions to the reporting procedure which would help to place the results in context.

The style of the approach adopted by the Director may show some lack of behavioural insight. The despatch of a memo to deal with a prototype report may result in lower staff morale and increased tension in the Homecare department. This may lead to inappropriate future decisions on spending and budget 'game playing' within the department. It may, of course, be a conscious decision of the Director to place the manager in the position of having to reduce spending to the allocated level.

Although this is the first month's report, in the future it may be helpful to use an additional column of the report to show the year-to-date figures. This would help to identify trends and assist discussion of whether costs are being controlled over the longer term. To show future results for only one month may be insufficient; for example, the repairs to equipment may not follow a regular pattern and this would be revealed if cumulative data existed.

335 WOODSIDE CHARITY (JUNE 2007)

(a) **Discussion of performance of Woodside Charity**

In a year which saw fundraising fall $80,000 short of the target level, costs were over budget in all areas of activity except overnight shelter provision. The budget provided for a surplus of $98,750, but the actual figures for the year show a shortfall of $16,980.

Free meals provision cost $12,750 (14%) more than budgeted. Most of the variance (69%) was due to providing 1,750 more meals than budgeted, although $4,000 of it was due to an increase of 20p in the average cost per meal.

Variable cost of overnight shelter provision was $26,620 (11%) less than budgeted. $31,000 was saved because usage of the service was 1,240 bed-nights below budget, but an adverse variance of $4,380 arose because of an increase of 50p in the average unit cost of provision.

Variable advice centre costs were $16,600 (37%) above budget. This was due to increased usage of the service, which was 17% up on budget from 3,000 to 3,500 sessions, and to an increase in the average cost of provision, which rose by 17% from $15 to $17.60 per session.

Fixed costs of administration and centre maintenance were $18,000 (28%) above budget and the costs of campaigning and advertising were $15,000 (10%) above budget.

While investigation of some of the variances in the reconciliation statement below may be useful in controlling further cost increases, the Woodside charity appears to have more than achieved its objectives in terms of providing free meals and advice. The lower usage of overnight shelter could lead to transfer of resources from this area in the next budget to the services that are more in demand. The reasons for the lower usage of overnight shelter are not known, but the relationship between the provision of effective advice and the usage of overnight shelter could be investigated.

Operating statement

	$	$	$
Budgeted surplus (W1)			98,750
Funding shortfall (W3)			(80,000)
			18,750
	Favourable	**Adverse**	
Free meals (W4)			
Price variance		4,000	
Usage variance		8,750	
Overnight shelter (W5)			
Price variance		4,380	
Usage variance	31,000		
Advice centre (W6)			
Price variance		9,100	
Usage variance		7,500	
Campaigning and advertising (W7)			
Expenditure variance		15,000	
Fixed cost (W8)			
Expenditure variance		18,000	
	31,000	66,730	(35,730)
Actual shortfall (W2)			(16,980)

Workings

(W1) Budgeted figures

	$	
Free meals provision	91,250	(18,250 meals at $5 per meal)
Overnight shelter (variable)	250,000	(10,000 bed-nights at $30 – $5 per night)
Advice centre (variable)	45,000	(3,000 sessions at $20 – $5 per session)
Fixed costs	65,000	(10,000 × $5) + (3,000 × $5)
Campaigning and advertising	150,000	
	601,250	
Surplus for unexpected costs	98,750	
Fundraising target	700,000	

(W2) Actual figures

	$	
Free meals provision	104,000	(20,000 meals at $5.20 per meal)
Overnight shelter	223,380	(8,760 bed-nights $25.50 per night)
Advice centre	61,600	(3,500 sessions at $17.60 per session)
Fixed costs	83,000	
Campaigning and advertising	165,000	
	636,980	
Shortfall	16,980	
Funds raised	620,000	

(W3) Funding shortfall – 700,000 – 620,000 = $80,000 (A)

(W4) Free meals price variance = (5.00 – 5.20) × 20,000 = $4,000 (A)

Free meals usage variance = (18,250 – 20,000) × 5.00 = $8,750 (A)

(W5) Overnight shelter price variance = (25.00 – 25.50) × 8,760 = $4,380 (A)

Overnight shelter usage variance – (10,000 – 8,760) × 25 = $31,000 (F)

(W6) Advice centre price variance = (17.60 – 15.00) × 3,500 = $9,100 (A)

Advice centre usage variance = (3,000 – 3,500) × 15.00 = $7,500 (A)

(W7) Campaigning and advertising expenditure variance = 150,000 – 165,000 = $15,000 (A)

(W8) Fixed cost expenditure variance = 65,000 – 83,000 = $18,000 (A)

(b) Financial management and control in a not-for-profit organisation (NFPO) such as the Woodside charity must recognise that the primary objectives of these organisations are essentially non-financial. Here, these objectives relate to helping the homeless and because the charity has no profit-related objective, financial management and control must focus on providing value for money. This means that resources must be found economically in order to keep input costs as low as possible; that these resources must be used as efficiently as possible in providing the services offered by the charity; and that the charity must devise and use effective methods to meet its objectives. Financial objectives could relate to the need to obtain funding for offered services and to the need to control costs in providing these services.

Preparing budgets

The nature of the activities of a NFPO can make it difficult to forecast levels of activity. In the case of the Woodside charity, homeless people seeking free meals would be given them, and more food would be prepared if necessary, regardless of the budgeted provision for a given week or month. The level of activity is driven here by the needs of the homeless, and although financial planning may produce weekly or monthly budgets that consider seasonal trends, a high degree of flexibility may be needed to respond to unpredictable demand. This was recognised by the charity by budgeting for a fundraising surplus for unexpected costs.

It is likely that forecasting cost per unit of service in a NFPO can be done with more precision if the unit of service is small and the service is repetitive or routine, and this is true for the Woodside charity. It is unlikely, though, that a detailed analysis of costs has been carried out along these lines, and more likely that an incremental budget approach has been used on a total basis for each service provided. It depends on the financial skills and knowledge available to the charity from its three full-time staff and team of volunteers.

Controlling costs

Because of the need for economy and efficiency, this is a key area of financial management and control for a NFPO. The costs of some inputs can be minimised at the point of buying, for example the Woodside charity can be economical when buying food, drink, crockery, blankets, cleaning materials and so on. The costs of other inputs can be minimised at the point of use, for example the Woodside charity can encourage economy in the use of heating, lighting, water consumption, telephone usage and postage. In an organisation staffed mainly by volunteers with an unpredictable clientele, cost control is going to depend to a large extent on the way in which responsibility and authority are delegated.

Collecting information

Cost control is not possible without collecting regularly information on costs incurred, as well as storing and processing this information. In the Woodside charity, provision has been made in the budget for fixed administration costs and the administration duties must hopefully relate in part to this collecting of costing information. Without it, budgeting and financial reporting would not be possible. Annual accounts would be needed in order to retain charitable status and to show providers of funds that their donations were being used to their best effect.

Meeting objectives

A NFPO organisation must be able to determine and demonstrate whether it is meeting its declared objectives and so needs to develop measures to do this. This can be far from easy. The analysis of the performance of the Woodside charity over the last year shows that it may be possible to measure objective attainment quantitatively, i.e. in terms of number of free meals served, number of bed-nights used and number of advice sessions given. Presumably, objectives are being met to a greater extent if more units of service are being provided, and so the adverse usage variances for free meals and advice sessions can in fact be used to show that the charity is meeting a growing need.

The meaning of quantitative measures of service provision may not be clear, however. For example, the lower usage of bed-nights could be attributed to the effective provision of advice to the homeless on finding housing and financial aid, and so may also be seen as a success. It could also be due to dissatisfaction amongst the homeless with the accommodation offered by the shelter. In a similar vein, the higher than budget number of advice sessions may be due to repeat visits by homeless people who were not given adequate advice on their first visit, rather than to an increase in the number of people needing advice. Qualitative measures of objective attainment will therefore be needed in addition to, or to supplement, quantitative ones.

336 ROBINHOLT UNIVERSITY (SEPT 2019)

(1) **To provide education which promotes intellectual initiative and produces confident and ambitious graduates who have reached the highest academic standards to prepare them for success in life and the workplace**

There are various performance indicators which can be looked at to ascertain whether RU is meeting this strategic aim. First, question 1 of the survey shows that 83% of students think that the course is intellectually stimulating and the quality of teaching is high. This has gone down by three percentage points since 20X5, which is not good.

In the NOS survey, the percentage of graduates agreeing that the course has developed them as a person has increased from 80% in 20X5 to 82% in 20X6. This would indicate that RU is indeed developing confident and ambitious graduates.

However, the number of graduates achieving first class degrees in 20X6 has fallen vastly from 28% to 20%. Given that the entry requirements were only relaxed in 20X6, this should not have had any impact on results. This infers that the quality of teaching may have declined and the ratio of students to academic staff has increased from 35:1 to 40:1. It appears that, although many new students were recruited in 20X6, there were not enough new academic staff recruited to deal with the influx of students. This is shown by the fact that student numbers increased by 13% but academic staff costs only increased by 6%.

As there was presumably a pay rise in the year too, it is clear that a proportionate amount of new staff were not recruited. This failing is also reflected by the fall in the answer to question 2 from 86% to 82%, with students being less satisfied in 20X6 with the advice and support they have received. Also, the staff retention rate has gone down in 20X6, meaning that staff are less familiar with RU and therefore more likely to provide a fragmented service.

However, in 20X5 74% of employers were happy with the graduates they recruited, in 20X6 this dropped to 72%. In addition, in 20X5 only 65% of students have managed to obtain graduate jobs within a year compared to previous years. Given that RU has relaxed the entry requirements for students in 20X6, this may mean that its 20X6 recruits are not as well qualified as its 20X5. This could mean that in the future the number of graduates obtaining graduate jobs within a year and the satisfaction percentages of employers could fall further. This decision has meant that there has been a 23% increase in fee income, but it compromises RU's ability to meet its first strategic aim.

(2)   To provide an organised, efficient learning environment with access to cutting edge technology and facilities

As regards premises, the money spent on maintaining these has decreased by 10% in 20X6, despite the increased student numbers. In the NOS survey, the percentage of students satisfied with these facilities has gone down nine percentage points from 92% to 83%. This suggests that this particular strategic aim has been neglected. Students seem far less satisfied with the way that the courses are run and administered now, with a fall of nine percentage points. Administration staff costs have only increased by 5% despite a 13% increase in student numbers and, presumably, a pay rise during the year. It can be inferred that staff are under increasing pressure and unable to cope with the increased numbers. This is again reflected by the fall in the staff retention rate from 90% in 20X5 to 75% in 20X6.

(3)   To be a leader in sustainable business practices which protect the environment and support local people

As with the above strategic aim, this one also seems to have been a little forgotten in 20X6. In 20X5, RU won an environmental award for its campuses. It also took part in a food sharing initiative which helped the local community. It has now got rid of its recycling bins and ceased to be involved in the food share project. RU's spending on sustainability and community assistance has actually halved in 20X6. This decline in activity is partly attributable to staff shortages. All in all, this is not very good as RU is now failing to meet one of its main strategic aims.

(4)   To provide attractive, innovative conference and event facilities, attracting clients both nationally and internationally

Conference and event income has gone up by 13% in 20X6, which is a good increase for RU. It has managed to control its costs relating to these events well too, since these have only increased by 4%. RU has also won an award for its conference facility and attracted a number of new clients. RU therefore appears to be focusing well on this strategic aim.

(5)   To be recognised both nationally and internationally for the scope and relevance of their research

Income from research at RU has actually gone down by 13% this year, as have the associated costs. Whilst a local university has won an award for their contribution to research, RU has not been successful in this regard. The suggestion is that this aim has not been focused on in 20X6.

Overall satisfaction

In addition to the above, it should be considered that the overall satisfaction percentage for students has decreased from 83% to 81%. This could have serious implications for RU as it is the main performance indicator used both internally and externally to assess how RU is performing. As well as meaning that RU may well now attract fewer students, it will also have an impact on the fees which can be charged to students in future years. The university needs to consider how it can improve the service it is providing in order to improve overall satisfaction.

Calculations

	20X6 $m	20X5 $m	% increase/ decrease
Income			
Tuition fees	148	135.6	9%
Research grants	3.5	4.5	(22%)
Conferences and other events	18	16	13%
Total income	169.5	156.1	9%
Expenditure			
Academic staff costs	80.8	76.2	6%
Administration staff costs	50.4	48	5%
Premises, facilities and technology costs	7.6	8.4	(10%)
Event and conference costs	8.3	8	4%
Research grants	3.1	4	(23%)
Sustainability and community assistance	1.2	2.4	(50%)
Total expenditure	151.4	147	3%
Surplus	18.1	9.1	99%
Student numbers	27,000	24,000	13%

ACCA Marking scheme	
	Marks
Calculations	4
Strategic aims discussion	16
Total	**20**

337 TONFORD SCHOOL (SEPTEMBER/DECEMBER 2020)

(a) The primary objective of commercial organisations is to maximise the wealth they generate for their owners (shareholders). In contrast, the objectives of NFPO's are often non-financial and reflect the interests which the various stakeholders have in an organisation. These stakeholders often have varying interests in the organisation, meaning that the organisation will also have a number of different objectives.

These conflicts may make it difficult to set clear objectives on which all stakeholders agree. Consequently, the organisation's management will face a dilemma when trying to decide which objectives are most important and therefore prioritised in the course of strategic planning and decision-making. This can be a particular problem when different objectives make different demands on resources or require different courses of action.

Another problem is that these organisations often do not generate revenue but simply have a fixed budget for spending which they have to keep to and are often subject to strong external influences which will influence the setting of objectives e.g. political factors.

(b)

Tutorial note

This solution is longer than one which candidates would need to produce to score the marks available. However, it is intended to illustrate the range of relevant points candidates could have identified from the scenario, and therefore the number of marks potentially available in this question.

Objective 1 – Strive for continuous improvement in performance standards.

The percentage of pupils achieving the target grades is not only below the national target, it is also lower than Tonford School achieved five years ago. As such, the school's does not appear to be achieving continuous improvement.

However, exam results alone are not necessarily an accurate indicator of a school's performance. For example, exam results will reflect the underlying ability of the pupils, as well as the quality of the teaching they receive.

There is a danger that if Tonford School focuses only on exam results it will become 'selective' and will only accept the most academically gifted pupils. However, such an approach would contradict the objective to provide 'all children' with access to high quality education, regardless of their background.

Pupil progress may be a more valuable measure than exam results, because the extent to which pupils' performance improves provides an indication of the value added by the school, rather than pupils' inherent ability.

Given the typical range of scores, Tonford School's performance in this respect (+0.4) is significantly above the national target (+0.25) and is at the upper end of the range.

The fact that pupil numbers have increased seems likely to suggest that the school is becoming more popular with parents. Given that parents can choose which school to select for their children, the increase in pupil numbers is likely to reflect a perception among parents that the school is performing well.

The results of the recent inspection visit would seem likely to reinforce this perception.

Note: An alternative interpretation could be that all the other schools in the area are already full, and Tonford has spare capacity, which is why its pupil numbers increased. However, such an explanation seems less likely given the context of the other performance indicators.

Objective 2 – Provide a supportive learning environment, which encourages a high standard of pupil achievement.

The 'pupil progress' score suggests the school is providing children with a high quality education and a learning environment which encourages a high standard of pupil achievement. The fact that Tonford School's 20X7 score is higher than its 20X2 score also suggests an improvement in the learning environment (although here again, to some extent the scores may reflect pupils' aptitude for learning as well as the efforts of the school).

The school's inspection grade is higher than five years ago, and is above the national target, which suggests the school is improving, and is performing relatively well. Although there is no indication that the DoE gives any more weighting to any single aspect of the performance data compared to other areas, the inspection grades could potentially be the most important indicator of how well as school is performing.

However, although Tonford School's grading is 'Very good' this suggests there is still room for further improvement, because the school did not achieve the top grade: 'Excellent'.

Tonford School's teacher/pupil ratio has remained essentially the same over the last five years – at 19 pupils per teacher, which is favourable compared to the national target of 22 pupils per teacher.

20X7: 662 pupils/35 members of teaching staff = 18.9 pupils per member of staff

20X2: 627 pupils/33 members of teaching staff = 19 pupils per member of staff

Having a low teacher pupil ratio is likely to be beneficial because it will allow teachers to give more time to each pupil, thereby providing a supportive learning environment.

Given that the school is funded by the DoE, it seems likely that the DoE would have had to authorise the budget needed to recruit the additional teachers. On this basis, the fact that Tonford School has been able to increase the number of teachers it employs suggests that the DoE is pleased with the way it is performing, and therefore authorised the additional budget.

Objective 3 – Ensure pupils are prepared for adult life and have the skills and character necessary to contribute to society and the economy.
The inspector has highlighted Tonford School's 'strong sense of community values and citizenship'. This suggests the school is performing well in relation to the objective of preparing students for adult life, and developing their social skills. Exam results and the 'pupil progress' scores in compulsory subjects indicate that the school is making a significant contribution in providing pupils with core knowledge and skills necessary for adulthood.
Objective 4 – Provide all children with access to high quality education, regardless of their location or background.
The inspector's report has highlighted that pupils at Tonford School come from diverse backgrounds' and awarded the school an improved grading over the last five years. Coupled with 'pupil progress' scores, this indicates that the school is fulfilling the objective to provide children which access to high quality education, regardless of their background.

(c) In order to assess any organisation's performance against its objectives, performance information needs to be available, and, in many cases, this information is obtained by measuring aspects of performance relevant to the objectives.

Difficulties of measurement

However, one of the inherent difficulties with qualitative objectives compared to quantifiable objectives is how to measure them.

For example, exam success rate (% of pupils achieving 5 grades A-C) is quantifiable, and relatively easy to measure, using exam results data. However, trying to measure the overall quality of education in a school or whether a school provides a 'supportive learning environment' is potentially much more difficult, because there aren't any specific outputs (e.g. results) which can be measured.

So, while exam results and pupil progress metrics are indicators of pupil achievement in schools – which can be measured – assessing them only provides a partial assessment of whether schools are providing children with 'access to high quality education' or whether they are providing 'supportive learning environment which encourages a high standard of pupil achievement.'

A related problem is that the aspects of performance which are monitored end up being the ones where performance can most easily be measured, rather than those which are most important in ensuring that the objectives are achieved.

The DoE has recognised these issues though and acknowledged the need for inspectors to visit schools on a regular basis, to gain an insight into the aspects of performance which cannot be reflected in statistical measures.

Subjectivity

Another major problem with assessing qualitative aspects of performance is that they tend to be subjective. For example, people are likely to have different expectations of what constitutes a high quality of education, a supportive learning environment, or the extent to which students are prepared for adult life.

In this respect, one of the key things the DoE has to ensure is that its inspectors are consistent in their grading of schools. For example, if one inspector rates a school as 'Good', but another inspector would have rated the same school as 'Excellent', this inconsistency would significantly reduce the validity of the performance data which is produced.

ACCA Marking scheme		
		Marks
(a)	Discuss the performance of Hammocks	4
(b)	Performance assessment of Tonford School	12
(c)	Explanation of difficulties in qualitative objectives	4
Total		**20**

338 MOBE (JUNE 2015 ADAPTED)

(a) From the group's perspective

For every motor sold externally, Division M generates a profit of $80 ($850 – $770) for the group as a whole. For every motor which Division S has to buy from outside of the group, there is an incremental cost of $60 per unit ($800 – ($770 – $30)). Therefore, from a group perspective, as many external sales should be made as possible before any internal sales are made. Consequently, the group's current policy will need to be changed. This does, however, assume that the quality of the motors bought from outside the group is the same as the quality of the motors made by Division M.

Division M's total capacity is 60,000 units. Given that it can make external sales of 30,000 units, it can only supply 30,000 of Division S's demand for 35,000 motors. These 30,000 units should be bought from Division M since. from a group perspective, the cost of supplying these internally is $60 per unit cheaper than buying externally. The remaining 5,000 motors required by Division S should then be bought in from the external supplier at $800 per unit.

In order to work out the transfer price which should be set for the internal sales of 30,000 motors, the perspective of both divisions must be considered.

From Division M's perspective

Division M's only buyer for these 30,000 motors (once external demand is exhausted) is Division S, so the lowest price it would be prepared to charge is the marginal cost of making these units and selling them internally, which is $740 per unit. However, it would ideally want to make some profit on these motors too and would consequently expect a significantly higher price than this.

From Division S's perspective

Division S knows that it can buy as many external motors as it needs from outside the group at a price of $800 per unit. Therefore, this will be the maximum price which it is prepared to pay.

Overall

Therefore, the transfer price should be set somewhere between $740 and $800. From the perspective of the group, the total group profit will be the same irrespective of where in this range the transfer price is set. However, it is important that divisional and staff remain motivated. Given the external sales price which Division M can achieve and the fact that Division S would have to pay $800 for each motor bought from outside the group, the transfer price should probably be at the higher end of the range.

(b) **(i)** **Return on investment**

Division S

Net Profit = $44,600 × 28% = $12,488

ROI = $12,488 ÷ $82,800 = 15.08%

Division M

Net Profit = $21,800 × 33% = $7,194

ROI = $7,194 ÷ $40,600 = 17.72%

(ii) **Residual income**

Division S

Divisional Profit = $12,488

Capital employed = $82,800

Imputed interest charge = $82,800 × 12% = $2,552

Residual income = $12,488 – $9,936 = $2,552

Division M

Divisional Profit = $7,194

Capital employed = $40,600

Imputed interest charge = $40,600 × 12% = $4,872

Residual income = $7,194 – $4,872 = $2,322

(iii) **Comments**

If a decision about whether to proceed with the investments is made based on ROI, it is possible that the Division S will reject the proposal whereas the of Division M will accept the proposal. This is because each division currently has a ROI of 16% and since the Division S investment only has a ROI of 15.08%, it would bring the division's overall ROI down to less than its current level. On the other hand, since the Division M investment is higher than its current 16%, the investment would bring the division's overall ROI up.

When you consider what would actually be best for the company as a whole, you come to the conclusion that, since both investments have a healthy return (as shown by the residual income), so they should both be accepted. Hence, the fact that ROI had been used as a decision-making tool has led to a lack of congruence between Division S and the company as whole. This backs up what the new manager of Division S is saying. If they used residual income in order to aid the decision-making process, both proposals would be accepted by the divisions since both have a healthy RI. In this case, RI helps the divisions to make decisions which are in line with the best interests of the company. Once again, this backs up the new manager's viewpoint.

It is important to note, however, that each of the methods has numerous advantages and disadvantages which have not been considered here.

339 FLAG CO (DECEMBER 2021)

(a) Profitability

	Flag Co	Budget Co
ROCE	12.8%	13.7%
Operating margin	10.93%	6.07%
Asset turnover	1.17	2.26

Budget Co has a better return on capital employed and is therefore making better returns for its investors. The main cause of this is Budget Co's ability to generate sales. For every $ of capital employed, it generates $2.26 of sales revenue as compared to only $1.17 in the case of Flag Co. Budget Co has much shorter flight times than Flag Co and therefore could be making more journeys and spending less time parked at airports.

Budget Co earns a lower operating margin than Flag Co, as Budget Co's operating costs as a percentage of revenue are 94% compared to Flag Co at 89%. This is probably due to Budget Co's pricing strategy. The lower operating margin is more than offset by Budget Co's higher asset turnover, resulting in a higher capital employed (asset turnover × operating margin = ROCE, therefore 6.07% × 2.26 = 13.7%).

Analysis of the other information provided shows that Budget Co has a much higher seat occupancy rate.

	Flag Co	Budget Co
Seat occupancy rate	66.29%	95.00%

This is probably a consequence of its low fares policy resulting in higher sales of seats relative to Flag Co and therefore a higher asset turnover.

Budget Co also appears more fuel efficient than Flag Co.

	Flag Co	Budget Co
Available seat kilometre per litre of fuel	8,802	12,001

The better fuel economy is probably related to Budget Co's newer fleet of aircraft. Better fuel economy would tend to improve Budget Co's operating margin, however, it is still lower than Flag Co's.

Liquidity

	Flag Co	Budget Co
Current ratio	0.60	0.79

The current ratios of the two businesses are below the text book norm of 2:1, however, they are both service companies which carry little inventory, so this is not surprising or worrying. There is no apparent reason for the difference between the two companies.

Risk

	Flag Co	Budget Co
Capital gearing (debt:equity)	110.44%	51.47%
Interest cover	4.96 times	8.08 times
Operating gearing	950%	820%

Flag Co has a relatively high level of long-term borrowings. This adds to the risks of the business as interest on these borrowings has to be paid no matter the company's operating profit. At present, its operating profit is nearly five times larger than its interest bill and it appears to be able to comfortably pay its commitments. Its operating gearing is 950%, indicating that if sales volume fell by 10%, then its profit before interest and tax would fall by 95% (that is 950% or 9.5 times more). This would cause Flag Co difficulty in covering its interest payments. As demand for business travel is very sensitive to economic conditions, there is a strong probability that at some point Flag Co will experience a fall in sales volume.

As a result of its owner's equity investment, Budget Co carries less financial gearing than Flag Co and has better interest cover. Its operating gearing is slightly lower and given its relative insensitivity to economic conditions, it can be considered a safer company than Flag Co.

(b) Fitzgerald and Moon's building block model provides a framework for service companies to design performance measurement systems which are linked to management rewards. It provides a system of targets (standards) which will motivate managers to improve business performance.

There are three building blocks in the model. The first block gives **six dimensions**, meaning the aspects of performance which must be measured in a service business. These are:

- Financial performance, for example, profitability and growth.
- Competitiveness which measures an organisation's standing against its competition.
- Quality of the service offered.
- Flexibility of the organisation in providing the service.
- Innovation which addresses the ability to introduce new processes and services.
- Resource utilisation which measures productivity and efficiency.

These six dimensions should be split into results (financial performance and competitiveness) which are the outcomes of past decisions and determinants (quality, flexibility, innovation and resource utilisation) which drive future performance and results.

The second block relates to setting **standards**. To motivate managers, it is important that they take ownership of standards (that is accept or internalise them) and the standards appear achievable and equitable (fair).

The third block relates to the **rewards** managers are offered for achieving the standards. These must have clarity (the performance measurement scheme must be understood by managers), they must be motivating (rewards must be attractive) and controllable (not subject to influences outside the manager's control).

	ACCA Marking scheme	Marks
(a)	Calculations	6
	Discussion	8
		14
(b)	Explanation	6
Total		20

Section 7

SPECIMEN EXAM QUESTIONS

Exam Summary

Time allowed: This specimen exam is not timed.

This exam is divided into three sections:

Section A

  • 15 objective test (OT) questions, each worth 2 marks.

  • 30 marks in total.

Section B

  • Three OT cases, each containing a scenario which relates to five OT questions, each worth 2 marks.

  • 30 marks in total.

Section C

  • Two constructed response questions, each containing a scenario which relates to one or more requirement(s).

  • Each constructed response question is worth 20 marks in total.

  • 40 marks in total.

Please note that the live exam is worth a total of 110 marks, 10 marks of which are for questions that do not count towards your final result and are included for quality assurance purposes. This specimen exam is worth a total of 100 marks, reflecting the element of the live exam on which your result will be based.

All questions are compulsory.

Section A

This section of the exam contains **15 objective test (OT) questions**.

Each question is worth **2 marks** and is compulsory.

This exam section is worth **30 marks** in total.

Select **Next** to continue.

Q1

A company manufactures two products, C and D, for which the following information is available:

	Product C	Product D	Total
Budgeted production (units)	1,000	4,000	5,000
Labour hours per unit / in total	8	10	48,000
Number of production runs required	13	15	28
Number of inspections during production	5	3	8

Total production set up costs	$140,000
Total inspection costs	$80,000
Other overhead costs	$96,000

Other overhead costs are absorbed on a labour hour basis.

Using activity-based costing, what is the budgeted overhead cost per unit of product D?

- $43.84

- $46.25

- $131.00

- $140.64

Q2

LPM Co has identified the trend line relating to its sales revenue as 2,000 + 25X.

X denotes the quarter number, with the first quarter of 20X5 being 13, the second quarter of 20X5 being 14, etc.

LPM Co uses the multiplicative model and has calculated the following seasonal variations:

Quarter 1: -0.20

Quarter 2: -0.08

Quarter 3: +0.04

Quarter 4: +0.24

What is LPM Co's seasonally adjusted sales revenue forecast for the second quarter of 20X7?

$ [   ]

Q3

P Co makes two products, P1 and P2. The budgeted details for each product are as follows:

	P1 ($)	P2 ($)
Selling price	10.00	8.00
Cost per unit:		
Direct materials	3.50	4.00
Direct labour	1.50	1.00
Variable overhead	0.60	0.40
Fixed overhead	1.20	1.00
Profit per unit	3.20	1.60

Budgeted production and sales for the year ended 30 November 20X5 are:

Product P1	10,000 units
Product P2	12,500 units

The fixed overhead costs included in P1 relate to apportionment of general overhead costs only. However, P2 also included specific fixed overheads totalling $2,500.

If only product P1 were to be made, how many units would need to be sold in order to achieve a profit of $60,000 each year (to the nearest whole unit)?

 units

Q4

Which TWO of the following statements, regarding environmental cost accounting, are true?

☐ The majority of environmental costs are already captured within a typical organisation's accounting system. The difficulty lies in identifying them

☐ Input/output analysis divides material flows within an organisation into three categories: material flows; system flows; and delivery and disposal flows

☐ One of the cost categories used in environmental activity-based costing is environment-driven costs which is used for costs which can be directly traced to a cost centre

☐ Environmental life-cycle costing enables environmental costs from the design stage of the product right through to decommissioning at the end of its life to be considered

Q5

To produce 19 litres of product X, a standard input mix of 8 litres of chemical A and 12 litres of chemical B is required.

Chemical A has a standard cost of $20 per litre and chemical B has a standard cost of $25 per litre.

During September, the actual results showed that 1,850 litres of product X were produced, using a total input of 900 litres of chemical A and 1,100 litres of chemical B.

The actual costs of chemicals A and B were at the standard cost of $20 and $25 per litre respectively.

Based on the above information, which of the following statements is true?

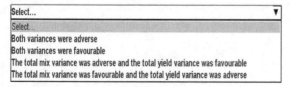

Select... ▼
Select...
Both variances were adverse
Both variances were favourable
The total mix variance was adverse and the total yield variance was favourable
The total mix variance was favourable and the total yield variance was adverse

Q6

A budget is a quantified plan of action for a forthcoming period. Budgets can be prepared using a variety of different approaches.

Match each of the following statements to the correct budgeting process.

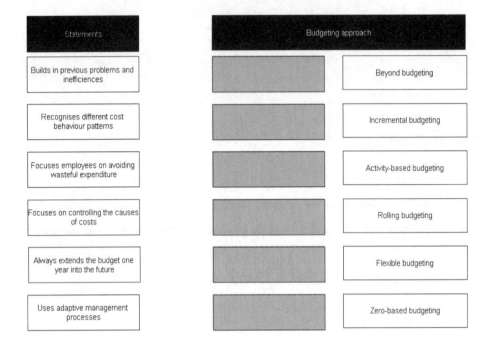

Statements	Budgeting approach
Builds in previous problems and inefficiences	Beyond budgeting
Recognises different cost behaviour patterns	Incremental budgeting
Focuses employees on avoiding wasteful expenditure	Activity-based budgeting
Focuses on controlling the causes of costs	Rolling budgeting
Always extends the budget one year into the future	Flexible budgeting
Uses adaptive management processes	Zero-based budgeting

Q7

A leisure company owns a number of large health and fitness resorts, but one is suffering from declining sales and is predicted to make a loss in the next year. As a result management have identified a number of possible actions:

(1) Shut down the resort and sell off the assets
(2) Undertake a major upgrade to facilities costing $4.5m
(3) Undertake a minor upgrade to facilities costing $2m

The upgrades are predicted to have variable results and the probability of good results after a major upgrade is 0.8, whereas the probability of good results after a minor upgrade is 0.7.

The company is risk neutral and has prepared the following decision tree.

Using the information below, identify, by clicking on the relevant branch of the decision tree, which action the company should take.

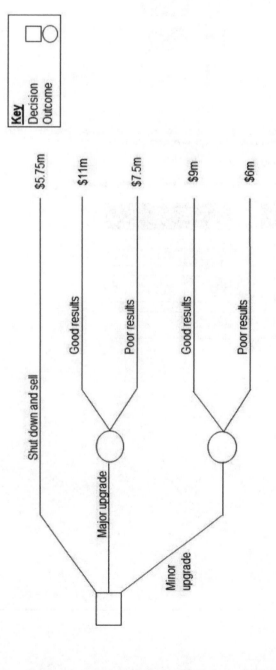

Q8

A company has the following production planned for the next four weeks. The figures reflect the full capacity level of operations. Planned output is equal to the maximum demand per product.

Product	A ($ per unit)	B ($ per unit)	C ($ per unit)	D ($ per unit)
Selling price	160	214	100	140
Raw material cost	24	56	22	40
Direct labour cost	66	88	33	22
Variable overhead cost	24	18	24	18
Fixed overhead cost	16	10	8	12
Profit	30	42	13	48
Planned output	300	125	240	400
Direct labour hours per unit	6	8	3	2

It has now been identified that labour hours available in the next four weeks will be limited to 4,000 hours.

Rank the products in the order they should be manufactured, assuming that the company wants to maximise profits in the next four weeks.

Q9

Def Co provides accounting services to government departments. On average, each staff member works six chargeable hours per day, with the rest of their working day being spent on non-chargeable administrative work. One of the company's main objectives is to produce a high level of quality and customer satisfaction.

Def Co has set its targets for the next year.

Match the correct value for money performance category to each of the following targets for Def Co.

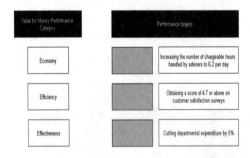

Q10

Different types of information systems provide the information which organisations need for strategic planning, management and operational control.

Match the following characteristics to the relevant information systems.

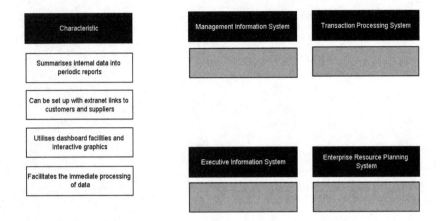

Q11

Which TWO of the following are examples of direct data capture costs?

☐ Use of bar coding and scanners

☐ Completion of timesheets by employees

☐ Payroll department processing time of personnel costs

☐ Input of data into the production system

☐ Emails sent to staff on matters that do not relate to them

Q12

Which TWO of the following statements regarding life-cycle costing are correct?

☐ It can be applied not only to products but also to an organisation's customers

☐ Often between 70% to 90% of costs are determined early in the product life-cycle

☐ It includes any opportunity costs associated with production

☐ The maturity phase is characterised by a rapid build up in demand

Q13

A company manufactures a product which requires four hours per unit of machine time. Machine time is a bottleneck resource as there are only ten machines which are available for 12 hours per day, five days per week. The product has a selling price of $130 per unit, direct material costs of $50 per unit, labour costs of $40 per unit and factory overhead costs of $20 per unit. These costs are based on weekly production and sales of 150 units.

What is the throughput accounting ratio?

- ○ 1.33
- ○ 2.00
- ○ 0.75
- ○ 0.31

Q14

Ox Co has two divisions, A and B. Division A makes a component for air conditioning units which it can only sell to division B. It has no other outlet for sales.

Current information relating to division A is as follows:

Marginal cost per unit	$100
Transfer price of the component	$165
Total production and sales of the component each year (units)	2,200
Specific fixed costs of division A per year	$10,000

Cold Co has offered to sell the component to division B for $140 per unit. If division B accepts this offer, division A will be closed.

If division B accepts Cold Co's offer, what will be the impact on profits per year for the group as a whole?

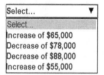

Q15

Identify, by clicking on the relevant box in the table below, whether each of the statements regarding Fitzgerald and Moon's Building Blocks model is true or false.

The determinants of performance are quality, innovation, resource utilisation and competitiveness	TRUE	FALSE
Standards are targets for performance and should be fair, achievable and controllable	TRUE	FALSE
Rewards encourage staff to work towards the standards and should be clear, motivating and controllable	TRUE	FALSE
It is a performance measurement framework suitable for service organisations	TRUE	FALSE

Section B

This section of the exam contains **three OT cases**.

Each OT case contains a scenario which relates to **five OT questions**.

Each question is worth **2 marks** and is compulsory.

This exam section is worth **30 marks** in total.

Select **Next** to continue.

Glam Co is a hairdressing salon which provides both 'cuts' and 'treatments' to clients. All cuts and treatments at the salon are carried out by one of the salon's three senior stylists. The salon also has two salon assistants and two junior stylists.

Every client attending the salon is seen first by a salon assistant, who washes their hair; next, by a senior stylist, who cuts or treats their hair depending on which service the client wants; then finally, a junior stylist who dries their hair. The average length of time spent with each member of staff is as follows:

	Cut (Hours)	Treatment (Hours)
Assistant	0.1	0.3
Senior stylist	1.0	1.5
Junior stylist	0.6	0.5

The salon is open for eight hours each day for six days per week. It is only closed for two weeks each year. Staff salaries are $40,000 each year for each senior stylist, $28,000 each year for each junior stylist and $12,000 each year for each of the assistants. The cost of cleaning products applied when washing clients' hair is $1.50 per client. The cost of all additional products applied during a 'treatment' is $7.40 per client. Other salon costs (excluding labour and raw materials) amount to $106,400 each year.

Glam Co charges $60 for each cut and $110 for each treatment.

The senior stylists' time has been correctly identified as the bottleneck activity.

Q16

What is the annual capacity of the bottleneck activity?

○ 2,400 cuts or 1,600 treatments

○ 4,800 cuts or 4,800 treatments

○ 7,200 cuts or 4,800 treatments

○ 9,600 cuts or 9,600 treatments

Q17

The salon has calculated the cost per hour to be $42.56.

Calculate the throughput accounting ratio (TPAR) for both services (to two decimal places).

Cuts ☐

Treatments ☐

Q18

Which THREE of the following activities could the salon use to improve the TPAR?

☐ Identify ways to reduce the material costs for the services

☐ Increase the time spent by the bottleneck activity on each service

☐ Improve the control of the salon's total operating expenses

☐ Increase the level of inventory to prevent stockouts

☐ Increase the productivity of the stage prior to the bottleneck

☐ Apply an increase to the selling price of the services

Q19

What would be the effect on the bottleneck if the salon employed another senior stylist?

○ The senior stylists' time will be a bottleneck for cuts only

○ The senior stylists' time will be a bottleneck for treatments only

○ The senior stylists' time will remain the bottleneck for both cuts and treatments

○ There will no longer be a bottleneck

Q20

Which of the following statements regarding the theory of constraints are correct?

(1) It focuses on identifying stages of congestion in a process when production arrives more quickly than the next stage can handle

(2) It is based on the concept that organisations manage three key factors - throughput, operating expenses and inventory

(3) It uses a sequence of focusing steps to overcome a single bottleneck, at which point the improvement process is complete

(4) It can be applied to the management of all limiting factors, both internal and external, which can affect an organisation

○ 1 and 2 only

○ 1, 2 and 3

○ 2, 3 and 4

○ 1, 3 and 4

Chair Co has several new products in development. Information relating to two of these products is as follows:

Luxury car seat
The estimated labour time for the first unit is 12 hours but a learning curve of 75% is expected to apply for the first eight units produced. The cost of labour is $15 per hour.

The cost of materials and other variable overheads is expected to total $230 per unit. Chair Co plans on pricing the seat by adding a 50% mark-up to the total variable cost per seat, with the labour cost being based on the incremental time taken to produce the eighth unit.

High chair
Another product which Chair Co has in development is a new design of high chair for feeding young children. Based on previous experience of producing similar products, Chair Co had assumed that a learning rate of 85% would apply to the manufacture of this new design but after the first phase of production had been completed, management realised that a learning rate of 80% had been achieved.

Chair Co uses cost-plus pricing when setting prices for its products.

Q21

In relation to the luxury car seat, what is the labour cost of the eighth unit?

⦿ $45.65

⦿ $75.94

⦿ $4.32

⦿ $3.04

Q22

The first phase of production has now been completed for the new car seat. The first unit actually took 12.5 hours to make and the total time for the first eight units was 34.3 hours, at which point the learning effect came to an end. Chair Co are planning on adjusting the price to reflect the actual time it took to complete the eighth unit.

What was the actual rate of learning which occurred (to two decimal places)?

[   ] %

Q23

In relation to the new design of high chair, which THREE of the following statements could explain why the actual rate of learning differed from the rate which was expected?

☐ Staffing levels were stable during the first manufacturing phase

☐ There were machine breakdowns during production

☐ Assembly of the chairs was manual and very repetitive

☐ There was high staff turnover during this period

☐ There were minimal stoppages in the production process

☐ The design of the chair was changed several times at this early phase

Q24

Identify, by clicking on the table below, whether each of the statements regarding cost-plus pricing strategies is true or false.

Marginal cost-plus pricing is easier where there is a readily identifiable variable cost	TRUE	FALSE
Full cost-plus pricing requires the budgeted level of output to be determined at the outset	TRUE	FALSE
Cost-plus pricing is a strategically focused approach as it accounts for external factors	TRUE	FALSE
Cost-plus pricing requires that the profit mark-up applied by an organisation is fixed	TRUE	FALSE

Q25

Chair Co has also developed a new type of office chair and management is trying to formulate a budget for this product. They have decided to match the production level to demand, however, demand for this chair is uncertain.

Management have collected the following information:

	Demand (units)	Probability
Worst possible outcome	10,000	0.3
Most likely outcome	22,000	0.5
Best possible outcome	35,000	0.2

The selling price per unit is $25. The variable cost per unit is $8 for any production level up to 25,000 units. If the production level is higher than 25,000 units then the variable cost per unit will decrease by 10% and this reduction will apply to all the units produced at that level.

Total fixed costs are estimated to be $75,000.

Using probabilistic budgeting, what is the expected budgeted contribution of this product (to the nearest whole $)?

$ [   ]

The Hi Life Co makes sofas. It has recently received a request from a customer to provide a one-off order of sofas, in excess of normal budgeted production. The order would need to be completed within two weeks.

The following cost estimate has already been prepared:

		$
Direct materials:		
Fabric	200 m^2 at $17 per m^2	3,400
Wood	50 m^2 at $8.20 per m^2	410
Direct labour:		
Skilled	200 hours at $16 per hour	3,200
Semi-skilled	300 hours at $12 per hour	3,600
Factory overheads	500 hours at $3 per hour	1,500
Total production cost		12,110
General fixed overheads at 10% of total production cost		1,211
Total cost		13,321

A quotation now needs to be prepared on a relevant cost basis so that Hi Life Co can offer as competitive a price as possible for the order.

Q26

The fabric is regularly used by Hi Life Co. There are currently 300 m² in inventory, which cost $17 per m². The current purchase price of the fabric is $17.50 per m².

The wood is regularly used by Hi Life Co and usually costs $8.20 per m². However, the company's current supplier's earliest delivery time for the wood is in three weeks' time. An alternative supplier could deliver immediately but they would charge $8.50 per m². Hi Life Co already has 500 m² in inventory but 480 m² of this is needed to complete other existing orders in the next two weeks. The remaining 20 m² is not going to be needed until four weeks' time.

What is the cost of the fabric and the wood which should be included in the quotation (to the nearest whole $)?

Fabric $ [   ]

Wood $ [   ]

Q27

The skilled labour force is employed under permanent contracts of employment under which they must be paid for 40 hours per week's labour, even if their time is idle due to absence of orders. Their rate of pay is $16 per hour, although any overtime is paid at time and a half. In the next two weeks there is spare capacity of 150 labour hours.

There is no spare capacity for semi-skilled workers. They are currently paid $12 per hour or time and a half for overtime. However, a local agency can provide additional semi-skilled workers for $14 per hour.

What cost should be included in the quotation for skilled labour and semi-skilled labour (to the nearest $)?

Skilled $ [   ]

Semi-skilled $ [   ]

Q28

Of the $3 per hour factory overheads costs, $1.50 per hour reflects the electricity costs of running the cutting machine which will be used to cut the fabric and wood for the sofas. The other $1.50 per hour reflects the cost of the factory supervisor's salary. The supervisor is paid an annual salary and is also paid $15 per hour for any overtime he works. The supervisor will need to work 20 hours' overtime if this order is accepted.

What is the cost which should be included in the quotation for factory overheads (to the nearest $)?

$ [   ]

Q29

Which statement correctly describes the treatment of the general fixed overheads when preparing the quotation?

○ The overheads should be excluded because they are a sunk cost

○ The overheads should be excluded because they are not incremental costs

○ The overheads should be included because they relate to production costs

○ The overheads should be included because all expenses should be recovered

Q30

Which FOUR of the following statements about relevant costing are true?

☐ An opportunity cost will always be a relevant cost even if it is a past cost

☐ Fixed costs are always general in nature and are therefore never relevant

☐ Committed costs are never considered to be relevant costs

☐ An opportunity cost represents the cost of the best alternative forgone

☐ Notional costs are always relevant as they make the estimate more realistic

☐ Avoidable costs would be saved if an activity did not happen and so are relevant

☐ Common costs are only relevant if the viability of the whole process is being assessed

☐ Differential costs in a make or buy decision are not considered to be relevant

Section C

This section of the exam contains **two constructed response questions**.

Each question contains a scenario which relates to one or more requirement(s) which may be split over multiple question screens.

Each question is worth **20 marks** and is compulsory.

This exam section is worth **40 marks** in total.

Important: In your live exam please show all notes/workings that you want the marker to see within the spreadsheet or word processing answer areas. Remember, any notes/workings made on the Scratch Pad or on your workings paper will not be marked.

Select **Next** to continue.

Q31

Carad Co is an electronics company which makes two types of television - plasma screen TVs and LCD TVs. It operates within a highly competitive market and is constantly under pressure to reduce prices. Carad Co operates a standard costing system and performs a detailed variance analysis of both products on a monthly basis. Extracts from the management information for the month of November are shown below:

		Note
Total number of units made and sold	1,400	1
Material price variance	$28,000 A	2
Total labour variance	$6,050 A	3

Notes:

(1) The budgeted total sales volume for TVs was 1,180 units, consisting of an equal mix of plasma screen TVs and LCD screen TVs. Actual sales volume was 750 plasma TVs and 650 LCD TVs. Standard sales prices are $350 per unit for the plasma TVs and $300 per unit for the LCD TVs. The actual sales prices achieved during November were $330 per unit for plasma TV and $290 per unit for LCD TVs. The standard contributions for plasma TVs and LCD TVs are $190 and $180 per unit respectively.

(2) The sole reason for this variance was an increase in the purchase price of one of its key components, X. Each plasma TV made and each LCD TV made requires one unit of component X, for which Carad Co's standard cost is $60 per unit. Due to a shortage of components in the market place, the market price for November went up to $85 per unit for X. Carad Co actually paid $80 per unit for it.

(3) Each plasma TV uses 2 standard hours of labour and each LCD TV uses 1.5 standard hours of labour. The standard cost for labour is $14 per hour and this also reflects the actual cost per labour hour for the company's permanent staff in November. However, because of the increase in sales and production volumes in November, the company also had to use temporary labour at the higher cost of $18 per hour. The total capacity of Carad Co's permanent workforce is 2,200 hours production per month, assuming full efficiency. In the month of November, the workforce were wholly efficient, taking exactly 2 hours to complete each plasma TV and exactly 1.5 hours to produce each LCD TV. The total labour variance therefore relates solely to the temporary workers, who took twice as long as the permanent workers to complete their production.

(a) Calculate the following for the month of November, showing all workings clearly:

(i) The sales price variance and sales volume contribution variance;

(4 marks)

(ii) The material price planning variance and material price operational variance;

(2 marks)

(iii) The labour rate variance and the labour efficiency variance.

(5 marks)

(b) Explain the reasons why Carad Co would be interested in the material price planning variance and the material price operational variance.

(9 marks)

(20 marks)

Q32

Thatcher International Park (TIP) is a theme park and has for many years been a successful business, which has traded profitably. About three years ago the directors decided to capitalise on their success and reduced the expenditure made on new thrill rides, reduced routine maintenance where possible (deciding instead to repair equipment when it broke down) and made a commitment to regularly increase admission prices. Once an admission price is paid customers can use any of the facilities and rides for free.

These steps increased profits considerably, enabling good dividends to be paid to the owners and bonuses to the directors. The last two years of financial results are shown below.

	20X4	20X5
	$	$
Sales	5,250,000	5,320,000
Less expenses:		
Wages	2,500,000	2,200,000
Maintenance - routine	80,000	70,000
Repairs	260,000	320,000
Directors' salaries	150,000	160,000
Directors' bonuses	15,000	18,000
Other costs (including depreciation)	1,200,000	1,180,000
Net profit	**1,045,000**	**1,372,000**
Book value of assets at start of year	13,000,000	12,000,000
Dividend paid	500,000	650,000
Number of visitors	150,000	140,000

TIP operates in a country where the average rate of inflation is around 1% per annum.

(a) Assess the financial performance of TIP using the information given above.

(14 marks)

During the early part of 20X4 TIP employed a newly qualified management accountant. He quickly became concerned about the potential performance of TIP and to investigate his concerns, he started to gather data to measure some non-financial measures of success. The data he has gathered is shown below:

Table 1

	20X4	20X5
Hours lost due to breakdown of rides (Note 1)	9,000 hours	32,000 hours
Average waiting time per ride	20 minutes	30 minutes

Note 1:
TIP has 50 rides of different types. It is open 360 days of the year for ten hours each day.

(b) Assess the QUALITY of the service which TIP provides to its customers using Table 1 and any other relevant data and indicate the RISKS it is likely to face if it continues with its current policies.

(6 marks)

(20 marks)

Section 8

ANSWERS TO SPECIMEN EXAM QUESTIONS

SECTION A

Q1 $46.25

Set-up costs per production run = $140,000/28 = $5,000
Cost per inspection = $80,000/8 = $10,000
Other overhead costs per labour hour = $96,000/48,000 = $2

Overhead costs of product D:

	$
Set-up costs (15 x $5,000)	75,000
Inspection costs (3 x $10,000)	30,000
Other overheads (40,000 x $2)	80,000
	185,000

Overhead cost per unit = $185,000/4,000 units = $46.25

Q2 $2,346

If the first quarter of 20X5 is quarter 13, the second quarter of 20X7 is quarter 22.

The forecasted sales revenue using the trend line is 2,000 + (25 x 22) = 2,550.

The seasonal variation for quarter 2 is -8%, so the seasonally adjusted sales revenue forecast is 2,550 x (1 – 8%) = $2,346.

Q3   18,636 units

The number of units required to make a target profit = (fixed costs + target profit)/contribution per unit of P1.

Fixed costs = ($1.20 x 10,000) + ($1.00 x 12,500) - $2,500 = $22,000

Contribution per unit of P1 = $3.20 + $1.20 = $4.40

($22,000 + $60,000)/$4.40 = 18,636 units

Q4   Statements (1) and (4) are correct.

Most organisations do collect data about environmental costs but find it difficult to split them out and categorise them effectively.

Life-cycle costing does allow the organisation to collect information about a product's environmental costs throughout its lifecycle.

The technique which divides material flows into three categories is material flow cost accounting, not input/output analysis

ABC does categorise some costs as environment-driven costs, however, these are costs which are normally hidden within total overheads in a conventional costing system. It is environment-related costs which can be allocated directly to a cost centre.

Q5

Mix variance:

Material	AQSM	AQAM	Difference (litres)	Standard cost ($/litre)	Variance ($)
A	800	900	100 A	20	2,000 A
B	1,200	1,100	100 F	25	2,500 F
	2,000	2,000			500 F

Yield variance:

Material	SQSM	AQSM	Difference (litres)	Standard cost ($/litre)	Variance ($)
A	779	800	21 A	20	420 A
B	1168	1,200	32 A	25	800 A
	1,947	2,000			1,220 A

Q6

Beyond budgeting attempts to move away from conforming to a rigid annual budget and uses adaptive management processes to encourage management to be responsive to current situations.

An incremental budget builds from the previous year's figures and so any inefficiencies will be carried forward.

Activity-based budgeting is based on the principles of activity-based costing and will attempt to identify the drivers of costs in order to formulate a budget.

Rolling budgeting are budgets which are continuously updated throughout the year by adding a new budget period once the most recent budget period has ended. This means that the budget is always extended one year into the future and so forces managers to reassess plans more regularly.

Flexible budgets are designed to show the changes in financial figures based on different activity levels and so will recognise different cost behaviour patterns.

Zero-based budgeting starts from scratch with each item justified for its inclusion in the budget and so should encourage the identification of waste and non-value adding activities.

Q7

EV for major upgrade = (0.80 x $11m) + (0.2 x $7.5m) = $10.3m
EV for minor upgrade = (0.70 x $9m) + (0.3 x $6m) = $8.1m

Decision

Shutdown and sell	$5.75m
Major upgrade (10.3m - 4.5m)	$5.8m
Minor upgrade ($8.1m - $2m)	$6.1m

As the minor upgrade has the highest expected return that should be the option chosen.

Q8

In a single limiting factor situation products should be ranked based on their contribution per unit of limiting factor, which in this case is labour hours.

Product	A	B	C	D
Contribution per unit ($)	46	52	21	60
Number of labour hours required per unit	6	8	3	2
Contribution per labour hour ($)	7.67	6.50	7.00	30.00
Ranking	2nd	4th	3rd	1st

Q9

Target 1 is measuring the rate of work handled by staff which is an efficiency measure.

Target 2 is assessing output, so is a measure of effectiveness.

Target 3 is a financial measure and so assesses economy factors.

Q10

Transaction processing systems facilitate the immediate processing of data.

Management information systems summarise data from TPS into periodic reports for management to use for decision-making.

Executive information systems draw data from the MIS and support senior managers to make strategic decisions. They usually have dashboard and interactive graphics so that the big picture can be seen.

Enterprise resource planning systems are software packages that integrate all the key processes in an organisation and so this permits data to be shared more easily between departments. It can also have extranet links set up with customers and suppliers.

Q11

Direct data capture is a type of data input in which there is no data entry but instead it is captured for a specific purpose. Therefore the use of bar coding and scanners and the completion of timesheets are examples of direct data capture costs.

Time spent by the payroll department processing personnel costs and the input of data into the production system are examples of process costs.

The sending of emails to staff regarding matters that are not pertinent to them is classed as an inefficient use of information cost.

Q12

Customer life-cycle costing can be used by organisations.

It has been reported that the majority of a products costs are determined early on, i.e. at the design phase.

Life-cycle costing does not include any opportunity costs associated with production.

The growth phase is characterised by a rapid increase in demand.

Q13

Return per factory hour = ($130 – $50)/4 hours = $20
Factory costs per hour = ($20/4) + ($40/4) = $15
TPAR = $20/$15 = 1.33

Q14

Increase in variable costs per unit from buying in ($140 - $100) =$40
Therefore total increase in variable costs (2,200 units x $40) = $88,000
Less the specific fixed costs saved if A is shut down = ($10,000)
Decrease in profit = $78,000

Q15

The determinants of performance are quality, innovation, resource utilisation and flexibility. Competitiveness is a result of the determinants.

Standards should be fair, achievable and staff should have ownership of them. Controllability is a feature of the rewards block.

Rewards should be clear, motivating and controllable.

It is a framework designed to attempt to overcome the problems associated with performance management in service companies.

Q16

Total salon hours = 8 x 6 x 50 = 2,400 each year.

There are three senior stylists, therefore total hours available = 7,200.

Based on the time taken for each activity, they can perform 7,200 cuts (7,200 hours/1 hour per cut) or 4,800 treatments(7,200 hours/1·5 hours per treatment).

Q17

Cuts
Return per hour = (Selling price - materials)/time taken on the bottleneck = (60 - 1.50)/1 = 58.50
TPAR = Return per hour/cost per hour = 58.50/42.56 = 1.37(to 2 decimal places)

Treatments
Return per hour = (Selling price - materials)/time taken on the bottleneck = (110 - 8.90)/1.5 = 67.40
TPAR = Return per hour/cost per hour = 67.40/42.56 = 1.58(to 2 decimal places)

Q18

The factors that are included in the TPAR are selling price, material costs, operating expenses and bottleneck time. Increasing the selling price and reducing costs will improve the TPAR.

Increasing the time which each service takes on the bottleneck (the senior stylists' time) will only reduce the number of services they can provide, so this will not improve throughput.

Throughput accounting does not advocate the building of inventory as it is often used in a just-in-time environment and there is no point increasing the activity prior to the bottleneck as it will just create a build-up of work-in-progress. Neither of these will improve the rate of throughput through the process.

Q19

The existing capacity for each activity is:

	Cut	Treatment
Assistants	48,000	16,000
Senior stylists	7,200	4,800
Junior stylists	8,000	9,600

If another senior stylist is employed, this will mean that their available hours will be (4 x 2,400) = 9,600.
This will give them capacity to now do 9,600 cuts (9,600 hours/1 hour per cut) and 6,400 treatments (9,600 hours/1.5 hours per treatment).

As a result, the senior stylists will still be the bottleneck activity for treatments but for cuts the bottleneck will now be the junior stylists as they can only do 8,000 cuts compared to the senior stylists of 9,600.

Q20

The theory of constraints is focused on identifying restrictions in a process and how to manage that restriction (commonly termed a bottleneck).

It is based on the concept of managing throughput, operating expenses and inventory.

It does use a series of focusing steps but it is not complete once the bottleneck has been overcome. In fact it is an ongoing process of improvement, as once the bottleneck has been elevated it is probable that another bottleneck will appear and the process will continue.

It cannot be applied to all limiting factors as some, particularly those external to the organisation, may be out of the organisation's control.

Q21

Learning curve formula = $y = ax^b$
Cumulative average time per unit for 8 units: $Y = 12 \times 8^{-.415} = 5.0628948$ hours.
Therefore cumulative total time for 8 units = 40.503158 hours.
Cumulative average time per unit for 7 units: $Y = 12 \times 7^{-.415} = 5.3513771$ hours.
Therefore cumulative total time for 7 units = 37.45964 hours.
Therefore incremental time for 8th unit = 40.503158 hours − 37.45964 hours = 3.043518 hours.
Total labour cost for 8th unit = 3.043518 × $15 = $45.65277

Q22

Actual learning rate:

Cumulative number of seats produced	Cumulative total hours	Cumulative average hours per unit
1	12.5	12.5
2	?	$12.5 \times r$
4	?	$12.5 \times r^2$
8	34.3	$12.5 \times r^3$

Using algebra: $34 \cdot 3 = 8 \times (12 \cdot 5 \times r^3)$

$4 \cdot 2875 = (12 \cdot 5 \times r^3)$

$0 \cdot 343 = r^3$

$r = 0 \cdot 70$

Therefore the learning rate was 70%

Q23

An 80% learning rate means that the learning was faster than expected.

Factors which are present for a learning curve to take effect are a highly manual and repetitive process (so staff can become quicker the more they perform the same series of tasks), no stoppages to production (so the learning rate will not be lost whilst staff are idle) and a stable workforce (so the learning process does not have to keep restarting).

If there is high staff turnover, stoppages in production and continual design changes, then the learning rate will not be effective and should be slower.

Q24

As marginal costing is based on variable costs it is easier when a readily identifiable variable cost has been established.

The budgeted volume of output does need to be determined for full cost-plus pricing as it would be used to calculate the overhead absorption rate for the calculation of the full cost per unit.

Cost-plus pricing is internally focused and a drawback of the technique is that it fails to consider external influences, like competitor pricing strategies.

The mark-up percentage does not have to be fixed; it can vary and be adjusted to reflect market conditions.

Q25

As the variable cost per unit is changing depending on the production level, contribution for each level needs to be calculated and then the probabilities applied to the outcomes.

Demand (units	Contribution (per unit)	Total contribution	Probability	Expected budgeted contribution
10,000	17.00	170,000	0.3	51,000
22,000	17.00	374,000	0.5	187,000
35,000	17.80	623,000	0.2	124,600
				362,600

Q26

Fabric is in regular use, so the replacement cost is the relevant cost $(200m^2 \times \$17.50) = \$3,500$.

$30m^2$ of wood will have to be ordered in from the alternative supplier but the remaining $20m^2$ which is in inventory and not needed for other work can be used and then replaced by an order from the usual supplier $(30m^2 \times \$8.50) + (20m^2 \times \$8.20) = \$419$.

Q27

Skilled labour:

There is no cost for the first 150 hours as there is spare capacity. The remaining 50 hours required will be paid at time and a half, which is $16 $\times$ 1.5 = $24.

50 hours x $24 = $1,200

Semi-skilled labour:

There is no spare capacity so the company will either need to pay overtime or hire in additional staff. The cost of paying overtime would be $18 per hour so it would be cheaper to hire in the additional staff for $14 per hour

300 hours x $14 = $4,200

Q28

The electricity costs are incremental as the machine will be used more to produce the new order (500 hours x $1.50) = $750.

The supervisor's salary is not relevant as it is paid anyway; however, the overtime is relevant (20 hours x $15) = $300.

Q29

The general fixed overheads should be excluded as they are not incremental, i.e. they are not arising specifically as a result of this order.

They are not sunk as they are not past costs. This is a common misconception.

Q30

An opportunity cost does represent the cost of the best alternative forgone, however, if it is an historic (past) cost, it would not be relevant.

Fixed costs can be incremental to a decision and in those circumstances would be relevant.

Committed costs are costs the organisation has already agreed to and can no longer influence and so are not relevant.

Notional costs are used to make cost estimates more realistic; however, they are not real cash flows and are not considered to be relevant.

Avoidable costs are saved if an activity is not undertaken and if this occurs as a result of the decision, then they are relevant.

Common costs are relevant if the whole process is being evaluated; however, they aren't relevant to a further processing decision.

Differential costs are relevant in a make or buy decision as the organisation is trying to choose between two options.

Q31

(i) Sales price variance and sales volume variance

Sales price variance = (actual price – standard price) x actual volume

	Actual price	Standard price	Difference	Actual volume	Sales price variance
	$	$	$		$
Plasma TVs	330	350	−20	750	15,000 A
LCD TVs	290	300	−10	650	6,500 A
					21,500 A

Sales volume contribution variance = (actual sales volume – budgeted sales volume) x standard margin

	Actual sales volume	Budgeted sales volume	Difference	Standard margin	Sales volume variance
				$	$
Plasma TVs	750	590	160	190	30,400 F
LCD TVs	650	590	60	180	10,800 F
	1,400	1,180			41,200 F

(ii) Material price planning and purchasing operational variances

Material planning variance = (original target price – general market price at time of purchase) x quantity purchased
($60 – $85) x 1,400 = $35,000 A

Material price operational variance = (general market price at time of purchase – actual price paid) x quantity purchased
($85 – $80) x 1,400 = $7,000 F

(iii) Labour rate and labour efficiency variances

Labour rate variance = (standard labour rate per hour – actual labour rate per hour) x actual hours worked

Actual hours worked by temporary workers:
Total hours needed if staff were fully efficient = (750 x 2) + (650 x 1·5) = 2,475.
Permanent staff provide 2,200 hours, therefore excess = 2,475 – 2,200 = 275.
However, temporary workers take twice as long, therefore hours worked = 275 x 2 = 550.

Labour rate variance relates solely to temporary workers; therefore ignore permanent staff in the calculation.
Labour rate variance = ($14 – $18) x 550 = $2,200 A

Labour efficiency variance = (standard labour hours for actual production − actual labour hours worked) x standard rate
(275 − 550) x $14 = $3,850 A

Marking scheme

Part	Sub Part		Maximum marks	Marks awarded
a	i	SP var - Plasma	1	
		SP var - LCD	1	
		SV var - Plasma	1	
		SV var - LCD	1	
a	ii	MP planning var	1	
		MP operating var	1	
a	iii	Actual hrs worked	3	
		Labour rate var	1	
		Labour eff var	1	

(b) Explanation of planning and operational variances

Before the material price planning and operational variances were calculated, the only information available as regards material purchasing was that there was an adverse material price variance of $28,000. The purchasing department will be assessed on the basis of this variance, yet, on its own, it is not a reliable indicator of the purchasing department's efficiency. The reason it is not a reliable indicator is because market conditions can change, leading to an increase in price, and this change in market conditions is not within the control of the purchasing department.

By analysing the materials price variance further and breaking it down into its two components − planning and operational − the variance actually becomes a more useful assessment tool. The planning variance represents the uncontrollable element and the operational variance represents the controllable element.

The planning variance is really useful for providing feedback on just how skilled management is in estimating future prices. This can be very easy in some businesses and very difficult in others. Giving this detail could help to improve planning and standard setting in the future, as management will be increasingly aware of factors which could create volatility in their forecasts.

The operational variance is more meaningful in that it measures the purchasing department's efficiency given the market conditions which prevailed at the time. As can be seen in Carad, the material price operational variance is favourable which demonstrates that the purchasing department managed to acquire the component which was in short supply at a better price than expected. Without this breakdown in the variance, the purchasing department could have been held accountable for the overall adverse variance which was not indicative of their actual performance. This is then a fairer method of assessing performance and will, in turn, stop staff from becoming demotivated.

Marking scheme

Part		Maximum marks	Marks awarded
b	Controllability	2	
	MP planning	3	
	MP operating	3	
	Other − plan/oper	1	

Q32

(a) TIP's financial performance can be assessed in a number of ways:

Sales growth

Sales are up about 1·3% (W1) which is a little above the rate of inflation and therefore a move in the right direction. However, with average admission prices jumping about 8·6% (W2) and numbers of visitors falling, there are clearly problems. Large increases in admission prices reduce the value proposition for the customer, it is unlikely that the rate of increase is sustainable or even justifiable. Indeed with volumes falling (down by 6·7% (W6)), it appears that some customers are being put off and price could be one of the reasons.

Maintenance and repairs

There appears to be a continuing drift away from routine maintenance with management preferring to repair equipment as required. This does not appear to be saving any money as the combined cost of maintenance and repair is higher in 20X5 than in 20X4 (possible risks are dealt with in part (b)).

Directors' pay

Absolute salary levels are up 6·7% (W3), well above the modest inflation rate. It appears that the shareholders are happy with the financial performance of the business and are prepared to reward the directors accordingly. Bonus levels are also well up. It may be that the directors have some form of profit related pay scheme and are being rewarded for the improved profit performance. The directors are likely to be very pleased with the increases to pay.

Wages

Wages are down by 12% (W5). This may partly reflect the loss of customers (down by 6·7% (W6)) if it is assumed that at least part of the wages cost is variable. It could also be that the directors are reducing staff levels beyond the fall in the level of customers to enhance short-term profit and personal bonus. Customer service and indeed safety could be compromised here.

Net profit

Net profit is up a huge 31·3% (W7) and most shareholders would be pleased with that. Net profit is a very traditional measure of performance and most would say this was a sign of good performance.

Return on assets

The profitability can be measured relative to the asset base which is being used to generate it. This is sometimes referred to as ROI or return on investment. The return on assets is up considerably to 11·4% from 8% (W8). This is partly due to the significant rise in profit and partly due to the fall in asset value. We are told that TIP has cut back on new development, so the fall in asset value is probably due to depreciation being charged with little being spent during the year on assets. In this regard it is inevitable that return on assets is up but it is more questionable whether this is a good performance. A theme park (and thrill rides in particular) must be updated to keep customers coming back. The directors of TIP are risking the future of the park.

Workings:

(W1) Sales growth is $5,320,000/$5,250,000 = 1·01333 or 1·3%.

(W2) Average admission prices were:
20X4: $5,250,000/150,000 = $35 per person
20X5: $5,320,000/140,000 = $38 per person
An increase of $38/$35 = 1·0857 or 8·57%.

(W3) Directors' pay up by $160,000/$150,000 = 1·0667 or 6·7%.

(W4) Directors' bonuses levels up from $15,000/$150,000 or 10% to $18,000/$160,000 or 12·5% of turnover. This is an increase of 3/15 or 20%.

(W5) Wages are down by (1 – $2,200,000/$2,500,000) or 12%.

(W6) Loss of customers is (1 – 140,000/150,000) or 6·7%.

(W7) Profits up by $1,372,000/$1,045,000 = 1·3129 or 31·3%.

(W8) Return on assets:
20X4: $1,045,000/$13,000,000 = 1·0803 or 8·03%
20X5: $1,372,000/$12,000,000 = 1·114 or 11·4%

Marking scheme

Part		Maximum marks	Marks awarded
a	Sales growth	3	
	Maintenance	3	
	Directors' pay	2	
	Wages	2	
	Net profit	2	
	Return on assets	2	

(b) Quality provision

Reliability of the rides
The hours lost has increased significantly. Equally the percentage of capacity lost due to breakdowns is now approaching 17·8% (W9). This would appear to be a very high number of hours lost. This would surely increase the risk that customers are disappointed being unable to ride. Given the fixed admission price system, this is bound to irritate some customers as they have effectively already paid to ride.

Average queuing time
Queuing will be seen by customers as dead time. They may see some waiting as inevitable and hence acceptable. However, TIP should be careful to maintain waiting times at a minimum. An increase of 10 minutes (or 50%) is likely to be noticeable by customers and is unlikely to enhance the quality of the TIP experience for them. The increase in waiting times is probably due to the high number of hours lost due to breakdown with customers being forced to queue for a fewer number of ride options.

Safety
The clear reduction in maintenance could easily damage the safety record of the park and is an obvious quality issue.

Risks
If TIP continues with current policies, then they will expose themselves to the following risks:

– The lack of routine maintenance could easily lead to an accident or injury to a customer. This could lead to compensation being paid or reputational damage.

– Increased competition. The continuous raising of admission prices increases the likelihood of a new competitor entering the market (although there are significant barriers to entry in this market, e.g. capital cost, land and so on).

– Loss of customers. The value for money which customers see when coming to TIP is clearly reducing (higher prices, less reliability of rides and longer queues). Regardless of the existence of competition, customers could simply choose not to come, substituting another leisure activity instead.

– Profit fall. In the end if customers' numbers fall, then so will profit. The shareholders, although well rewarded at the moment, could suffer a loss of dividend. Directors' job security could then be threatened.

Workings:

(W9) Capacity of rides in hours is 360 days x 50 rides x 10 hours per day = 180,000.
20X4 lost capacity is 9,000/180,000 = 0·05 or 5%.
20X5 lost capacity is 32,000/180,000 = 0·177 or 17·8%.

Marking scheme

Part		Maximum marks	Marks awarded
b	Reliability of rides	2	
	Av queuing time	2	
	Risks	2	